THE DRAMATIST
AND THE
RECEIVED

THE DRAMATIST
AND THE
RECEIVED IDEA

STUDIES IN THE PLAYS OF
MARLOWE & SHAKESPEARE

BY

WILBUR SANDERS

CAMBRIDGE UNIVERSITY PRESS

CAMBRIDGE

LONDON   NEW YORK   NEW ROCHELLE

MELBOURNE   SYDNEY

Published by the Press Syndicate of the University of Cambridge
The Pitt Building, Trumpington Street, Cambridge CB2 1RP
32 East 57th Street, New York, NY 10022, USA
296 Beaconsfield Parade, Middle Park, Melbourne 3206, Australia

Library of Congress catalogue card number: 68-13542

ISBN 0 521 29800 8 paperback

First published 1968
First paperback edition 1980

Printed in Great Britain at the
University Press, Cambridge

FOR IAN

CONTENTS

v

A NOTE ON EDITIONS

The text of Marlowe used is the Methuen edition (1930–3, published under the general editorship of R. H. Case), with the exception of *Doctor Faustus*, where I quote from the Revels Plays edition (ed. J. D. Jump, London, 1962). For *Richard III* I have used A. H. Thompson's old Arden edition (1907) which, though outmoded in its textual *theory*, is nevertheless more scrupulous in avoiding gratuitous emendation than many more recent editions. *Richard II* is cited in Peter Ure's Arden edition (1961); and in the case of *Macbeth* I have reverted to the *editio princeps*, the Folio—for reasons given in note 8 to chapter 13.

In the case of certain other standard works, to which frequent reference was being made, I have omitted full publication details, and used only the following cue-titles:

Hol.   R. Holinshed, *The Chronicles of England, Scotlande and Irelande* (2nd edn., London, 1587).

Eccl. Pol.   R. Hooker, *Of the Laws of Ecclesiastical Polity*, in *Works*, ed. J. Keble (Oxford, 1863).

Institutes   Jean Calvin, *Institutes of the Christian Religion*, tr. F. L. Battles, ed. J. T. McNeill (London, 1961).

Discourses   *The Discourses of Niccolò Machiavelli*, tr. L. J. Walker (London, 1950).

Prince   Niccolò Machiavelli, *The Prince*, tr. Luigi Ricci (World's Classics, London, 1935).

SCG   St Thomas Aquinas, *Summa Contra Gentiles*, tr. English Dominican Fathers (London, 1928).

ST   *Summa Theologica*, tr. English Dominican Fathers (London, 1915). (Since the volumes are not numbered in these editions of Aquinas, I give section numbers which will serve to identify the volume, followed by a bracketed page reference to facilitate the location of the precise passage.)

PREFACE

Acknowledging one's debts is a relatively simple matter if one confines oneself to tangible benefits received: my thanks on this score are due to the administrators of the Commonwealth Scholarship scheme, who made this piece of work possible in the most literal sense.

But one's indebtedness to friends and teachers, and especially to those who are both, is such that, the larger it is, the less one tends to be conscious of it: it gets built into the structure of one's thinking. The many hours spent arguing out the details and the design of this book with Professor L. C. Knights have issued, I suspect, in my coming upon many insights that I am now presenting confidently as my own. His generosity with his time, however, goes with a magnanimity which regards ideas as no man's private oyster, and I'm confident he will forgive me my inadvertent plagiarisms as readily as he forgave me for disagreeing with him at times.

Professor S. L. Goldberg—though he may be surprised to hear it, and might not always relish the imputation—was another presence of which I was conscious in writing, though there were regrettably few opportunities to discuss progress with him. And my wife, on more occasions than I can count, helped me to disentangle myself from factitious complications, by bringing a fresh intelligence to problems that were beginning to moulder in the close air of 'the mental life'.

Other friends, too, who submitted to an excessive number of cups of coffee, or who overloaded an already crowded teaching programme, in order to inspect minutely various corners of this edifice, have earned my gratitude. In the first (coffee) category, Mr Ian Nelson, Dr David Gillham, Mr Alan Powell and Mr David Spooner were invaluable parts of a kind of continuous three-year post-graduate seminar, and in some cases undertook the further tedium of checking the manuscript. In the second category, Mr Roy Littlewood frequently provided the inspiration, and Mr Morris Shapira on several occasions the constructive resistance, that I needed to take my problems one stage further. In the early months, I spent a good deal of time in heated argument with Dr B. L. Joseph, only to discover later that I had silently appropriated several of his points. I hope he will take these amends in part-satisfaction for my intransigence. Other friends, particularly Mr Andrew Deacon and Fr Tim Kelly, helped with proof-reading out of sheer goodwill, and to them, and to Mrs Judy Faulkner who typed the manuscript, I can only offer my best thanks. Parts of chapters 1, 11 and 13, which have appeared in *The Critical Review* (Melbourne and Sydney), are reprinted here by courtesy of the editors.

As this is a bulky volume, I have not been as thorough in acknowledging the work of other critics as I would have liked. The perspicacious reader will frequently be able to track me in other people's snow in places where no footnote confesses a trespass. My plea is firstly, space; secondly, that in these much-annotated plays there can hardly be a single local point which has not been made by somebody somewhere, and it seemed pointless to load the text with references, unless I felt convinced that the particular article or book was worth consulting for more than that local point. But there are other cases, I'm sure, where the failure to acknowledge a borrowed idea is due simply to my not being aware of having borrowed at all—and that, unfortunately, is likely to have happened most persistently with the critics I read with most pleasure. I have tracked down a few cases of this unconscious absorption of congenial material; for the rest I am penitent.

One final apology: the manuscript was prepared at a distance of twelve thousand miles from the British Museum (where I consulted some of the more obscure primary material cited in the text). Consequently, I had to rely on notes which, though carefully kept, were certainly not utterly reliable. Anyone, therefore, whose exploration of my sources meets a check from a false reference, or whose sense of decency is outraged by an inaccurate quotation, is asked to grant me his indulgence, and to accept my apologies.

Sydney   W. S.
November 1966

1

LITERATURE AS HISTORY:
WITH SOME QUESTIONS ABOUT
'HISTORICAL IMAGINATION'

I

The reader who has arrived at page one by way of the table of contents
will have noticed, perhaps with some misgivings, that the argument of
this book is fairly heavily weighted with historical material. The reason
is not that I believe this kind of erudition is a necessary pre-requisite for
reading Marlowe or Shakespeare profitably. Quite the reverse: one of
the things that I hope may emerge incidentally from the discussion is
the surprising extent to which it is *not* a pre-requisite. It is that, as well
as reading Marlowe and Shakespeare, I am trying to do something else
—to look again at that puzzling relationship one is sure exists between
artist and culture, yet which seems to be perennially in need of scrutiny,
qualification and re-formulation.

Anyone who storms this citadel will find it extremely well defended.
Many of the inhabitants have been in residence for several decades. They
draw on well-stocked arsenals, and they are always capable of felling
one with a single well-aimed Fact. Hence my own coat of mail, such as
it is—not, I am sure, bullet-proof, but I hope serviceable.

Radiating outward from any responsive interest in literature runs a
network of threads and filaments leading to other areas of human
concern—philosophy, history, sociology, theology, politics—and it is
not my intention to sever these living connexions in the interests of
this or that critical orthodoxy—not while they are living. But one of
the unfortunate by-products of the literary historicism that has come
into bloom this century has been to turn the living connexions into
dead ones. By the imposition of a static, schematic conception of the
major epochs of our literature, the historicists have contrived to confine
that literature within little closed compartments, so that the living
interests of the general reader cannot hope to achieve any vital engagement with it. The Elizabethan–Jacobean period has suffered particularly
acutely from this constriction. Our conception of the Elizabethans has

been codified for us into an 'orthodoxy', a world-picture which, if it has not yet induced complete apathy about these dull, conformist people, has only failed to do so because generation after generation of readers and playgoers has known that the literature itself offers much more.

Yet genuine historical curiosity, fed on this meagre fare, is pretty soon starved into submission: it concludes, perhaps, that the literature is one thing and the culture another, and is content to marvel at their contemporaneity; or perhaps it accepts the scholarly redactions of the literature as the dismal truth, and either learns to cultivate an anti-quarian taste for Elizabethan oddities, or gives up trying to relate the literature at all to its own living concerns. When this takes place, not only does literature become an academic matter in the very worst sense of that opprobrious term, but the real historical questions are by-passed: What precisely does an artist do with the material his culture offers him? Is intellectual history simply, in Collingwood's phrase, 'the decanting of ready-made thoughts out of one mind into another',[1] or is the process more complex? What happens when ideas received from a contemporary culture are 'dramatised'? And into what kind of relationship with this dramatisation can the inhabitant of another culture and another age enter?

To answer these questions we must obviously do two things, but do them better than the scholars I'm complaining about—read the litera-ture and study the history. Read the literature first, because the scholarly simplification which has produced this gelded Elizabethanism would have been impossible if the literature itself, in all its rich complexity, had been the real point of departure—the discrepancy would have been patent. But study the history too, because it would have been equally impossible if the historical investigation had been more painstaking; for, ironically, the scholars, who have been so stern in the reproof of subjective readings of literature, have frequently come to their Shake-speare or their Marlowe so armed with historical *idées fixes*, that they have been unable to see the work for the theory, or the writer for the 'influence'. For an age that was, to those that lived in it, 'full of agonies, uncertainties and conflicts, and seemed, as every age does, a time of crisis, chance and change, as well as a time of confidence, advance and new knowledge', they have substituted 'a kind of Golden Age of the Mind, when the difficulties which we feel as historical beings were not felt, when faith was easy, and man, knowing his place in an ordered system of things, happily saw correspondences everywhere, only slightly disturbed by the possibility that the universe might not be geo-centric'. Such a patronising attitude to the past, as Helen Gardner goes on to observe, reveals, not respect for the past, but contempt for it.[2]

And it arises because of a failure to distinguish between the things an age likes to think about itself and its real nature. H. A. Mason draws a helpful analogy from our own century:

When, for example, people tell us that the literature of the 1930s and the mental climate of the thirties were essentially what C. D. Lewis thought they were, we must salute the enterprise of the group that was able to impose its view of things on those too weak or too vacant to resist, but we must also apply another test; that of reality and real achievement. This is in fact one of the main tasks whatever the period we are studying: to distinguish what may be called the *Zeitgeist* or spirit of the times from the true spirit of those really 'making it new'.[3]

Any civilisation can be mistaken about itself—one suspects that most are. The Elizabethan ego-image is not the *ipse dixit* which puts an end to argument but, like all fantasy-projections, it is something to be earnestly scrutinized and sharply cross-questioned. Nor is there any dearth of primary material on which to base the scrutiny.

My aim, then, is not to campaign for the abolition of 'historical criticism'—although its perversity sometimes provokes one to this kind of extremism—but to do the job better. I have tried to test the relevance of historical material in each particular case, without too eager a commitment to a general theory of what that relevance must be. Tried too, to remain alive to the dangers of quick, one-way solutions to these complex problems. Above all, I have tried to treat the plays which are my historical data with the kind of respect for their essential nature that they deserve and demand.

But here one runs immediately into a sharp conflict between historical and critical methodologies: for the work of literature is no mere historical object, something to be converted into 'evidence', but something we have to enter into imaginative partnership with, something that is approached personally or not at all; and to treat it as 'historical data' looks very much like not treating it at all. So it seemed best to begin by considering in pretty broad terms the relationship between historical and literary studies, in the hope of characterising more precisely that play-of-mind which takes place when we read the literature of the past.

II

At first sight the historian and the critic appear to share a common pre-occupation—the desire to render intelligible the whole of man's past and present. Both historical and literary studies, that is to say, attempt to achieve that 'intellectual deliverance' which Matthew Arnold a century ago diagnosed as one of the deepest needs of his age—a deliverance from the pressure of mere information, from that 'vast multitude of facts awaiting and inviting…comprehension'. Arnold's development of this idea provides the wider context within which I would like this essay to be read. Our intellectual deliverance is perfected, he says,

> when we have acquired that harmonious acquiescence of mind which we feel in contemplating a grand spectacle that is intelligible to us; when we have lost that impatient irritation of mind which we feel in the presence of an immense, moving, confused spectacle which, while it perpetually excites our curiosity, perpetually baffles our comprehension.[4]

'Acquiescence' is perhaps putting the matter too passively, and even the 'harmonious' presupposes some restriction of discord in the interests of 'resolution'; yet in so far as 'harmonious acquiescence' is an ideal that commands respect, it reminds us that the study of literature is a part of the larger operation of self-knowledge to which man's nature commits him. So it seems worthwhile enquiring whether a rigid partitioning of the historical and the literary aspects of that operation does not impoverish both parties to the division. Can they not meet as friends and allies?

One would have hesitated to attempt any such reconciliation a century ago, when the techniques of natural science had achieved such a methodological hegemony that the historian tended to view himself as a kind of higher collector-of-facts bent on the discovery of Universal Historic Law; or when von Ranke's innocent remark that the task of the historian was 'simply to show how it really was' could be hailed as a profound truth. But both science and the philosophy of history have undergone marked changes since then. We now know—or think we know—that a law is not *in nature*, waiting to be discovered; that facts will lie inert for ever if the breath of an hypothesis does not resurrect them, and that the best of our systematic knowledge of the world is no more than a mental construct, an internally consistent and pragmatically verified model which enables man to establish a kind of intellectual suzerainty over certain tracts of his environment.

4

Now it is as true of history as of physics that our formulations do not describe *what is*, but our own state of mind while intelligently contemplating what is. As Johan Huizinga puts it,

Every event (even the very simplest fact) conceived by the faculty of historical cognition presumes an arranging of the material of the past, a combining of a number of data out of the chaos of reality into a mental image...[5]

This interpretative—one might almost say, creative—dimension of historical thought deserves some attention, the more so since the nineteenth-century conception of history (as facts interrelated in a system of quasi-mechanical laws) still lingers on—especially in works of literary history, which are very prone to invoke the historical arm of the law to suppress, by force of facts, rebellious literary interpretations. As I hope to show, such a use of history is based on a misconception.

Perhaps the best way into the matter is provided by Croce's dictum that 'all history is contemporary history'. This is so, he argues, even when it concerns events long past, since the very condition of history is that the factual matter of which it is woven should 'vibrate in the mind of the historian'.

And if contemporary history springs directly from life, equally directly from life rises that history which is customarily called non-contemporary, because it is evident that only an interest in this present life can move us to investigate a fact of the past.[6]

This being so, the historian must establish an imaginative commerce with the past:

If I have no feelings (however quiescent) of Christian love, of salvation by faith, of gentlemanly honour, of Jacobin radicalism or of reverence for ancient tradition, I shall vainly scan the pages of the Gospels or the Pauline epistles or the Carolingian epics, or the speeches made in the National Convention, or the lyrics, dramas and romances in which the nineteenth century recorded its nostalgia for the Middle Ages. Man is a microcosm, not in the natural sense, but in the historical sense, a compendium of universal history.[7]

To enter into living relationship with the past does not involve a withdrawal from one's present concerns, but is a natural extension of them.

When the cultural development of my particular historical moment...opens up to me the problem of Greek civilisation, of Platonic philosophy, or of a particular attitude characteristic of Attic life, that problem is as much bound up with my being, as the history of a transaction I am handling, or a friendship I am cultivating, or a danger that threatens me; and I investigate it with the same eager desire, I am troubled by the same sense of uneasiness, until I succeed in resolving it. Greek life is, in this case, present in me...[8]

As Collingwood points out, it is not the past in general that is the concern of the historian, but 'the past of this present, the present in which the act of imagination is going on, as here and now perceived'.[9]

It might be thought that so strongly 'subjective' an emphasis is some kind of Italianate aberration in Croce. But apart from Collingwood, who is an avowed admirer, historian after historian is to be found insisting on the Crocean historical imagination as a fundamental element in historical thought. Thus Huizinga talks of the 'historical sensation', 'a contact with the past, which is accompanied by an utter conviction of genuineness'.[10] And E. H. Carr, the historian of the Russian Revolution, who has not much time for Collingwood, and who, one suspects, would have even less for Croce's *filosofia dello spirito*, nevertheless allows, indeed insists on, the 'imaginative' component in historical thought.[11] We can take it, I think, that Collingwood's distillation—'History as re-enactment of past experience'[12]—however incomplete an account it may be of historical thought as a whole, still represents for modern historians an important component of it.[13]

This being so, there are some interesting consequences for a study of literature which attempts to be historical. For one thing, the possibility of complete objectivity, always questionable on literary grounds, turns out to be equally dubious historically. Collingwood again:

Thought can never be mere object. To know someone else's activity of thinking is possible only on the assumption that this same activity can be re-enacted in one's own mind. In that sense, to know 'what someone is thinking' (or 'has thought') involves thinking it for oneself.[14]

As Croce saw, the pursuit of historical objectivity is founded on a false opposition of *verità di ragione* to *verità di fatto*, truth of reason to truth of fact—truth of reason being regarded as subjective and therefore fallible, truth of fact as objective and therefore knowable. One is a subjective construct of the observer's, the other an emanation of the observed fact. For Croce, on the other hand, these are not two different kinds of truth, but parts of a 'unique, indivisible truth'.[15] The cognitive act, for both historian and critic, is one in which he *enters into relationship with the object*. And whatever the epistemological difficulties that stand in the way of conceiving this kind of cognition, they must simply be

6

faced; for, as E. H. Carr insists, any epistemology which enforces 'a rigid separation between the observer and the thing observed' is inappropriate to historical thought; 'we need a new model which does justice to the complex process of interrelation and interaction between them'.[16] Inappropriate too, one may add, to the critical process, where a new model is equally necessary.

Once we grasp the interpenetration of subjective and objective, of interpretation and fact, in an act of historical cognition, we are freed from the necessity of pursuing that phantom objectivity which was the *ignis fatuus* of nineteenth-century historiography. And at the same time, and for the same reasons, we can abandon the search for that 'authorised version' of a work of literature which would turn it finally and irrevocably into a *fact*.* The play of mind upon the historical or literary 'object' immediately lifts it out of the category of simple fact.

There is a second consequence of this recognition of the role of interpretation in history: the facts become, in a sense, subsidiary to the questions that are put to them. The historian stands in a new relation to his data. No longer is he their obsequious servant, opening his mouth only when, and as wide as, they permit him. No longer does he sit in contemplation, patiently awaiting the ineluctable epiphany of the Fact from Above; he does not find his facts, he makes them. They only become historical facts because they promise to answer the question he puts to them—before he had framed that question they were only a part of that 'chaos of reality' of which Huizinga speaks.[17] 'Sources,' says Croce, 'in the extrinsic sense of the empiricists, as things, are... not anterior but posterior to history.' And he classifies such sources, before the historical imagination has been to work on them, as *chronicle* not history: 'first History, then Chronicle. First the living man, then the corpse'. 'An object gives birth to an object, not to thought: the history that proceeded from objects, would be itself an object...' The significance of historical thought, therefore, depends not upon the facts that are adduced but upon the questions that are asked of those facts; and those questions are most properly historical when—to quote Croce again—they 'come out of the heart of life'.[18]

Because there is a kind of modernity, then, which is not unhistorical, but a necessary condition of historical intelligibility, because all history is contemporary history, I shall not allow myself to be intimidated by literary historians who mutter and grind their teeth whenever a

* I have been obliged to use this highly ambiguous word for lack of any more precise synonym.

'modern' question is asked of an Elizabethan author. They are simply trying to confine historical intelligence to the realm of chronicle, trying to veto that play of intelligence over the material of man's past which is at the heart of history. If I can be accused of being unhistorical, it will not be because I ask these questions, but because I answer them in the wrong way.

III

For, of course, there is a wrong, unhistorical way of answering questions which are, from an historical point of view, perfectly legitimate ones. It arises, one might say, from an excessive emphasis on the interpretative element in history. Accordingly, it would be best to pause here and give ear to a not altogether imaginary objector who has been getting increasingly restless during the last few paragraphs. 'But look here,' he says, 'what is to prevent your interpreter from imposing any pattern he likes upon history? Surely the nineteenth-century historians you so much deplore are important precisely because they tied clogs to the mere indulgence of fantasy under the pretext of history? Without the checking action of historical fact, without the resistance offered by the intractable but undeniable reality of the past, man merely recreates the past in his own image, never submitting his present to real critical appraisal, and thus he by-passes the true discipline of history, turning it into mere self-indulgence and self-congratulation. Facts matter. Without their bracing effect, historical thought becomes spineless, complacent, flabby.'

Now all this is true too. Part of the value of history, as Huizinga observes, is that it is one of the important ways open to man of 'reaching beyond oneself'.[19] And if we are to reap the benefit of this check on our habitual presuppositions and unrecognised prejudices, we must submit to the alien, the intractable and *the other*, in the period we are studying. In any case, to deny satisfaction to the appetite for facts, is to stunt a very natural and fruitful side of human nature—curiosity. 'As there is a curiosity about intellectual matters', wrote Arnold, 'which is futile, and merely a disease' (the 'chronicler's' affliction, we might say),

so there is certainly a curiosity,—a desire after the things of the mind simply for their own sake and for *the pleasure of seeing them as they are*,—which is, in an intelligent being, natural and laudable. Nay, and the very desire to see things as they are, implies a balance and regulation of mind which is not often attained without fruitful effort, and which is the very opposite of the blind and diseased impulse of mind which is what we mean to blame when we blame curiosity.[20]

History as a factual science is a legitimate exercise of natural curiosity. And the curiosity is purposive, as Arnold's remarks (in another context) on the importance of knowing the past, will indicate:

To know how others stand, that we may know how we ourselves stand; and to know how we ourselves stand, that we may correct our mistakes and achieve our deliverance—that is our problem.[21]

This then is one of the values the past can have for us—as the challenge to self-definition offered by a fact which resists our attempts to assimilate it to our habitual modes of thought and feeling.

But the factual dimension of history also saves us from the ravages of total relativism. E. H. Carr defines this danger well:

It does not follow that, because a mountain appears to take on different shapes from different angles of vision, it has objectively no shape at all or an infinity of shapes. It does not follow that because interpretation plays a necessarily large part in establishing the facts of history, and because no existing interpretation is wholly objective, one interpretation is as good as another, and the facts of history are in principle not amenable to objective interpretation.[22]

By recalling us to the necessary assumption of intelligibility in history, the factual approach prevents us from losing ourselves in a dense fog of pyrrhonistic relativism.

But having said this, it must also be pointed out that the factual approach, taken in isolation (like the interpretative approach pursued in isolation), has a characteristic defect—it tends to lack any anchorage in the present which could justify its activity. Arnold's 'natural curiosity' tends to dissipate itself in motiveless intellectual vagrancy, becoming 'merely a disease'. And it does this because it has separated the subject of its studies from its actual living concerns. It has made a separation, in Croce's terms, between *la vita teoretica* and *la vita pratica*, 'between moral life and the life of truth, with the absolute closure of communication between the two'. This separation, which takes away from history 'the current and heat of sentiment and moral effort', is responsible, says Croce, for

those so numerous histories that have been written and are still being written without motivation, which do not have at their origins, as an antecedent, a moral uneasiness and solicitude, and at their end do not leave the mind disposed to action, and lack for that reason problems, or even content that could be called historical. In reality, the life of moral consciousness, and of historical investigation and contemplation, are so mutually involved that the one grows along with the other...[23]

In the course of this essay I shall be concerned with many works of literary history which suffer from just this impoverishment—the lack of any living involvement with the contemporary life from which they spring and to which they are addressed.

The recognition of a distinction between the factual and the interpretative dimensions of historical thought should also alert us to the confusions that surround conceptions like 'the representative man' or the 'orthodoxy' of an age. It is perhaps naïve to point out that we have no Elizabethan public opinion polls, and that, even if we had, they would be in need of rigorous interpretation; but some literary historians are apt to forget it. 'What the majority of Elizabethans thought' on a given subject is beyond recovery, not only for lack of evidence, but also, more importantly, because it is not a 'fact' but a mental construct of the interpretative kind. Nor is it by any means certain that a statistical head-count of prevalent opinions, where Richard Hooker's counts for as much as a Lincolnshire poacher's, is what is wanted for purposes of historical intelligibility. The way one formulates 'Elizabethan opinion' is directly related to the purpose to which the formulation is to be put. In a study of the stresses and strains to which English Protestantism was subject in the sixteenth century, the testimony of one widely read, well-informed and sensitive observer like Hooker is worth a wilderness of pamphleteering ephemerids or oratorical parsons. In other words, our enquiries are oriented in relation to the interpretative function they are to serve, rather than in relation to the objective-factual state of affairs—which is (objectively) structure-less and chaotic.

Talk about the *representative* in an age, or a culture, is thus to be eschewed, because it commits one too deeply to the statistico-factual criterion, and neglects the interpretative dimension of historical under-standing (that is, where the word is not being used illicitly to cover an evaluation or an interpretation with a veil of spurious 'factuality'—a very common abuse in the writing of literary history). It is more proper to concern ourselves with the *significant*. I do not mean to use the word in a purely evaluative sense. Historically speaking, a thinker may be significantly muddle-headed and a poet significantly bad. Their significance resides in the help they offer in the answering of the questions we have set ourselves. If those questions are themselves insignificant, the 'significance' of this thinker, this writer, is illusory; for the whole value of historical studies depends upon our asking the right questions. (It may perhaps be worth adding that what is the right question for one age may not be the right question for the next: the self that is defining itself by the historical act changes, and with it, the questions that are central.) My aim then, in the historical part of this study, is to ask the significant questions, and to ask them of the men of the period who can best answer.

In framing the question and finding witnesses I shall inevitably be guided by personal judgments about the nature of the 'significant'; but there is no way round this kind of subjectivism. This historian exists in history, not outside it. 'When we seek to know the facts', E. H. Carr observes wisely,

the questions which we ask, and therefore the answers which we obtain, are prompted by our system of values. Our picture of the facts of our environment is moulded by our values, i.e. by the categories through which we approach the facts; and this picture is one of the important facts of which we have to take account...Progress in history is achieved through the interdependence and interaction of facts and values. The objective historian is the historian who penetrates most deeply into this reciprocal process.[24]

This last remark makes it clear that we are being befogged here by a false dichotomy. There is not interpretative history *and* factual history. There is only history—which consists in the proper interrelation and interaction between the two. As Carr has argued so persuasively, the historian's thought is a kind of dialectic, 'a continuous process of moulding his facts to his interpretation and his interpretation to his facts. It is impossible to assign primacy to one over the other.' It is a dialogue between the present and the past.[25]

In this dialogue the two modes of thought, factual and interpretative, merge into each other. Croce, who, following Vico, calls them 'philological' and 'philosophic' respectively, describes the process:

The philosophic mind, even if it brings before itself the whole mass of facts uncovered and corrected and set in order by the philologists, though it accepts for its own ends (and with due gratitude) a large or small part of these facts and checks them on its own account, is never satisfied within itself, because the very course of the investigation propounds new philological problems to which it must attend, thereby making itself philological. On the other hand, how can a philologist carry out his researches if he does not have in mind some problem or other—however vague—of historiography, which guides him in the selection that he makes from the factual data awaiting elucidation...?[26]

Croce's nomenclature for the two hypothetical types of historian brings to the surface an important conflict—for one tends to think of philosophy and philology as two mutually exclusive extremes, almost temperamental incompatibilities: one requiring the virtues of minute scholarship, the other demanding a rarer talent for large conceptions and bold leaps of imagination. But historical thought demands just these antithetical powers of mind—common enough in isolation, but rarely found co-existing in one mind in their fully developed form. It is the same twofold qualification that literature demands of its reader.

On the one hand he must bring all his normal modes of thought and feeling, his deepest concerns and his most profound convictions, and try to interpret what the past offers him in the light of those concerns and convictions, incorporating the past into an inclusive personal view of life. He must try to assimilate the past to his present self, and do so at the deepest level. He cannot rest content with the kind of effete indifference that shrugs it all off with a murmured 'De gustibus...'. On the other hand, he must possess the scholar's scrupulousness about seeing things 'as they really are'; he must respect the 'document'; he must recognise, indeed welcome, the unassimilable, the unpalatable, the indigestible. He must realise that the past, in so far as it diverges from the present, constitutes a challenge to the present—'Justify yourself! Can you afford to dispense with modes of thought which were fruitful and illuminating to us? Are your mental categories appropriate here? How can you be sure you have progressed? Answer for yourself!' He must be prepared to discover that his interpretative tools must be abandoned, because they do too much violence to the data they are trying to encompass.

In this way the recognition of the alien and the inimical in the past, far from enervating contemporary consciousness, rather sharpens it—by providing the kind of constructive resistance to thought that a grindstone offers to a knife. It is only those who fear that the cutting edge of contemporary consciousness may be turned against their own throats, who wish to legislate, in the name of scholarship, for a permanent divorce between knife and grindstone.

This parallel between the dialectic of historical thought, the process by which the historian transforms documents or chronicle-matter into history, and the literary critic's attempt to penetrate imaginatively a literary work of the past, throws some light on the epistemology of both historical and critical cognition: in both cases the significance uncovered is both created and objectively there; and in both cases the breadth and importance of that significance is dependent, firstly, on the rigorous submission of preconception and predilection to the test of the 'document', and, secondly, on the writer's having wide, living, intelligent and profound relations with his own culture, and with himself as a human being, in the light of which he makes his interpretation.

Nor is this simply a matter of the thought that is specifically concerned with the past. Clearly the paradoxical tension between interpretation and fact is present in any balanced approach to literature—to contemporary literature as much as to the literature of the past. There must be a poise, an equilibrium, between imaginative re-enactment (the assimilative movement in any act of comprehension), and an attention to fact, a willingness to grapple with the 'not-ourselves' in the work; 'and it is impossible to assign primacy to one over the other'. Seen in this light, the apparently special problem posed by the literature of the past shows itself to be simply one manifestation of a much larger problem—the problem of assimilating the products of other minds without destroying their characteristic shape and contour. It is (to follow the scent a little further) the basic problem of human relationships, in which, ideally, there should be a simultaneous assimilation of the person one meets to one's own modes of thought and feeling, *and* a reckoning with, a response to, that in him which is not assimilable in this way. Without the attempt to grasp inwardly and imaginatively the personal significance of this man's being he remains for me an uninterpreted hieroglyph on the surface of life; yet if the assimilative movement is too strong I see only my own image, and the liberating meaning of the encounter is perpetually lost. By this double motion of absorption and separateness we enlarge our world in the most important of ways, and our experience becomes an *experience of the other*, while remaining truly *our experience*. It is in the seminal nature of this complex response to reality-outside-ourselves that the studies of history, and of literature, find one of their most important justifications.

IV

But here we have reached a *ne plus ultra* in the attempt to subsume the study of literature under the study of history. And so as not to jeopardise a useful formulation by woolly syncretism, it would be wise to attend to some necessary distinctions that are beginning to present themselves.

If one ponders the analogy from personal relations, it becomes clear that it is much more apposite to literature (which *is* a person-to-person situation) than to historical thought (which confronts an age rather than an individual). Not only does literature make a more personal demand on the inner resources of the student, but it concerns itself, much more than history does, with the individual case, the writer, the work. History, that is to say, is a more theoretical science, in the sense that, however chary it may be of the concept of Law, its gravitation is always toward the generalisation, without which it would be mere chronicle. The critic, by contrast, has as his necessary anchorage the particularity of the text he is studying, and he refuses to abate one jot or tittle of the written word in the interests of generality.

Consequently there is a considerable difference between the historian's evaluation of the significance of his raw material, which is closely tied to its relevance as *evidence* for or against a general proposition, and the critic's evaluation of a work, which refuses to submit the work to categories outside the work, refuses, that is to say, to use the work as evidence at all, but rather approaches it as a completed structure of meaning which will dictate its own categories. He may perhaps put questions to the work, but his aim is not to press it into the service of generality, but to elicit, in a new historical context, the meaning which, he takes it, is already *there* in some real sense.

In historical thought the preoccupation is with process, in the light of which the event acquires its significance; whereas the critic is more concerned with continuity, with the past seen as heritage rather than process, and with the event as unique and intrinsically significant. The concept of progress, with which most modern historians seem to have made their peace in one way or another,[27] is, in the field of art, essentially meaningless. Literature has not progressed since the time of Shakespeare, any more than it has declined. Art is not in this sense subject to history. Nor does it acquire its significance by being plotted against the coordinates of historical evolution: the significance is intrinsic. The literary stance toward the past is thus radically evaluative: it is concerned, in Arnold's phrase, with 'the best which has been thought and said in the world',[28] and it tries to salvage from the past all that is of perennial interest and value. The critic is less concerned to distinguish one age from another than to discern their common ground. He contemplates what Burckhardt, in a suggestive phrase, called the 'continual metempsychosis of acting and suffering man through countless incarnations',[29] and he notes that, though man is always learning, at the deepest level the lessons remain oddly the same.

But when one tries to treat Elizabethan literature historically—which is what this study aims at doing—one is committed, in some measure at least, to treating it as evidence. And this is where we came in. Is there simply a flat methodological contradiction which leaves one with nothing but a choice of mutually exclusive alternatives—history *or* literature? Or can the two modes of thought be entertained together? Can the contradiction be forced to yield up a single truth?

The past as cultural heritage, as against the past as evolutionary process: it is hard to see on what grounds, philosophical or human, one could deny validity to either notion. They are both necessary: the first, literary, stance if we are to evaluate properly our own existence, make vital discriminations between the healthful and the malignant in contemporary culture, and learn to understand our own nature; the second, historical, stance if we are to change that culture and exercise any kind of control over the evolutionary process; necessary, that is to say, if we are to implement the insights and evaluations we bring from literature. And I have already suggested that this kind of practical concern with the quality of contemporary life is something that grows naturally out of a responsive reading of literature. Nothing but impoverishment results from forbidding criticism to cross the frontier between *la vita teoretica* and *la vita pratica*.

What do we do then, about the methodological conflict which seems so often to make historians bad critics, and critics bad historians? We have seen that it cannot be resolved at the theoretical level—modern historiography is still too suspicious of direct evaluation of the event to be ready to absorb the literary attitude to the past. But it is still open to us to be historical on a broader basis than contemporary theory would permit us; realising that some of the documentary matter the past offers us has reached us through the refracting medium of a great mind and requires, consequently, a more respectful and submissive attention than is suggested when we refer to it as 'evidence'. (The good historian, I suspect, makes this kind of compensation automatically.)

But even if we accept an essential discontinuity between historical and literary studies, it is still open to us to strain our faculties to encompass both views of the Elizabethan world, to try to keep a foot in both camps, remaining ready at all times to translate cultural *tradition* into historical *process*, and back again into cultural tradition; aware simultaneously that human nature is always the same, and that it is always changing; knowing that ideas grow with, and out of, a specific historical context, yet also that some ideas possess the kind of substantial truth which cuts right across historical relativism; recognising the major thinkers and artists as in some sense the products of an age, yet also as the makers of an age and the perennial possession of mankind thereafter; remembering that, while for convenience we regard history as a system of rational causal relationships, there is a mystery about that regenerative vitality which throws up from time to time the man of creative genius, and that explanation in this area must stop short of impertinence; approaching the Elizabethans, then, for evidence about the process that produced the modern world, but approaching them, too, for the direct personal stimulus and inspiration that can only come out of 'conversation'; bearing in mind all the while what Lionel Trilling observes in an excellent essay on 'The Sense of the Past': that 'the refinement of our historical sense chiefly means that we keep it properly complicated'.[30] This is asking a lot of human fallibility, and by these standards I shall certainly not escape condemnation. But I have yet to be convinced that a conscious inability to live up to them disqualifies one from formulating one's ideal objectives, and I take some comfort from the case of Dr Johnson: 'There are two things which I am confident I can do very well: one is an introduction to any literary work, stating what it is to contain, and how it should be executed in the most perfect manner; the other is a conclusion, shewing from various causes why the execution has not been equal to what the author promised to himself and to the publick.'

v

I now approach the particular focus of this study—the relationship between artist and culture. The historical 'explanation' of the artist (as the product merely of his environment), which promises to throw a flood of light on the relationship, is in reality no more than a half-truth: the inevitable result of asking a causal question is that one gets a causal answer. Even if we remain within the realm of causation, the matter is more complex than this, for causation, as Lionel Trilling points out, is a two-way process:

The poet, it is true, is an effect of environment, but we must remember that he is no less a cause. He may be used as the barometer, but let us not forget that he is also part of the weather. We have been too easily satisfied by a merely elementary meaning of environment; we have been content with a simple quantitative implication of the word, taking a large and literally environing thing to be always the environment of a smaller thing. In a concert room the audience and its attitudes are of course the environment of the performer, but also the performer and his music make the environment of the audience.[31]

The two-way traffic implicit in the artist–audience relationship is something that should not be forgotten.

But the artist also enters into a relationship with his culture, in which he is much more the receiver. The process extends over his entire life-span within society. Throughout this period he is being moulded, incited, balked or infuriated by the multilateral pressures that go to make up social existence. Here again the relationship is one neither of dependence nor independence. It is a kind of *creative assimilation*. I use the organic metaphor because the assumption of an instrumental relationship, as of sculptor to marble, seems to me highly misleading—artist and material are inextricably confounded. The intellectual climate in which the artist lives is partly his own creation. He can only receive the 'received ideas' of his age by making them part of his own meta-bolism. And who, in the face of this obscure and inherently private mystery, will venture to determine how much or how little of purely personal insight he has added to what he received? 'Before the idea of an influence', writes Trilling in the same essay,

we ought to be far more puzzled than we are; if we find it hard to be puzzled enough, we may contrive to induce the proper state of uncertainty by turning the word upon ourselves, asking, 'What have been the influences that made me the person I am, and to whom would I entrust the task of truly discovering what they were?'[32]

And yet this impenetrably mysterious personal activity emerges in the social activity we call literature, literature which, in the words of L. C. Knights, is 'the exact expression of realised values'. He goes on,

and these values are never purely personal: even when they conflict with accepted modes they are conditioned by them, and it is part of the artist's function (whether he is a 'representative man' or not) to give precise meaning to ideas and sentiments that are only obscurely perceived by his contemporaries.[33]

It is only by a paradoxical synthesis of historical and literary methodo-logies that we can even begin to grasp the nature of this interaction of personal and social in the creative act—and it should never be forgotten that the paradox is there.

I have spoken of 'creative assimilation' as if this is what every artist does with the material his culture offers him. But in reality it is a very rare, almost miraculous equilibrium—the poise of a mind utterly sure of itself, yet immensely responsive to the manifold life of humanity around it. It is a quality one can claim for the mature Shakespeare but for few others; for lesser men there is a whole spectrum of more or less unsatisfactory adjustments, ranging from ruinous dependence on a debased social code to an independence which is in danger of toppling over into mere assertiveness or a random impulse to *épater-les-bourgeois*. I have cast Marlowe to play this second and unenviable role: not only because I want to propose some limits to his already distended reputation, but also because he exemplifies very clearly the way alertness to the currents of contemporary life can be quite unavailing to an artist, as long as the inner stability, the central core of assured humanity, is lacking. Indeed Marlowe's sensitivity to the flux of Elizabethan feeling and belief, a quality which makes him a magnificent instrument for registering the tensions of his age, was artistically his downfall. But it is best to leave assertions of this kind to emerge from a more particular context where they can be weighed and tested. It is enough at this stage to be awake to the manifold shapes this independent-dependence can take, and to be prepared to see the relationship substantially modified by the nature, and the growth, of individual artistic sensibility.

But Shakespeare's creative partnership with his own culture, in terms of which we can give some meaning to this creative assimilation, ultimately raises questions which lead us out of the purely literary sphere. Because he is able to give imaginative body and weight to so much of Elizabethan life and thought, Shakespeare makes us directly aware of a whole range of beliefs and attitudes which, though we know them to be historically conditioned and very much of an age, nevertheless seem to carry in their dramatised form guarantees of a much higher validity and permanence. Many of these conceptions are no longer part of our normal consciousness, and they present us, consequently, with the historical challenge of the foreign and the 'other'. Yet here they are, built into the foundations of an art that is still, and very properly, a part of modern consciousness. It is a very teasing paradox. But the appropriate response to it is not to attempt to resurrect the lost conditions by an act of will—propounding once more the cultural myth of an ideal Elizabethan society, and turning ourselves in the process into earnest literary anachronisms. It is rather to consider whether those conditions are indeed lost, and whether our failure to discern them is not a failure to think creatively about our own historical environment. We cannot be content to label the assumptions, which are woven into the very fabric of so impressive a web of meaning, merely 'out-of-date'.

Shakespeare forces us to enquire whether an intelligence to which his view of the state, or his Christianity, are affairs of the past, is not an intelligence that has failed to encompass the full significance of being alive in the twentieth century.

The factors that I single out as central to the lost Elizabethan wisdom will inevitably be taken as selected on the basis of a personal quarrel with contemporary culture. No doubt this is true. I can only say, first, that to have no quarrel with contemporary culture would be more reprehensible; and secondly, that my very tentative conclusions in this area have been (for me at least) genuine discoveries, a drawing to the light of certain half-formed uneasinesses and dissatisfactions under the stimulus of Shakespeare's broad and profound humanity.

2

DRAMATIST AS JINGOIST:
'THE MASSACRE AT PARIS'

I

If space were to be allotted to a play only in proportion to its dramatic merit, I should not be writing this chapter. But if one can postulate a spectrum of possible adjustments to the cultural environment, ranging from disastrous capitulation to triumphant partnership, then *The Massacre at Paris* is clearly at the lower end of that spectrum; and there is always something to be learned about norms, from the study of extremes. Furthermore, a play as bad as this, written by an author whose reputation is as much in the ascendant as Marlowe's is at present, raises too many interesting questions to be entirely by-passed. What, for instance, does the brutal, chauvinistic propagandist who produced this piece reveal about the author of *Doctor Faustus*? Or again, what is the explanation for the extraordinary faithfulness with which Marlowe mirrors the extreme protestant view of sixteenth-century French history—mirrors it to such an extent that it is possible to provide an exact 'source', not only for the version of events which Marlowe gives us, but even for the sentiments to which the play gives voice, to account for its moral climate? And this implies a further question: what happens within the creative sensibility of a man who capitulates so completely to the lowest appetites of his audience? How did Marlowe permit himself to write the play?

And here, as with nearly all Marlowe's plays, we are dogged with textual difficulties—for can we really say with any show of accuracy that Marlowe wrote the text we now have? F. S. Boas has made great play with the so-called 'Collier Leaf', a leaf of manuscript, previously thought to be a forgery, but now shown by Quincy Adams to be probably genuine.[1] It is a considerably expanded version of the first part of Scene xvi, and one may legitimately infer that other scenes have been similarly cut and distorted in the printed text. There is, however, no warrant for the further inference which Boas proceeds to make, that the missing passages are of a kind to redeem a patently feeble play; for the Collier Leaf text differs from the printed text only in being longer—it is not, in any obvious way, of better quality. Indeed, it would be reasonable to argue that the printed version gains as much in conciseness as it lost by excision. We are not faced here with a textual problem comparable to the problem posed by *Doctor Faustus*, where there is evidence in the surviving text of considerable imaginative power. *The Massacre at Paris* as we now have it is so dismally consistent that the putative additions would need to be of staggering quality to change substantially our estimate of the play. I am, of course, being cavalier about the science of bibliography—though not inadvertently so. In fact, it might be wisest to pause here at the outset to consider the claims of the bibliographers, since parts of my argument rest on the assumption that the 'badness' of Marlowe texts is, as yet, unproven.

Like the converted sinner who magnifies his unregenerate depravity, to the greater glory of God, the bibliographer is inclined to magnify the corruptness of his text as an oblique compliment to the bibliographical art which can redeem such unpromising material. What he often obscures, however, is the subjective way in which he has decided the text is bad in the first place.[2] I am continually astounded at the ease with which Marlowe's editors arrive at the conclusion that a certain passage is not Marlowe's, but the work of an interpolator, yet do so without offering any account of the qualities they regard as specifically Marlovian. Even the redoubtable Greg has some sins of this kind to account for—though he at least has the wisdom to admit the role of 'personal Impressionism' in his judgments.[3] But this kind of editorial activity is not so much 'impressionism' as a systematic attempt to rehabilitate a poet whose reputation must suffer if all the texts published under his name are acknowledged to be his own work.

It seems to me less tendentious to start from just this assumption—that the published texts of the plays are Marlowe's texts—and to derive our conception of the Marlovian from those texts, and not from a Marlowe anthology compiled according to the personal preferences of each successive editor. At least then we have some agreed common ground instead of a confusion of tongues. There is, after all, no law of nature which prevents a poet capable of the *Faustus* soliloquy from writing lumpish bombast and unfunny farce. In fact, the co-existence of these 'incompatible' strains is one of the most notable features of the group of plays that have come down to us under Marlowe's name. Even the straight-laced and solemn *Tamburlaine* had the usual supply of 'fond and friuolous Iestures', if we can trust the word of the printer who decorously suppressed them.

Returning to *The Massacre*, then, I would argue that, while there is evidence to suggest that our text is, at least in places, a memorial reconstruction,[4] and to suspect that quite a lot has been lost,[5] there is no evidence that what we have is not Marlowe's. Nor does the play lead us to expect that a complete text would reveal any hitherto unsuspected depth or subtlety in Marlowe's mind—it is plainly the work of a man whose heart is not in the enterprise. So we are left with our initial question: how did Marlowe come to write this nasty piece of journalistic bombast?

Some obvious answers spring to mind. The Guise is a creation of a familiar type, clearly cast in the same mould that produced Tamburlaine, Barabas and Faustus. He is Icarus, Lucifer, the overreacher and highflyer:

> Set me to scale the high Pyramides,
> And thereon set the diadem of France:
> I'll either rend it with my nails to naught,
> Or mount the top with my aspiring wings,
> Although my downfall be the deepest hell.   ii. 43

He is the villain-hero for whom 'peril is the chiefest way to happiness,/ And resolution honour's fairest aim' (ii. 38). Like Barabas and Mortimer he is an exponent of *Realpolitik*, and a Machiavellian:

> The gentle king, whose pleasure uncontroll'd
> Weakeneth his body, and will waste his realm...
> Him, as a child, I daily win with words,
> So that for proof he barely bears the name;
> I execute, and he sustains the blame.   ii. 70

Like Tamburlaine, he has grandiose visions, in the future tense, of brazen, despotic power:

> As ancient Romans o'er their captive lords,
> So will I triumph o'er this wanton king;
> And he shall follow my proud chariot wheels.   xviii. 51

The attraction of this motif for Marlowe is indicated by its appearance, not only in *Tamburlaine*, but also in *Edward II*:

> ...I think myself as great
> As Caesar riding in the Roman street,
> With captive kings at his triumphant car.   I. i. 172

The Guise's power-lust provides opportunities, not only for bloody spectacle, but for that 'bombast circumstance, / Horribly stuff'd with epithets of war' which had been so successful in *Tamburlaine*.

> Give me a look, that, when I bend the brows,
> Pale death may walk in furrows of my face;
> A hand, that with a grasp may gripe the world...   ii. 100

With which we might compare this description of Tamburlaine:

> Pale of complexion, wrought in him with passion,
> Thirsting with sovereignty and love of arms,
> His lofty brows in folds do figure death...   *I Tam.* ii. i. 19

There are times, indeed, when the speakers in *The Massacre* sound like ventriloquists' dummies for the ghost of the Scythian war-lord:

> NAVARRE. The power of vengeance now encamps itself
> Upon the haughty mountains of my breast:
> Plays with her gory colours of revenge...   xiii. 20

Then Henry III, the weak king with homosexual leanings, has obvious affinities with Edward II (though which play came first is largely a matter for conjecture). From the repetition of this homosexual motif, both in the opening scene of *Dido* and in Leander's encounter with the amorous Neptune, we may suppose this to have been one reason for Marlowe's becoming interested in this particular stretch of French history.

But *Tamburlaine* or *Edward II*, however much they may tell us about the attraction the subject held for Marlowe, are misleading analogues, if they lead us to suppose that the centre of gravity of *The Massacre* is to be found in these Marlovian 'themes'. They may have provided the initial impetus for the play, but their energy was very quickly expended, as the terrible thinness of both drama and poetry bears witness. In their place, a far more prosaic process supervenes. Marlowe stands here in a special relationship to the material of his drama. He is a kind of mechanical transcriber of events which are *given* in a sense that the imaginative facts of Tamburlaine's career are not 'given' in Perondinus or Fortescue. The play is notable for a crippling dependence on source material which was, in itself, vacuous: the public declarations, apologies and manifestoes published by the official parties; the flood of polemic ephemerae (pamphlets and newsbooks) dealing with European affairs between 1570 and 1589; and the various partisan histories of the Religious Wars in France.

This ground has been well charted by Paul Kocher in a series of three articles,[6] and I have found no evidence to modify the clear-cut conclusions he advances. These are, briefly, that Marlowe almost invariably follows the accounts of the protestant propagandists where he is directly dependent on his sources, and his own inventions or re-arrangements are either in the direction of blacker villainy contrasted with more astonishing virtue, or they represent a strong predilection for the lurid and bloody. The same judgment applies to the cases where he chooses one of several rival accounts of the same event.

II

In order to understand the nature of Marlowe's dependence on his sources, we need at least a thumbnail sketch of the events between the St Bartholomew massacre of 1572 and the assassination of Henry III in 1589—the time span of the play.

In 1572 the chronic hostilities between Catholic and Protestant seemed to have given way to an *entente cordiale*: for the Catholic sister of King Charles IX was to marry the protestant Henry of Navarre, who together with Admiral de Coligny and the prince of Condé formed the nucleus of the Huguenot party. Shortly afterwards, how-ever, the Huguenots who had assembled in Paris for the wedding were put to the sword in the St Bartholomew massacre, amongst them the admiral himself. The papal reaction staggered protestant opinion, for Gregory XIII declared himself better pleased than with fifty Lepantos and held services of thanksgiving in Rome.

Charles, whose role in the massacre had been equivocal, and who had offered successively a series of incompatible reasons for the atrocity, died in 1574, and rumours were abroad that it was no natural death— that he had imprudently sworn vengeance on the executors of the massacre. He was succeeded by Henry III, formerly duke of Anjou, who, like his brother Charles, found himself under continual pressure from the Guise faction (which, in 1585, consolidated itself as the 'Holy League') and from his mother Catherine de Medici. The League was an organisation aimed ostensibly at the extirpation of protestant heresy in France and it had ambiguous liaisons both with the papacy and the king of Spain. There seems no doubt that Philip was using the faction of discontent in France as a lever against Navarre, as a means of weaken-ing the English alliance, and as an insurance policy in the Low Coun-tries; at the same time Henry, duke of Guise, was playing his own game, and paying his bills in Spanish pistolets. Under League pressure Henry III was finally persuaded, in 1587, to send an army against Henry of Navarre, now the heir presumptive to the French throne and a thorn in the flesh of the Catholic party. The French forces, however, were defeated at the battle of Coutras, and the Guise faction turned its energies to domestic affairs. There seems little doubt that Guise himself was aiming at the crown of France—to judge from the bogus propaganda published to prove his lineal right to it—and in 1588 he entered Paris with an army (the 'Day of the Barricades') and Henry was obliged to retire, in view of the popular enthusiasm for his rival. Soon afterwards, though, at Blois, he had the Guise assassinated, to the great joy of protestant Europe.

The house of Guise put up considerable resistance, but after the strangling of the cardinal of Lorraine it was plain that treachery could only be met by treachery; thus, in 1589, a friar who had gained access to the king stabbed him with a poisoned knife. Again papal reception of the news confirmed the worst suspicions of the protestants, for Sixtus V delivered himself of an Apologia for the deed and forbade the solemnisation of Catholic funeral rites for the dead king. Navarre succeeded to the French throne as Henry IV, amid great Huguenot rejoicing.

Ironically, it was only four years later, in 1593, that he decided that 'Paris vaut une messe' and turned Catholic. Of course, this last reversal, which sheds such an equivocal light on the protestant hero of the propagandists, lies outside the purview of Marlowe's play, which was probably produced no later than 1591, after which the fortunes of the Huguenot party went into a steep decline.

The obvious interest of this tract of French history for the English audience lay in the apparent centrality of the religious conflict between Huguenots and Catholics. The English protestants saw enacted on the stage of France their own tragedy—but for the grace of God and of Queen Elizabeth—and their intense sympathetic involvement was heightened by the threat of Catholic domination, whether in the shape of Mary Stuart (a cousin of the Guise), Jesuit missionaries, popish assassination plots, or Spanish invasion. After the 1570 papal bull, which excommunicated Elizabeth and absolved her Catholic subjects of their vows of allegiance, every agglomeration of Catholic power could justifiably be regarded as the massing of the army which was to depose the heretic queen at the instigation of the pope.[7]

In such an atmosphere of preternatural anxiety and chronic suspicion, the only history likely to be written was moralistic history, and English versions of French affairs, where they are not merely translations, rely exclusively on the views of the besieged and embattled Huguenots themselves. So we can hardly blame Marlowe for neglecting the Catholic accounts of these events (although there are, interestingly enough, two points in the play where only a French Catholic pamphlet could have supplied him with a fact that he uses).[8]

Commentators on both sides, however, saw themselves not as reporters of the Wars of Religion, but as moralists assisting the just gods and the gentle reader to find out their enemies so as to oppose and destroy them, and their true friends so as to support them. Consequently, those personages like Henry III who in life vacillated between the two causes inevitably have their careers split into two halves (one villainous, the other heroic) separated by a decisive change of heart, if not a conversion.

As I have suggested, it is not surprising to find Marlowe following the protestant party line and attributing all kinds of villainy to the Guise, turning Navarre into the model Christian prince, underlining the enormity of the massacre or condoning the assassination of the Guise. What is more interesting, though, is the consistency with which he outdoes his models; for the crude melodrama of the play surpasses the crudity of its sources.

While there is general agreement, for instance, that the Guise is a villain, Marlowe invents and adapts incidents to enhance this villainy. There is no authority in the sources for attributing to him the poisoning of the old queen of Navarre (ii. 10–25). The malignity which makes him trample on the dead admiral's body (v. 42) is either an invention or a detail deliberately sought out in a book which he does not use elsewhere. The murder of Loreine (Leranne in the sources) by the Guise (v. 64 ff.) is another fabrication, for in all the available sources the preacher escapes, and his assailant, in any case, is not the Guise. Nor was he present at the murder of Ramus (Scene vi) in which Marlowe gives him a major part. Similarly, the murder of Navarre's 'pedants' (vi. 77 ff.) is committed by the king's guard of Switzers, not, as in Marlowe, by the Guise personally. One of the most repulsive and ludicrous pieces of butchery, the massacre of the open-air conventicle of Huguenots (Scene ix), is borrowed from an exploit of the Guise's father, Francis duke of Guise, and dates from a time ten years earlier.[9] Even the hated Catholic seminary at Rheims—to English minds the seed-bed of popish plots against Elizabeth—is fathered upon the Guise (xviii. 102–3); and it is perhaps the same indiscriminate malice which leads Marlowe to rake up the incident of the duchess of Guise's lover from sources now lost,[10] thus making the Guise not only vicious, but ridiculous as a cuckold.

The kind of dramatic licence which aggregates events around a central character is perhaps excusable, but at the same time as he is blackening the Guise's character and representing him as the chief instigator and enactor of the French wars, Marlowe is also pursuing a similar campaign of vilification against the queen-mother and Henry of Anjou. In Scene i, Catherine declares her intention of dissolving 'with blood and cruelty' the marriage celebrations of Navarre and his bride—a clear hint that she is plotting the massacre; and Marlowe goes to extraordinary lengths to present her as the super-manipulator at the heart of events:

> Tush, all shall die unless I have my will;
> For, while she lives, Catherine will be queen.   xi. 66[11]

In this emphasis he is following Catherine's vindictive protestant biographer, Henri Estienne; but Estienne at least has the grace to realise that Catherine's sole responsiblity for the ills of France is incompatible with the Guise's, and he paints him as a comparatively white sheep.[12] Marlowe, by contrast, is happier the more villains he can find.

He even compromises the future Henry III, by permitting him, as Anjou, a far more active and bloody role in the massacre than the authorities warranted.[13] And in the emphasis on the king's homosexual passion for his 'minions' (xi. 16–21, 45—7; xiii. 10–22) Marlowe is either indulging an obsessive preoccupation of his own, or following the most libellous of the Catholic propagandists. Protestants, on the whole, did their best to smooth over or ignore this weakness of the French king.[14] But Marlowe's indiscriminate appetite for vice garners it from any source. As a result he has a hard job shifting gear when Henry becomes a protestant sympathiser and opponent of the League. In order to smooth over this transition, he is obliged to invent another incident—Henry's dismissal of his council (xvi. 78–81) and his adherence to the anti-League hero, Epernoun.[15] This is in line with the pro-Navarre propaganda which sought to woo Henry away from the Guisians by insisting that all his misdeeds were done under compulsion from bad advisers—thus making a change of face possible without loss of face.[16] But none of these writers records a dismissal of the council at this point; and the intimacy between the king and Epernoun, however gratifying to the opponents of the League, has no foundation in contemporary reports.[17] All the 'sweet Epernouns' of Scene xxi are part of a systematic rehabilitation of Henry, the erstwhile *massacreur*.

Just as the monumental villainy of the Catholic party is constructed upon falsification of the facts as Marlowe knew them, so his glorification of Navarre draws on the most inflated panegyrics of that prince.[18] There were at hand, if he had wanted them, sane and balanced accounts of this key figure, weighing his virtues against his deficiencies.[19] But the kind of drama which permits a hero to have weaknesses is foreign to the chop-logic of this play, and Navarre remains so sublime an example of protestant virtue braving Catholic vice that he hardly exists at all. It is a gratuitous bounty that places Du Bartas, poet and protestant, at the side of Navarre: although he was in the court, he played no such role as Marlowe gives him.[20]

When I talk of 'falsification of facts' and a 'campaign of vilification', I do not mean to imply a conscious didactic aim on Marlowe's part. In all these alterations and amplifications there is a curiously random air which is only compatible with an instinctive adaptation of material in a congenial direction. And it is the debased nature of this *instinct* that concerns me here.

The extent to which Marlowe has sold out to the basest elements in himself and his audience is plainest in his treatment of the papal and Spanish dimensions of his story. He opens his case for the prosecution by an assertion for which I can find no authority in the most rabid of the anti-Leaguers, that the Guise has some sort of plenary dispensation from the pope, a blank cheque on the mercy of God:[21]

> For this, have I a largess from the Pope,
> A pension, and a dispensation too;
> And by that privilege to work upon
> My policy hath fram'd religion.   ii. 62

But this is less a comment on the Guise than an attempt to call into play the turbulent emotions associated with the Catholic plots against Elizabeth; it is a reminder of the Throckmortons, the Babingtons and the Parrys who were rumoured to have possessed some kind of papal indulgence for their treachery. It is the kind of thing that ill-educated Englishmen necessarily believed of papists—more or less an emphatic way of asserting a complete absence of moral scruple.

But more important than this kind of systematic libelling, is the tone of the utterances, which is set very early in the play. The Guise is reported to have planned a massacre of the protestants. Condé remarks,

> My lord, you need nor marvel at the Guise,
> For what he doth, the pope will ratify,
> In murder, mischief, or in tyranny.   i. 39

The objection is not that Marlowe holds this view of Vatican policy—which was, after all, a fairly common one[22]—but to the tone of petulant and savage vindictiveness which marks all the utterances about the papacy. And this tone, while it may be paralleled in some of the more extravagant pamphleteers, is unmistakably Marlowe's own. Thus the dying Henry III announces,

> ...I hope to live;
> Which if I do, the papal monarch goes
> To wrack, and [th'] antichristian kingdom falls.
> These bloody hands shall tear his triple crown,
> And fire accursed Rome about his ears;
> I'll fire his crazed buildings, and enforce
> The papal towers to kiss the lowly earth.
> Navarre, give me thy hand: I here do swear
> To ruinate that wicked Church of Rome,
> That hatcheth up such bloody practices;
> And here protest eternal love to thee,
> And to the Queen of England specially,
> Whom God hath bless'd for hating papistry.   xxi. 59

This from a Catholic prince who has, even in the protestant accounts, just received the sacrament and made his confession to a friar,[23] patently has no reference to history, or to the historical Henry III. Rather it is the indulgence of a mood which Marlowe several times allowed to run away with his pen—as when the mild Edward II gives vent to these resounding sentiments:

> Proud Rome, that hatchest such imperial grooms,
> For these thy superstitious taper-lights,
> Wherewith thy antichristian churches blaze,
> I'll fire thy crazed buildings, and enforce
> The papal towers to kiss the lowly ground.
> With slaughter'd priests may Tiber's channel swell,
> And banks rais'd higher with their sepulchres.
>   *Edward II*, I. iv. 97

I mention this parallel (and notice how extraordinarily exact it is, even down to the scornful use of the word 'hatch') not simply as a stick to beat Marlowe with, but to point up a curious element in his work—the recurrence of certain obsessive motifs.[24] This particular motif—the vision of the Babylonian destruction of Rome—is part of a larger complex of images of bloody destruction and fire. The thought recurs in *The Jew of Malta*:

> I'll be reveng'd on this accursed town...
> I'll help to slay their children and their wives,
> To fire the Churches, pull their houses down... v. i. 62

and is almost the *idée fixe* of *Tamburlaine*, where the iconoclastic animus is directed against the Turks.[25] Faustus, we recall, vows

> To burn [God's] scriptures, slay his ministers,
> And make my spirits pull his churches down. vi. 100

There is a bad breath of psychic decay about these lines, a kind of motiveless aggression for which no object can provide sufficient provocation; and its poetic equivalent is the ranting monotone for which these speeches are notable. A psychological drive of this kind would certainly account for the puerile-hysterical tone of *The Massacre at Paris*.

Thus it seems possible that the reworking of lines, which Eliot has noted as a feature of Marlowe's poetic practice[26] (and it is much more extensive than the cases he records), is less a craftsman's concern than an expression of a mind that tends always toward the obsessive, and which only needs to be jogged a little in a familiar direction for the whole complex of ideas and associations to force its way into the foreground. It would be plainly unfair to argue from this anti-papist animus to so large a generalisation, and there are other considerations which modify the judgment: the fact, for instance, that the preoccupation with destruction gives rise to the symbolic vision of Troy burning, impressively formulated in *Dido*, II. i. 166–301, and crystallised in 'the topless towers of Ilium'. Nevertheless, the point is worth raising, for, if I have diagnosed a real tendency of Marlowe's mind, it goes a long way towards explaining his failure—as I shall argue—to free his drama from the mere 'ideas' which gave rise to it. The ideas are ministering to urges which are only partially understood.

To return to *The Massacre*—the vengeful passion which has smouldered throughout the play blazes forth into open threats in the final speeches:

> NAVARRE. ...I vow so to revenge his death
> As Rome, and all those popish prelates there,
> Shall curse the time that e'er Navarre was king,
> And rul'd in France by Henry's fatal death. xxi. 110

This seems no more than a fitting response to Henry's injunction:

> Henry, thy king, wipes off these childish tears,
> And bids thee whet thy sword on Sixtus' bones,
> That it may keenly slice the Catholics.   xxi. 99

If one looks for sources for this savage elation—and for the wooden rhythms—one finds it only in the most violent of the pamphleteers. Yet the parallel is illuminating, for there is the same admixture of obnoxious self-congratulation, and the same inescapable sense that, at the level where it really matters, the writer is not serious, but is playing a brutal schoolboy game:

let men say and thinke what they please, but I doe well know that we are in a marueilous periode and great Catastrophe, at the point to see a straunge alteration. For it is most certaine that Babylon shall fall, and that shortly with a sodein fall...It shalbe a wonderfull doome, when by the effectes, we shall heare the voyce of the maister of the house...saying, Bring vnto me these my enemies, that would not, that I should raigne over them, and slay them before my face.

The writer goes on to describe this Armageddon of slaughter as 'the banket of the·Lambe',

wherein there shall be such and so great plĕtie of flesh, that the very foules of the aire shall haue enough...for the very foules are also inuited to the banket of the Lambe, there to be satisfied with the flesh of Kings, Princes and mightie persons.[27]

I shall try, in a moment, to penetrate behind the merely repulsive in this view of history, but let me simply put the question for the present—What must happen to a mind which freely entertains this kind of thinking, and admits it as material for art?

The second area where Marlowe sells out to his own and his audience's vulgarity is the area of Spanish affairs. Again, the charge is not that he took a conventional view of Spanish villainy—three years after the Armada, it would have been as hard for him to adopt a neutral position, as it would have been to write a pro-Nazi play in 1948. Rather I am objecting to the inconsistency of introducing yet another prime villain and to the crude way in which this villainy is asserted:[28]

> Spain is the council-chamber of the Pope,
> Spain is the place where he makes peace and war;
> And Guise for Spain hath now incens'd the king.   xiii. 12

Navarre is to be crowned king of France

> In spite of Spain, and all the popish power
> That holds it from your highness wrongfully.   x. 46[29]

We have already seen how an insatiable appetite for villainy led Marlowe to assert simultaneously the sole responsibility of the Guise and of Catherine; and in the treatment of the Papacy and of Spain he introduces a third term. It is nevertheless naïve to suppose that, if he holds the Hispano-papal bloc responsible for all the ills of France, he will therefore present the Guise as some sort of tool. In point of fact the Guise is never sufficiently characterised to be able to exist in any social or political *context*. Indeed there is no social or political context in this play—only a chaos of religious platitudes and nationalist war-cries, gigantic self-assertions of gigantic non-entities, resounding in a poetic void. So perhaps 'inconsistency' is the wrong charge, implying as it does some whole with which the part is to be integrated. The only unity the play possesses resides in the ferocious protestant nationalism which it presupposes in the audience.

It is easy enough to see what appeal an exposure of papal and Spanish machinations would have had for an Elizabethan in the 1590s. It elicits the kind of gloating satisfaction which informs Greene's post-Armada lampoon, *The Spanish Masquerado* (London, 1589). In woodcut cartoons (now lost) the delighted reader could watch

The Pope, hauing put off his triple Crowne, and his Pontificalibus, sitting malecontented, scratching of his head throwing away his keies and his sword, in great choller...[or].

The Cardinals of Rome, seeing that the Pope was malecontented for the bad successe of the Spanish Fleet, apparelled like Mourners, go solemnly singing *De Profundis*, from Castel Angelo to S. Peters church...[or]

The rest of the rascall Rable of the Romish Church, as Monkes, Friers, and dirging Priestes, storming at these newes, sitting banquetting with the fair Nunnes, hauing store of daintie Cates, and wines before them, stall-fed with ease and gluttony, grone out of their fat paunches this passion:

> *Quanta patimur pro amore Christi...*

At the same time, international tensions did not disappear with the last galliass: there was anxiety about Jesuits at large in England, and invasion scares persisted throughout the 'nineties.[30] One of the readiest ways of purging this chronic anxiety was to find a scapegoat big and black enough to carry away the load of evil and perturbation. In the figures of the pope and Philip, the common man, oppressed by the complexity of diplomacy and intrigue, found just such a broad-backed sin-bearer. And Marlowe did the common man the further service of linking the Guise and Catherine to this potent concatenation of diabolical enemies. It was a sovereign salve for the wound of unrest, and the obscure sense that one was being 'got at' might well have been appeased by it. That each of these figures should be an absolute villain in his own right was simply an additional way of ensuring that they could serve their therapeutic function the better. (It is a tempting hypothesis that the Machiavel villain-hero, who emerged on the stage at about this time, grew out of just this immature need for moral simplification, and is a manifestation of a characteristic neurotic trend of the time.)

But the obstinate fact remains that Marlowe himself was not one of these common men, and we have still to account for what appears to be a voluntary degradation of both artist and man—also, one might add, a degradation of the audience. The first recorded performance drew a bumper crowd (takings totalled £3.14s.) but one suspects it was composed largely of those for whom the theatre offered a boisterous holiday from reality, rather than those who, with the gradual maturing of Elizabethan drama, were coming to see it as a way of confronting reality. The very title of the play—an inept index of its subject—appealed to this kind of appetite.

I suppose really bad art, like really good art, defies causal analysis. It is the mystery of iniquity which can only be marvelled at or shunned. All one can say is 'thus it must have been', and discuss the assumptions from which the iniquity proceeds.

One of these assumptions, in the case of *The Massacre*, appears to be the view that history is a series of monodramas, each epoch being dominated by the colossal figure of the great man whose star is in the ascendant. This is of a piece with the moral simplification I have discussed, for it absolves everyone else of responsibility for events. It postulates a special sphere—the political—which is totally distinct from the human. And consequently it robs the political of all meaning. One has only to compare Marlowe's political monodrama about French history with Shakespeare's treatment of the (equally urgent) Wars of the Roses, to see how everything has been sacrificed—dramatically and humanly—to a kind of childish puppetry. The closest relationship between the Guise and the common herd of humanity is that of suborner to murderer (Scene ii); yet even here Richard III and his conscience-ridden instruments provide an instructive contrast. The very act of murder, the strange relationship between agent and patient (cf. Clarence and *his* murderers), is emptied of all content. There is no sense of interaction. The victims might as well be blocks of wood; this is why the preposterous brutality of the play (nineteen mortalities in twenty-one scenes), in the end, merely evokes laughter—it is all so unreal; and the unreality is a direct result of the suppression of the human in the interests of the 'political'.

It is rather as if Marlowe set out to be a kind of passive register of the crudest political rationalisations of his age, but the inevitable disciplines of dramatic form frustrated this neutrality. The composer Mussorgsky once remarked that the act of creation 'bears within itself its own laws of refinement. The verification', he went on to add, 'is inner criticism.' Art has a knack of betraying the practitioner who tries merely to *use* it, thinking to by-pass the 'inner criticism': the dramatic medium has left Marlowe exposed nakedly as the purveyor of the establishment lie, as a time-server. Thus, when Henry III, soon to become the enemy of Rome and friend of Navarre, has to detach himself from a dubious past, the moral charlatanism involved is blazoned forth by the speech of explication which the dramatic form requires:

> ...here in presence of you all, I swear,
> I ne'er was king of France until this hour.
> This [i.e. Guise, who is dead at his feet] is the traitor that
>   hath spent my gold
> In making foreign wars and civil broils.
> Did he not draw a sort of English priests
> From Douay to the seminary at Rheims,
> To hatch forth treason 'gainst their natural queen?
> Did he not cause the king of Spain's huge fleet
> To threaten England, and to menace me?...
> Hath he not made me, in the Pope's defence,
> To spend the treasure that should strength my land,
> In civil broils between Navarre and me?...
> Let Christian princes, that shall hear of this...
> Rest satisfied with this, that here I swear,
> Ne'er was there king of France as yok'd as I.   xviii. 98

There can have been few occasions in drama when erring man has been able to lock so many skeletons in the one capacious cupboard. In the world of the 'political', as distinct from the human world, the sins of one's past are shed like an outmoded garment with every change of policy. When Marlowe tries to use drama to endorse so superficial a view of human action, the very language turns against him and betrays it for the arrant sophistry it is.

Drama, which is political in this disastrously limited sense, can only be melodrama; and its morality must be the morality of melodrama—something to be turned on like a tap at the critical moment, and turned off again when that moment has passed. In no sense can it grow out of the existential realities of the action, since there are no such realities. It separates the evil action, both from its agent, and from its roots in the common consciousness of humanity, and makes of it something portentous, absolute—and meaningless; for the morality of melodrama ultimatedly denies all moral sanctions by making them the subject of manipulation.

I think it is this equivocation at the moral heart of *The Massacre at Paris* which accounts for the equivocal role played by the Guise. It is never entirely certain what Marlowe expects us to make of him. As the only character granted an opportunity for self-revelation (in the Scene ii soliloquy) he immediately tends to fill more of the imaginative stage than his homiletic function would lead us to expect; and in that soliloquy it is impossible to miss the exultant lilt of the virtuoso in evil inviting the audience's tacit approval:

> Religion ! O *Diabolo* !
> Fie, I am asham'd, however that I seem,
> To think a word of such a simple sound,
> Of so great matter should be made the ground!   ii. 66

It is the voice (and the sentiments) of Machiavel in *The Jew*, titillating the audience with 'advanced thought', under the all-licensing cloak of the melodrama villain. In a drama of schematic morality this is bound to happen. Virtue cannot be other than colourless—it is defined by its passivity in the hands of vice—and vice, consequently, usurps the stage. The Guise dies as Caesar. The protestant martyrs merely expire.

This kind of moral ambiguity is a problem in other plays of Marlowe's besides this one. What else accounts for the rival interpretations of *Tamburlaine*—as a Christian fable against presumption, or as a humanist manifesto of the free spirit? Isn't there an analogous problem with the damnation of Faustus, the problem of deciding where precisely Marlowe stands? *The Massacre* is a useful focus for these perplexities, because it articulates the possibility, which cannot be dismissed out of hand, that perhaps he stands precisely nowhere.

III

Admirers of Marlowe have been ready enough to regard *The Massacre* as an aberration; but the implication of this admission seems often to be that the play can therefore have no bearing on our estimate of the real Marlowe. It seems to me that the creative sensibility is far too delicate a mechanism to admit of such ruthless compartmentalisation. It is, after all, a function of the total moral consciousness of the man who creates, and an artistic betrayal of this kind both modifies and expresses the consciousness which is guilty of the betrayal. The whitewash, which in melodrama can obliterate Henry III's past, cannot avail for a poet in life. To have been capable once of a prostitution of art, is to create an abiding potentiality for further prostitutions. The alarming thing about the play, moreover, is the fact that it is so thoroughly Marlovian—echoing (or foreshadowing) themes of the other plays, sometimes with a surprising verbal exactness. And, as a result, it raises most pressingly the question of Marlowe's real stature.

I would like to put this question in an extreme form by quoting one of Marlowe's most bitter critics—G. B. Shaw. For Shaw, Marlowe is objectionable in himself, a fool whose folly 'not only expresses itself in blank verse, but invents that art form for the purpose', but he is also the founder of a school of 'clumsy horse-play and butcherly rant', of 'falsehood, bloody-mindedness, bombast and intellectual cheapness'.

I admit that Marlowe's blank verse has charm of colour and movement; and I know only too well how its romantic march caught the literary imagination and founded that barren and horrible worship of blank verse for its own sake which has since desolated and laid waste the dramatic poetry of England. But the fellow was a fool for all that. He often reminds me, in his abysmally inferior way, of Rossini. Rossini has just the same trick of beginning with a magnificently impressive exordium, apparently pregnant with the most tragic developments, and presently lapsing into arrant triviality. But Rossini lapses amusingly; writes 'Excusez du peu' at the double bar line which separates the sublime from the ridiculous; and is gay, tuneful and clever in his frivolity. Marlowe, the moment the exhaustion of the imaginative fit deprives him of the power of raving, becomes childish in thought, vulgar and wooden in humour, and stupid in his attempts at invention. He is the true Elizabethan blank-verse beast, itching to frighten other people with the superstitious terrors in which he does not himself believe, and wallowing in blood, violence, muscularity of expression and strenuous animal passion as only literary men do when they become thoroughly depraved by solitary work, sedentary cowardice, and starvation of the sympathetic centres. It is not surprising to learn that Marlowe was stabbed in a tavern brawl: what would be utterly unbelievable would be his having succeeded in stabbing anyone else. On paper the whole obscene crew of these blank-verse rhetoricians could outdare Lucifer himself: Nature can produce no murderer cruel enough for Webster, nor any hero bully enough for Chapman, devout disciples, both of them, of Kit Marlowe. But you do not believe in their martial ardour as you believe in the valor of Sidney or Cervantes. One calls the Elizabethan dramatists imaginative, as one might say the same of a man in delirium tremens; but even that flatters them; for whereas the drinker can imagine rats and snakes and beetles which have some sort of resemblance to real ones, your typical Elizabethan heroes of the mighty line, having neither the eyes to see anything real nor the brains to observe it, could no more conceive a natural or convincing stage figure than a blind man can conceive a rainbow or a deaf one the sound of an orchestra.[31]

This reaction, for all its crudity, strikes me as more authentic than the vein of pious adulation that has become the fashion in Marlowe criticism; at least there can be no doubt that the critic has come into real contact (or should I say, collision?) with his subject. It will not account for all of Marlowe; but then neither will the idolatry of a Swinburne. And where Swinburne's panegyrics merely anaesthetise the critical faculties, Shaw's unambiguous 'Damn!' does at least brace us to consider Marlowe's real achievement. There is no doubt that he has characterised the author of *The Massacre at Paris* very aptly.

3

DRAMATIST AS REALIST: 'THE JEW OF MALTA'

'Marlowe's Jew', complained Charles Lamb, 'is a mere monster brought in with a large painted nose to please the rabble. He kills in sport, poisons whole nunneries, invents infernal machines. He is just such an exhibition as a century or two earlier might have been played before the Londoners "by the royal command", when a general pillage and massacre of the Hebrews had been previously resolved upon in the cabinet.'[1] In a sense this is no more than a just reaction to one aspect of The Jew of Malta; at least Lamb diagnoses correctly the element of pandering to a debased public taste which links the play with The Massacre at Paris. Yet he does it less than justice; for there is also some truth in Eliot's contention that it is a 'farce of the old English humour, the terribly serious, even savage comic humour...which spent its last breath on the decadent genius of Dickens', and in his claim that Marlowe 'develops a tone to suit this farce, and even perhaps that this tone is his most powerful and mature tone'.[2] We may grant the farce and the savagery, but the very real critical question concerns the powerfulness, the maturity and the seriousness of the comic humour. To my mind, The Jew of Malta is neither as successful as Eliot would have it to be, nor as crude as Lamb implies.

Perhaps it is best to begin by considering the 'mere monster' in Barabas, whose radical deviation from the human is immediately registered by the huge 'artificiall nose' to which Ithamore repeatedly draws our attention:[3]

O mistress! I have the bravest, gravest, secret, subtle, bottle-nosed knave to my master, that ever gentleman had!

III. iii. 9[4]

The monster is a composite figure. Partly it is the ethnic stereotype of the Jew—a stereotype all the more tenacious in England for the fact that it went largely unchallenged by first-hand acquaintance with Jews;[5] partly the stock figure of the usurer who is intimately allied to the Vice Avarice in such a play as Udall's Respublica[6] (and this mixed ancestry traces back further to an earlier forbear—the Judas–usurer–Jew of the mystery cycles); but also, as Marlowe's Prologue makes explicit, the monster is an Italian monster, a Florentine to be precise (II. iii. 23), and one of the earliest of a long line of stage Machiavels. Barabas thus has his dramatic roots deep in the soil of popular, not to say vulgar, folk-lore and superstition, and the vulgar origins contribute much that is crudely superficial in the play—the heavy-handed dramatic technique, for example, which has Marlowe continually drawing black lines under what he has already written in heavy type—'I must dissemble', shouts Barabas when it is evident to the veriest infant that this is what is happening (VI. i. 50). The explicitness is the mark of a dramaturgy which can endure nothing unexplained, subtle or ambiguous—'I am betray'd' (IV. v. 41); 'I must make this villain away' (IV. v. 30); 'So now, I am reveng'd upon 'em all' (IV. vi. 42). Or there is the melo-dramatic aside which works, if it works at all, by presenting the humane in violently incongruous juxtaposition with the inhuman, undying love with inveterate malice—

> Please you dine with me, sir;—*and you shall be most*
> *heartily poisoned.* IV. v. 30

> Here, take 'em, fellow, with as good a will—
> *As I would see thee hang'd*; O, love stops my breath. IV. v. 53[7]

Or there is the preposterous exaggeration of Barabas's egomania—

> Nay, let 'em combat, conquer, and kill all.
> So they spare me, my daughter, and my wealth. I. i. 150

> Down to the cellar, taste of all my wines...
> And, if you like them, drink your fill and die;
> For, so I live, perish may all the world! V. v. 7[8]

—or Ithamore's random destructiveness—'But here's a royal monastery hard by; / Good master, let me poison all the monks' (IV. i. 13); this same motiveless aggression is displayed against the friars who are the butts of endless lewdly unfunny jests about monastic lechery and conventual pregnancy.[9] One is inclined to conclude from this kind of evidence that Marlowe is too childish-vicious for this world, and that *The Jew*, like *The Massacre*, merely reflects some of the least savoury aspects of Elizabethan society. Certainly this side of the play cannot be described as either mature or serious.

However, Lamb and those who accept his estimate of the play, would extend this judgment to the whole play, claiming perhaps that it is 'modern and romantic' to see in Barabas anything more than a monster held up for abomination, because 'his Jewishness defines his condemnation'.[10] But this is to ignore the qualities to which Eliot has pointed, and in any case it is fairly easy to show that 'his Jewishness' actually defines nothing at all—it is, in fact, a subject the play investigates.

A stereotype like that of the Jew (or the Machiavel) is not something which is necessarily accepted in a simple unqualified way, but it implies by its very existence the possibility of modification. The fact that many Elizabethans felt in a certain way about (say) political order, so that it is moderately meaningful to talk about 'the Elizabethan concept of the State', did not, as we shall see, preclude other ways of feeling about the State. The Elizabethans were probably less prone to this sort of mass thinking than the literary historians at whose hands they have suffered. Neither did the existence of a Jew stereotype prevent individual Elizabethans from adapting, modifying or simply rejecting the stereotype. Thus we find in an undistinguished play of the 1580s a Jew, and a usurer at that, favourably contrasted with an unscrupulous Christian merchant who seeks to evade his financial responsibilities by turning Turk. His Jewish creditor, appalled at this mercenary apostasy, immediately cancels the debt, and the judge moralises, 'Jews seek to excel in Christianity and Christians in Jewishness.'[11] The semantic implications of this interesting sentence will occupy me in a moment, but it might be noted now that the traditional anti-semitism of the Elizabethans could be not only modified, but stood on its head.

The truth of the matter is that the Elizabethan audience—that peremptory hangman so frequently called in to effect the execution of this or that critical judgment—is so nebulous an entity as to be useless in an operation calling for precise definition. In so far as there is an Elizabethan mind, it is as much moulded by the playwrights who sought to educate its sensibility and broaden its horizons, as it moulds those playwrights. The 'orthodoxy' of a period is not an ideological steamroller that subdues all humanity to its ruling passion for the horizontal, but itself the product of the delicate, breathing organism of human society, in which cause and effect are never very sharply distinguished. The play itself not only offers something concrete for us to get to grips with, but it also constitutes *prima facie* evidence for the state of mind of the audience to which it is addressed; so that the primary question is the critical one—What is actually there in the play? To ask this question, even about a play as superficially barren as *The Jew of Malta*, is to discover a great deal more than a vulgar anti-semitism and a melodramatic Machiavellism.

I

Take the Jew-component first. For many Elizabethans the very word 'Jew' was a term of miscellaneous abuse: thus Thomas Coryat reflects on 'our English prouerbe: to looke like a Jewe (whereby is meant sometimes a weather beaten warp-faced fellow, sometimes a phrenticke and lunaticke person, sometimes one discontented)'; or Gobbo puns, 'I am a Jew if I serve the Jew any longer', thus separating the ethnic and pejorative senses of the word for the sake of a joke.[12] But it had other usages at once more precise and more derogatory—'Jews seek to excel in Christianity and Christians in Jewishness' (where the primary meaning of 'Jewishness' is almost certainly the avarice the Christian merchant had shown, and the word is used as an antonym for 'Christianity', meaning 'charitable self-sacrifice'). As a smug Antonio puts it, 'This Hebrew will turn Christian: he grows kind.'[13] The connexion between the word 'Jew' and the practice of usury (recorded in the verb 'to judaise', one meaning of which was 'to lend at interest') was strengthened by the similarity of sound in Elizabethan pronunciation—Iew, iudaize, usurer; and the hard-hearted attributes of the money-lender were thereby fathered on the entire Hebrew race, so that Antonio, faced by the implacable Shylock, despairs of ever softening 'that—than which what's harder?— / His Jewish heart'.[14] Add to this the implication of double-dealing reflected in the common linking of 'Iudas' and 'Iew' and we have a semantic complex of infidelity, treachery, inhumanity and rapacity informing the very use of the word 'Jew'.

This usage can be found in Marlowe's play, where the word is sometimes employed for purposes of comprehensive denigration—'Then, like a Jew, he laugh'd and jeer'd, and told me he lov'd me for your sake...' (IV. v. 116); in Ferneze's smug reference to Barabas's diabolical engine as 'a Jew's courtesy' (v. v. 108) or Ithamore's drunken imprecation, 'Hang him, Jew' (IV. iv. 88). But these references on the whole represent the ignorant hostility of the speaker better than they give the tone of the play. True, we get a few easy laughs at the expense of Jewish cupidity—'O, that I should part with so much gold!' (IV. v. 52) or Barabas's reaction when Ferneze brings the gratuity of £100,000: 'Pounds say'st thou, governor? well, since it is no more, / I'll satisfy myself with that' (v. v. 21)—but the strongest tendency in the play is to assail the facile and hearty complacency of Christian anti-semitism with persistent inversions and permutations of the Jew–Christian antithesis. Thus, when Barabas gives a parody version of the usurer-Jew—

> I have been zealous in the Jewish faith,
> Hard-hearted to the poor, a covetous wretch,
> That would for lucre's sake have sold my soul.
> A hundred for a hundred I have ta'en—   IV. i. 54

the context (he is being blackmailed by two avaricious and lecherous friars on the strength of information revealed in shrift) turns the ironic shaft back into the flank of the Christians for whose benefit he is performing: at the same time as the friars accept this preposterous confession of the Jewish faith, the audience sees that it is, for all practical purposes, the Christian creed as well.

This technique of ironically undercutting Christian superiority is supplemented by a whole series of inversions by which Barabas simply pays the Christians with their own bad coin. The affectation of sanctified hauteur, well caught in Katherine's 'Converse not with him; he is cast off from heaven' (II. iii. 159), is neatly parodied by the Jew:

> This offspring of Cain, this Jebusite,
> That never tasted of the Passover,
> Nor e'er shall see the land of Canaan,
> Nor our Messias that is yet to come;
> This gentle [Gentile] maggot, Lodowick, I mean,
> Must be deluded...   II. iii. 302

and again:

> these swine-eating Christians,
> Unchosen nation, never circumcis'd;
> Such as (poor villains) were ne'er thought upon
> Till Titus and Vespasian conquer'd us...   II. iii. 7

Perhaps the most exquisite of these parody-revenges comes when the Jew takes the medieval libel of the *foetor judaicus* (a vile-smelling bodily secretion due to alleged menstruation in Jewish males, which good Christians found intolerable and which could only be obliterated by the waters of baptism)[15] and maliciously re-applies it:

> LODOWICK. Whither walk'st thou, Barabas?
> BARABAS. No further: 'Tis a custom held with us,
>   That when we speak with Gentiles like to you,
>   We turn into the air to purge ourselves;
>   For unto us the promise doth belong.   II. iii. 44

The parody is exact and devastating.

It is by the same process that Barabas turns the Christian blank charter for aggression against heretics[16] ('To undo a Jew is charity and not sin'—IV. vi. 80) into a weapon in his own Jewish armoury:

> It's no sin to deceive a Christian;
> For they themselves hold it a principle,
> Faith is not to be held with heretics:
> But all are heretics that are not Jews;
> This follows well, and therefore, daughter,
>   fear not.　　　　　　　　　　　　　　　　　　II. iii. 310

Barabas here confronts his Christian assailants with their mirror-image: the syllogism is identical in form; only the major premiss has changed. By reversing the direction of the Christian morality of anti-semitism, Marlowe reveals the destructive potential of its thoroughly pernicious logic—and the reversal is the more telling for the fact that the accent of pert self-congratulation is authentic.

If we are to have any quarrel with Marlowe's treatment of the Jew–Christian theme, then, it cannot be because (as Lamb suggests) he has capitulated to vulgar anti-semitic prejudice. The objection is rather to this technique of ironic inversion—it is almost the basic poetic strategy of the play—and the limitations that it imposes on the play's grasp of human realities. I shall be returning to this matter, but perhaps I can observe at this point that when a writer contents himself with a parody-inversion of the attitude he is attacking he commits himself to the narrow categories of that attitude. The results of the inversion may be, as they are with Barabas, acidly witty and mordant; but there is a certain shallowness and constriction which is the consequence of a refusal to allow parody to deepen into exploration. One can be grateful to Marlowe for mounting a courageous attack on a powerful and particularly vicious social prejudice, without regarding it as a very profound contribution to the understanding of anti-semitism to turn on the Christians and cry, 'Woe unto you hypocrites; for you are villains every bit as unconscionable as the Jews you abominate.'

Nevertheless, within these self-imposed limits, Marlowe achieves a good deal. There are moments in the play which seem to sum up the whole tortured history of anti-semitism: as when Barabas, with a furious self-loathing, assumes the role the Christians have cast for him:

> We Jews can fawn like spaniels when we please;
> And when we grin we bite;...
> I learned in Florence how to kiss my hand,

> Heave up my shoulders when they call me dog,
> And duck as low as any bare-foot friar;
> Hoping to see them starve upon a stall,
> Or else be gathered for in our synagogue...   II. iii. 20

At the same time as we are given the whining, ingratiating Jew with an almost tactile concreteness (and note how lively and gestural the verbs are), we also feel the pull of an alarming logic of circumstance, feel the historical roots of this irremovable rancour in repeated and unceasing acts of Christian 'injury' (l. 19). We recognise the 'teachers' who have forced the Jew to 'learn' this degrading trade.

Throughout the play, there is a steady drive to undermine Christian complacency about the Jews, and to reveal the common ground of rapacious self-interest which perpetuates their mutual enmity. As Barabas puts it,

> This is the life we Jews are us'd to lead;
> And reason too, for Christians do the like.   v. ii. 115

His little joke about the 'golden cross' (a gold coin stamped with a cross and bearing a superscription—a 'posy'—round the perimeter) focuses these themes with a sly lucidity. Lodowick, he expects,

> would disdain
> To marry with the daughter of a Jew:
> And yet I'll give her many a golden cross,
> With Christian posies round about the ring.   II. iii. 295

The subtle identification of religious 'profession' with financial advantage—if the wooden cross divides Jew and Christian, the golden one unites them—is a central motif in the play, and gives rise to some quite delicious comedy. The method is again parody, but parody so consummate as momentarily to break out of the limitations of that mode. The repenting Barabas, for instance—

> A hundred for a hundred I have ta'en;
> And now for store of wealth may I compare
> With all the Jews in Malta; but what is wealth?
> I am a Jew, and therefore am I lost.
> Would penance serve for this my sin,
> I could afford to whip myself to death...
> To fast, to pray, and wear a shirt of hair,
> And on my knees creep to Jerusalem.   IV. i. 57

But what is wealth? The answer is instantaneous: 'O good Barabas, come to our house!' 'O no, good Barabas, come to *our* house!' 'O

Barabas, their laws are strict!' '*They* wear no shirts, and they go barefoot too.' 'Good Barabas, come to me.' The juxtaposition is brilliant, as is the comic insight which makes this sanctified haggling issue in Jacomo's attempted murder of an already dead Barnardine. The Friars sequence ends with an unctuously regretful Barabas feeling himself morally obliged to carry Jacomo to the magistrates:

> No, pardon me; the law must have his course:
> I must be forc'd to give in evidence,
> That, being importun'd...   IV. iii. 24

and discovering that a new scruple has arisen in connexion with his proposed conversion:

> No; for this example I'll remain a Jew:
> Heaven bless me! what, a friar a murderer?
> When shall you see a Jew commit the like?   IV. iii. 34

The comic texture is very dense, but one perception that hovers at the edges of laughter is that Barabas's use of the language of religion and piety as a weapon against his personal and commercial enemies is not different in kind from the uses of that language elsewhere. It is just more explicit and less self-deceiving:

> As good dissemble that thou never mean'st
> As first mean truth and then dissemble it.   I. ii. 290

The one thing that none of these purveyors of religious platitude ever does is to turn the prescriptive edge of Christianity against his own breast.

The comic probing goes deep enough, too, to show up the sub-human nature of the acquisitive urge itself—as when, for instance, we watch Barabas hugging his newly recovered bags and capering about in a grotesque travesty of joyous emotion:

> Now, Phoebus, ope the eye-lids of the day,
> And, for the raven, wake the morning lark,
> That I may hover with her in the air;
> Singing o'er these, as she does o'er her young.
> *Hermoso placer de los dineros.*   II. i. 60

This kind of workmanship *does* merit the title of 'serious farce', and it also, incidentally, makes nonsense of that curious myth of a Marlowe who had no sense of humour. The unforced gaiety of some early Shakespearian comedy may be outside his range, but a critic who fails to find anything funny in these scenes is in no position to accuse others of lacking humour. Whatever one may think finally of *The Jew of Malta* as a whole, one must admit that it gives evidence at times of a very lively wit and intelligence in its creator.

II

Almost all these trends—the comic exposure of rapacity, of the politic abuse of religion, and the assault upon gentile complacency—run in one channel in the play's second scene, a passage that deserves detailed scrutiny, not least for its sharp exposure of the ruinous assumptions that have underlain the history of anti-semitism: the assumption for instance that the Jews, being alien and accursed, represent a kind of National Deficit Liquidation Fund which can be drawn upon in any crisis; the assumption that their very presence in the community is the cause of ill-fortune, and, conversely, that when a national disaster occurs, it may be directly traced to the activity of the Jews; that Christians, as the chosen people, are the divinely appointed scourge of the wickedness of the rejected people; and that the Jews are collectively accountable for the blood-guilt invoked by their forbears who crucified the Messiah (that this doctrine had to wait until 1963 for official repudiation by the Catholic Church indicates how deeply rooted it is in Western Christian consciousness). The assumption, in short, that to be a Jew is to be *ipso facto* inexcusable. At the same time the depiction of state extortion provides Marlowe with an opportunity for a more general investigation of the ethics of acquisition—another aspect of his subject in *The Jew of Malta*.

Part of the scene's mastery resides in the subtle gradations of tone—the elevation of moral sentiment varying directly with the speaker's rapacity, politeness being merely a function of greed, and innocence a preliminary affectation. Ferneze opens with suave urbanity—'Hebrews, now come near'—and expostulates mellifluously—'Soft, Barabas! there's more 'longs to't than so'. The Jew counters with a pretended ignorance of their drift which pierces the euphemistic mist, and the First Knight, enraged by Barabas's feigned belief that they are asking him to fight in the army, explodes,

> Tut, Jew, we know thou art no soldier;
> Thou art a Merchant, and a money'd man,
> And 'tis thy money, Barabas, we seek.   I. ii. 52

The swift transition, from surly contempt to an oily servility before the personification of Mammon, represents dramatic economy of a high

order. Barabas's tone undergoes a complementary series of transforma-
tions: at first affected innocence ('How, my lord! my money!'), it
modulates through mock incredulity to moral indignation ('The man
that dealeth righteously shall live'), dying away finally in stoical indifference ('take it to you, i' the devil's name'). Ferneze, on the other
hand, preserves a uniformly lofty tone—extortion is no occasion for
indecorum—and is at some pains to cloak his expediency in moral
rectitude. He offers the Jew the kind of supercilious mock-explanation
that comes naturally to the consciously impregnable when dealing with
a helpless victim.

His sophistries, however, expose in a lucid syllogism the logic of
anti-semitism: Barabas will contribute to the Turkish levy, not
'equally', but 'like an infidel':

> For through our sufferance of your hateful lives,
> Who stand accursed in the sight of heaven,
> These taxes and afflictions are befall'n.   I. ii. 63

Ferneze's primary intention is to justify the levying of the entire tax
upon a tiny fraction of the population, but he cannot resist the additional
gratification of a moral, as well as economic, vaunt: Observe, O Jew,
the self-sacrificial charity of the Christians who, even at the risk of
incurring the divine wrath, have graciously permitted Jews to trade in
Malta. The logical form, with its *post hoc propter hoc* fallacy, is also
characteristic: Jews are under a curse; we are suffering under the curse
of Turkish extortion; *ergo* our misfortune is due to your accursed
presence. If there were no more here than this syllogistic expediency,
the comment would be perceptive. But the factor that lifts it out of
the field of social commentary, and elevates it to the comic plane, is the
lofty moral tone in which Ferneze chooses to enunciate his logical
travesty. It is the timeless voice of pious dissimulation.

Evidently, however, he fears a retort, for he hastily draws the naked
sword of ordinance and waves it over Barabas's head. Only now do we
discover that the regulations are already drawn up and that the preliminary discussion has been the merest façade. The proclamation follows
the traditional formula for squeezing the Hebrew orange dry—either
you pay, or you pay. When Barabas demurs, the Governor, who is
clearly tired of the game, immediately dispatches his officers. 'Corpo di
Dio!' exclaims the Jew, as if only a Christian oath could do justice to
this Christian villainy.

Ferneze's next justification is pure Pharisee: 'Better one want for the common good, / Than many perish for a private man', and calls up the memory of Caiaphas dealing with another recalcitrant Jew. The indirect effect of this echo is to put Barabas in the place of Christ, as the innocent victim of pharisaical expediency—another parody of Christian self-righteousness.

The Knight, however, sees events in a dimly religious light: are there not signs of a divine hand in Barabas's downfall?

> If your first curse fall heavy on thy head,
> And make thee poor and scorn'd of all the world,
> 'Tis not our fault, but thy inherent sin.   I. ii. 108

The principle by which a person can proceed against his fellow-man, while complacently regarding himself as some kind of supra-moral scourge of God, is the principle of anarchy. On this basis the action is his, but he has not performed it: the left hand cannot be brought to justice because the right hand knows nothing of the crime. The function of religion in Malta is always like this—the introduction of the imponderable and the irrefragable in order to drive a wedge between the agent and the consequences of his own act; it 'hides many mischiefs from suspicion'. 'Villains', exclaims Friar Jacomo, 'Villains, I am a sacred person, touch me not' (IV. iii. 40). But of course the sophistical invocation of the moral order merely sets up reverberations which drown the protestations of sanctity.

Refusing, however, to be 'preached out of his possessions', Barabas makes his appeal against the Christian doctrine of corporate Jewish guilt, and to a principle of individual responsibility. In so doing he reaches the heart of his apology, for it is precisely this determination to think of the Jews *en masse* which makes the present extortion possible. Barabas turns Christian totalitarian thinking in their own teeth, thus revealing its absurdity:

> Some Jews are wicked, as all Christians are;
> But say the tribe that I descended of
> Were all in general cast away for sin,
> Shall I be tried by their transgression?
> The man that dealeth righteously shall live:
> And which of you can charge me otherwise?   I. ii. 113

Barabas has been somewhat carried away by the lofty tone of his opponents, and, forgetting for the moment that he is a Machiavellian, lays claim to a nobility of spirit which is rather incongruous, if not blasphemous (cf. Christ's claim—John viii. 46). It is too much for Ferneze, who splutters,

> Out, wretched Barabas!
> Sham'st thou not thus to justify thyself,
> As if we knew not thy profession?   I. ii. 119

(there can be no justification for being a usurer-Jew) and proceeds to exercise his considerable dialectical skill in cutting the ground from under Barabas's feet: 'If worldly success is the inevitable result of righteousness' (this is not quite what the Jew had said, but it is a reasonable extension of it) 'and if you are, as you say, righteous, there is no possible cause for anxiety.' This leaves Barabas neatly impaled on the horns of his own dilemma, unless he is to confess that he thrives, not by righteousness, but by 'policy'—and the confession would be monstrously impolitic.

Having won this point, Ferneze goes on to his last and most extravagant casuistry, which he offers with a pompous fatuity that is truly heroic:

> Excess of wealth is cause of covetousness:
> And covetousness, O, 'tis a monstrous sin!   I. ii. 124

The responsibility for the Christian lust for Jewish gold is thus laid squarely on Barabas's shoulders; a responsibility of which Ferneze has obligingly relieved him, by yielding to that lust. This is the height of Marlowe's mordant irony, which, despite its extravagance, has secure historical roots in the habitual Christian, and human, practice of laying the entire burden of moral responsibility at one's neighbour's door, and elevating oneself above the merely moral plane into a minister of abstract justice. Later in the play, Barabas is to demolish Ferneze's affected righteousness, by the simple device of singing the same tune after him—and doing it better. He is promising the Governor's son a 'diamond', which he proposes to give him 'with a vengeance'; Lodowick insists on 'deserving' it, which moves the Jew to an ecstasy of *double entendre*:

> Good sir,
> Your father has deserv'd it at my hands,
> Who, of mere charity and Christian ruth,
> To bring me to religious purity,
> And, as it were, in catechising sort,
> To make me mindful of my mortal sins,
> Against my will, and whether I would or no,
> Seiz'd all I had, and thrust me out a doors,
> And made my house a place for nuns most
>   chaste.   II. iii. 69

The scene is more than an essay in the dialectic of religious intolerance. Neither party is, in any case, greatly moved by the events that take place, both having taken the necessary decisions, and made the necessary arrangements, before this encounter took place. What Marlowe leads us to perceive behind the verbal and rationalistic fencing, is the perennial comedy of acquisition and the substratum of universal Machiavellism which makes nonsense of the division into Jew and Gentile.

III

I have lingered over the second scene because, as one of the best and most sustained pieces of writing in the play, it does indicate where the real creative currents are flowing—into an exposure of the ferocious egocentricity upon which the structures of material acquisition and temporal power are erected. The method is a dialectical demolition of the moral superstructure until the brute facts show their real nature.

Yet although the points are trenchantly made, and the satiric barbs stick fast, there is a certain constriction and a certain emptiness attendant on the dialectical method, just as there was on the ironic inversions I have already discussed. The kind of laughter upon which it trades has a hard, self-righteous timbre. It does not, like the wit of the best comedy, get in behind the egotistic defences, and engage creatively an audience's capacity for self-criticism and self-ridicule. It draws too heavily on contempt for that. It is demonstrative satire, inviting us to indulge the secure guffaw; and the guffaw tends to swamp the genuinely exploratory satire as the play moves to its conclusion. In the First Knight's sophistry, for example ('If your first curse fall heavy on thy head... 'Tis not our fault...'), there is an explicitness, an overplus of assertiveness, which passes judgment on the sentiment almost before it has been expressed. If one considers the sanctimonious Richard of Gloucester hypocritically excusing Margaret's hair-raising curses—

> I cannot blame her: by God's holy mother,
> She hath had too much wrong; and I repent
> My part thereof that I have done to her—[17]

one senses a significant difference: though the didactic point is there, it is refracted through the enriching medium of Richard's character, and the utterance has a human weight and body behind it that may properly be termed dramatic. The implied dissimulation, and the notion of playing a part, are enacted in Shakespeare's verse—'by God's holy mother'—whereas for Marlowe this is merely a premiss appropriately expressed in melodramatic asides—'How! a Christian? Hum, what's here to do?' (I. ii. 75). Marlowe's verse, that is to say, has the wrong kind of clarity—a clarity which permits us to see what is being done, instead of enabling that which is being done to act more immediately on the imagination.

Barabas's famous autobiographical sketch (II. iii. 175–202) is faintly unsatisfactory in the same way; not because it is shocking—it is far too frivolously and slyly enunciated to be that—but because we can see it is meant to be shocking. Barabas confesses to most of the criminal occupations with which anti-semitic polemists had credited the Jews—poisoning wells (the alleged origin of Bubonic plague), practising a murderous physic, working as a military engineer, as inventor of diabolical devices and as diplomatic traitor, besides of course the conventional occupational role of usurer—and on this level the speech is a quiet jibe at the Christians who can believe such tales.[18] Barabas clearly makes no great effort to convince Ithamore or us of its accuracy: the syntax is of the 'throw-away' kind—'As for myself, I...sometimes I...and now and then...Being young I...And, after that... Then, after that...some or other...'—and he puts the lid on the whole performance by enquiring blandly, 'But tell me now, how hast thou spent thy time?'

Yet, for all the nonchalant airs, what is the speech included for at all, if not to shock? And what is this affectation of bland indifference, if not an oblique attempt to strengthen the effect? The under-statement is a sop to our sophistication, but it is the eternal Machiavel monster who is being put on show for our wonderment.

'Machiavel' is an especially appropriate denomination if I am right in detecting the same equivocation in the Prologue. Certainly there is the same affected nonchalance—'I come not, I, / To read a lecture here in Britain...' (ll. 28–9)—the same casual and loose-limbed syntax, the same exaggeration of sentiment in the most equable of rhythms—'I count religion but a childish toy, / And hold there is no sin but ignorance'. And over it all there hangs a strong sense that Machiavel is rather aimlessly exhibiting himself and his intellectual emancipation; further, that behind him stands the figure of an iconoclastic young man, very much up with the latest intellectual fashions, trying to goad us into protest or reproof, so that he can then laugh in our faces and claim that he is only joking. But in fact he is half-committed to the very monster he invites us to ridicule. He is not so much teasing the audience as giving expression to his own ambiguous liaison with Italianate vice. It is this immature and unacknowledged fascination, I suggest, which accounts for the persistent tendency to overstate villainy, or to write verse in which the organising principle is a systematic assault on all our normal moral expectations—'Do you not sorrow for your daughter's death?' 'No, but I grieve because she liv'd so long' (IV. i. 17); or this of Barabas—

> There is no music to a Christian's knell:
> How sweet the bells ring, now the nuns are dead,
> That sound at other times like tinkers' pans!
> I was afraid the poison had not wrought.   IV. i. 1

This is the brutal schoolboy humour of the 'sick' joke, whose only charm is that of perversity; and it is clearly related to that drive for random destruction which is so dominant in *The Massacre* and *Tamburlaine*.

All of which would suggest that it is to the vulgarised Machiavel-myth, not to Machiavelli himself, that we must look for Barabas's genesis and for the origins of the peculiar moral climate of the play. It is true that Barabas displays a preoccupation with the techniques of power, divorced from a consideration of the ends of power, which is congruent with Machiavelli's discussion of princely *virtù*, true also that there is a preoccupation with the politic uses of religion (which 'hides many mischiefs from suspicion') and friendship ('he from whom my most advantage comes, / Shall be my friend'), and that this can be paralleled in *The Prince* and *The Discourses*. But Barabas as dissembler, as poisoner, as inveterate malice personified, owes more to the flourishing legend of the Machiavel than to whatever first-hand acquaintance with the Florentine Marlowe may have had. And what had been in Machiavelli a dispassionate contemplation of the wolvish habits of men, a clinical dissection, tends, in the myth, to degenerate into a predilection for drawing men who are precisely the reverse of what we would like to think them to be. When Marlowe indulges this predilection at any length, the result is just as unreal as the idealised version of man that he is attacking. Again he has been betrayed by the 'mere idea'.

Yet, as so often with this desperately uneven play, one must qualify. For it seems probable that the plot is deliberately organised with a view to offering a serious critique of a society founded on the free operation of individual power-lust. This surely is the point of showing us Barabas frying to death in his own Machiavellian engine. Although one may hesitate to ascribe his final foiling, as Ferneze does, 'to Heaven', it is clearly intended to exemplify a kind of poetic, if not divine, justice. It is the development of a theme Greene stated two years earlier, in his death-bed exhortation to Marlowe:

What are his [Machiavelli's] rules but meere confused mockeries, able to extirpate in small time the generation of mankind. For if *sic volo, sic iubeo* hold in those that are able to command; and if it be lawfull *Fas & nefas* to do anything that is beneficiall; onely Tyrants should possesse the earth, and they striuing to exceed in tyrannie, should each to other be a slaughter man; till the mightiest outliuing all, one stroke were left for Death, that in one age mans life should end.[19]

As a refutation of Machiavelli this is less than adequate. It ignores, amongst other things, the way in which morality, ejected by Machiavelli at the pragmatic front-door, re-enters at the utilitarian back-door as a practical necessity of existence in society. But we can grant it a certain limited kind of truth: universal Machiavellism, supposing it to be possible, would entail universal annihilation. On this basis there need be no divine intervention to wreak vengeance on these cynical opportunists, because, given time, they will destroy each other. This Marlowe sees clearly enough to be able to dispense completely with the transcendental order in this play. There is never the slightest suggestion that anything but terrestrial processes are involved in Barabas's downfall. It is a simple failure of 'policy'—he makes the fatal mistake of allowing another Machiavellian to 'partake' his policy (v. v. 24), and his fortunes are thereafter dependent on the good-will of an accomplice who is his bitterest enemy. And so the long, murderous jockeying for power reaches its inevitable, and morally meaningless, stasis. The mightiest outlives all, to make a final cynical appeal to what Miss Mahood calls 'those truths which are outworn from a materialist viewpoint, but which are retained for the commercial value of their respectability':[20]

> So, march away; and let due praise be given
> Neither to Fate nor Fortune, but to Heaven. v. v. 123

Having complacently accepted the fruits of 'a Jew's courtesy' while smugly deploring 'the unhallow'd deeds of Jews', having exploited the situation for its maximum financial and political yield, having cannily repudiated Calymath's disingenous offer to negotiate Malta's peace in person, and having generally shown himself superior to either Fate or Fortune, Ferneze, with acute theological impertinence, identifies his own Machiavellian *virtù* with divine justice. On this note of exquisite casuistry Marlowe ends, leaving his unconscionable prince in command of the situation, his dead hero quietly simmering in his own juice, and no sign that Heaven cares sufficiently about the affairs of men to repudiate the gigantic blasphemy.

That this is effective enough in its cynical way, I don't dispute. It is one way of confronting the contradiction between the conception of a morally ordered universe and the amoral realities of the power-game— namely, with a moral shrug. At least in this way Marlowe preserved his hard shell of sophisticated mockery intact in a way that Shakespeare, faced with the same contradiction in *Richard III*, failed to do when he opted for Providence in the teeth of the dramatic facts.[21] Yet in a young writer ingenuousness is far less damaging than a premature cynicism. At least he can grow out of the ingenuousness; but cynicism is one of those galloping diseases that is exacerbated by time.

Furthermore, by accepting the premiss of universal Machiavellism— one which Machiavelli, who regarded perfection in evil as a very rare endowment, would certainly not have granted[22]—Marlowe has cut the knot which a more scrupulous mind would have tried to untie. If all men were indeed devoid of scruple, the matter would be comparatively simple—we would at least know where we stood, and could take measures accordingly. But part of the difficulty of living in society stems from the fact that men are neither uniformly moral nor uniformly immoral. The total contempt for principle which prevails in Marlowe's Malta is simply not to be found in nature. The exaggeration which makes all the personages in *The Jew* either knaves or fools, though it has the charm of all such summary solutions to the uneasy doubleness of life, committed Marlowe to a kind of unreality which became increasingly damaging as the action moved to its melodramatic conclusion. At the level where it really matters, Marlowe was not serious.

In any case, the attempt to depict the self-destructive dynamic of Machiavellism involved Marlowe in difficult structural complication: the plot is necessarily the representation of a machine that is running down. It is a kind of anti-drama, a theatre of disintegration in which the moral emptiness of the characters is a premiss of the action. In the early scenes there is some attempt to foist the spurious splendours of mere wealth upon the audience—the 'infinite riches in a little room' phase— but as the action progresses there is less and less that can engage us imaginatively. Barabas, robbed of the very bread of his existence (for his Machiavel cannot operate without the assistance of Mammon), degenerates into that repellent curmudgeon which he played in jest in the earlier scenes: he squirms, he whines and he cajoles.

> 'Tis not five hundred crowns that I esteem;
> I am not mov'd at that: this angers me,
> That he, who knows I love him as myself,
> Should write in this imperious vein. Why, sir,
> You know I have no child, and unto whom
> Should I leave all, but unto Ithamore?
> PILIA-BORZA. Here's many words, but no crowns: the crowns!
> BARABAS. Commend me to him, sir, most humbly,
> And unto your good mistress as unknown.   IV. V. 42

The cold-blooded ruthlessness of Marlowe's portraiture has a certain impressiveness, but it alienates the audience to such an extent that in the latter part of the play he is obliged to sustain the interest by a frenetic proliferation of intrigue and counter-intrigue. The alienation is complete by the time Barabas is in the cauldron breathing forth his 'latest fate':

> And, had I but escap'd this stratagem,
> I would have brought confusion on you all,
> Damn'd Christians, dogs, and Turkish infidels!   V. V. 84

One can see that this is one way of making the point that the Machiavellian deprived of success is grotesquely sub-human; but dramatically it is a cul-de-sac. The road *in* is completely logical—given the existence of this kind of villainy—but there is no road *out*. Perhaps it is some awareness in Marlowe of being trapped, that gives to Barabas's last speech a hysteric intensity which is not entirely explained by reference to the 'extremity of heat' and the 'intolerable pangs' he is suffering. It is not a poetic intensity, because the aggressive energies are not *in* the verse but erupting through it, so that one has the impression of a wounded beast lashing about in the dark, a beast for whom Barabas is no more than a vehicle.

IV

There is one further respect in which *The Jew of Malta* engages directly with the social environment in which it was reared—in its treatment of the new world of international mercantilism:

> Warehouses stuff'd with spices and with drugs...
> At Alexandria merchandise unsold;
> But yesterday two ships went from this town,
> Their voyage will be worth ten thousand crowns:

> In Florence, Venice, Antwerp, London, Seville,
> Frankfort, Lubeck, Moscow, and where not,
> Have I debts owing; and, in most of these,
> Great sums of money lying in the banco...   IV. i. 67

From the first scene of the play onwards, this milieu is created. Barabas initiates us into the cosmopolitan freemasonry of the great plutocrats—

> There's Kirriah Jairim, the great Jew of Greece,
> Obed in Bairseth, Nones in Portugal,
> Myself in Malta, some in Italy...   I. i. 122

—talks easily of 'mine argosy at Alexandria', bills of entry, seeing the freight discharged, custom houses, and so on, displaying that mastery of detail combined with expansive opulence that marks him as the Renaissance merchant-prince—

> Here have I purs'd their paltry silverlings.
> Fie; what a trouble 'tis to count this trash.   I. i. 6

There is the concrete particularity of a real world in this opening scene —in such details, for instance, as Barabas's quizzical scrutiny of the weather-vane (in the later scenes, as his gestures become increasingly flamboyant and imprecise, we tend to forget that ships are dependent on mere winds); and at the same moment that he is expending his most opulent verse on the varnishing of the higher cupidity—

> Bags of fiery opals, sapphires, amethysts,
> Jacinths, hard topaz, grass-green emeralds...   I. i. 25

—Marlowe is also subtly bringing our sense of moral constriction into play:

> Thus trowls our fortune in by land and sea,
> And thus are we on every side enrich'd:
> These are the blessings promis'd to the Jews,
> And herein was old Abraham's happiness.   I. i. 101

In Barabas's world, the patriarch's flocks and herds weigh more than the divine promise: Messiah has already come in the guise of 'fiery opals' and 'grass-green emeralds'. Throughout the scene there is this continuous appeal to the substantial facts of worldly prosperity, against the moral view of what *ought* to prevail:

> They say we are a scatter'd nation:
> I cannot tell; but we have scambled up
> More wealth by far than those that brag of faith.   I. i. 119

Birds of the air will tell of murders past? Barabas is ashamed to hear such fooleries. His own career of extortion has disproved these notions of a natural moral order:

> But mark how I am blest for plaguing them;
> I have as much coin as will buy the town.   II. iii. 200

The hard metallic glitter of Barabas's world is striving to outshine the hidden riches of morality and religion.

> Happily some hapless man hath conscience,
> And for his conscience lives in beggary.   I. i. 117

The Jew's is a Machiavellian realism for which moral sanctions have been abolished by the hard facts of predatory human nature; the 'wind that bloweth all the world besides' is simply 'desire of gold' (III. v. 3), and with good reason: for 'who is honour'd now but for his wealth?' (I. i. 111). When the half-strangled Friar Barnadine enquires, 'What, will you have my life?' Barabas appeals to the (by now) axiomatic equivalence of life and material prosperity—'Pull hard, I say. You would have had my goods' (IV. ii. 20).

Parallel with this opening of the sepulchre of universal cupidity runs a study of the various moral whitewashes which are employed to conceal the worms and the corruption. We have seen Ferneze's theological sophistries performing this function, but the issue is continually cropping up in the play. It is at its most blatant in the persons of the two contractor-friars, offering rival tenders for Barabas's soul, and making it plain in the process that even salvation can be had at cut rates if the market is good and your credit stands high. Religion for Barnadine and Jacomo is simply a technique of spiritual blackmail.

The same sanctified rapacity is shown to be at work in Act II, Scene ii, where Ferneze finds himself caught in the cross-fire between Spaniard and Turk. It is an extremely embarrassing diplomatic crisis: he must either alienate Christian Spain by refusing trading rights to their vice-admiral, or incur the wrath of the Turk, who is only being held at bay by ruinous cash payments and a somewhat one-sided treaty. The solution proposed—a Spanish alliance, followed by war with the Turk—brilliantly satisfies security, self-esteem and fiscal considerations. The funds extorted to pay the Turkish levy can be diverted to the Department of Defence (l. 27); the threatened expulsion by Spain can be averted (ll. 37–41); the stain on the honour of the Knights Templar is expunged (ll. 28–33); Maltese resistance is buttressed by

Spanish aid (l. 40); trade, that deity of the mercantilist cult, can proceed unhindered (l. 42); and Ferneze may again congratulate himself on being a good Christian as he and his 'warlike knights' sally forth 'against these barbarous misbelieving Turks' (l. 46). With so many offered advantages, moral and economic, the mere breaking of faith with an ally (and an infidel at that) could carry no weight at all. Marlowe sums up this fox's wisdom of the Governor in the resounding accents of triumphant nationalism:

> Claim tribute where thou wilt, we are resolv'd—
> Honour is bought with blood, and not with gold.   ii. ii. 55

(He nevertheless keeps the gold.)

There is a strain of tough honesty in *The Jew* which commands some respect; a refusal to be deflected by the moralistic smokescreen with which rapacity tries to conceal its activities, and as such it is an entirely healthy strain. I am reminded of some remarks of Eric Voegelin's on the subject of Machiavelli's 'realism'. Machiavelli's generation, he claims, was strongly moulded by the traumatic experience of the French invasion.

The more intelligent and sensitive members of such a generation have seen the reality of power at the moment of its existential starkness when it destroys an order, when the destruction is a brute fact without sense, reason or ideas. It is difficult to tell such men any stories about morality in politics. With the experienced eye of the moraliste [sic] they will diagnose the moralist in politics as the profiteer of the status quo, as the hypocrite who wants everyone to be moral and peace-loving after his own power drive has carried him into the position he would retain...In this aspect a man like Machiavelli...is a healthy and honest figure, most certainly preferable as a man to the contractualists who try to cover the reality of power underneath an established order, by the moral ...swindle of consent.[23]

In so far as Marlowe's (or Machiavelli's) contemplation of economic and political power is 'realistic' in this sense, no one will cavil. For it is a potentially tragic vision in which the inalienable ideal is held in tension with the brutal reality, and man is torn between them. But the tragic way of confronting life was, as I shall argue in the next chapter, totally foreign to Machiavelli's cast of mind. And Marlowe wrote neither a tragedy nor a tragicomedy: he wrote a farce. That is to say, he succumbed to the inevitable tendency of 'realism' to become so insensitive to the bitter truths it tells that it degenerates into self-indulgence. This 'realist's sentimentality' revels in the *sensation* of honesty that comes from resolutely contemplating hard facts, without ever paying the price of mental anguish that such a contemplation should entail. Realism, from being a mental discipline, has become a mental habit, and leads eventually to neglect of the facts that gave rise to it—the characteristic failing of a social-critic-cum-dramatist like Bertolt Brecht, in whose early work particularly the unmasking of bourgeois vice became an end in itself, and the revelation of the power-structure behind the stately façade of morality a joyful mission. As with Marlowe and Machiavelli, there is something stunted about the humanity that emerges from Brecht's reductive analysis. The up-to-the-minute enlightenment is too brash, the traditional values too glibly surrendered. Indeed there are signs in all three writers that they derived positive satisfaction from scuttling the old hulk and watching it sink beneath the waves of history.

The sentimentality of realism is perhaps less vicious than the more immediately recognisable brutality of realism, but it has its roots in the same diversion of the energies of perception from object to subject. In *The Jew* we have both the sentimentality and the brutality; but they are simply two phases of the one process—the application (as distinct from the realisation) of an *a priori* tough-mindedness which, because it is *a priori*, can never sufficiently divest itself of the doctrinaire and the abstract to clothe itself in the human and the dramatic. The ideas Machiavel promulgates in the Prologue (which are lively enough as ideas) are deprived of imaginative sustenance because they are not held by men, but by ideological constructs designed specifically for their ability to hold them. And the world within which the ideas are held is not a human world, but a diagrammatic representation of that world. The objection is not to the schematisation which is indispensable to comedy, but to a certain brittle and defensive hardness, which tries to hold the real world, as it were, at arms' length. When Marlowe tires of the didactic constriction of his satirical microcosm, he relieves his feelings with those outbreaks of destructive violence with which the play is dotted: brutality masquerading as realism is the degenerate end-product of that subjugation of the human to the 'truth', in which realism begins.

V

Considerations such as these lead directly to *Richard III*. For in a sense Shakespeare is there trying to be realistic about the same facts of human greed and lust for power. It is no coincidence, for example, that he

borrows Marlowe's image of the treacherous dog, the cunning cur
equipped to draw profit from murderous competition—

> We Jews can fawn like spaniels when we please;
> And when we grin we bite...   II. iii. 20

—and applies it to Richard—

>   take heed of yonder dog!
> Look, when he fawns, he bites; and, when he bites,
> His venom tooth will rankle to the death;
>
>   *Richard III*, I. iii. 289

for the investigation of this kind of vicious dissimulation is at the heart
of both plays. Again, there is in both the same hypocritical adoption of
pious poses, so that the invocation of religious sanctions usually arouses,
rather than calms, our suspicions. And there is a nagging suggestion
that, in a world as corrupt as this, the only alternative to 'unseen
hypocrisy' may be (as Barabas urges) 'a counterfeit profession'. The
hypocrisy of both Barabas and Richard is a response to a social order in
which the ideal and the actual are so sharply at odds that genuine virtue
is indulged at the risk of temporal disaster. Both plays confront that
new social and political world which is presided over by the tutelary
genius of Machiavelli.

But to see Marlowe and Shakespeare merely as sharing a common
Machiavellian realism is to neglect some important distinctions: the
way, for instance, *Richard III* makes us aware of the scaling-down of
humanity in *The Jew*: whereabouts in that play could one find a place
for Clarence's dream? A category of realism broad enough to include
both plays strikes me as a not very useful instrument of thought. But it
also neglects some necessary judgments about the *level* on which
Machiavelli's own realism operates—which is the subject of the next
chapter.

4

MACHIAVELLI AND THE
CRISIS OF RENAISSANCE POLITICAL
CONSCIOUSNESS

So far I have been avoiding the question of Machiavelli's direct influence on Marlowe—largely because there is so little to be said on the subject. There is every likelihood that Marlowe was acquainted with the 'odd crewe' of Cambridge Machiavellists that Gabriel Harvey mentions in a letter of ca. 1580, the more so since Marlowe appears to have borrowed the idea for his Prologue from Harvey's Latin Epigram in which *Machiavellus ipse loquitur*.[1] He could have read *The Prince* and *The Discourses* in John Wolfe's surreptitious Italian editions, or in one of several manuscript translations—and it is well to remember what a recent historian of the subject has pointed out, the 'manuscripts and printed books are like snakes: for every one you see there are a hundred others hidden in the undergrowth'.[2] There is no reason, therefore, to assume that Marlowe, who showed enough interest in Machiavelli to introduce him to the English stage, would have been beholden to Gentillet (who was not in print in Marlowe's lifetime and never much read in England anyway)[3] for his knowledge of the Italian theorist. But beyond this the evidence is very thin, and depends heavily on the individual reader's reaction to Marlowe's plays. The radical disagreement of Marlowe scholars indicates, at the very least, that we are not dealing here with anything so definite as allusion—which has never been established—but with an 'influence' so diffuse and imprecise as to be hardly worth discussing.[4] Certainly very little has emerged from the learned debates of the last thirty years or so. The matter is made more inconclusive by the innumerable occasions when, as A. H. Gilbert has shown, what looks like a Machiavellian maxim could equally well have been derived from the common stock of medieval political commonplace.[5] The direct influence of Machiavelli on Marlowe we may, I think, dismiss as a useless, because unanswerable, question.

The Machiavel-myth, as we have seen, is rather more relevant. But it is worth enquiring how relevant. When we have read Professor Praz's pioneering study, or followed Meyer through his 395 allusions, or discovered by dint of honest sweat that his list is incomplete, it is questionable whether we are any better equipped to read Marlowe.[6] Most readers know a bogey when they meet one, and it is far more interesting to ponder what Marlowe has done with his, than to trace its configurations in the vulgar error and superstition from which it takes its rise. The most that can be said is that some of the gross simplification implicit in the myth has rubbed off on Marlowe's drama—in the naïve delight in monumental villainy or the monstrous dissimulation of the Machiavel. But this is a matter of intellectual history (if we may so dignify it) and a not very elevated part of it at that.

Why then have I been talking so insistently about Machiavellism? Briefly, because Machiavelli, whether read or not, whether distorted by popular fancy or judiciously pondered by the wise, represents one of the central facts of Elizabethan culture. Even if Marlowe had not read him, he (and any other intelligent Elizabethan) was certainly aware of the movement in European thought which made Machiavelli appear important to later historians. Machiavelli, and the kind of mind he represented, was the radical yeast in the traditional loaf. As H. B. Parkes puts it,

the Elizabethans were in process of discovering by empirical methods that man's natural energy was an amoral force which did not appear to conform with any traditional notions of goodness. On the one hand they had been taught that nature was fundamentally good, that evil was a mere imperfection or aberration, and that the maintenance of moral and political order depended upon this belief in the identity of natural and divine law. On the other hand, they were confronted by a natural world in which the central reality was not reason or morality, but power, and the manifestations of power were, by traditional standards, evil. Evil, including all its destructive potentialities, thus appeared to be natural. They found themselves, therefore, torn between two kinds of knowledge, with no way of bridging the gulf between them...[7]

There is no separating the change in the *realities* of power from the change in the *conception* of power: each derives from, and modifies, the other. But change there certainly was, and Machiavelli is one of the clearest symptoms of that change.

When men find themselves committed in this way to two irreconcilable conceptions, there are various ways of dealing with the problem. One method, which appeals to the impatient, is to cut the knot and espouse one cause in opposition to the other: thus the conservative mind is driven into blind assertion of the old values, while the type of mind misleadingly described as 'emancipated' enthusiastically adopts the new and the radical, either ignoring the traditional conceptions or expending its energy on their demolition. The other solution—and it is the only one open to the mind which feels both pressures deeply—is to attempt the laborious yet constructive task of discovering a new frame of reference which will contain the new without sacrificing the old. Machiavelli and Marlowe (in *The Jew*) fall into the 'emancipated' category, agreeing to disregard the claims of morality in public life and to concentrate exclusively on the techniques of power. The bulk of Elizabethan opinion inhabited the conservative camp, though it is to the credit of many of these traditionalists that they did so with considerable misgivings.[8] The only unequivocal attempt at reconstruction and retrenchment that I have been able to find is embodied in Shakespeare's history plays—which is one reason for regarding them as centrally important to any understanding of the Elizabethan period.[9]

My inverted commas around the word 'emancipation', however, constitute insinuation rather than demonstration. I have implied that Machiavelli's emancipation is a fairly limited affair, and that there is a serious partiality about his political thought, of which Shakespeare cannot be accused; and these contentions call for a closer look at his writings.

In Machiavelli, the contradiction between ideal and actual is already familiar enough to have lost all its poignancy—hence probably the flat assurance with which he enunciates the dilemma:

Many have imagined republics and principalities which have never been seen or known to exist in reality: for how we live is so far removed from how we ought to live, that he who abandons what is done for what ought to be done, will rather learn to bring about his ruin than his preservation. A man who wishes to make a profession of goodness in everything must necessarily come to grief among so many who are not good.[10]

Machiavelli is here well on the way to the self-congratulatory hardheadedness of which I have accused Marlowe. It is not simply that he recognises the gulf between ideal and actual, for this was the hoariest of commonplaces: as Gentillet remarked, *Il Principe* was a well-known personage in the old political treatises, only there he was known as 'the Tyrant'.[11] It is that he unequivocally accepts it; and in this consists his newness. (Marlowe, too, as we have seen, accepts it—with fewer qualms, indeed, than Machiavelli; he makes it the comic premiss of his play and proceeds to exploit the discrepancy between moral expectation and amoral actuality for all that it's worth.)

I am aware that the neglect of moral considerations in Machiavelli is deliberate; that he is attempting the modern laboratory technique of isolating the subject of study in order to understand it in a more precise context. I am aware too of the historicist contention that Machiavelli is the product of a very particular political situation in sixteenth-century Italy and that his conclusions were only intended for application in that limited area. This last contention, relying as it does on the judgment that the most outstanding feature of Machiavelli's style—its epigrammatic generality—is somehow an irrelevant matter of external form, seems to me indefensible.[12] In both style, and the intention revealed by that style, he is a general theorist, and, as Cassirer observes, an over-confident one at that.[13]

But the attempted isolation of the political sphere raises several very important questions: first, whether the isolation is even possible—and Machiavelli's own final failure to exclude the moral order makes this more than dubious; second, whether the consequences of the isolation are not so pernicious as to render the whole operation suspect; third, whether the tendency of modern thinkers to endorse the Machiavellian compartmentalisation is not symptomatic of a dangerous debility in the political thought of our own age, one which suggests that we have something still to learn from Machiavelli's renaissance critics; and finally, whether the discovery that the actual is flagrantly at odds with the ideal entitles the discoverer to dismiss the ideal as irrelevant to reality.

Is the separation of the political and moral spheres even possible? What happens, for instance, when issues that are inescapably moral are discussed in purely technical terms, as in the following consideration of the expedience of poisoning one's political rivals?

It is true that the use of poison is more dangerous owing to its being more uncertain, for not everybody has the commodity, so that those who have it must needs be consulted and the necessity of consulting others means danger to yourself. Again, for a variety of reasons, a poisoned drink may not prove fatal, as those discovered who were to kill Commodus, for, on his throwing up the poison they had given him, they were forced to strangle him if they wanted him to die.[14]

The moral issues have not been excluded; they have been blinked. And as a result they re-enter as a powerful irony which is the more damaging because Machiavelli, either out of naïvety or perversity, refuses to recognise it. If one turns to the chapter in *The Prince* where he discusses the treatment to be accorded to the conquered, one finds the same flaw:

the injured parties...must either be caressed or annihilated; they will revenge themselves for small injuries, but cannot do so for great ones; the injury therefore that we do to a man must be such that we need not fear his vengeance.[15]

As Una Ellis-Fermor remarks, 'there are passages in [*The Prince*] set forth in all good faith, that read like Swift at the height of his irony'.[16] The equable tone is staggering because of the staggering insensitivity, innate or acquired, which it implies. Can this woodenly humourless man be a great thinker?

At this point Machiavelli's apologists send us back to square one, by reasserting the Machiavellian dichotomy. 'Nothing', declares Federico Chabod,

nothing is further from Machiavelli's mind than to undermine common morality, replacing it with a new ethic; instead, he says that in public affairs the only thing that counts is the political criterion, by which he abides: let those who wish to remain faithful to the precepts of morality concern themselves with other things, not with politics...The truth is that Machiavelli leaves the moral ideal intact, and he does so because it need not concern him.[17]

It may have been far from his mind, but if so that merely indicates how inadequately he understood his own thought-processes. If this is 'leaving the moral ideal intact', the moral ideal has no more deadly enemy than such neglect. In fact Chabod's flat dichotomising simply betrays a profound indifference to the 'moral ideal'. Our initial question remains: can the moral and the political be kept separate?

Machiavelli himself fails to maintain the dichotomy. As long as his discussion concerns itself exclusively with means—the 'how' of politics —he is reasonably consistent, and, from a descriptive point of view, often illuminating. But these means, questionable as they so often are, were to be finally sanctioned by the end.[18] The suspension of moral norms is performed in the interests of some higher objective.

How laudable it is for a prince to keep good faith and live with integrity, and not with astuteness, every one knows. Still the experience of our times shows those princes to have done great things who have had little regard for good faith.[19]

There is no blinking the fact that the 'great things' (*gran cose*) are being morally endorsed as more *laudabile* than 'good faith' and 'integrity'. From the ashes of superseded convention rises the new morality of princely glory, which, in Machiavelli's case, is to subserve the grand aim of the unification of Italy—as we discover in the final chapter.

With that chapter, the inconsistency of his position *vis-à-vis* morality becomes completely disabling. The same men of whom 'it may be said...in general that they are ungrateful, voluble, dissemblers, anxious to avoid danger, and covetous of gain', the very men whose evil dispositions make necessary the abrogation of moral codes and the deliberate use of deception: these men are to become the selfless supporters of the leader 'appointed by God' for Italy's 'redemption', 'for you cannot have more faithful, or truer and better soldiers'.

I cannot express the love with which he would be received in all those provinces which have suffered under these foreign invasions, with what thirst for vengeance, with what steadfast faith, with what love, with what grateful tears. What doors would be closed against him? What people would refuse him obedience? What envy could oppose him? What Italian would withold allegiance?[20]

Machiavelli is, of course, quite right to recognise the indispensability of this kind of moral fervour if his *gran cose* are to be accomplished. It is just that his whole effort elsewhere has been directed to rendering it meaningless. Machiavellism, writes Friedrich Meinecke,

already contained the poison of an inner contradiction, from the very moment it began its ascent. On the one hand, religion, morality and law were all absolutely indispensable to it as a foundation for its existence; on the other hand, it started off with the definite intention of injuring these whenever the needs of national self-preservation would require it.

This contradiction Machiavelli effectively concealed from himself by believing that the same force (*necessità*) which, in Meinecke's words, 'impelled princes to refrain from being good under certain circumstances, also impelled men to behave morally; for it is only from necessity that men perform good actions'.[21]

In the end, Machiavelli's empiricist exclusion of morality from his scrutiny of political life means only that he is free to invoke the first moral sanction that comes to hand, while leaving his implicit value-system completely unscrutinised and uncomprehended. The question that cries out for an answer is, 'Wherein lies the overriding importance of the ideal of unity, or stability, these "great things", that so much can be sacrificed to it?' And this question can only be answered by plunging boldly into the moral speculation which Machiavelli consistently eschews.

As soon as one takes this plunge, the dichotomy begins to break down. *Raison d'état* does not operate independently of morality. It draws its strength from it. Meinecke, in a long and brilliant passage, forces the confusion into the open:

If a statesman feels himself obliged by 'necessity of State' to violate law and ethics, he can still feel himself morally justified at the bar of his own conscience, if in doing so he has, according to his own personal conviction, thought first of the good of the State entrusted to his care. Thus the realm of values is capable of shedding an ennobling light far into the inmost recesses of problematical conduct. But nevertheless such conduct still remains problematical and dualistic, because the conscious infringement of morality and law must in any circumstances...be a moral stain, a defeat of Ethos in its partnership with Kratos. Thus all conduct prompted by *raison d'état* fluctuates continuously back and forth between dark and light.

Nor is this the end of the matter. Once entered upon the region of motives, the road leads even deeper into obscurity: when a statesman

sets the goal of power above justice and ethics...is he then really impelled by the welfare of the State, disclosing itself as a moral value? By a sore anxiety regarding the existence, the future and the environment of the State entrusted to his care? Is there no more here than a conflict between divergent moral duties? Or do we also perceive the intrusion of some amoral motives? The striving for power is an aboriginal human impulse, perhaps even an animal impulse, which blindly snatches at everything around it until it comes up against some external barriers. And, in the case of men at least, the impulse is not restricted to what is necessary for life and health. Man takes a wholehearted pleasure in power itself, and, through it, in himself and his heightened personality.

What Meinecke calls 'unfathomable transitional zones' are perhaps the fundamental reality of political motivation. On the one hand, the State cannot do without the animal impulse, 'for without such a contribution of personal pleonexia on the part of the strong-willed man with nerves of steel the State could never succeed in acquiring the power that is indispensable to it'. On the other hand, the power drive has

a natural tendency...to restrict itself to whatever bare egotistical advantages can be attained for the State, and to make its calculation with reference to these alone. And the advantage of the State is always at the same time blended with the advantage of the rulers. So *raison d'état* is continually in danger of becoming a mere utilitarian instrument without ethical application, in danger of sinking back again from wisdom to mere cunning, and of restraining the superficial passions merely in order to satisfy passions and egoisms which lie deeper and are more completely hidden.[22]

Machiavelli—even without his famous lion-and-fox exempla— is the exponent of this mere animal cunning. He is oblivious of, indeed indifferent to, the 'unfathomable transitional zones' of political behaviour. Not even in his espousal of ends is he aware of the moral problems involved. A whole hemisphere of political speculation, which was so obvious to his contemporaries as to be self-evident, is non-existent for him. Because it expressed itself in platitude, he assumed it to be dead. But his interment of morality was as premature as the burial service that Darwinians read over the quasi-corpse of theism in the 1860s: what has lived so long and fully does not die overnight. Machiavelli thus represents a truncation of renaissance political consciousness—an attempt on the part of the tree to grow without its roots. The fact that he represents also the 'modern' face of that consciousness should not betray us into thinking that he is therefore more important than his opponents. Progress may be a valid conception, but progress in a straight line is certainly an invalid one.

For the immediate losses sustained when, in Cassirer's phrase, the State 'won its full autonomy' were so huge as to set men thinking urgently.

The sharp knife of Machiavelli's thought has cut off all the threads by which in former generations the state was fastened to the organic whole of human existence. The political world has lost its connexion not only with religion or metaphysics but also with all the other forms of man's ethical and cultural life. It stands alone—in an empty space.[23]

The obligation of ruler to subject was dissolved. The 'common weal', for all that Machiavelli invoked it, was an essentially obsolete conception; for, although it might be built again on grounds of expedience and utility, that process was to take centuries. The Elizabethans, caught between the upper and lower millstones of historical evolution, made their peace as best they could: hoped, with Bacon, that decency would prevail—

certainly with these [Machiavelli's and others'] dispensations from the laws of charity and integrity, the pressing of a man's fortunes may be more hasty and compendious. But it is in life as it is in ways, the shortest way is commonly the foulest, and surely the fairer way is not much about;[24]

or granting, with Hooker, the accuracy of Machiavelli's description, deplored its adoption as a norm, hinting that such unbridled pursuit of personal advantage would in the end defeat itself;[25] others contented themselves with vilification and angry invective. Those like Marlowe who indulged a kind of tongue-in-cheek Machiavellism had to pretend an obliviousness to traditional values, and to the answers that had been made to Machiavelli, which was damagingly disingenuous. There is a certain element of display, a shallow and self-conscious modernity, in Marlowe's championship of the Florentine which goes with a refusal to grapple with the rival claims of traditional political wisdom. None of Machiavelli's English admirers at this period was able to rid himself of this curious double-mindedness.[26]

I have suggested that there is still something to be learned from Machiavelli's sixteenth-century detractors. But it is not the answers they propounded, for they were all in one way or another unsatisfactory. It is that there is a problem. I have already instanced Chabod's dangerous insensitivity to the problem, and it appears to be fairly widely shared by Italian historians who seem bent on having Machiavelli as some kind of secularist saint. It is present in a remark of Trevor-Roper's which I can only regard as wilfully misleading:

> What was the new science which Machiavelli had invented; which had so outraged the world that only revolutionaries, a hundred and fifty years later, could dare to praise him openly?...Machiavelli humanised the study of politics.[27]

There may be a single word for what he did to politics, but it is not 'humanised'. There is something in modern political consciousness which still responds so strongly to Machiavelli's 'realism', that it is unable to see that it is only realistic in a very limited area. Machiavelli speaks the kind of truth which, especially since the political disenchantment of the late 'thirties, twentieth-century man likes to hear. But it is not the whole truth. And one of the great advantages to be reaped from attending to a great mind like Shakespeare's speaking out of the heart of the Elizabethan dilemma, is that we may learn to correct our own partial insights. As Bernard Spivack remarks,

> For all their distortion of his doctrine and their hysterical denigration of his character, the Elizabethans, standing as they did at the crossroads of two realities, probably grasped the import of the Florentine better than do we today, who have been carried four centuries out of sight of the great corner turned. That for us he is no longer of the Devil's party means chiefly that we have got rid of the Devil...[28]

Shakespeare stands at these crossroads, before the onset of modern cynicism about 'politics' had emptied the public realm of moral significance. Machiavellian 'policy' he knew and faced—knew it perhaps more thoroughly than anyone else whose writings have come down to us. But there was still 'religious policy' too. 'The generall name of Policie', wrote a seventeenth-century anti-Machiavellian, (like the double face of *Ianus*) respecteth two seueral obiects; the better hath regardful eie to honesty, and lawfull warrant onely, the other beholdeth all things with indifferent eie, not respecting lawfulness, but conueniency in euery practise.[29]

This coalescence in a single noun, 'policy', of two universes of political discourse is the semantic axis of the Shakespearian political vision, and it indicates why he was able to include so much of known reality within that vision.

And so to *Richard III*, where the Machiavellian dilemma is, one might almost say, the structural principle. The same play which presents most vigorously an amoral philosophy of power (in the mouth of Richard: 'Conscience is but a word that cowards use, / Devis'd at first to keep the strong in awe', v. iii) also embodies an elaborate attempt to demonstrate the operation of Providence, and thereby to validate the whole moral order on a cosmic scale. And Shakespeare's political imagination is particular where so many of the theorists are general. He sees that, even if the political sphere *were* sealed off from the moral, there would still be the individual casualties of amoral statecraft whose sufferings would provide the soil in which morality might grow again. It is a mark of a certain frivolity in Marlowe that the sufferings of an Abigail, a Lodowick or a Barnadine are either so unreal or so preposterously well-deserved, that the moral balance of the play registers not a flicker of deviation as they go to their deaths. Shakespeare, on the other hand, presents us with a long procession of victims past and present, and far from shirking the destructive implications of Machiavellism, he devotes one of the longest and most powerful scenes (Clarence's death) to a steady contemplation of it. He sees too that, however much conscience, in the hands of the unscrupulous, may become an instrument of 'policy', it still retains its own unique life, and cannot finally be wrested from its true nature to subserve the aims of policy. It remains, to a surprising extent, the intransigent accuser that cannot be suborned. Even so complete a Machiavel as Richard III is liable to be betrayed by the 'babbling dreams' of conscience, when the decline of his fortunes has made a breach in the apparently impregnable self-assurance. And yet, at the same time, Shakespeare is so far from being unaware of the positive energies of Machiavellism that he embodies them in one of the most zestful, energetic characters of the whole canon.

This is to take the Machiavellian dilemma seriously in a dramatic way. Not, like Machiavelli himself, simply to shelve the moral issue, nor, like Marlowe, to use it as a stick to beat the establishment with, but, in the Shakespearian manner, to submit it to the searching test of dramatic embodiment, forcing the general and abstract to yield up its particular, human meaning. How successful he is in resolving the dilemma, we shall see. To enter imaginatively into the reality of the dilemma is an experience we can still undergo with profit.

One thing we may, however, find puzzling: how can it be that a dramatist, who perceives so clearly the capacity of power to have its own way in the world, can still insist on so anachronistic a conception as Providence? The answer lies partly in a belief in nature-as-providential which we have lost; but also in that a certain type of logical connexion, which is so natural to the modern mind as to seem almost axiomatic, is for Shakespeare neither natural nor logical. I can illustrate, conveniently, from Machiavelli:

a prudent ruler ought not to keep faith when by so doing it would be against his interest, and when the reasons which made him bind himself no longer exist. If men were all good, this precept would not be a good one; but as they are bad, and would not observe their faith with you, so you are not bound to keep faith with them. Nor have legitimate grounds ever failed a prince who wished to show colourable excuse for the non-fulfilment of his promise. Of this one could furnish an infinite number of modern examples, and show how many times peace has been broken, and how many promises rendered worthless, by the faithlessness of princes, and those that have best been able to imitate the fox have succeeded best.[30]

What is interesting here is the logical relation between the last sentence the 'infinite number of modern examples', and the 'ought' of the first sentence. The implication—and it is by now so thoroughly familiar that we scarcely notice it—is that ideals of behaviour can be altered, even invalidated, by a consideration of the way men actually behave. It is the axiom of the Machiavellian. and of much modern political science. But is it really true?

Shakespeare appears to have thought not.

PROVIDENCE AND POLICY
IN 'RICHARD III'

I

In the closing scene of *Richard III*, the victorious Richmond, having just announced the marriage which is to join the warring houses of York and Lancaster, declaims,

> Smile Heaven upon this fair conjunction,
> That long have frown'd upon their enmity,   v. v. 20

and adds, with a gesture which I cannot help thinking was intended to embrace the audience as well as his retainers,

> What traitor hears me, and says not amen?

The rest of the speech sounds more like 'an act of common worship', to borrow Tillyard's phrase,[1] than the concluding lines of a play:

> Abate the edge of traitors, gracious Lord,
> That would reduce these bloody days again
> And make poor England weep in streams of blood!
> Let them not live to taste this land's increase,
> That would with reason wound this fair land's peace.

(Perhaps the 'traitors' are the Rheims jesuits, one of whom—Parsons— had recently smuggled a tract against Elizabeth into the country;[2] perhaps the Spanish sympathisers—traitors anyway.)

> Now civil wounds are stopp'd, peace lives again:
> That she may long live here, God say Amen!

I take the liberty of regarding these sentiments as referring rather to the Elizabethan than to the alleged historical situation, partly because they refer to nothing precise in Richmond's situation—the 'traitor' is routed and his followers have largely defected to the victorious side— and to much precisely in Elizabethan England in the early 1590s; and also because the tone of the speech is an appeal to group participation— non-participation is indulged on pain of declaring oneself a traitor. Amen, therefore.

I should have thought that it was equally clear that the kind of effects the speech aims at are those open to an election speaker, addressing an audience cleared of hecklers and packed with supporters, as he scores easy points against the abominated and unrepresented opponent and paints a rosy future for right-thinking men. But the followers of Dr Tillyard are still with us—able, apparently, to see all this and, swallowing their judgment, to excuse this identification of 'Shakespeare's official self' with 'an obvious and simple phase of public opinion' because the identification is 'entirely sincere, and the opinion strong, to be shared alike by the most sophisticated and the humblest.' ³ Faced with the alternative of this kind of sincerity, one is tempted to hope that Shakespeare was, for once, insincere.

For the fact is, that if this is the deeply felt centre of the play and the fount of its profoundest discoveries—that is to say, if the sincerity is appropriately deployed—then the play offers only a profound platitude, and most of the rest is either botched or totally irrelevant. If the operation of Providence means no more than the factious manipulation of the commonweal to the achievement of the Tudor settlement, whereupon the whole process is arrested, mankind divided into traitors and patriots (traitors being defined as those who are less than satisfied with the *status quo*), and if Shakespeare wished this state of petrification to rejoice in the title of 'Peace', then we can only conclude that the political evolution of the last four hundred years has carried us beyond the point where he can speak to us and be understood.

But, on the contrary, there is plenty of life in *Richard III* still. And it is in order to cherish that life that certain amputations must be performed—starting, I suggest, with this speech. It is carrying flexibility to the point of dishonesty to pretend that one can be equally enthusiastic about such patriotic banner-waving, and about the extended demonstration elsewhere that mere patriotism is at the mercy of the more complex mechanisms of power, greed and self-deception. Richmond's speech is almost as tenuously integrated with *Richard III* as is the Bastard's analogous curtain speech with the play *King John*. In both cases, the kind of human/critical awareness which Shakespeare has set in motion in the course of the play makes short work of the platitude with which he tries to wind it up. He has created an audience which is now too wary of simplifications to be fobbed off with this one, and which quickly reduces it to a pious shell and a hard core of prudential self-interest. It is interesting to note that, in both cases, the didactic simplification is signalled by a retreat from the dramatic complexities of

Shakespearian history, into the mode of the political morality, with the introduction of the personification 'England', who has 'long been mad', and has wept 'in streams of blood', and who now has only to rest true to herself in order to baffle all her enemies.

We are of course continually being told by critics that the marriage of Richmond and Elizabeth was the great and never-to-be-forgotten nexus of Elizabethan political consciousness, the dawning of a new age, the advent of the messiah-king.[4] This, perhaps, is the view the Tudors liked to take of the matter, and the unoriginal minds of Hall and Holinshed found the legend sufficiently attractive to perpetuate and disseminate it. But we are not talking here about the conservative-royalist wing of Elizabethan opinion (and it is no more than that), but about a particular and original Elizabethan mind—a mind which could read Holinshed and think otherwise, as Shakespeare clearly did on this issue. For he gives the marriage the bare minimum of treatment consistent with its function in the plot. While he devotes 230 lines to Richard's wooing of Elizabeth, he disposes of Richmond's courtship in two:

> Withal say that the queen hath heartily consented
> He should espouse Elizabeth her daughter.   IV. V. 7

This is all that is left of the transports of delight with which, in Holinshed's version,[5] the idea inspires all those who hear it. And the only other allusion to the matter which is not a mere exigency of exposition is Richmond's surprisingly laconic

> And then, as we have ta'en the sacrament,
> We will unite the white rose and the red.   V. V. 18

One wonders whether the commentators who make such great play with the dynastic theme in *Richard III* have not inadvertently been reading the *True Tragedie of Richard III* and thinking it Shakespeare's play. For here indeed we are given the full treatment. Elizabeth (an off-stage phantom in Shakespeare) has been seen on stage from the beginning of the action (Scene ii); the marriage is discussed at length (Scene xv) and Elizabeth herself appears after the Battle of Bosworth Field to be presented to her betrothed (Scene xx). And lest we should miss the point that more than one 'Elizabeth' is involved, there are forty lines of potted history to bring the story up to date, winding up with a fulsome panegyric of the latter-day Elizabeth:

> She is that lampe that keeps faire Englands light,
> And through her faith her country liues in peace:

And she hath put proud Antichrist to flight,
And bene a meanes that ciuill wars did cease.
Then England kneele vpon thy hairy knee,
And thanke that God that still prouides for thee.

Malone Society Reprint, ll. 2202–7

Now this (apart from the striking flight of fancy which endows England with hairy knees) is more like the jejune versification one would expect from a playwright setting out to extol a dynastic union and hymn the *status quo*. That Shakespeare did not, even in his weakest moments, write this sort of verse, despite the model provided by the *True Tragedie*, might sow a discreet doubt whether he had quite the same aims in view.[6] In fact it seems plain enough that if there were any spectators who came to see celebrated the 'union of the two illustre families of Lancaster and York' (an odd enough reason for attending a theatre, even in the sixteenth century) they were doomed to disappointment. It fills only a small corner of Shakespeare's canvas.

II

The more conservative proponents of monarchical theory can scarcely have been pleased either; for while all the right things are said, the orthodox attitude is continually being caught in compromising postures. Thus Rivers, trying to prove his faithfulness to Edward, despite the damaging fact that he has fought against the Yorkist cause in the past, expostulates,

> My Lord of Gloucester, in those busy days,
> Which here you urge to prove us enemies,
> We follow'd then our lord, our sovereign king:
> So should we you, if you should be our king.   I. iii. 145

The apparent worthiness of the sentiments is clouded when we recall that the strife in those 'busy days' was precisely over the question of who *was* the 'sovereign king'; that Rivers now gives allegiance to the issue of a traitor to that 'sovereign king'; and that he can even envisage bestowing the same doggish fidelity on a King Richard. In point of fact he can envisage nothing of the sort, and the whole speech is a nasty piece of equivocation, but it remains that Shakespeare has here shown the total inadequacy of blind obedience to whatever head happens to be under the crown. Within a few lines the point is reinforced by the appearance of the widow of the murdered King Henry, who demands

75

rites of allegiance from all present (I. iii. 160 f.). No simple rule of thumb can extricate us from the intense confusion about the nature of kingship which is generated in this short space. Interestingly enough, the only invocation of the divine sanction of kingship that occurs in the play comes from the lips of Richard, the usurper:

> A flourish, trumpets! strike alarum, drums!
> Let not the heavens hear these tell-tale women
> Rail on the Lord's anointed!   IV. iv. 149

At this stage the divinely appointed ruler is using the 'clamorous report of war' to silence the truth about his own murderous career—the allusion is rich in irony.

Indeed one has only to pause for a moment to realise that, in choosing to treat this turbulent stretch of English history, Shakespeare has plunged into the very waters where the concept of kingship was fraught with the profoundest complexities. If he was planning to exemplify the simplified monarchic theory of Tudor propaganda, it was a singularly unhappy choice of subject. One might as well try to justify papal infallibility by writing a play about the Avignon schism. Furthermore, it is precisely Rivers's equivocating use of the cloak of allegiance to screen him while he turns his coat that is repeatedly challenged in *Richard III*—most notably in the long dialogue between Clarence and his murderers, to which I turn now (I. iv. 162 f.).

One is tempted to call it a debate; but it is more, for behind the dialectical manoeuvring for position, there is the heat of urgent self-justification informing and qualifying the theoretical positions taken up by the disputants. When challenged to justify an act which has no formal legal sanction, the Murderers take the expected line:

> FIRST MURDERER. What we will do, we do upon command.
> SECOND MURDERER. And he that hath commanded is our king.
>   I. iv. 192

But Clarence will not let the matter rest there:

> Erroneous vassals! the great King of kings
> Hath in the table of His law commanded
> That thou shalt do no murder. Will you then
> Spurn at His edict, and fulfil a man's?

This is the sixteenth-century debate over the right to rebellion in a nutshell—Does not the final sanction of sovereignty reside outside the sovereign's will? But the confrontation is more than a confrontation of ideologies: 'What we will do, we do upon command' is offered as an answer to 'The deed you undertake is damnable', and its tone is both defensive and evasive. The Murderers, by their alternate repugnance to the idea of the murder, have already shown how its 'damnable' character disturbs them. Both have had trouble with conscience (ll. 121, 143), and Clarence would not now be speaking had not the First Murderer lost his nerve at the moment when the Second cried 'Strike!' (l. 158). Thus for them the royal command is no more than a desperate means of shoring up a crumbling resolution, so that the force of their prosaic enunciation of their legal position is changed by the tone of evasion and self-justification with which it is coloured. Yet, at the same time, when the First Murderer declares 'My voice is now the king's' (l. 167), Shakespeare allows full force to the identification and the Murderers' prose modulates into a verse which, shortly afterwards, has developed sufficient power to hold Clarence's (and our) attention rivetted to the realities of his situation.

Clarence's appeal to 'the king's King' does not stand unqualified either. His self-righteous tone of patrician immunity—'Erroneous vassals...Take heed...'—so clearly covering a frantic, animal fear, is quickly reduced to

> Alas! for whose sake did I that ill deed?
> For Edward, for my brother, for his sake.   i. iv. 210

And although all he says may be the purest doctrine, it is for him a sophistry (just as his later concern for the souls of the Murderers—'Have you that holy feeling in your souls?...'—however sincere, is also a sophistry: it is his own soul, not theirs, which so intensely concerns him at that point).

The Murderers, meanwhile, have established a new offensive position: in a series of machine-gun accusations—perjury, murder, treason—they beat back Clarence's defence; the First Murderer concludes,

> How canst thou urge God's dreadful law to us,
> When thou hast broke it in such dear degree?   i. iv. 208

As with so many of the rationalisations advanced in this play, this is a point which carries considerable objective weight—as Shakespeare makes clear by intermitting the more idiosyncratic speech of the Murderers in the early part of the scene; and it is a point which Clarence must and does take to heart (he has, indeed, already spent a season in hell face to face with it); but it is a point which cannot be the whole truth for the person who utters it. In so far as the First Murderer addresses Clarence, he is right; in so far as he speaks to silence his own guilt, he is wrong. In this encounter, truth—even the historical truth about Clarence's defection and betrayal—is a double-edged weapon which wounds the wielder as well as his quarry.

I need not pursue the debate much further, for its basic pattern is clear: Clarence is asserting his right to live when he has no right to live; the Murderers their right to kill, which is no right. Between these two passionate self-interests the issues of allegiance and justice are tossed and jostled back and forth, every rationalisation being undercut by the next. Every principle of abstract justice that Clarence can invoke, he can be shown to have himself violated; yet every blackening stroke that is added to the picture of Clarence's guilt makes it clearer that, even were his faults without end, the Murderers would still be 'warring with God' in exterminating him in this illicit way. And in taking it upon themselves to be the scourge of his evils, they tacitly license the powers who will punish them for their own deed. It is an infinite regression of crime and punishment, and the only hope Clarence has of shattering the twin mirrors of retaliatory justice is to appeal to a principle outside the whole nightmare mechanism—

> If God will be avenged for the deed,
> O, know you yet, he doth it publicly.
> Take not the quarrel from his powerful arm.   I. iv. 214

Vengeance is mine, saith the Lord. But it is the only point in the play where retributive justice is alienated from the natural order and handed over bodily to the Divine Will. On this principle, there would have been no Yorkist wars, no forsworn Clarence, no murdered Henry. But, as the First Murderer is quick to point out, however ideally true this may be, Clarence is the one man who cannot claim protection from its truth:

> Who made thee then a bloody minister,
> When gallant-springing brave Plantagenet,
> That princely novice, was struck dead by thee?   I. iv. 219

Again, whether he *was* the scourge of God, a 'minister', is an open question; but that he can thereby claim moral immunity is most certainly false. Likewise, the Second Murderer, who had claimed to hurl God's vengeance on Clarence, discovers that, though this may be his true role *sub specie aeternitatis*, it cannot exempt him from the operation of an accusing conscience:

> How fain, like Pilate, would I wash my hands
> Of this most grievous murder.   I. iv. 272

I have done scant justice to the richness of this scene, but I think a limited point is now clear—we have travelled so far from the simplicities of kingly sovereignty and subject-ly submission, that it is hard to recall what that sharply-lit, black-and-white country looked like. What had begun as a simple question put to puzzled allegiance, finishes as a study of the transformation of ideas in the mouths of the disingenuous. What answers there are, are paradoxical: Clarence has no right to live, the Murderers none to kill. One may punish justly and be justly punished for it. What is true in one man's mouth is false in another's.

But perhaps the most compelling sound that remains in our ears is the voice of the victim of judicial murder, stripped of all logical cover, his moral integrity hanging in tatters about him, but pleading still for life simply—no more:

> Which of you, if you were a prince's son,
> Being pent from liberty, as I am now,
> If two such murderers as yourselves came to you,
> Would not intreat for life? As you would beg
> Were you in my distress—

The sentence is cut off by the harsh voice of the First Murderer,[7] but it echoes through the play as successive victims of naked power go to their deaths. It is worldly power seen from the passionate vantage-point of the executioner's block.

III

So far I have been trying to lay the dust that previous scrimmages have raised in the arena, and to suggest that Tudor political orthodoxy, simply conceived, is the kind of irrelevance that simply prevents us from seeing what is going on. In the process, certain deeper concerns of the play have begun to emerge: the concern with the orientation of the individual toward the moral order, which is coupled, of course, with an acute awareness of the difficulty of locating that order in a world dominated by mere force and greed of power; the concern with power itself, its methods, its sophistries and its moral casualties; and, informing the whole analysis, a steady drive toward that level of understanding where the outcome of the action will not appear a merely fortuitous aggregation of amoral forces, a meaningless and temporary stasis in the endless turmoil of man's communal existence. The short shrift Shakespeare gives to the glib rationalisations of triumphant injustice implies no anxious doubts about the possibility of Justice; it is part of a purposive effort to discover a meaning for the word which can encompass the patent *injustices* of human existence without denying their painful reality. This last concern—which gives rise to the the 'providential' movement in the play—I shall be discussing later. I want now to look at Shakespeare's assault on the problem of conscience.

I suggested in the last chapter that Shakespeare has gone more deeply than Machiavelli into the amorality of actual human behaviour; but his investigation begins in the Machiavellian recognition that 'how we live is...far removed from how we ought to live'. He does not need to be instructed in the complications that conscience introduces into everyday life:

> It makes a man a coward: a man cannot steal, but it accuseth him; a man cannot swear, but it checks him; a man cannot lie with his neighbour's wife, but it detects him. 'Tis a blushing shamefast spirit, that mutinies in a man's bosom; it fills a man full of obstacles:...it beggars any man that keeps it; it is turn'd out of towns and cities for a dangerous thing; and every man that means to live well endeavours to trust to himself and to live without it. I. iv. 132

Not only the attitudes, but the very voice of the politic realist is alive in these lines. But Shakespeare recognises, with the First Murderer, that the operation of conscience does not fall entirely under the jurisdiction of a man's conscious will:

> Zounds, 'tis even now at my elbow, persuading me not to kill the duke! I. iv. 143

It is an involuntary, probing sensitivity to the far-reaching consequence of action—even the action for which one has abundant 'warrant':

> FIRST MURDERER. What, art thou afraid?
> SECOND MURDERER. Not to kill him, having a warrant; but to be
> damn'd for killing him, from the which no warrant can
> defend me. I. iv. 108

Around the finite, temporal action, laps a whole sea of infinite and impalpable scruple; and conscience grows out of the recognition, however dim, that there is too much one does not and cannot know. The black void of unbeing, that 'blind cave of eternal night', continually menaces the self-possession of those who try to reduce the moral problem to a mere question of technique. The intensely serious comedy of the Murderers' dialogue shows up the Machiavellian manipulator, for whom conscience is a mere instrument of policy, as a chimera.

There is something solid and substantial about this pair that makes *il principe* look thin and theoretical.

What the Murderers do in this sequence, of course, is to consolidate a position that has been established in the earlier part of the scene, in the long dream-investigation of the concealed underside of moral consciousness. Clarence's dream has a haunting fascination which it is hard to rationalise in terms of theme or dramatic action; but its imaginative power is sufficient to guarantee its centrality in Shakespeare's conception.

Clarence's undersea world is a kingdom of inestimable and yet irrecoverable riches, the spoils of human shipwreck and disaster:

> Methoughts I saw a thousand fearful wracks,
> A thousand men that fishes gnaw'd upon,
> Wedges of gold, great anchors, heaps of pearl,
> Inestimable stones, unvalu'd jewels,
> All scatter'd in the bottom of the sea.
> Some lay in dead men's skulls; and, in the holes
> Where eyes did once inhabit, there were crept,
> As 'twere in scorn of eyes, reflecting gems,
> That woo'd the slimy bottom of the deep,
> And mock'd the dead bones that lay scatter'd by.   I. iv. 24

To descend into this realm of lost opulence is to drown, to be submitted to the catastrophic disruption of normal modes of perception which protect man from the knowledge of his own forfeited magnificence. It is a kind of death precipitated by a tempest of the body.

But the 'tempest to the soul' of which Clarence speaks (I. iv. 44) connects the appalling wastage directly with acts of moral capitulation and cowardice:

> then came wandering by
> A shadow like an angel, with bright hair
> Dabbled in blood; and he squeak'd out aloud,
> 'Clarence is come, false, fleeting perjur'd Clarence,
> That stabb'd me in the field at Tewkesbury:
> Seize on him, Furies, take him into torment!'   I. iv. 52

The vivid actuality of these phantoms of retribution, and the logic by which violated trust gives birth to the Furies of self-accusation, are political facts of prime importance: a man may founder and lose himself in the unfathomable depths of consciousness if this vision once takes hold of him. The realm of conscience is one of infinite richness, but also one of desperate peril. Violated conscience breeds infernal torment.

Richard on Bosworth Field is puzzled by the tendency of his disturbed consciousness to threaten a revenge of 'myself upon myself' (v. iii. 189); but this is only puzzling because, thorough-going Machiavellian that he is, he has failed to recognise the powerful ligament that binds the conscience to the self. As a stranger to the laws of his own nature, Richard finds this bond merely baffling; but the play that contains him also contains a Clarence who knows only too well that it is an earlier, less guilty self which rises now to accuse him of an unpardonable betrayal of the self.

Machiavellian realism has no place on its charts for this region of moral awareness. For Shakespearian realism, the undersea world is half —and perhaps the more important half—of terrestrial reality. The contrast with *The Jew* is sharp here: whereas Marlowe met the Machiavellian world head-on and dealt with it at the level of maxim and plot-manipulation, Shakespeare goes straight to the inner world of consciousness and deals with conscience in terms of persons, not ideas. The result of this oblique approach is that he can penetrate the armour-plated ideational shallowness of Machiavelli's analysis and guide the discussion into areas where the veto on moral considerations is revealed for the evasion it is—the neglect of a central political, and human, fact. Yet this sensitivity to the inner world of moral consciousness does not entail *in*sensitivity to hard political facts. Shakespeare knows very well what power is, and what it can do. It is indeed a large part of his aim in *Richard III* to show us how nearly omnipotent it can become.

In his consideration of power, Shakespeare's debt to More's life of Richard III can hardly be over-estimated. More's close scrutiny of the minutiae of political existence, his ironic contemplation of the self-betrayals that virtuous obtuseness can be induced to make, and his penetration into the knack of 'vile politicians' for simultaneously achieving the evil goal and appeasing the violated good, provides Shakespeare with the text for much that is excellent in the first half of the play. And it is a sign of Shakespeare's dramatic intelligence that when Holinshed's transcription of More comes to an end, and the pedestrian Hall takes over, the dependence becomes much less marked and much less detailed.[8]

In More, too, we can find the double vision of the world of power: the exalted viewpoint of the active makers of policy side by side with the worm's-eye-view of those who merely suffer the results. The impotent wisdom of the man who, clearly perceiving that he is oppressed, is yet still oppressed, was More's insight before it was Shakespeare's.

And so they said, that these matters be kings games, as it were stage plaies, and for the more part plaied vpon scaffolds, in which poore men be but lookers on. And they that wise be will meddle no further.[9]

But the insight grew in the dramatist's mind into that preposterous farce entitled *The Reluctant Monarch* (III. vii), or, less spectacularly, into the muted comedy of the Three Citizens (II. iii): one (First Citizen) vacuously optimistic, one (Third Citizen) portentously doom-ridden—the authentic pot-house Jeremiah—and the other (Second Citizen) feather-headed, carried with every wind of doctrine to contradictory conclusions and involving himself, in his only personal contribution, in a syntactical tangle from which he escapes panting (ll. 12–15). The citizens pass on to the Justices, but another window has been opened, and another implication of the exercise of power has been laid before us. Through this window we observe the Londoners at Guildhall, gaping 'like dumb statues, or breathing stones' (III. vii. 25) at the flood of Buckingham's menacing eloquence; or the Recorder, repeating the whole speech, yet contriving to speak nothing 'in warrant from himself' (III. vii. 33); or even more interestingly, the Scrivener, an unwilling party to the whitewashing of Hastings's tomb, warily weighing his conscience against his skin, and knowing that he, like the rest, will choose to save his skin:

> Who is so gross,
> That cannot see this palpable device?
> Yet who so bold, but says he sees it not?   III. vi. 10

The Scrivener is one of the many minor characters who present themselves to our understanding as beings who have made *per viltate il piccolo rifiuto*—not great apostates, nor great cowards, but the small moral casualties of the fray in which others lose their heads. The Second Murderer is another of these lesser damned. So is Brackenbury:

> I will not reason what is meant hereby,
> Because I will be guiltless from the meaning.
> There lies the duke asleep, and there the keys.   I. iv. 93

Like the Cardinal, when he agrees to violate what he has just (and justly) termed 'the holy privilege / Of blessed sanctuary', Brackenbury

83

imagines that there is some kind of limited liability in doing evil under duress; the Cardinal's words might be his:

> My lord, you shall o'er-rule my mind for once.   III. i. 57

There is a sour pathos in that 'for once'. When once a man has allowed his conscience to pass into another man's keeping, it is not so easy to recover it. The Cardinal must henceforth live with the knowledge that he is responsible for the fact that *two* princes, not one, fall to Richard's avenging sword.

A whole lifetime of these small betrayals, the accumulation of innumerable sacrifices of the human particular to the political abstract, gushes from its subterranean hiding-place in Edward's death speech (II. i). Two thoughts run through the speech—the necessity for actions of state to be tempered by the kind of human awareness symbolised in the word 'brother', which Edward reiterates with a mounting hysterical horror; and the way in which this humanisation of the political sphere has been perverted into the mere sporadic exercise of favouritism:

> But when your carters or your waiting vassals
> Have done a drunken slaughter, and defac'd
> The precious image of our dear Redeemer,
> You straight are on your knees for pardon, pardon;
> And I, unjustly too, must grant it you.   II. i. 121

It seems consonant with the play Shakespeare gives us to conclude that this appalling vision, of a life spent gaining and maintaining an order that is rotten at the heart, kills King Edward.

But of all the moral casualties of Richard's power-game, Anne is the most fully presented. I say 'moral' casualty because I believe the conventional view of Act I, Scene ii, as a pretty piece of undramatic rhetoric, is wide of the mark. On one level the scene presents the rout, by the Machiavel for whom the dialectical and rhetorical skills are an instrument of policy, of a woman for whom the rhetorical inflation of reality is an habitual and dangerous addiction. The addiction (which I think is Anne's rather than Shakespeare's) is plain enough in the first thirty lines of the scene, but it is not clearly placed until it encounters Richard's ice-cold delivery.

> ANNE. ... Either heav'n with lightning strike the murderer dead,
> Or earth, gape open wide and eat him quick,
> As thou dost swallow up this good king's blood,
> Which his hell-govern'd arm hath butchered!

> RICHARD. Lady, you know no rules of Charity,
>   Which renders good for bad, blessings for curses.
> ANNE. Villain, thou know'st no law of God nor man:
>   No beast so fierce but knows some touch of pity.
> RICHARD. But I know none, and therefore am no beast.
> ANNE. O wonderful, when devils tell the truth!
> RICHARD. More wonderful, when angels are so angry.   I. ii. 64

The level of the discussion is not very lofty, but its childishness proceeds less from a Shakespearian weakness for stichomythia, than from Anne's spluttering anger which is clearly overspending its capital resources of real feeling. She is not as outraged as she pretends to be. It is on the element of the factitious in her position that Richard launches his attack. He invites her to play with the situation—

> RICHARD. Say that I slew them not?

—and she accepts the terms proposed—

> ANNE.   Why, then they are not dead...
> RICHARD. I did not kill your husband.
> ANNE.   Why, then he is alive.   I. ii. 89

And when, realising how pervasively flippant the interchange is becoming, she attempts to recover her resentment, her patent lack of conviction is exploited by Richard.

> ANNE. O, he was gentle, mild, and virtuous!
> RICHARD. The better for the King of heaven, that hath him.
> ANNE. He is in heaven, where thou shalt never come.
> RICHARD. Let him thank me, that holp to send him thither;
>   For he was fitter for that place than earth.
> ANNE. And thou unfit for any place but hell.
> RICHARD. Yes, one place else, if you will hear me name it.
> ANNE. Some dungeon!   I. ii. 104

If we are in any doubt about the reality of Anne's outrage, a quick glance at Elizabeth's utterances in the same situation should settle the matter. For there we find the authentic note of passionate grief:

> But that still use of grief makes wild grief tame,
> My tongue should to thy ears not name my boys,
> Till that my nails were anchor'd in thine eyes;
> And I, in such a desperate bay of death,
> Like a poor bark, of sails and tackling reft,
> Rush all to pieces on thy rocky bosom.   IV. iv. 230

There, too, the verbal fencing is in deadly earnest, and blood is drawn
(as the sharpness of Richard's tone attests)—

> RICHARD. Your reasons are too shallow and too quick.
> ELIZABETH. O no! my reasons are too deep and dead;
>   Too deep and dead, poor infants, in their graves.
> RICHARD. Harp not on that string, Madam; that is past.
>
> IV. iv. 364

This is poles apart from the querulous vindictiveness which Shakespeare gives to Anne's utterance—'Some dungeon!'—and thus it is not
a complete surprise to find that Richard's lascivious insinuation—
'Your Bed-chamber'—instead of provoking an explosion of incredulous
indignation, produces only a low-keyed, uneasy

> Ill-rest betide the chamber where thou liest.
> RICHARD. So will it, madam, till I lie with you.
> ANNE. I hope so.

There is a terrible ambiguity about Anne's 'hope', a hope, specifically,
I suppose, that ill-rest will betide the chamber where he lies by himself.
But it also, by a kind of syntactical 'Freudian slip', implies equally a
hope that the ill-rest will be only *until* he lies with her, and a hope that
he *will* lie with her. One can almost hear her blush in terror. It is a
beautiful enactment of the frightening moral confusion that lies beneath
Anne's easily adopted rhetorical postures.

From now on her resistance goes in a series of declining waves. She
attempts again to beat him at the verbal game, but Richard has already
indicated the futility of what is merely 'the keen encounter of our wits'.
With her physical faculties in insurrection, she betrays the ineffectual
nature of her vituperative passion by spitting at him—whereupon
Richard, the spittle hanging from his face, enacts a monstrous parody
of the patient, spurned lover—

> Never came poison from so sweet a place.   I. ii. 146

Finally she is reduced to looking scornfully at him (S.D. l. 170), and the
charade with the sword seals her fate. He is so preposterous that she is
almost laughing:

> Arise, dissembler: though I wish thy death,
> I will not be thy executioner.   I. ii. 184

Thus the morally uncorrupt surrenders itself to evil known, at the
moment of surrender, to be evil of the most virulent and destructive
kind—'Arise, dissembler...' By now the passion of outrage has
given way to an intense curiosity—'I would I knew thy heart' (l. 192);

and finally, Anne drops her pinch of incense on the altar of the Abomination, like the Cardinal, and the Second Murderer and Brackenbury, and accepts Richard's ring, protesting, as they all do, that it is no great matter:

> To take is not to give. I. ii. 202

By her exit, she has found her true tone in a light flaunting badinage:

> RICHARD. Bid me farewell.
> ANNE. 'Tis more than you deserve;
> But, since you teach me how to flatter you,
> Imagine I have said farewell already. I. ii. 222

It is like—indeed it is—coquetry at the edge of a grave.

Part of the power of this scene is that, while it is rooted in a clear perception of psychological realities and follows minutely the fluctuations and interactions of a critical personal relationship, this particularity nevertheless sets in motion much larger significances and meanings. It is as if the tidal movement in Anne's moral being were an abiding possibility of human nature; and the situation, preposterous though it is (wooer murderer confronting widow over corpse of his victim), were archetypal. The unthinkable is not only possible, but has a malign fascination of its own. And giving in to it is really such a simple matter.

Shakespeare thus shows the potency of Richard's evil to rest, at least partially, upon the moral cowardice of a Brackenbury, the moral laxity of an Edward, and the moral impotence of an Anne. But it also rests on the folly of a Hastings. Hastings is well enough aware that Richard is 'full of danger'—

> To fly the boar before the boar pursues,
> Were to incense the boar to follow us
> And make pursuit, where he did mean no chase— III. ii. 28

so he reasons with Stanley. But he is sufficiently muddle-headed to believe that the beast which is a ruthless opportunist in all other relationships will 'use us kindly'. He knows that the states of political personages are insecure in the extreme, but excepts himself:

> Think you, but that I know our state secure,
> I would be so triumphant as I am? III. ii. 81

He knows Richard aims at the crown; has before his eyes the spectacle of one group of opponents going to the block for their opposition; but declares blithely his own opposition while, in the same breath, referring to himself as dear

> To princely Richard. III. ii. 67

The weakness of his mind is its ability to avoid connecting general truth with his own particular situation: opportunism exists in the world—indeed, Hastings rather glories in the fact that his enemies can be so summarily 'let blood'—but he is able to contemplate it with jocular equanimity because he believes himself exempt from its operation.

Richard, as the machiavellian *diabolus ex machina*, believes in the most rigorous economy in evil-doing, and he is always happy to build on the vices and follies of others—to allow Hastings to pronounce his own sentence (III. iv. 65 f.), to induce others to beg him to do what he will in no wise be prevented from doing (III. vii), or to take the petty animosities of court faction and set them to work fomenting the state of intense mutual suspicion which is his working milieu (I. iii). One leg of his machiavellian enterprise does rest on this alarming species of human fallibility. But the other leg is his own formidable political *virtù*.

His command of the techniques of persuasion—from 'Off with his head', to the rigged political rally (III. vii. 34 f.) and the staged press-conference ('*Enter Richard, aloft, between two Bishops*')—has been sufficiently remarked upon elsewhere.[10] But if it is a study of the techniques of power that we want, we can find it, more fully, in More's *Life*, from which many of Shakespeare's most telling points are borrowed. What the dramatist offers in addition, is a perception of the way in which habitual dissimulation and pious fraud interact with the moral order which they are engaged in parodying; for one of the effects of Richard's sustained role-playing, I suggest, is to envelop the moral and the Christian in a cloud of ambiguity. Shakespeare uses Richard to call into play a kind of wary alertness about the invocation of moral sanctions—an alertness which, as I have argued, is dangerous to the pretensions of a Richmond.

We can see the nature of that interaction focused to a fine point when the nobles are disputing over the size of the train that is to accompany the Prince from Ludlow (II. ii). It has become clear, first, that neither faction will trust the other with the Prince's custody, and that both expect civil disorder to result from division of responsibility —all this despite the resounding oaths that have been sworn in the previous scene. In this impasse, Richard intones sweetly,

> I hope the king made peace with all of us;
> And the compact is firm and true in me.   II. ii. 132

This throws everybody into confusion: for the kind of righteous constancy which Richard has parodied is at once an object of conventional veneration, and, at the same time, so foreign to their experience that they are unable to detect that it *is* a parody. Rivers does the best he can:

> And so in me; and so, I think, in all:
> Yet...

and proceeds to argue on the assumption that the compact is anything but firm.

Now, parody of this kind is the most consistent feature of Richard's technique. We see him successively in the roles of stern and reprehending moralist ('O, he hath kept an evil diet long...', I. i. 139 f.), the plain man slandered ('They do me wrong, and I will not endure it... Because I cannot flatter, and look fair...', I. iii. 42 f.), the compassionate brother in a hard world ('I would to God my heart were flint, like Edward's...', I. iii. 140 f.), the wronged man forgiving his enemies ('I cannot blame her: by God's holy mother / She hath had too much wrong...', I. iii. 306 f.), the innocent lamb rejoicing in his innocence ('I do not know that Englishman alive, / With whom my soul is any jot at odds...', II. i. 69 f.), the sage counsellor to youth, instructing in the wiles of wickedness ('Sweet Prince, the untainted virtue of your years / Hath not yet div'd into the world's deceit...', III. i. 7 f.), and his final triumphant impersonation of the holy man disturbed at his devotions (III. vii). All but one of these impersonations are signally successful, drawing polite murmurs of sympathetic approval from the bystanders—and successful, not simply because they are consummately staged and performed, but also because virtue of this complexion is so rare a visitor to the arena of court life that no one is in a position to call Richard's bluff, at least not without revealing that, at the heart of their political practice, there lies a contempt for the pious values Richard simulates.

The exception, of course, is Prince Edward who, precisely because he has not yet 'div'd into the world's deceit', is able to meet Richard's 'God keep you from them [the incarcerated uncles], and from such false friends' with the verbal equivalent of a cool stare:

> God keep me from false friends! but they were none.
>
> III. i. 16

The others, however, are too deeply implicated in the world's deceit to be able to place any such ingenuous reliance on sincerity. As with

Clarence, their own behaviour has rendered any appeal to the moral order treacherously disingenuous. At times they, too, attempt to simulate the externalities of righteousness: in Act I, Scene iii, threatened with a common enemy in the person of Margaret, the dogs who have been 'snarling all' before she came, 'Ready to catch each other by the throat', suddenly turn all their rancour on her and join in a howling chorus of mock piety:

> HASTINGS. O 'twas the foulest deed to slay that babe,
>   And the most merciless, that e'er was heard of.
> RIVERS. Tyrants themselves wept when it was reported.
> DORSET. No man but prophesied revenge for it.
> BUCKINGHAM. Northumberland, then present, wept to see it.   I. iii. 183

But there is no sign here of the redeeming irony of Richard's performance: the consort has in fact burst into song only after Richard, in the preceding lines, has given them the *canto fermo*. The sham moralists are taken in by their own counterfeit passion. Small wonder therefore that Richard's infinitely superior impersonations pass unchallenged, thus serving to expose the continuity between his open-eyed villainy and the self-deceiving hypocrisy of the 'virtuous'.

Another effect of the parody comes to light if we enquire why these scenes come across as so authentically comic. I think the answer is that Richard releases a sense of incipient absurdity about the very postures that he hypocritically adopts. In the world of cut-throat intrigue and bloody reprisals (the world of the *Henry VI* plays, as well as the specific creation of Richard himself) there is something faintly absurd about a lofty motive. It is this dormant sense of incongruity which Richard exploits to comic effect. He even succeeds in insinuating that the moral structure of Christianity is some sort of intrusive irrelevance:

> But then I sigh, and with a piece of Scripture,
> Tell them that God bids us do good for evil;
> And thus I clothe my naked villainy
> With odd old ends, stolen forth of Holy Writ.   I. iii. 334

And when, in the opening soliloquy, he equates 'these fair well-spoken days' of a peaceful regime with 'sportive tricks', courting 'an amorous looking-glass' and strutting before 'a wanton ambling nymph', the energetic vigour of his contempt leaves 'Peace' somewhat shrunken as a term of approbation. In short, we are presented with a world where the 'gentle, mild and virtuous' Henry VI is most appropriately housed in heaven, 'for he was fitter for that place than earth' (I. ii. 104–8).

Richard, indeed, in a pregnant phrase, attempts to father his own moral deformity on the whole natural order: he claims that he has been 'Cheated of feature by *dissembling Nature*' (I. i. 19), suggesting thereby that it is in the nature of Nature to dissemble, and that his deformity is of a piece with the great swindle which curtails a man of his 'fair proportion' (one meaning of 'proportion' being 'distribution according to share'). Although this charge against the organisation of the macrocosm does not finally stick, it does represent one pivot of the axis on which the play revolves, and helps to shape the sense of moral misrule which pervades the action.

Frequently the references to the Deity and to heaven are tainted by this sense. It is remarkable in how many contexts heaven appears to be no more than a receiving depot for the souls of the massacred, God being reserved as Richard's factor to take delivery. Here is a characteristic example:

> Which done, God take King Edward to his mercy,
> And leave the world for me to bustle in.   I. i. 151[11]

Provided God's in his heaven, all's right with Richard's world. The last thing he wants is to have his 'bustling' interrupted by providential interference. The radically anti-Christian orientation of this thinking is in tune with a view of the after-life which is only loosely related to the Christian view of the matter—for it is a classical underworld, Hades not heaven, which figures most prominently in the play. Richard, Margaret declares (IV. iv. 71–3), is 'hell's black intelligencer', 'their factor, to buy souls, / And send them *thither*', i.e. to hell. This cannot be because of any notable depravity in the victims, but rather because Shakespeare, through Margaret, is visualising an underworld populated with all the dead of the Wars. It is to this underworld that Charon ferries Clarence (I. iv), and its inhabitants whom Buckingham visualises as 'moody discontented souls' that 'through the clouds behold this present hour' (V. i. 7–8).

I have, of course, been propounding a view of the moral order which Richard would have found highly congenial. But my point is that Richard is not the only one who is implicated in this view, nor does his extremely vigorous address to the world leave that world untouched. To some extent his assumptions hold good: earth *is* no place for mild virtue; Nature does appear to dissemble; heaven does allow remarkable latitude for the 'bustlers' of this world; and indeed the only kind of after-life consonant with this life appears to be one populated by 'moody discontented souls' thirsting for revenge.

I would like it to be clear, however, that I am not trying to pin this sceptical outlook on Shakespeare personally—though he was clearly capable of some degree of imaginative identification with it. Nor am I claiming *Richard III* as a thesis or problem play, explicitly launching an assault on the fixities of Elizabethan thought—though its questioning need be no less disruptive of traditional categories for being unobtrusive. To products of a culture so deeply involved with classical thought as the Elizabethan culture, an audience acclimatised to the Christianised Virgil (say), there would have been nothing startling in this kind of pagan naturalism. What I *am* suggesting is that all these features combine to create a dramatic environment and a philosophical climate in which the threshold of orthodoxy is lowered and the mind is free to play over a wider range of possibilities than would otherwise be available to it. And the special colouring with which the supernatural order is transfused is a part of this silent transformation of the moral landscape—a transformation of which Richard himself, the atheist-hero, is the most salient feature.

IV

However, against this pessimistic naturalism, Shakespeare places in the scales a concept of Providence which is clearly a central part of the design. What, then, are we to make of it?

Richard himself offers one answer—the providential order is a delusion, perhaps (like conscience) 'devis'd at first to keep the strong in awe'. It leaves the world at the disposition of the powerful, the 'bustlers'. Thus Richard, galled by King Henry's prophetic nomination of Richmond as king, takes grim pleasure in affirming that force which shapes its own ends, without consulting divinity:

> How chance the prophet could not at that time
> Have told me, I being by, that I should kill him?　　iv. ii. 99

(It is, of course, a part of the play's essential ambivalence that Richmond does become king.) In the same vein, though with less conviction, Richard dismisses the ominous tardiness of the sun on the morning of his last battle:

> Not shine today? Why, what is that to me
> More than to Richmond?　　　　　　　　　　　v. iii. 286

He goes into battle under a heaven void of omens and cleared of all watching presences, the 'babbling dreams' of uneasy conscience consigned to oblivion:

> Our strong arms be our conscience, swords our law.
> March on, join bravely, let us to't pell-mell,
> If not to heaven, then hand in hand to hell!   v. iii. 312

And in his final appearance he is making adherence to his philosophy of chance a kind of moral duty, demonstrating to the world that he has the courage of his Epicurean convictions:

> Slave, I have set my life upon a cast,
> And I will stand the hazard of the die!   v. iv. 9

It is an intransigent naturalism that will yield no ground to the supernatural; and again, it cannot be dismissed as the mere fulminations of villainy, for Richard as a theatrical creation, and especially as a Captain, is a force to be reckoned with. Shaw has reminded us of 'the curious recovery by Richard of his old gaiety of heart in the excitement of battle...He is again the ecstatic prince of mischief of the "Shine out, fair sun, till I have bought a glass" phase, which makes the first Act so rapturous...The offer of his kingdom for a horse is part of the same thing: any means of keeping up the ecstasy of the fight is worth a dozen kingdoms.'[12] This aspect of Richard's impact should not be under-estimated; it was this famous gesture, after all, which made such a lasting impression on the minds of contemporaries.[13] And one might point, in the same connexion, to the contemptuous bravado of Richard's oration to his army—

> If we be conquer'd, let men conquer us,
> And not these bastard Bretons, whom our fathers
> Have in their own land beaten, bobb'd, and thump'd... v. iii. 333

—which has an earthy vernacular vigour totally foreign to Richmond's tongue:

> God and our good cause fight upon our side;
> The prayers of holy saints and wronged souls,
> Like high-rear'd bulwarks, stand before our faces.   v. iii. 241

It is not necessarily to a wooden rectitude that we give our imaginative allegiance; where we can never approve, we may nevertheless admire.

Furthermore, there are frequent occasions in the play where the invocation of Providence, far from relieving that right-thinking moral awareness which has been under siege, proves to be a flagrant sophistry. We are familiar enough with this in Richard's mouth—'God will revenge it', he announces suavely, so that when God's avenger arrives in his own person no one need be too greatly shocked. But Dorset uses the same spurious theological rationalisation to cover *his* sins (I. iii. 186) and Elizabeth, confronted with the termagant Margaret, is sufficiently conscienceless to support Richard in maintaining Margaret's misfortunes to be the divine judgment on her crimes—'So just is God to right the innocent' (I. iii. 182). In point of fact, Elizabeth has serious doubts about the infallible operation of Providence (elsewhere she accuses God of sleeping when he should have been taking positive action—IV. iv. 24), and what we really have here is a very nasty piece of self-congratulation, a complacent acceptance of the fruits of evil under the gratuitous title of 'divine justice'. Indeed, throughout this scene (I. iii), the invocation of divine sanctions is so deeply intertwined with personal malice and unappeased rancour that it is dangerous to take any of it at face value. This is especially true of Margaret, the chief exponent of the philosophy of Providence in the play—a point to which I shall return.

One has a great deal of sympathy with an angry Victorian Christian who, protesting against a current elevation of Shakespeare into some kind of religious teacher, rightly saw that the kind of thinking about Providence implicit in this scene is radically inimical to Victorian and other varieties of Christianity.

They who pretend to believe in a Providence [Richard and the others, ll. 175-87], in their turn disbelieve it [ll. 285-6]; and she who scoffed at the idea when it was called to witness in their favour [i.e. Margaret], believes it [l. 287] when they assert their disbelief to escape its consequences. But what else does such a dialogue convey but doubt and contempt of its interference—a satire upon its supposed operations, alternately accepted and rejected, and chiefly proclaimed by the religious buffoon, Richard. The issue of all which would seem to point out that Providence cared not to prevent, could only second, the effusion of blood; and in that all his [*sic*] power lay.[14]

Pious indignation aside, Mr Birch does here admirably indicate the kind of realities which any account of Providence in this play must confront: namely, that it easily becomes an instrument of faction, and that when it does, one very naturally enquires what validity the concept has at all.

That Shakespeare confronts these realities is sufficiently proved by the liveliness with which he dramatises them; but that the confrontation leads to a resolution of the dissonance between a Machiavellian philosophy of power, and a Christian one of Providence, seems to me extremely doubtful—though there *is* a movement toward the kind of resolution that we get in *Macbeth*.

In fact, he attempts two not entirely distinguishable yet different answers. The first is the cyclic pattern of nemeses which R. G. Moulton has analysed so thoroughly, and which has become a commonplace in the criticism of the play.[15] Shakespeare seems to be offering this cyclic pattern as an answer to the demand for justice in human affairs—as a way of asserting Providence, without denying that the wicked do indeed prosper. But there is something willed and rhetorical about this aspect of the play, something relying too heavily on external manipulation to be wholly convincing. It is in fact an abstracted and attenuated version of his second, and more intrinsically dramatic, assault on the problem: the development of a conception of 'natural providence', an organic human process by which the diseased soul disintegrates under the weight of its own evil, and the diseased society purges itself. This insight was not to be fully embodied until much later in his career, but it does enable him, in *Richard III*, to get beyond the confusions and absurdities of a providential theory of divine *intervention*.

For a doctrine of Providence very readily degenerates into a gross over-simplification of the complex phenomenon of evil. The causal network of human affairs is turned into a series of isolated acts which are then rewarded or punished *in vacuo* by extra-human agency. The observable continuity of crime with its nemesis is sacrificed to a series of arbitrary acts which are unsatisfactory in proportion as the evil they punish, or the good they reward, is problematical.

Now this dangerous simplification was ready to Shakespeare's hand in his Holinshed, and it is well to ponder it, in order to decide how much (or how little) the play owes to this line of thought.

And thus it well appeared, that the house of York shewed it selfe more bloudie in seeking to obteine a kingdome, than that of Lancaster in vsurping it: so it came to passe, that the Lords vengeance appeared more heauie towards the same than towards the other, not ceasing till the whole issue male of the said Richard duke of Yorke was extinguished. For such is Gods iustice, to leave no vnrepentant wickednesse vnpunished, as especiallie in this caitife Richard the third...[16]

Such a view of the Wars of the Roses has serious limitations: it is clear enough that the interpretation is only possible retrospectively, and will offer small comfort to those actually caught in the machinery of 'the

Lords vengeance' (if that is what it is). Despite the hallucinatory weighing of relative bloodiness (how *does* one decide which side in a war has been 'more bloudie'?), the judgment can really only be made from the secure vantage point of the Tudor establishment. If we accept Holinshed's terms, Providence becomes the handmaid of the successful. The wicked are those who fail, and those who fail are, by that token, revealed to be wicked. The whole notion proclaims its absurdity once one realises that the next revolution in the state which unseats the 'righteous' house of Lancaster will necessitate a rewriting of history to make *them* 'the wicked'. Holinshed's little moralisations are, indeed, all of this *ad hoc* variety, and display the same drastic inconsistency with each other. Providence is for him no more than a theological rationalisation of the *status quo*.

Although there was no dearth of contemporary objections to it,[17] some such simplified account of the operation of Providence does seem to have left its mark on *Richard III*. The deity is continually invoked by the wronged to intervene in a direct and arbitrary way. The curses called down on the heads of their oppressors form a continual chorus to the extension of that oppression. The problem, of course, is to be certain to what extent, and in what way, Shakespeare is behind the curses and the mechanism of retribution which brings about their fulfilment.

There is considerable evidence that we are meant to take it seriously; the procession of the condemned whom we meet on their way to execution—Rivers, Vaughan and Grey (III. iii), Hastings (III. iv. 82 f.), Buckingham (v. i)—all see their fate as divinely ordained and link it explicitly with Margaret's curse. Elizabeth fears she will 'die the thrall of Margaret's curse' (IV. i. 45); Anne knows she is 'the subject of her own soul's curse' (IV. i. 80); and Buckingham phrases this aspect of the action for us:

> Thus doth he [God] force the swords of wicked men
> To turn their own points in their masters' bosoms.   v. i. 23

I called this a *mechanism* of retribution with deliberate intent—for there is something mechanical about even the recognition of the providential order. One has only to compare Buckingham's loosely platitudinous grasp of his situation with Macbeth's intensely imaginative apprehension of the 'bloody instructions' that constitute our 'judgement here', to realise that Buckingham's is an idea *about* Providence not an idea *of* Providence. There is a stratum of moral platitude in this play which reveals Shakespeare grappling with an idea for which he has not yet been able to find a body. I think it is significant that, when someone like Moulton tries to justify this aspect of the play, he is obliged to take as central to his argument scenes and passages which are poetically barren, expository in tone and dramatically static. Thus Act III, Scene iii, becomes the pivotal point of the action, and Grey's 'Now Margaret's curse is fall'n upon our heads' the great discovery of the play.[18] Any member of an audience could have told him that it is nothing of the sort. The kind of satisfactions that the patterns of retributive reaction offer an audience are of a very limited geometrical kind—one grasps them with the mind, perceiving their symmetric felicity, but somehow they fail to mesh with the human complexities which are the stuff of the play. The heart beats elsewhere.

Not, however, in the kind of irony which is released when the victim of Fortune recalls how easily he might have evaded catastrophe —a recurring motif in the play, from Hastings (III. iv. 83 f.) to Buckingham (v. i). These formal recapitulations, of which Anne's (IV. i. 65 f.) is the most elaborate, operate by viewing the event from behind, where its face is inscrutable and problematical, and from before, when events have uncovered the reality. But it is an unresonant device, this wisdom after the event, with its explicit and unhelpful moral of human blindness. It is the wisdom of 'I could kick myself!' in which the realisation is eternally divorced from the possibility of action, a realisation of the irrevocable intolerable—static and unproductive. Or, more precisely, the only action open to Anne and her companions in woe is inner action of the Lear kind—and this the play hardly envisages, and certainly not for these people. Hence perhaps the feeling of rhetorical self-indulgence which hangs about their laments.

The rigid artifice of the nemesis patterns is indeed fairly intimately related to the much noted rhetorical patterning—though some distinction needs to be drawn between the two wooing scenes (where the formalities of stichomythia are like the formalities of a fencing match, decorum and punctilio merely heightening the awareness that the issue is life or death), and the scenes of choric lament and execration (I. ii. 1–32; I. iii; II. ii; II. iv; IV. i and IV. iv) where there is no such dramatic sanction for the artifice, unless it be the attempt to enact the ghoulish tedium of the endless, repetitive slaughter:

> I had an Edward, till a Richard kill'd him;
> I had a Henry, till a Richard kill'd him:
> Thou had'st an Edward, till a Richard kill'd him;
> Thou had'st a Richard, till a Richard kill'd him.   IV. iv. 40

Yet, if this is the function of these scenes, they succeed only too well in evoking tedium, and one is still left with the uneasy question, 'Why should calamity be full of words?' (IV. iv. 126), which it is tempting to regard as a Shakespearian misgiving on the subject. At times, the mechanical nature of the rendering becomes explicit, as, for instance, in the mathematical imagery of the Duchess of York's

> She for an Edward weeps, and so do I;
> I for a Clarence weep, so doth not she:
> These babes for Clarence weep, and so do I;
> I for an Edward weep, so do not they.
> Alas! you three on me, threefold distress'd,
> Pour all your tears...   II. ii. 82

It is this limiting confidence that the affairs of the heart can be thus totted up, weighed and parcelled which is so convincingly exploded in Act I of *Lear*; yet the only qualification to the Duchess's quantitative computation of grief is a verbal irony which merely undercuts the reality of the grief which so expresses itself. It is, of course, arguable that the stylisation is aimed at leading us beyond the 'grief' itself, to a perception of cosmic order that informs the 'calamity'—but that order is so rhetorical in conception as to be equally unsatisfying. 'Rhetorical', I mean, not in the generic Elizabethan sense, but rather in Yeats's sense of the word—'what is rhetoric but the will trying to do the work of the imagination?' [19] This terse little *aperçu*, I believe, throws more light on the experience of watching or reading *Richard III* than many a lengthy attempt to validate the artificial mode of Elizabethan poetry. There is a certain sterility about this side of the play, and it is a sterility which is rooted, I suggest, in the externality with which the operations of Providence are conceived. It is only appropriate that a mechanical justice should be enunciated in poetry whose most notable feature is mechanism. Shakespeare's imagination will not fully respond to a moral order which is so alien to 'this breathing world'—so he gives us, instead, the rhetoric of the will, the shallow irony, and the arbitrary patterns of retributive justice.

v

But, as I have suggested, there is another prong to Shakespeare's attack on the question of cosmic justice. Just as, in the wooing scenes, the rhetorical may merge imperceptibly into the dramatic, so the external meddlesome Providence is at times transmuted into a natural providence, part of the organic processes of individual consciousness and society. Where the two modes are in close proximity it is difficult to be sure which is chiefly operative, and I shall be content if I show, firstly, that the two modes do co-exist in the play; secondly, that they are, in their extreme forms, antithetical, and finally, that the tensions set up by their opposition prevent *Richard III* from being the play it shows signs of becoming.

These tensions can be seen in the treatment of the curses, all of which are meticulously fulfilled, that Buckingham (in II. i. 32–40) and Richard (IV. iv. 400–8) call down on their own heads. On the one hand, the revenge of an outraged moral order is figured in the fulfilment of the curses; but on the other, there is remarkably little hint of the supernatural about either the invocation of the penalties, or their fulfilment. Buckingham follows the succession of petty schemers who have been ordered by Edward, 'Dissemble not your hatred, swear your love'— and whose discomfort in performing this self-contradictory task is expressed in the grudging brevity of their oaths. Buckingham, however, though he has no more intention than they of keeping it, makes his oath needlessly elaborate. With a kind of dissembler's *hybris* which is entirely in character, he brazenly defies heaven, which, if it were to fulfil the conditions of his oath, would strike him down upon the spot. It is the same with Richard's oath to Elizabeth:

> As I intend to prosper and repent,
> So thrive I in my dangerous affairs
> Of hostile arms! myself myself confound!...
> Day, yield me not thy light; nor, night, thy rest!
> Be opposite, all planets of good luck,
> To my proceeding, if with dear heart's love,
> Immaculate devotion, holy thoughts,
> I tender not thy beauteous princely daughter!   IV. iv. 400

This is not so much an oath as a gesture of defiance towards the supernatural order which is shamelessly invoked to buttress dissimulation. Shakespeare's view of divine retribution is clearly less mechanical than some, for the thunderbolt does not immediately transfix the false forswearer. Neither does the way in which the two curses come to fulfilment involve any occult processes: Buckingham's 'friend' Richard, has always been 'deep, hollow, treacherous, and full of guile', so it is only a matter of time before he proves so to Buckingham; and Richard himself is clearly headed for the catastrophe where the self he has so assiduously cultivated will confound itself; his sleeplessness is no more than the operation of conscience, and the sun does not shine every day.

Nevertheless, Buckingham, faced with the fulfilment of his curse, explicitly and needlessly moralises the event, and presents us with a neatly packaged universe where 'Wrong hath but wrong, and blame the due of blame'—the symmetry is both the appropriate rhetorical equivalent of this view of Providence, and its most severe limitation.

In Richard's case, however, the fulfilment is not signalled by platitude: he is apparently never aware that it has taken place. The irony thus remains implicit; the audience is left to reach its own conclusions about the explicable, yet mysterious confluence of events on Bosworth Field: not, I suggest, concluding that God has avenged himself, but that this is the kind of thing that happens to the kind of person who perpetrates this kind of defiance of the moral order. By remaining particular and mysterious, this ironic justice does more to reinforce a sense of universal justice than Buckingham's moralising could ever do.

The same kind of tension between natural and supernatural views of events is apparent in the treatment of Margaret. We have seen (and been told often enough) to what extent she may be regarded as Nemesis personified, the vatic mouthpiece of the Providential order, and this is clearly one of her dramatic functions. Yet even in this role she speaks primarily for herself and her wrongs, and her voice at its most powerful is the individual voice of a neurotic and grief-crazed woman—'Urge neither charity nor shame to me...My charity is outrage, life my shame...' (I.iii.274). There are appalling glimpses of a seething misanthropic hell, a consciousness in which the primary values of generation and 'kind' have been converted into the energy of implacable hatred:

> From forth the kennel of thy womb hath crept
> A hell-hound that doth hunt us all to death:
> That dog that had his teeth before his eyes,
> To worry lambs and lap their gentle blood,
> That foul defacer of God's handiwork,
> The excellent grand tyrant of the earth,
> That reigns in galled eyes of weeping souls,
> Thy womb let loose to chase us to our graves.
> O upright, just, and true-disposing God,
> How do I thank thee, that this carnal cur
> Preys on the issue of his mother's body,
> And makes her pue-fellow with other's moan!   IV. iv. 47

We are even given, in her instructions on how to curse, some insight into the means by which Margaret has created this internal hell:

> Forbear to sleep the night, and fast the day;
> Compare dead happiness with living woe;
> Think that thy babes were sweeter than they were,
> And he that slew them fouler than he is.
> Bettering thy loss makes the bad causer worse:
> Revolving this will teach thee how to curse.   IV. iv. 118

To some extent this vision of pathological disorder invests Margaret's imprecations with a thoroughly evil potency, and shows her conception of God (a supernatural agency under contractual obligation to exterminate the house of York) to be the product of a diseased mind. But I cannot help feeling that we are confronted with two distinct concepts of her dramatic function—one, as the specially sanctioned spokesman for wronged humanity, employing a deliberately stylised diction to indicate her ideal function; the other, as a particular sick woman, vomiting up her corruption—a demented prophetess in the grip of an eternal rancour which has eaten out the heart of her humanity. Later in his career, Shakespeare would have been able to fuse the personal and the choric functions into a single mode of dramatic speech; he would not perhaps even have needed the explicit comment of a Margaret, in order to make us aware of the cycles of nemesis which overtake the evil-doer and the opportunist. But at this stage there is much in his art which is still explicit; and it seems to be at odds with the things we would most readily call Shakespearian.

Nevertheless, it is Margaret who enunciates the organic providence most clearly:

> So! now prosperity begins to mellow
> And drop into the rotten mouth of death.   IV. iv. 1

It is a process which cannot be hastened or retarded; it follows a cycle, of which the very rottenness of the fruit is a part. As in *Macbeth*, the providential purposes are assimilated to their natural analogue: when the fruit 'Is ripe for shaking', *then* 'the Powers above / Put on their instruments' (*Macbeth*, IV. iii. 237). There is a suggestion that Time itself is a healing process: as we have it in *Lucrece*, that

> Time's glory is to calm contending kings,
> To unmask falsehood and bring truth to light...
> To wrong the wronger till he render right...   (ll. 939–43)

It is proper to add that this formulation occurs in a passage where 'injurious, shifting Time' is being accused of failing in his office—a reminder that 'Time's glory' is not, for Shakespeare, annulled by his vision of 'devouring Time'. It is rather that, by a simultaneous contemplation of the fortuitous and the meaningful in time, he is able to impart to the concept of Providence a range and depth which it could never have if the fortuitous were excluded. It is the germ of an insight that Tolstoy so magnificently embodied in *War and Peace*—a cosmic justice whose proper medium is the mutually contradictory, infinitely complex, and apparently meaningless sum of a myriad free acts of human choice. It is a tower of meaning erected in the quicksands of time.

In *Richard III* the providential process seen as continuous with 'mellowing' time is shown in two dimensions: in the inner world of conscience where evil brings self-betrayal, and self *does* self confound; and in the commonweal where tyranny creates, by its own excesses, the opposition which will overthrow it. Since the treatment of the inner disintegration of Richard brings to a focus what I believe is the play's central limitation, I shall leave that question till last, and consider first the ways in which the purgative action of the political organism is presented to the imagination.

Because the process is intimately related to the operation of time, much of its dramatic representation depends on a sense of fitness in events, an unseen ripening which is manifested only in symptomatic changes in the political landscape—and since this sense reaches us at an almost pre-conscious level, being apprehended 'musically' as a kind of proportion and symmetry in the temporal ordinance of the action, it is exceedingly difficult to analyse. I can only point to the symptomatic changes and hope that their temporal and dramatic coherence is not a private delusion of my own.

We have already seen one such change in the Scrivener's speech (III. vi), when we are made conscious of the eyes turned accusingly toward the tyrant, from faces which seem sealed for ever from speaking their knowledge. The same dumb faces, this time multiplied to a sea, meet Buckingham in the Guildhall; and a conviction forms at the back of one's mind that this soundless opposition must some day find words for its discontent. From the moment of Richard's coronation, the wave of reaction begins to gather itself, 'as a sea without wind swelleth of himselfe...before a tempest', as More puts it[20]—and first among his own followers. Buckingham, who has so long 'held out untir'd' with Richard, 'stops for breath' at the knowledge that the prudential slaughtering of the innocent is not to abate (IV. ii. 44–5). Catesby, too, faced with a new judicial murder, this time of Anne, is sufficiently bewildered to be caught dreaming (IV. ii. 50 f.). Tyrrel, at the very moment of performing the tyrant's command for the extermination of the Princes, sees the 'bloody king' for what he is, and loathes him (IV. iii. 22); and before this scene is out the news of the first rebels in arms is brought to Richard. From this point onward the messengers come with an accelerating frequency which exasperates Richard. Even the 'queen of sad mischance' finds it in herself to outface Richard to an extent that no one has done before (IV. iv).

By the last act, the sense of momentum which has always attended Richard's exploits has transferred itself to Richmond, marching 'with drum and colours':

> Thus far into the bowels of the land,
> Have we march'd on without impediment...   v. ii. 3

And the Ghost sequence, though a little stilted, brings this movement to a culmination. The measured monotony of the Ghosts' utterance— the formal correlative, perhaps, of their monotonous 'taking off'— their clockwork apparition and disappearance, are ways of freeing the audience for the contemplation of their sheer numerical weight, and, by consequence, of Richard's colossal villainy. They crystallise for us a sense of the overwhelming violence he has done to human feeling. And crowding in behind their personal thirsting for revenge come all the incidental hints we have had about subterranean movements of resentment and revolt in Richard's England—particularly the complaint we have just heard from Stanley's lips:

> the fearful time
> Cuts off the ceremonious vows of love
> And ample interchange of sweet discourse,
> Which so long sunder'd friends should dwell upon.   v. iii. 98

His 'God give us leisure for these rites of love!' is reinforced by the conviction that these things can only be 'cut off' for a limited time. Human mutuality is a powerful current. It only gains in strength from being dammed up.

The point I want to make about all this, which could be the merest plot manipulation, is that its timing within the dramatic movement is such as to release for the audience the sense of a ripening supra-personal purpose, a process which, though the result of individual decision, somehow adds up to a revenge of nature upon the usurper. 'Providence' may still be an appropriate term for it, but it is a Providence which has emerged out of the natural, an enactment of universal moral law, not a mere proclamation of it; and it grows out of the soil of human life, rather than descending supernaturally from above.

VI

But the development most pregnant with possibilities of dramatic growth is that which was foreshadowed in the Clarence scene (I. iv) and which is taken up after Richard's coronation—an exploration in depth of the personal consequences of commitment to evil. Interestingly enough, the beginning of this movement coincides precisely with the termination, in Holinshed, of More's narrative, and a new freedom in the treatment of source material; and this is not surprising, for More's Richard is almost entirely conceived from the outside, as the Machiavellian politician and super-manipulator, and could thus have acted as a brake on any tendency to internalise the meaning of events. (The Clarence scene, with its exceptional preoccupation with the inner life, offers some confirmation of this view—for it, too, is a Shakespearian invention, independent of More, and so free to develop along different lines.)[21] To More's Machiavellian, Shakespeare has wedded, in the first three acts, the stage convention of the Vice,[22] the consummate dissembler, trader in double meanings, and natural enemy of peace and virtue, thus producing his own version of Marlowe's invention, the stage Machiavel.[23] This is Richard in his comic dimension, 'the Prince of Punches' (to borrow Shaw's phrase) who 'delights Man by provoking God, and dies unrepentant and game to the last'.[24] Like Punch and the Vice, his very existence depends on a kind of conspiratorial collaboration with the audience, a relationship which Shakespeare establishes in the first speech of the play. There is such an immense gusto and vernacular body in those lines that one never suspects Richard of being less than 'real'; but the tongue-in-cheek self-exposition ('I am determined to be a villain'), the patronising airs of the master-of-ceremonies ('Plots have I laid, inductions dangerous'), the infectious and question-begging contempt ('this weak piping time of peace')—all combine to make him a being less vulnerable and subject to change than any mere man could be. He is, rather, a magnificent theatrical fiction.

But immediately after the coronation we see a Richard who is unwilling to name the deed he proposes to execute, begging Buckingham to 'think now what I would speak' (IV. ii. 10), and when forced to specify his proposal, demanding, 'Say, have I thy consent that they shall die?' It is a brief glimpse, closely woven into the dramatic texture, of a mind momentarily unnerved by its own depravity, an eye that wishes to wink at the hand. Almost at once the familiar stony-hearted egotism supervenes—

> I will converse with iron-witted fools
> And unrespective boys; none are for me
> That look into me with considerate eyes—   IV. ii. 28

but before this, in a fine touch, Shakespeare has given us the isolated, fretful king surrounded by whispering courtiers—

> CATESBY. [aside] The King is angry; see, he gnaws his lip.

Almost all the light shed on Richard's inner turmoil comes through such a crack in the shutter—this perhaps being Shakespeare's recognition that introspection and self-revelation is foreign to the character he has accepted from More. So when, a few lines further on, there is a momentary regret at the failure of Buckingham to stay with the chase, the reflective 'Well, be it so' is promptly engulfed in a new outburst of plotting. But the curtain is closed only to part a few lines further on with

> But I am in
> So far in blood, that sin will pluck on sin...   IV. ii. 63

This is the organic principle of retribution—the law by which evil is self-propagating and thus self-destructive. It is the principle in *Macbeth* which corresponds to Nemesis in this play.[25] But Richard, at the very moment that he enunciates it, denies it access to his moral nature, for he immediately snarls,

> Tear-falling pity dwells not in this eye;

and again we are left darkling.

This inexplicit but extremely revealing vacillation in Richard is superbly dramatised in the series of minor *faux pas* that close Act IV, Scene iv—sequences so perfectly adapted to the theatrical medium that I can only refer the reader to them: ll. 436–59—the hard-pressed administrator growing absent-minded as larger questions than those of immediate action crowd into his mind; ll. 459–500—thrown off balance by his previous blunders, Richard relieves his feelings by bullying Stanley mercilessly; ll. 501–17—Richard, now a little rattled, seeks the relief of a gesture of dominance, and is obliged instead to apologise to an underling. A great deal about flagging morale and uneasy sovereignty is implied in these simple exchanges, and it is not hard to guess at the state of mind which produces the symptoms. But Shakespeare goes no further into the nature of Richard's sickness until we meet him on Bosworth Field, his spirits sagging under the weight of the gloomy faces around him, and attempting a leaden-footed jocularity:

> RICHARD. My Lord of Surrey, why look you so sad?
> SURREY. My heart is ten times lighter than my looks.
> RICHARD. My Lord of Norfolk!
> NORFOLK.   Here, most gracious Liege.
> RICHARD. Norfolk, we must have knocks: ha! must we not?
> NORFOLK. We must both give and take, my loving Lord.
> RICHARD. Up with my tent! here will I lie to-night.
> But where to-morrow? Well all's one for that.   v. iii. 2

This, in its way, is very fine: Shakespeare has implied a great deal with simplicity and economy; but it is still the glimpse through the shutter. If this development of Richard is to be carried through, we must be at once led into the recesses of his consciousness, and liberated to contemplate the larger significance of this very personal depression. Richard needs to be enlarged poetically to include the Clarence in his nature— for there has been nothing since Act I, Scene iv, which has engaged our attention on quite so deep a level. It is a logic of this kind which leads to the soliloquy which follows the appearance of the Ghosts, and which takes up the theme of conscience last broached by Clarence.

There is nothing else in the play (one is tempted to say, in Shakespeare) which is quite like this soliloquy. The one which opened the play was basically an actor–audience interchange in which Richard exposed those parts of his nature which suited him, and established a working *rapport* with the audience. This soliloquy has nothing of that kind about it; indeed there are strong indications that it is to be played as if Richard were still in the grip of his dream, until he finally recalls what has precipitated the crisis—

> Methought the souls of all that I had murder'd
> Came to my tent...   v. iii. 204

Yet it has no relation to the mature Shakespearian soliloquy of introspection, unless it be the relationship of parody. It promises to take us into the world of conscience and shine the light on the inner results of Richard's obsessive power-seeking; but if it is, as John Palmer claims, 'no empty catechism, but a dialogue pointed at the heart of the eternal problem of conscience and personality',[26] one can only retort that it is exceedingly wildly aimed, and, in any case, too clumsy a blunderbuss to do more than disintegrate the object of its activity. It has become common to explain the speech as a case where the dramatist has bitten off more than he can chew, claiming that it marks 'a stage in Shakespeare's development at which he was unequal to the psychological skill which such a speech required'.[27] This may be so. But it seems to me that he has also been confronted with a choice of evils—a choice between the evil of extending Richard in depth to the point where he parted company with his 'Punch' self, and the evil of failing to investigate questions raised by the action.

Faced with this dilemma, Shakespeare attempts a compromise—a 'Punch-soliloquy'—sacrifices profundity to consistency, and, after permitting Richard to dance about on the brink of moral awareness, restores him to the certainties of the Machiavellian world where 'Conscience is but a word that cowards use'.

I call it a 'Punch-soliloquy' because there is something more than faintly comic about it. Shakespeare's instinct tells him that introspection in Richard will require a special mode—a dramatic representation of the geometric precision and ironic alertness of his mind, and, at the same time, a revelation of the limiting simplicities in which such a mind deals.

> Is there a murderer here? No. Yes, I am,
> Then fly. What, from myself? Great reason: why?
> Lest I revenge. What, myself upon myself?   v. iii. 185

The onslaught of conscience is resisted by the mobilisation of the forces of self-love, invoked half-playfully—

> Alack, I love myself.

Nowhere is there a hint that these antithetical warring selves are just the dialectical result of a failure to realise the deep involvement of 'conscience' with the 'self'. Richard simply hops like a flea from one antithesis to another. The movement of deepening seriousness, which begins when he admits the term 'conscience' shorn of the epithet 'coward' (l. 194), and which is marked by the ironing out of the nervous fragmentary rhythms of debate—'I shall despair. There is no creature loves me; / And, if I die, no soul will pity me'—is halted abruptly by a return to that which has greater reality than any regret he can generate in himself—a grasp of his own pitiless immunity, even from self-pity:

> Nay, wherefore should they, since that I myself
> Find in myself no pity to myself?   v. iii. 203

This, the nearest approach to self-discovery that he ever achieves, has a force and justice which the probing of conscience in the earlier lines cannot rival. The only relationship that Richard can enter into with himself is one of indifference mingled with contempt, and in such a consciousness self-knowledge can find no foothold. Substantially, this is his final address to the world. The flirtation with the moral order is over. More's Richard, a liability which Shakespeare gladly incurred and triumphantly exploited, can go no further—except for the proclamation of a brazen-throated physical courage, where the last scruple is swallowed up in the jaws of the threatened dissolution:

> A thousand hearts are great within my bosom.
> Advance our standards, set upon our foes;
> Our ancient word of courage, fair Saint George,
> Inspire us with the spleen of fiery dragons...   v. iii. 348

As martial music goes, this is pretty good stuff; but I don't think it is merely a temperamental antipathy to brass bands that sets other echoes ringing in my ears. The echo set up, for instance, when Richard momentarily faces his 'tomorrow' and turns aside abruptly with 'Well, all's one for that' (v. iii. 8), and we recall a very different tyrant on the eve of battle, fixed in stony contemplation of the endless tomorrows that process before him—not taking refuge in Richard's easy insouciance, but consumed by a kind of infernal knowledge. Faced with a vacuum where his life once was, Macbeth grapples with the unmeaning in an attempt to understand and come to terms with it, submitting himself to the despair which is part of the cosmic cycle of seasons and decay:

> I have liv'd long enough: my way of life
> Is fall'n into the sere, the yellow leaf...   *Macbeth*, v. iii. 22 f.

When Richard's 'alacrity of spirit' and 'cheer of mind' desert him, he calls for a bowl of wine: despairing self-knowledge can find no lodgement in his mind.

And thus the pledge given in the Clarence scene is never honoured; for the world of power-lust and political opportunism, and the curious fixity of the Machiavel character, combine to render implausible the kind of investigation Shakespeare proposed in that scene.

In one other direction *Macbeth* indicates what *Richard III* is not. I am thinking of the contrast between the external manipulating Providence of the earlier play and the dramatic providence of the later.

In *Macbeth* the purposes beyond time are wholly assimilated to time; the sanctions of divine law become the laws of human consciousness, and the vengeance of God becomes the purgative action of the diseased social organism. The supernatural order remains, as it were, in abeyance: whether one *can* jump the life to come, here—but here—remains an open and unanswered question. But the question is rendered peripheral by the certainty of judgment here, and by the infallible return of bloody instructions upon the head of the inventor. And the surprising fact is that the sense of moral order, far from being stunted by this pruning away of the transcendental leafage, merely strikes deeper roots into the soil of consciousness, and grows more compelling as it is less definable.

It is, of course, a dangerous practice to reprehend one play for not being another, and one has some sympathy with A. P. Rossiter when he suggests that the 'early work' label, as applied to *Richard III*, is an evasion and a refusal to accept what the play does offer.[28] If I am right, however, in thinking that the play offers us two incompatible insights, the matter becomes more complicated than Rossiter admits. If *Richard III* does not have that 'unity' which he detects, it is idle to submit ourselves to the guidance of Shakespeare's master-intelligence—for it has not yet achieved mastery. Rather, I would suggest, Shakespeare is at that creatively frustrating stage of his career when he has more philosophical souls on his shelves than he has dramatic bodies for them to inhabit; and the excess of the disembodied Idea floats like a disturbing phantom over some passages of the play—above all, over the idea of Providence, which, disconcertingly allied with a naïve chauvinism, leaves the closing minutes of the play sadly contracted to the stature of Tudor propaganda.

6

PROVIDENCE AND HISTORY IN ELIZABETHAN THOUGHT

In the previous chapter I have tried to put the objections to the mechanical, intervening, retributive Providence in terms of its unfortunate dramatic results in *Richard III*; and this is certainly the primary judgment upon which all others depend. But the matter does not end there. When a playwright of real ability fails to find a satisfactory dramatic embodiment for an idea, a conception, it is natural and probably inevitable to trace this failure back to an inherent inadequacy in the conception itself. Form is a revelation of what the content always was, and a dramatic weakness is a more than literary matter. The critical judgment reaches back to, perhaps necessarily implies, a judgment about the truth of the conception which has failed to achieve dramatic depth and coherence.

When one looks closely at the theoretical foundations of the providential historiography which lies at the base of the lament-and-retribution movement in *Richard III*, two things become plain: one, that the conception is shallow, over-schematic and internally inconsistent; the other, that in order to hold it at all an Elizabethan mind had either to be ignorant of, or suppress knowledge of, certain important and contradictory conceptions which were part of the Elizabethan milieu—particularly in the field of historiography. Thus the critics who want us to accept as 'the Elizabethan conception of history', the view that history is the triumphal march of Providence toward universal beatitude, have neglected (as this kind of mind usually does) to note that 'Elizabethan conceptions' in this field, as in any other, are growing and evolving by a process which is dialectical. The received doctrine of the period is only one-half of this process—a kind of natural precipitate from the cultural compound which, at the very moment of its formation, becomes assailable by those other active ingredients in the compound which it has implicitly denied the right to exist. Or—to change the metaphor—the culture of any one period necessarily contains the seeds of the culture which will supersede it. If it did not it would be eternal and immutable, without origin and incapable of further development.

It is at the heart of this dialectic, at the point of confluence where the established shore-line of *ideés reçues* is assailed by the incoming tide of creative and radical innovation, that the real insights—the ones which, while grounded in it, yet rise above the flux and turmoil of the historic process—are fought for and won. That is the place where we expect to find the great thinker taking his stand. We do not expect to find him, Canute-like, enthroned on the dry land of current orthodoxy, refusing to accept that it will soon be sea.

That is why the overtly 'providential' element in *Richard III* is disappointing. It simply asserts something which is, quite literally, *reçu*, something for which Shakespeare has not had to fight, and it ignores the fairly obvious objections to which the *idée* was, and still is, open. That these objections are largely theoretical (logical, philosophical and so on) does not mean that they are irrelevant to a dramatist's problems: we have only to glance over the partisan literature of our own century to realise how certain types of intellectual dishonesty can place a complete embargo on creative fruition. Mind is a part of man, and its malfunction is a distortion of the whole psyche, not just of the intellect. Intellectual dishonesty of this damaging kind is, it seems to me, involved in any unqualified espousal of the so-called 'orthodox protestant conception' of Providence in Shakespeare's age. It is the intellectual dishonesty that is born of a fear of complexity. It lives in emotional bondage to those simplifying conceptions which promise to make the world a less awesome place to live in, and man's responsibility a little less terrifying. It is not surprising that an imagination as alive as Shakespeare's to the complexity of human affairs ran into difficulties when he tried to dramatise this view of history; not surprising, either, that once he had outgrown it he never returned to it. The lack of conviction about the passages in *Richard III* explicitly devoted to its exposition seems to indicate that he never succeeded in believing in this external, meddlesome Providence in the way that is essential to a creative artist.

The temper of protestant providentialism in the sixteenth century goes a long way towards explaining why Shakespeare failed to transform it into the master-idea behind the first tetralogy. The conception depends upon a view of the divine activity in history as a continual and arbitrary interference in earthly affairs. The protestant God has everything at his fingertips. As Calvin never tires of telling us, he is *not* the detached observer in the watch-tower, contemplating the operations of immutable law. Rather he is the super-technician in the control room of his latest invention.

If God's governance is so extended to all his works, it is indeed a childish cavil to enclose it within the stream of nature. Indeed, those as much defraud God of his glory as themselves of a most profitable doctrine who confine God's providence to such narrow limits as though he allowed all things by a free course to be borne along according to a universal law of nature.

The units of nature are, for Calvin, 'nothing but instruments to which God continually imparts as much effectiveness as he wills, and according to his own purpose bends and turns them to either one action or another'. There is no such thing as chance or fortune, only 'a secret operation of providence'—'it is certain that not one drop of rain falls without God's sure command'.[1] 'If there is a God,' remarks one ingenuous theologian, 'it is necessary and requisite that he be occupied.'[2] The protestants gave him plenty to get on with.

A God so directly in control of human affairs is, of course, open to charges of maladministration and injustice; and it is here that the providential theory immediately begins to reveal its evasiveness. Why do the wicked prosper? For prosper they certainly do. Why are the righteous desolate? The kinds of answer that are given to these questions depend upon taking each alleged case of injustice singly, and rationalising it in terms of an unquestioned morality of nature. Yet when we put the rationalisations together they annihilate each other. The ill fortune of the wicked is a sign of God's wrath; but the ill fortune of the just is a sign of his love. The good man who prospers is being rewarded for his righteousness, but the evil man who prospers is being deluded with worldly success in preparation for his eventual condemnation at the Day of Judgment. Justice is always done in this life; but when it is not, the faithful need have no fear, it will be done in the next. God, says Calvin,

by open and daily indications declares his clemency to the godly and his severity to the wicked and criminal. For there are no doubts about what sort of vengeance he takes on wicked deeds. Thus he clearly shows himself the protector and vindicator of innocence, while he prospers the life of good men with his blessing...And indeed the unfailing rule of his righteousness ought not to be obscured by the fact that he frequently allows the wicked and malefactors to exult unpunished for some time, while he permits the upright and deserving to be tossed about by many adversities, and even to be oppressed by the malice and iniquity of the impious. But a far different consideration ought, rather, to enter our minds...that, when he leaves many sins unpunished, there will be another judgment to which have been deferred the sins yet to be punished.[3]

The problem of temporal injustice and the inequality of fate can hardly ever have received an answer so glaringly inadequate.

The spectacle of the good Christian wriggling on the horns of the providential dilemma must have been a fairly familiar one in the sixteenth century:

And though [God] suffreth the wicked for the most part to liue in prosperitie, and the good in aduersitie: yet we maye see by many notable examples, declaring as well his wrath, and reuenge towardes the wicked, as also his pittie and clemencie towardes the good, that nothing is done by chaunce, but all things by his foresight, counsell, and diuine prouidence.[4]

We *may* see; but we may also have difficulty in reconciling the 'pittie and clemencie' with the 'aduersitie', the 'wrath, and reuenge' with the 'prosperitie'. Not only is this having your cake and eating it, but there is a central equivocation: Is justice done in this life, or is it not? And if not, on what grounds do we infer a just God?

It is like Aquinas who claims to have proved 'that natural bodies are moved and work towards an end...from the fact that *always or nearly always* that which is best happens to them'.[5] Even if one admits the 'nearly always' (and it is a huge admission) the nature of these exceptions is crucial and makes the 'proof' highly suspect. In that little self-correction, which Aquinas clearly regards as marginal, the whole realm of bitter and manifest injustice, human and cosmic, is relegated to an insignificant corner. It is no more than a parenthesis in the universal well-being. One need not hesitate before labelling this a retreat from painful reality into a comfortable simplification and self-deception of a very dangerous kind. In this kind of context the 'will of God' becomes the magical refuge for the timid mind that wants a single principle of order so urgently that it will sacrifice anything for it. (And there *is* an intellectual timidity which is entirely compatible with the production of vast *Summae* or definitive theological systems like the *Institutes of the Christian Religion*. The System has an abiding capacity to become, not a way of understanding reality, but a way of avoiding it.)

When the providential conception is applied to national destinies, the discrepancies become even more glaring: 'Realmes and nations are either preserved if they be Godlie, or vtterly distroyed, and shamefullie oppressed if they be vngodlie', declares Christopher Goodman.[6] But by the time he has accounted for the numerous godly nations which are oppressed, and the equally numerous wicked ones preserved, his initial confident assertion has been qualified out of existence. One is left with the assurance that, one way or another, now or else later, anyway in God's good time, all is for the best; but with not a shred of a conception how this can come about. The realm of the natural has been handed over bodily to the supernatural, and man can only wonder at the inexplicable operations of what he is assured is Providence. One can no more make drama out of this conception, than one can make history. It is fundamentally and incurably arbitrary.

But the conception was, naturally enough, under assault. As Hooker remarked, they who 'peremptorily avouch that there is no manner why to be rendered of anything which God doth, but only this, It was his absolute will to do it', simply make it impossible to conceive of God as 'just' at all.[7] For Hooker, God and nature are not so desperately at odds as these men would suggest. And for some thinkers, they are very nearly the same thing—so much so that God is in danger of becoming a superfluity: 'The ignorant vulgar,' remarks the Spanish humanist Huarte,

seeing a man of great wit and readinesse, straightwaies assigns God to be the author thereof, and looke no further...but naturall Philosophers despise this manner of talking, for...it groweth from not knowing the order and disposition which God placed amongst naturall things...and [t]o couer their ignorance with a kind of warrantise, and in sort, that none may reprehend or gainsay the same, they affirme that all befals as God will, and that nothing succeeds, which springs not from his diuine pleasure.[8]

(As so often, the medieval conception of natural law—that 'order and disposition...amongst naturall things'—lies ready at hand to be wielded against protestant extremists.) Though this be never so true, Huarte continues, yet 'as not euerie kind of demaund...is to be made after one fashion, so not euerie aunswer (though true) is to be giuen'. This rushing to the supernatural explanation he sees largely as a result of mental indolence:

Men are for the most part impatient, and desirous to accomplish speedily what they couet. But because the natural means are of such prolixitie, and work with length of time, they possesse not the patience to stand marking thereof... Wherefore they would haue God demeane himself towards them, after his omnipotencie, and that (without sweating) they might come to the wellhead of their desires.

Why do the wicked prosper? Well, says Huarte,

the true solution of this demand is, that the lewd sort are verie witty, and haue a gallant imagination, to beguile in buying and selling, and can profit in bargaining, and employing their stocke where occasion of gain is offered. But honest men want this imagination: many of whom haue endeuoured to imitate those bad fellowes, and by trafficquing and trucking, within few daies haue lost their principall.[9]

This is one mode of attack on the over-simplifications of providentialism—a naturalistic appeal to rationality and law within the realm of the human, and an eschewal of those quick and easy solutions which, while they offer to save 'sweating', prove ultimately to be mere evasions.

Sometimes, however, Huarte's urbane rationality took a more bitter turn, and became the railing voice of the malcontent—in this case, Quadratus in Marston's *What You Will*:

> None but a mad man would terme fortune blind.
> How can shee see to wound desert so right,
> Just in the speeding place? to girt leud browes
> With honord wreath? Ha! Fortune blinde? Away!
> How can she, hud-winkt, then so rightly see
> To starve rich worth and glut iniquitie?[10]

Not only is the world not uniformly just, it is actively malevolent. And this too is part of the 'Elizabethan world picture' which we ignore at the risk of over-simplification. Hooker apparently found the complaint sufficiently serious and widespread to preface a discussion of Providence with four pages in which he takes the full force of the accusation against divine justice. The passage provides evidence that, even for the devout, it was a real and pressing problem.[11]

H. R. Patch has shown how at this period the medieval assimilation of Fortune to the providential activity of God was being reversed, while there was a revival of interest in the more cynical pagan goddess of antiquity—a malicious and irrational creature, who was perhaps (as Machiavelli alleged) the friend of the bold, but certainly no fit ally of the Deity.[12] Indeed the discrepancy between merit and reward had become so glaring that Pontano, in Italy, had felt obliged to invent a new class of men, the *fortunati*, whose irresistible success in this world was an endowment given them at birth, and one completely devoid of moral implications.[13]

But perhaps the most important attack on providentialism came from the historians. Like Huarte, they were annoyed by the way Divine omnipotence was used as a shield for human indolence. 'Christian authors,' complains Edmund Bolton, with some asperity,

while for their ease they shuffle up the reasons of events, in briefly referring all causes to the Will of God, have generally neglected to inform their Readers in the ordinary means of Carriage in human Affairs, and thereby singularly maimed their Narratives.[14]

'The ordinary means of Carriage in human Affairs' is increasingly being recognised as the true subject-matter of history, though it will be some time before the historian dispenses altogether with the notion that by the study of the past 'we may learne...to acknowledge the prouidence of God'.[15] Nevertheless, Renaissance historiography shows a consistent, and relatively new, determination to take only the rational and the explicable as its province. It presupposes, in Bodin's words, 'an inevitable and steadfast sequence of cause and effect', which is only broken by 'spectacles of distorted nature and huge monsters'—and these not the concern of the historian. Bodin's rationalism carries him to the point where he will exclude from 'human history' even the spontaneous and uncalculated in *human* behaviour:

Those activities are human, then, which spring from plans, sayings, and deeds of men, when volition leads the way. For will power is mistress of human activity.[16]

The distance from the Calvinist position, where human freedom stood dwarfed and cowering in the huge shadow cast by the will of God, could hardly be greater. The humanism of Graeco-Roman historiography has begun to erode the providentialism of the Christian historians.[17]

Providential historiography required, further, a quick and easy location of the godly and the wicked, so that the moral plaster could be promptly applied to the running sore of history; and about this the more scrupulous historians were growing rather cagey. Impartiality they saw as an essential virtue of the historian, and they tended to become enraged with the man who continually gave his opinion of the moral significance of events, 'although not asked'. Let the reader make his own judgments. 'History ought to be nothing else than...a record of events which is placed in the clearest public view for the decision of all.'[18] The historian, 'unless he mean only to serve a Side and not to serve Truth and Honesty', should simply 'set forth without Prejudices, Depravations, or sinister items, things as they are', and leave 'the Judgment of all to the competent Reader, which Judgment we ought not to forstall'.[19] Moralised history, of which Holinshed is such a damaging example, was becoming increasingly difficult for the intelligent—a truth which is witnessed by the huge gulf between Holinshed's and Shakespeare's versions of English history.

And yet, like the nineteenth-century historians they so often seem to anticipate, Renaissance historians, in their reaction against simplifications, had abdicated a whole province of historical thought—the province of ultimate significance. Here they are discreetly agnostic, leaving it to the theologians and philosophers. It is not out of any disrespect for the scruples that induced that abdication that I suggest they were wrong; it is simply that I doubt whether any profound contemplation of human affairs can dispense with the concept of purpose. And Providence, or Fate, or Fortune, all of which the historians tended to minimise or deny, are ways of thinking about purpose in history.

We have seen that Shakespeare's commitment to the protestant kind of providentialism is, in *Richard III*, a liability which he incurs with a bad grace and fails to make much of. His imagination will not adhere to this material—which is hardly surprising when all the most enlightened opinion is ranged against it. And yet Providence of some kind lies at the heart of the dramatic logic of the play (as it does in *Macbeth*), and he will not permit the naturalism of his political vision to loosen his grasp on the meaning of the whole historical spectacle. His position, fairly clearly, lies between the older providential historiography and the new Renaissance naturalism, and he retains elements of both. The emergence of what I called a 'natural providence' in the play is an attempt to wed the two, an attempt to be realistic and naturalistic about human affairs, without emptying them of all meaning; and, on the other hand, to achieve a wholeness of vision which does not persistently blink awkward facts in the manner of the providentialists. It is an attempt to gather up the conflicting elements in his own culture into a synthesis which preserves the virtues of both old and new.

It is interesting to note that the few Elizabethans who are thinking seriously about the problem of Providence are also making similar suggestions. Hooker, for instance, admits the validity of the classical conception of 'natural destiny':

The natural generation and process of all things receiveth order of proceeding from the settled stability of divine understanding. This appointeth unto them their kinds of working; the disposition whereof in the purity of God's own knowledge and will is rightly termed by the name of Providence. The same being referred unto the things themselves here disposed by it, was wont by the ancient to be called natural Destiny.[20]

The implication seems to be that these matters can be legitimately discussed on the naturalistic plane, although a total view will relate the logic of the natural realm to the supernatural purpose which it subserves.

The other movement in providential theory I want to mention is one which attempts to make the scope of Providence increasingly large, to encompass longer periods of history, and to look beyond merely local, or even national, destinies. Many of the accusations against Providence, suggests a seventeenth-century writer, result from a certain self-centred preoccupation with a small local area of human life, whereas

what was lost to one part, was gained to another; and what was lost in one time, was to the same part recouered in another; and so the ballance by the divine providence over-ruling all, kept vpright.

Thus there is a certain cyclical rise and fall in human and national affairs. Certain things decay here, rise elsewhere. It is this vast and complex process which is presided over by Providence, rather than the meticulous allotment of rewards and punishments to each peccadillo and act of virtue.[21] Hooker, in a similar mood, quotes the proverb that 'Truth is the daughter of Time' and warns against premature attempts to impose a providential gloss on the historical text.[22]

But Hooker's great contribution to the discussion lies in a discrimination which cuts right through the confusions that attend the attempts to make God the simple rewarder of virtue and punisher of vice. Worldly prosperity, he suggests, is too shallow a criterion. Does justice require, he asks,

that the righteous have every desirable thing, the unrighteous nothing which is naturally good permitted them? Then that which never as yet any man was so senseless as to imagine notwithstanding must needs be; to wit, that if only the just be not beautiful, if they only be not strong, if any be healthful besides them, if they alone do not see the fruit of their bodies increased to the third and fourth generation, God doth deal unjustly with them.

Not only is this a madman's justice, it implies manifest injustice to all but the righteous.

Wicked men, although they be their own workmanship as they are wicked, yet as they are men being his handywork, are we not rather injurious unto them than God to us, if so be we envy them all participation even in those things which they are capable of as men?

Here he touches the nerve-centre of the Calvinist providentialism—a chronic envy of the wicked whose lives are so much more manifold than those of the elect. The Calvinist, for all his high-minded concern with the next life, is materialistically bent on getting his rewards in a very concrete way—even his heaven is materialistically conceived as a reward. For Hooker, however, the true reward of righteousness does not come in the shape of bonus payments from the hands of the Almighty—which may or may not be forthcoming—but in righteousness itself.

It had been more than childishness in Moses to choose a fellowship in the bitter afflictions of the people of God, refusing the offered pleasures of sin, if the just man's estate, be it whatsoever, were not by infinite degrees happier than the wicked's in their chiefest ruff...The righteous therefore may have their phancies; they may, being carried away with grief or distempered with passionate affections, conceive worse of their own estate than reason giveth: but surely there was never yet that hour, wherein, if mortal eyes could discern the things that belong unto solid happiness, the hearts of the most unhappy would not wish, as Balaam's did, 'O that we were as the just and righteous!'[23]

Not only is this a much more intelligent approach to the problem of justice, avoiding some of the inconsistencies and absurdities of a simple-minded providentialism, but, by focusing attention on the natural level, it offers the kind of 'dramatic' solution which we have seen Shakespeare moving towards in *Richard III*. The *deus ex machina*, both a theological and a theatrical embarrassment, is rendered superfluous.

It is possible, I suppose, to see this enlargement of the scale of providential operations as an attempt to defend the indefensible by moving the argument into a region where the imponderables are so vast as to preclude discussion. But I am inclined to regard it rather as an act of faith in the morality of the universe, a refusal to restrict speculation to the verifiable and the observable (as the historians increasingly were doing), or to fall back cravenly on an Epicurean primacy of chance. True, when this act of faith is made *before* the powerful objections to it have been throughly faced, it is no more than a retreat into delusive simplicities. But Hooker makes his affirmation after a very thorough consideration of those objections, and the affirmation is, one might say, heightened and given added seriousness by its obviously paradoxical nature.

I think there is much in the history plays to suggest that Shakespeare, too, has made this act of faith. At times, regrettably, it is no more than a convenient fiction which does not carry much conviction. At others it seems to release a sense of order grounded in the deepest levels of the personality. One is prompted to ask whether some such faith in the essential morality of the universe is not a necessary faith for the dramatist. Whether this is not one of those seminal conceptions Shakespeare inherited from his culture, refined in his own unique way, and built into the foundations of his art. Whether our own twentieth-century difficulties about such a faith, real and pressing though they are, do not inhibit something essential in our drama, and in our way of looking at the world. One thinks of that courageous, but defeated, playwright, Samuel Beckett, or the less courageous and more acutely defeated Pinter. The problems of affirmation are enormous now, but to be able to assert from the heart of known injustice, evil, muddle, fortuity, calamity, an order which is still moral, is a great achievement of Shakespeare's art which we cannot regard as irrelevant. In *Richard III* we can see him trying his wings, being misled by the wrong kind of providential conception, but pressing nearer to his objective in moments of insight which tend to fuse the historic event and its moral significance in a single, intensely dramatic vision.

HISTORY WITHOUT MORALITY:
'EDWARD II'

Perhaps the most remarkable thing about Marlowe's *Edward II* is the fact that, although it has every appearance of being a play on a national and political theme, a play about kingship, it is yet an intensely personal play in which the public issues hardly arise. It's true that there is a fair deal of talk about 'our country's good' (see II. iii. 1; IV. i. 2; IV. v. 74–7; and v. i. 38), and no scarcity of criticisms against Edward's mode of ruling, but on these occasions one is primarily conscious either of the slackness of unfelt platitude, or of a very bald sophistry on the part of egocentric power-seekers. The sentiments do not seem to mesh with any larger scheme of political morality in the drama. When Isabella exults,

> Successful battles gives the God of kings
> To them that fight in right and fear his wrath,   IV. v. 28

one's first impulse is to sneer, for the introduction of providential sanctions seems quite gratuitous in the world of this play. It is not that Marlowe has created a dramatic context, like the world of *Richard III*, within which the rationalisations of violence stand nakedly revealed for pious cant: what would have been clearly placed, in *Richard III*, as a sophistical cloak for unscrupulous opportunism, remains, in *Edward II*, oddly unplaced. Like the frequent appeals to an overriding common good, the queen's theology is neither imaginatively ratified nor used to expose the egocentricity of her motivation: it is simply a statement thrown up in the course of conflict.

This strange moral indeterminacy—and it is thoroughly typical of the play—is a quality that is familiar enough to readers of modern newspapers: it is the reporter's studious policy of non-involvement, the uncommitted neutrality that operates by means of the reported speech and the eye-witness account. It is an early essay in the documentary mode. But it is rather startling to find it in an Elizabethan play. Marlowe appears to have assimilated the naturalistic trend of Renaissance historiography so thoroughly as to exclude altogether the providential tradition. As Irving Ribner puts it,

Marlowe sees no pattern in history simply because...he does not see in history the working out of a divine purpose, and therefore he cannot see in it any large scheme encompassing God's plans for men and extending over many decades. Marlowe sees history entirely as the action of men who bring about their own success or failure entirely by their own ability to cope with events.[1]

Though I am unconvinced by the rest of Ribner's argument, this is, I think, an accurate charting of the sphere of action in *Edward II*; and it might seem to imply a very proper concentration on the dimension of human behaviour which lends itself naturally to dramatisation. And yet it is a very different kind of naturalism from the Shakespearian; for it is without moral anchorage. Marlowe displays no faith in the natural order; he does not seem to regard it, indeed, as anything more than material to be reported, and the play, consequently, provides us with an interesting test case for the question raised in the last chapter: whether a fundamental faith in the morality of nature is not a necessary faith for the dramatist? We can examine here, in a particular context, the consequences that ensue when a playwright chooses to put 'providential' thinking resolutely behind him.

But because Marlowe 'sees no pattern in history', it is exceedingly difficult to get hold of the pattern in the play. Theoretical views of monarchy bear on it only to the negative extent that they are largely ignored. The shape of the dramatic movement does not in any obvious way reveal a general conception lying behind the plotting. We cannot even take our bearings in the historical theorising of Marlowe's contemporaries, for his apparent obliviousness to providentialism makes him a veritable phoenix of Elizabethan thought—though many were prepared to challenge it, few could affect to be unaware of the existence of providential historiography. The only way into the play seems to lie in an attempt to discover the personal sources from which it stems—the thematic nodes in the source material which could account for Marlowe's interest in it.

F. S. Boas pointed out some time ago the remarkable similarity between the political and personal situations of the king in *Edward II* and Henry III in *The Massacre at Paris*. It is a parallelism which extends, as he shows, as far as a number of quite close verbal echoes.[2] He was not, however, the first to note the analogy:

The Duke [of Espernon] was then in his Cabinet, attending the houre of masse: where hee red the history of *Pierce Gaueston*, in old time deerely fauored by *Edward* the second King of *England*, prefered before all others in Court, inriched with the Kings treasure, and the people's wealth, but after banished the realme, and in the end beheaded at the sute of the Parliament.

This slanderous libell being printed at *Paris*, not so much against the Dukes honour as the Kings, compared the Duke with *Gaueston*, and concluded that vnder Henry the third, hee should ende his daies by the like tragedie...[3]

Since the first recorded printing of these words was after Marlowe's death, it is most unlikely that he saw them—though he may have read the scurrilous pamphlet to which De Serres refers.[4] Be that as it may, the connexion made libellously by Espernon's enemies in the Holy League indicates that some assumptions, which have been very much in dispute in the interpretation of Marlowe's history play, may legitimately be made: first, that there is a path leading directly from the weak be-minioned king of *The Massacre* to King Edward II, and that to see a common preoccupation with homosexual friendship in both plays is not a post-Freudian delusion, but the kind of thing a contemporary might have noticed; secondly, that an allegation of this kind (*pace* L. J. Mills and his scholarly contentions about the normality of such relationships for platonically enlightened Elizabethans[5]) was regarded as 'slanderous', even in those broad-minded days. It is thus, from an historical point of view, entirely possible that Marlowe was attracted to the reign of Edward by the opportunity it offered him to treat a forbidden sexual deviation. Whether this is really what the play is about is a critical question that I shall try to answer by critical methods. All I want to establish here is the historical admissibility of such a view.

A second possible point-of-entry for Marlowe is one which has been frequently noted—the overreaching figure of Mortimer, who so clearly swims in the mainstream of the Marlovian heroic tradition; though (I am bound to add) one is more conscious of the considerable amplification which takes place in dramatisation, than of the fitness of Holinshed's Mortimer for the role.[6] For in Holinshed, the man is a fairly conventional aspirant for temporal power, and his method of ascent is undivulged. We are told simply that 'what he willed the same was doone, and without him the queene in all these matters did nothing'. The fullest account we get of his career is in the five articles of his Attainder, by which time it is at an end.[7] The character of Mortimer, it would seem, is less dependent on source material and more truly Marlowe's creation than most of the other characters in the play. Consequently he reveals very little about the preoccupations which sent Marlowe to this particular section of English history.

There is, however, one striking passage in Holinshed which cannot have escaped his notice, and which also forms the most obvious climax in the play—the murder of Edward. Here is Holinshed's rather too circumstantial account:

they came suddenlie one night into the chamber where he laie in bed fast asleepe, and with heauie featherbeds or a table (as some write) being cast vpon him, they kept him down and withall put into his fundament an horne, and through the same they thrust vp into his bodie an hot spit, or (as others haue) through the pipe of a trumpet a plumbers instrument of iron made verie hot, the which passing vp into his intrailes, and being rolled to and fro, burnt the same, but so as no appearance of any wound or hurt outwardlie might be once perceived...[8]

This is strong meat, so strong that the play's most recent editors question whether Marlowe dared to stage it.[9] Yet it is a fact that he specifies feather-bed, table *and* spit in Lightborn's instructions to his assistants (v. v. 29–32) and it seems gratuitous to assume that the spit was requisitioned yet not used. Clearly the whole gruesome scene is enacted unexpurgated in full view of the audience. After all, the cry of a man smothered under a feather-bed is not so horrific as to provoke fears that it 'will raise the town' (v. v. 113), nor does it leave that indelible mark in the memory of a spectator which would account for a strange digression in a State Poem by Peele—

> Edward the Second, father to this king,
> Whose tragic cry even now methinks I hear,
> When graceless wretches murder'd him by night...[10]

Since no stage direction describes the actual performance of the murder, we are justified in assuming that this ferocious execution was performed as Holinshed gives it. This is disturbing enough.

But if we look more closely at the murder we see that the physical horror masks a more profound psychological horror; for the spit of Lightborn is a diabolic phallic parody of the perversion which is hinted at in the rest of the play—the so-called 'talion' punishment which psychoanalysis has diagnosed as one *modus operandi* of a guilt-ridden mind revenging itself on the world or on itself.[11] One does not have to accept the Freudian account of such matters to feel the malign fascination of this symbolic torture, and the ferocious concept of justice which lies behind it. And it is hard to believe that a man who could pretend to read sodomy into the intimacy of Christ with St John—and on this point Kyd and Baines corroborate each other—and who accounted those 'that loue not Tobacco & Boies' 'fooles', would have been totally insensible to the significance of the punishment which a plodding Holinshed dutifully reports.[12] Though such extrinsic arguments are always inconclusive, it seems that in Edward's symbolic torture we have another at least plausible reason for Marlowe's interest in this chapter of English history.

If I say that this last point-of-entry—the murder of Edward—raises doubts in my mind, I hope I shall not be suspected of merely scenting perversion afar off and evading the issue. Partly it's an uneasiness I have about the internal balance of the play: such a blazing *fortissimo* of physical and psychic horror runs in peril of destroying whatever dynamic integrity the drama possesses. But the climax also raises questions about the pressures under which Marlowe writes. Does he, in short, *use* the homosexual motif, or does it use him? Does it simply gush up from that great storehouse of insurrectionary compulsions that goes by the name of the Unconscious? Clifford Leech, less disturbed by the death-scene than I am, has remarked,

Here in *Edward II* [Marlowe] stages the ultimate physical cruelty. He was a man who speculated on, and brought alive to his mind, the furthest reaches of human power and human suffering and humiliation. These things, he saw, men could do and had done, could suffer and had suffered, and his wondering mind gave them dramatic shape.[13]

My problem with *Edward II*, to try to crystallise the matter, is that Marlowe's mind in this play does not strike me as a 'wondering' one. Rather it is alternatively a wandering one, playing over an historical landscape in which he finds nothing to stimulate his imagination, and a compulsively driven one, delivered up to deep internal drives which he cannot bring into any satisfactory relation with the world of the human and the historical. It is as if the concerns which, in the first place, directed his attention to this reign—the weak homosexual king, the sensational violence of his death, the Machiavellian ambition of a Mortimer—take charge of his pen; and when their momentum is spent, he is obliged to trace meaningless patterns on the paper until the imaginative fit seizes him again.

This, it seems to me, is what happens to the Gaveston–Edward liaison, colourfully (if somewhat inconsistently) adumbrated in Gaveston's early soliloquies: before very long it has sunk into a lethargy of barren and repetitive protestations of love, from which it never recovers. If one must choose, the quartan fever of imaginative possession seems preferable to the lethargy. But neither is the mark of 'a man in his wholeness wholly attending'—to borrow a phrase from Lawrence. There seems a singular absence of any guiding and shaping intelligence behind the presentation of the historical material.

Perhaps I can focus this dissatisfaction by asking in what sense this is an historical play at all. We have seen that it is not historical in the religious-providential way—Marlowe is largely indifferent to the great epochal tides in human affairs, and certainly does not see them in theological terms—but this is only one way of looking at history and can hardly be regarded as the *sine qua non* of historical drama. A more serious lack in *Edward II*, as an historical play, is its consistent subjugation of the political and the public to a very narrowly conceived pattern of personal conflict. It is not, as with Shakespeare, a simultaneous vision of the political and private dimensions of the public man, but a determined attempt to ignore the political sphere. The king's fatal defiance of the duties imposed by his position ('for but to honour thee, / Is Edward pleased with Kingly regiment'—I. i. 164) is a violent insurrection against the exigencies of political existence which, though eloquent, merely comes into collision with those exigencies, without generating any new insight either in the king or in the play.

Edward II is indeed (as so many of the commentators find themselves saying) a play about a man who happens also to be a king; and the chief use to which his kingly status is put is to enhance the pathos of his situation as a man:

> Within a dungeon England's king is kept.   v. iii. 19

> They give me bread and water, being a king.   v. v. 61

This indifference to the possible significances of kingship, except as a personal cross to be borne by Edward, is one side of the coin; its obverse, by an apparent paradox, is the absence of any common human context for the political action that *is* presented. How unusual (and how refreshing) it is to find Pembroke making a little detour in order to visit his home:

> We that have pretty wenches to our wives,
> Sir, must not come so near and baulk their lips.   II. v. 102

This kind of placing of the action in a context of everyday reality, which is integral to Shakespeare's historical vision, is a stranger to Marlowe's. There is only one other scene in *Edward II* where we are made aware, as we constantly are in *Richard III*, that high-level political decisions devolve infallibly on the backs of the commonalty. This is in

the joint attack that Mortimer and Lancaster launch against the king
in Act II, Scene ii:

> MORTIMER JUNIOR. The idle triumphs, masks, lascivious shows,
> And prodigal gifts bestow'd on Gaveston,
> Have drawn thy treasure dry, and made thee weak,
> The murmuring commons overstretched hath.
>
> . . . .
>
> LANCASTER. Thy garrisons are beaten out of France,
> And, lame and poor, lie groaning at the gates.
> The wild Oneyl, with swarms of Irish kerns,
> Lives uncontroll'd within the English pale.
> Unto the walls of York the Scots made road,
> And unresisted drave away rich spoils.
>
> . . . .
>
> MORTIMER JUNIOR. Libels are cast against thee in the street:
> Ballads and rhymes made of thy overthrow.
> LANCASTER. The Northern borderers seeing their houses burnt,
> Their wives and children slain, run up and down,
> Cursing the name of thee and Gaveston.   II. ii. 155 f.

This, though rhythmically wooden, is effective enough in the way it
plots Edward's movements against the coordinates of a larger social
necessity; but it is also quite uncharacteristic. Indeed it would not be
so effective if it were not so different from the writing that surrounds it.
One feels that a great weight is being lifted off the play, and that its
terms of reference are being radically enlarged. The claustrophobic
constriction of a political action which is no more than an administrative extension of obsessive personality patterns (as much in the barons
as in Edward) begins to break up and there is movement in the air.
But it is a false dawn. The nearest we get to action on the basis of a
conception of the common weal is in the last scene, with young
Edward's belated bout of pruning in the garden of the State, and his
recognition that there is a clash between the public function and the
private nature of a king:

> If you be guilty, though I be your son,
> Think not to find me slack or pitiful.   v. vi. 81

No doubt this is to get priorities straight, but the rest of the play has
recognised the dilemma only to deny it. Although it provides a formal
coda to the piece, this final scene has no organic relation to the action it
concludes. Moreover, its function as a resolving cadence is subverted

by two very different gestures which, theatrically speaking, dominate the last few moments—Mortimer's of stoic defiance, 'Weep not for Mortimer, / That scorns the world...' and Isabella's of despair, 'Then come, sweet death, and rid me of this grief'. Marlowe's uneasiness with the kind of monarchic synthesis, which Shakespeare indulges at the end of *Richard III*, is apparent in the unfinished air of the concluding lines, which merely recapitulate a pathos of which we've already had a good deal too much:

> And let these tears, distilling from mine eyes,
> Be witness of my grief and innocency.   v. vi. 101

Young Edward's grief and innocency are neither in question nor to the point.

Of course, I am not deploring the absence of a platitudinous Richmond to tie all up in a neat parcel and bow himself out, but rather recognising the justice of the instinct which leads Shakespeare to attempt such a summation. For if we are to have more than a psychological study of faction war, if the moral meaning is to encompass more than a personal ethical dilemma, the action must be placed in a larger frame. It must be seen to have both context and consequences. The crown must become more than a symbol of personal power-lust, more than a piece of jewellery which one wears or gives away as the caprice takes one: for the abdication scene (v. i), with its now-you-see-it, now-you-don't whimsy, surely borders on the burlesque. Such a performance would be unthinkable if the crown had been imaginatively clothed with the kind of significance Shakespeare gives it—

> Here, cousin, seize the crown.
> Here, cousin,
> On this side my hand, and on that side thine.
> Now is this golden crown like a deep well
> That owes two buckets...   *Richard II*, iv. i. 181

Edward's crown is not 'a deep well' but a glittering bauble (v. i. 60), another in the long line of theatrical properties with which he has adorned himself as the player-king. It sparkles; but one cannot look down into it, glimpsing at the bottom that ghostly reflection of one's own face which is a haunting presence behind so many lines of Shakespeare's play. Nor is there any cross-fertilisation between Edward's vacillating anguish and the moral awareness of his tormentors—no more than he, can they learn anything from the experience, frozen as they are in postures of stereotyped and uncomprehending revolt. One has only to recall Bolingbroke tensed in unwilling fascination on the edge of this throne—'Mark, silent king, the moral of this sport...' —to realise how two-dimensional Marlowe's dramatic imagination really is.

Now of course many admirers of the play have noted the abdication of social responsibility implicit in the barons', and more especially in Edward's, behaviour. The difference is that they have seen it as a Marlovian insight and a masterly piece of dramatic analysis. And so it might have been, if certain conditions had been fulfilled: if, for instance, Edward's weakness had been firmly placed, if he had been presented through a dramatic verse subtle and poised enough to permit a consistent ironic detachment in the audience, if his manner of speech had made us aware of the things he didn't know at the very moment he enunciated those he did—poetic refinements, all of them, largely foreign to the verse of this play; or if there had been a dramatically realised social context which provided an implicit critique of Edward's imperfect adjustment to his public responsibilities—something we have already seen to be sadly lacking; or if Edward had been attended by a Gaunt or a York, instead of by the faceless ciphers Lancaster, Mortimer Senior, Warwick: *then* we might have had the penetrating study of royal weakness and baronial faction that these critics credit Marlowe with producing. But the activities of power are not, in *Edward II*, given a fully human context.

The serious limitations of Marlowe's conception of the human can be illustrated by a small piece of source-study. The episode in Act v, Scene iii, where Edward is shaved with puddle water, is one of the few occasions in the play where Marlowe goes outside his Holinshed for material, and it can be traced indirectly to the Latin chronicle of Geoffrey le Baker (though we cannot be sure how the passage in question was actually transmitted to Marlowe).[14] In the play, the king requests water to cool his thirst and to clear his body of 'foul excrements'. His warders offer him 'channel water' and proceed to shave off his beard, to prevent recognition and rescue. The emphasis of this short scene is principally on the humiliation and indignity of the operation—

> Traitors, away! What, will you murther me,
> Or choke your sovereign with puddle water?   v. iii. 29

and the chief effect generated is one of a generalised pathos attendant on the contrast between Edward's status and the treatment he receives. In Marlowe's source, however, there is much more.

These champions bring *Edward* towardes Barkeley, being guarded with a rabble of helhoundes, along by the Grange belonging to the Castle of Bristowe, where that wicked man *Gorney*, making a crowne of hay, put it on his head, and the souldiours that were present, scoffed, and mocked him beyond all measure, saying, Tprut auaunt sir King...[Since] they feared to be met of any that should knowe *Edward*, they bent their iourny therefore towardes the left hand, riding along the Marish grounds lying by the riuer of Seuerne. Moreouer, deuising to disfigure him that hee might not bee knowne, they determined for to shaue as well the haire of his head, as also of his beard: wherefore, as in their iourny they travailed by a little water which ranne in a ditch, they commaunded him to light from his horse to bee shauen, to whom, being set on a moale hill, a Barbar came vnto him with a basen of colde water taken out of the ditch, to shaue him withall, saying vnto the king, that that water should serue for that time. To whom *Edward* answered, that would they, noulde they, hee would haue warme water for his beard; and, to the end that he might keepe his promise, hee beganne to weepe, and to shed teares plentifully.[15]

It is possible to see why a playwright chary of official vengeance on blasphemy might omit the suggestive scene of the mock-crowning. But why, having decided to present the shaving sequence, does Marlowe suppress that intensely human gesture of Edward's as he demands—in the midst of the desolate 'Marish grounds'—warm water for his beard? Or why is nothing made of the incipiently powerful identification of warm water and tears? One is tempted to mutter piously, 'What a scene Shakespeare would have made of it!' But perhaps the truth is that Marlowe ignores these details because they are nothing to his point: this is not the kind of drama he is writing. He does not want to take us into that inner world of poignant self-delusion where royalty can only assert itself in a ludicrous demand for the luxurious appurtenances of kingship, nor to make us see in a single vision the absurdity and the dignity of Edward's nature. The marriage of the incongruous with the tragic implicit in the conceit of a king who provides his own shaving water by weeping is too deeply disturbing to subserve the effects of generalised pathos at which Marlowe is aiming here. The marriage may be native to Shakespeare's art—

> That bucket down and full of tears am I,
> Drinking my griefs...   *Richard II*, IV. i. 188

—but Marlowe is content with, indeed he is committed to, a surface pathos founded upon the simple opposition of good and evil, tyrannical oppression and innocent suffering—

> The wren may strive against the lion's strength,
> But all in vain: so vainly do I strive
> To seek for mercy at a tyrant's hand.   v. iii. 34

The activities of power are not given a fully human context: instead they are schematised in a kind of vectorial diagrammatic reduction. The world is populated by wrens and lions. The metaphor implies a kind of imaginative extremism—since there are, after all, intermediate beasts—which is magnified when we recall that only two scenes earlier it was Edward, not Mortimer, who was 'the imperial lion' (v. i. 11 f.). It seems largely a matter of convention which way the arrows in the force-diagram point; and whichever way it is, they are always the generalised components, not the unique human force they set out to account for. It is this breaking up of a complex conflict into its vectorial components, which explains those violent reversals of feeling, those inversions of the moral 'sense' of a character, of which Isabella's infamous desertion is the most familiar, and the most frequently deplored, example. For if one is committed to this kind of diagrammatic representation there can be no gradual transitions—the only angles are right-angles, and the third dimension must be systematically suppressed.

And yet, to do the play justice, the tyranny of the schematic is not ubiquitous; indeed, it is precisely because there are signs of a very human ambivalence in the first two acts that the supervention, in the second half, of over-systematic moral conceptions is disappointing. This is particularly true of the two characters who, in the last act, have hardened into mere monsters of turpitude—Isabella and Mortimer. Listen to the Isabella of Act I, pleading with the barons for the repeal of Gaveston:

> MORTIMER SENIOR. Plead for him he that will, I am resolv'd.
> LANCASTER. And so am I, my lord: dissuade the queen.
> Q. ISABELLA. O Lancaster, let him dissuade the king,
>   For 'tis against my will he should return.
> WARWICK. Then speak not for him, let the peasant go.
> Q. ISABELLA. 'Tis for myself I speak, and not for him.
> PEMBROKE. No speaking will prevail, and therefore cease.
> MORTIMER JUNIOR. Fair queen, forbear to angle for the fish
>   Which, being caught, strikes him that takes it dead.   I. iv. 214

Despite a certain metrical inflexibility, much of Isabella's torturing dilemma has been captured in the sharp reciprocating movement of the

131

stychomythia, and the whole agonising ambivalence of Gaveston's lethal attractiveness is precipitated in Mortimer's metaphor. But the precariousness of the achievement is sufficiently indicated by the next two lines, in which the tight knot of meaning is unravelled with bathetic explicitness:

> I mean that vile torpedo, Gaveston,
> That now, I hope, floats on the Irish seas.

The metaphorical fusion of ideas has given place to their whimsical association, and Mortimer's tone of earnest compassion and admonition relapses into the old monotone of inflexible opposition.

Yet however violent may seem Isabella's transition from a dogged, doomed loyalty to a conscienceless callousness (see especially v. ii. 68–74), the germs of the dramatic implausibility are already present in the verse Marlowe gives her in Act I:

> Like frantic Juno will I fill the earth
> With ghastly murmur of my sighs and cries;
> For never doted Jove on Ganymede
> So much as he on cursed Gaveston:
> But that will more exasperate his wrath;
> I must entreat him, I must speak him fair;
> And be a means to call home Gaveston:
> And yet he'll ever dote on Gaveston;
> And so I am for ever miserable.   I. iv. 178

Soliloquy in this vein may sketch the outline of a conflict but it cannot present it. Instead of an imaginative initiation into the inner condition of the speaker ('How weary, stale, flat, and unprofitable / Seems to me all the uses of this world'), we are given a succession of hypothetical reconstructions which replace each other like cards in a shuffled pack ('But that will...I must...And yet...And so...'). Figurative language does not so much explore and deepen the sense of inner conflict ('Oh, that this too too solid flesh would melt, / Thaw, and resolve itself into a dew...'), as give a kind of enamelled fixity to a rhetorical posture already chosen ('Like frantic Juno...'). The style of the verse is the poetic counterpart in unrealised intention of a dramatic action which is often no more than 'a good idea for a play'. Those who, with Clifford Leech, wish to see the Queen's betrayal as 'one of the most perceptive things in Marlowe's writing', are obliged to add, 'at least in the planning' for it is a dramatic perception deprived of a poetic body.[16]

There is a similar disappointment in the treatment of Mortimer, whose sturdy masculinity and bursts of impetuosity reveal something of an embryonic Hotspur:[17]

> Q. ISABELLA. Ah, Mortimer! now breaks the king's hate forth,
>   And he confesseth that he loves me not.
> MORTIMER. Cry quittance, madam, then; and love not him.   I. iv.193

Or this—

> WARWICK. Bridle thy anger, gentle Mortimer.
> MORTIMER. I cannot, nor I will not; I must speak.
>   Cousin, our hands I hope shall fence our heads,
>   And strike off his that makes you threaten us.
>   Come, uncle, let us leave the brain-sick king,
>   And henceforth parley with our naked swords.   I. i. 121

Yet this is another of the play's unfulfilled promises. Just as Isabella's divided loyalties are resolved by transforming her into the ferocious caricature of Act v, so Mortimer's irascible ambivalence is reduced to a monolithic and herculean Machiavellism—

> Mine enemies will I plague, my friends advance;
> And what I list command who dare control?   v. iv. 67

> Fear'd am I more than lov'd;—let me be fear'd,
> And when I frown, make all the court look pale.   v. iv. 52

> As for myself, I stand as Jove's huge tree,
> And others are but shrubs compar'd to me.   v. vi. 11

This is familiar Marlowe country and the playwright seems to be very much at home in the facilities of the old rhodomontade; but dramatically and poetically it is as much of a blind alley as the earlier characterisation of Mortimer was fraught with possibilities.

The one determined attempt Marlowe makes to grapple with the complexities of self-division—in the person of Kent—yields only a hectic series of changes-of-heart, whose rapid succession is very nearly comic. In Kent's soliloquies we are presented, not with the process of moral debate, but with its end-product, which is submitted to the usual varieties of rhetorical embellishment and inflation:

> Rain showers of vengeance on my cursed head,
> Thou God, to whom in justice it belongs
> To punish this unnatural revolt...   IV. v. 16

Since, on the last occasion we heard from him in this vein (IV. i), Kent was performing the same operation to the extenuation of the rebellion he now abhors, there is a singular lack of conviction in this apostrophe. In any case, the worthy earl barely has time to establish which side he is on now, before he is whisked away to vacate the stage for those monuments of undeviating will in whom Marlowe is so much more interested.

Yet the preoccupation with Mortimer and his kind is hardly justified. They are not so much characters as character-postulates, aggregations of certain selected characteristics, like a child's drawings with the guiding lines left in, or, in Rossiter's phrase, 'fractional-distillations of Man, not men'.[18] This bondage to generalised and simplified outline is apparent even in Marlowe's attempts to represent complexity of motive— Gaveston, within forty lines of declaring himself desirous of dying on Edward's bosom, is busy devising means to 'draw the pliant king which way I please' (I. i. 53), and there is no dramatically realised 'self' in the lines which could mediate between the passionate lover and the cynical opportunist in his character. The two traits are simply juxtaposed and we (or the actor) must make of it what we can. (A skilful director can indeed make a great deal of it, but he should not fool himself that he is interpreting Marlowe. He is merely making up Marlowe's mind for him.) Anyway, it's not long before the genuinely individual in Gaveston—his superb effrontery, for instance, when he parries Isabella's 'Villain! 'tis thou that robb'st me of my lord', with 'Madam, 'tis you that rob me of my lord' (I. iv. 160)—is submerged by the spring tide of lamentation which laps about the whole play, until the characters can only 'stand metaphorically back-to-back and bawl and counterbawl about their fates to the stars'.[19]

With many of the characters there is not even as much raw material of human ambiguity as we find in Gaveston. The baronial opposition is from the start frozen in the least interesting of postures, and condemned in its utterances to a monotone of recrimination, as they inveigh interminably against 'that base and obscure Gaveston', 'accursed Gaveston', 'that villain Gaveston', 'that base peasant', 'hateful Gaveston', and so on. Succumbing to the creeping paralysis, Edward responds with equally tedious praises of 'my Gaveston', 'sweet Gaveston', 'my dearest Gaveston', thus bogging the action down in the elaboration of feelings which have passed beyond all possibility of modification or growth.[20] It is hard to imagine anything less instructive than this head-on collision of meaningless obsessions. Nor are we much further forward when the Spencers replace Gaveston, for the same peevishly repetitive malice is diverted into the new channel with hardly a break in the steady flow of abuse. The Spencers, we are told (twice), are revelling in 'England's wealth and treasury' (IV. iv. 27 and IV. v. 61), but since Marlowe ignores Holinshed's fairly detailed accounts of these depredations, the hostility of the barons remains a mere postulate, a piece of creaking plot machinery unrelated to the favourites we actually see on the stage.

I suppose there are admirers of *Edward II* who would be prepared to admit most of these charges, but who would, at the same time, invite us to consider the crucial case of Edward himself as an exception to such strictures. This view is sufficiently general to demand consideration and I had best begin by indicating the extent to which it is true. For there are several points, in the first two acts particularly, where Marlowe strikes a chord rich with possibilities of development. In each case the suggestiveness derives from an objectification of feeling, an ironic detachment, which makes it possible for us to contemplate Edward steadily and dispassionately, instead of being swamped in a hot wave of generalised emotion.

In the fourth scene, Edward has been raining titles and offices on the implacable barons in a vain attempt at conciliation. He goes on, in the stony silence which has greeted his concessions,

> If this content you not,
> Make several kingdoms of this monarchy,
> And share it equally amongst you all,
> So I may have some nook or corner left,
> To frolic with my dearest Gaveston.   I. iv. 69

In these lines, the extravagance of Edward's affection ('Ere my sweet Gaveston shall part from me, / This Isle shall fleet upon the Ocean, / And wander to the unfrequented Inde'—I. iv. 48) makes a decisive break with an extravagance native to Marlowe's style (the 'fleeting land' conceit is an old weapon in the Marlovian armoury—See *Dido*, IV. iv. 134–5) and stands firmly in its own dramatic right. For the first time we begin to *see* Edward, to sense that appalling inner vacuum which makes him fling kingdoms about like dust in the wind. We see that his dedication to the personal values of friendship is a neurotic dedication to pure nullity—that telling verb 'frolic' occurs several times in this connexion (cf. I. ii. 67 and II. iii. 17)—a last frantic attempt to build banks against the black wave of emptiness and self-doubt that rises against him. The poignancy of the last two lines is due in part to his unadmitted knowledge that no such 'nook or corner' exists in the real world. An intense personal anguish is released a few lines further on, when Mortimer questions in exasperation, 'Why should you love him whom the world hates so?' and the king replies,

> Because he loves me more than all the world.   i. iv. 77

This is a genuine *cri de coeur* (contrast the rhetorical posturing implicit in a line like 'O shall I speak, or shall I sigh and die!'—iii. ii. 122) and its effect is arresting. Again we find ourselves really *hearing* Edward on the emotional level where human sensitivity is activated. The vision of agonising *ab*normality functions normatively in directing attention to the springs of true feeling, here irremediably fouled and muddied.

The other example I would like to adduce is an external and hostile view of the same internal turmoil; yet its visual immediacy and precision of observation make it an imaginative gateway to the same insight:

> When wert thou in the field with banner spread?
> But once, and then thy soldiers march'd like players,
> With garish robes, not armour, and thyself,
> Bedaub'd with gold, rode laughing at the rest,
> Nodding and shaking of thy spangled crest,
> Where women's favours hung like labels down.   ii. ii. 180

Through the lens of Mortimer's contemptuous masculinity—'When wert thou in the field...But once, and then...'—our doubts about Edward are sharply focused in details of costume, in diction keen as a scalpel—'bedaub'd', 'spangled', 'labels'—and in a verse movement which is superbly gestural—'nodding and shaking of thy spangled crest'. The tinsel flimsiness of Edward's very triumphs revives again the sense that he treads a thin crust of glittering ice which, if it cracks, will plunge him into the black waters of self-negation—though here it is the political implications of his psychic malady that are stressed.

If we put these two passages together we have the germ of a powerful tragic encounter, in which neither the personal dimension is sacrificed to the political, nor the social vision obscured by the inward vision, but in which they exist in a mutually enriching symbiosis. Why then do we not get it—for even the play's loudest advocates talk of pathos rather than tragedy?

Pathos, indeed, has a great deal to do with the failure of *Edward II*; for pathos is a paralysed form of imaginative sympathy, a self-imposed embargo on all ways of looking at the subject but one—the pathetic. Before I attempt to give an account of the 'why' of this substitution of pathetic *attitude* for tragic *insight*, it would be well to examine the 'how'. What means does Marlowe use to elicit this pathos?

The process can be studied most fully in the Neath Abbey scene (IV. vi), where the king is finally overtaken by his pursuers.

> O, hadst thou ever been a king, thy heart,
> Pierced deeply with sense of my distress,
> Could not but take compassion of my state.
> Stately and proud, in riches and in train,
> Whilom I was, powerful, and full of pomp:
> But what is he whom rule and empery
> Have not in life or death made miserable?
> Come, Spencer; come, Baldock, come, sit down by me;
> Make trial now of that philosophy,
> That in our famous nurseries of arts
> Thou suckedst from Plato and from Aristotle.
> Father, this life contemplative is heaven.   IV. vi. 9

The chief effect of this passage—and it is entirely representative of the Edward of Acts IV and V—is to force us to surrender the tragic insights given in the kind of writing I've just been discussing. We, through the Abbot whom Edward addresses, are urged insistently to abandon that hard-won detachment, and to indulge in a very simple kind of identification—'O, hadst thou ever been a king...'—'Put yourself in my shoes'; and the moral duty of a 'compassion' which swallows up all distinct apprehension of its object is made to supersede the more painful obligation to see weakness for what it is. A generalised, and so anaesthetising capitulation to the *de casibus* cycle is to replace our very clear perception of what it really means to be 'stately and proud, in riches and in train'—that is, to be 'bedaub'd with gold...laughing at the rest, /Nodding and shaking of thy spangled crest...'. It is only by dint of forgetting that it is '*mis*rule and empery' that has made Edward miserable, that we can receive fully the voluptuous gratification of indulged emotion which this passage offers (and I take it that Marlowe wants us to receive it, since he repeats the strategy so often as the play draws to an end). Philosophy, we note, is not the art of understanding reality, but simply a means of keeping an intolerable reality at bay, a 'life contemplative' conducted in monastic isolation from the world. The very personalities of the real world are taboo here:

> Mortimer, who talks of Mortimer?
> Who wounds me with the name of Mortimer,
> That bloody man?

And then follows a most revealing passage:

> Good father, on thy lap
> Lay I this head, laden with mickle care.
> O might I never open these eyes again,
> Never again lift up this drooping head,
> O never more lift up this dying heart!

Friends and foes of Marlowe alike regard this as a central passage; but what does it amount to? Isn't it the old, old song of the lotus-eaters, the drug-pedlars, the death-worshippers? Certainly it presents nothing precisely, with its 'drooping heads' and 'dying hearts'; its rhythms are the rhythms of rhetorical anaesthesia—'O might I never...Never again ...O never more...'; it is the child's lapse out of responsibility on the lap of a 'good father'.

In the nature of things, it is difficult to demonstrate (what I believe to be the case) that Marlowe is trying to carry us, along with Edward, into the phantasmic world of oblivion. But we are entitled to ask where else, if not in the broken king, the imaginative centre of gravity is located. Is it in Mortimer? Isabella? in vacillating Kent? Clearly not, yet all the other central characters are mere shadows of Edward's grief. Nor is the answer to be found in the energies of the verse; for it has lost its capacity for dramatic presentment and has become either enervated and bonelessly 'lyrical', meandering in a despairing arc of subordinate appendages—

> I wear the crown, but am controll'd by them,
> By Mortimer, and my unconstant queen,
> Who spots my nuptial bed with infamy;
> Whilst I am lodg'd within this cave of care,
> Where sorrow at my elbow still attends,
> To company my heart with sad laments,
> That bleeds within me for this strange exchange; v. i. 29

or violently emotional, with such drastic imprecision that one is hard put to it to guess what effect was aimed at—

> For such outrageous passions cloy my soul,
> As with the wings of rancour and disdain
> Full often am I soaring up to heaven,
> To plain me to the gods... v. i. 19

or (a short step) we are back in the old 'Stygian vein' of *Tamburlaine*—

> A litter hast thou? lay me in a hearse,
> And to the gates of hell convey me hence;
> Let Pluto's bells ring out my fatal knell,
> And hags howl for my death at Charon's shore.   IV. vi. 86

Much of this is no more than Marlowe's familiar stylistic vices at large again. As Mortimer is made to remark, in an attempt to apply the brakes to the runaway carriage of high-astounding diction, '*Diablo!* What passions call you these?' But when the verse does get a grip on itself, it does so primarily to enforce our acquiescence in Edward's self-destructive pilgrimage to Killingworth:

> Whither you will; all places are alike,
> And every earth is fit for burial.   v. i. 145

It is not 'Whither you will, so I were from your sights'—Richard's anguished protest against an intolerable humiliation—but 'Whither you will; all places are alike...'—a capitulation so complete that Edward almost ceases to exist as a human entity. To call this tragic is to strain the word too far from its proper usage.

With the explicit emergence of this strain in the play, the life-denying stoic abdication of the human, we are very near to grasping the central failure of *Edward II*. Wilson Knight has observed that 'Marlowe, like Tamburlaine, is a king-degrader';[21] but *Edward II* sets me (for one) wondering whether he is not also a man-degrader. What other motive can be advanced for staging the exquisite humiliation of Edward's death? Why else the long enumeration of the squalid conditions of his incarceration in Act v, Scene v? What possible satisfaction can the spectator derive from that scene, unless it is the satisfaction of seeing 'inhuman cruelty presented more or less for its own sake'?[22]

Several attempts have been made to resist the force of this argument. Miss Mahood would have us believe that Marlowe is displaying, with impartial tragic insight, the self-destructive dynamic of 'false humanism'. But such a demonstration would require a moral framework within which the self-destructive dynamic worked itself out, and to which it was referred, and this Miss Mahood fails to locate.[23] Clifford Leech claims for Marlowe's exhibition of suffering, a dispassionate scientific objectivity:

There is no theory here which Marlowe illustrates, no warning or programme for reform, no affirmation even of a faith in man. The playwright merely directs our attention on certain aspects of the human scene...[24]

But if this is what it means to have 'no theory', it can hardly be claimed as a virtue in a playwright. It seems almost indistinguishable from having no point of view—and indeed this is the clearest impression I have of the Marlowe who wrote *Edward II*, that he has no firmly-grounded centre of consciousness from which to conduct his exploration of human life. And thus the obsessive and the compulsive is free to burst into surface conflagration until it has burnt itself out—as in the anti-papist frenzy of Act I, Scene iv, the anti-clerical animus of the bishop of Coventry sequence (I. i), or in the images of violent destruction which need surprise only those readers unacquainted with Marlowe's chronic partiality for circumstantial bloodiness:

> If I be England's king, in lakes of gore
> Your headless trunks, your bodies will I trail,
> That you may drink your fill, and quaff in blood,
> And stain my royal standard with the same,
> That so my bloody colours may suggest
> Remembrance of revenge immortally...   III. ii. 135

We cannot pretend that the mild Edward is the real speaker of these lines.

But the most disturbing thing that bubbles up in the dark pool of the playwright's consciousness is an ecstatic impulsion to 'do dirt on humanity', to humiliate and grind into the dust, and then again to humiliate. I am not disputing that the process generates a good deal of theatrical power—though that power is somewhat dissipated by the bludgeoning monotony of it all—I am questioning the health of the imagination which so dwells on it.

It was known before the age of psychoanalysis that misanthropy was the uneasy bedfellow of self-contempt and guilt, and I am making no revolutionary proposal if I suggest that there is a strange congruency in the fates of Edward, the dabbler in sodomy, and of Faustus, the religious sceptic, which might be accounted for as a neurotic desire for symbolic punishment and expiation. If this were merely a matter of biographical curiosity, such a theory might well remain unexpressed. But it is worth serious consideration if it enables us to offer an account of puzzling features in the play *qua* play—the unbalanced and apparently motiveless violence of its catastrophe, for instance; or Marlowe's fascinated circling around objects in his consciousness which Wilson Knight has characterised as 'things at once hideously suspect yet tormentingly desirable',[25] things like the homosexual theme, or the sadistic horrors of Edward's last days (Swinburne, disciple of de Sade, once observed that Marlowe was not exempt from a certain 'hideous lust of pain').[26] It's precisely because it is a 'circling' that the psychodynamic hypothesis is so tempting, since one distinguishing mark of neurosis is a simultaneous incapacity either to leave the painful subject alone or to do anything constructive about it. The irrelevant outbursts of violence are similarly intelligible if we posit a creative process disrupted by explosions and eruptions of the unresolved tensions below the level of consciousness.

But there is another way in which a 'psychiatric' explication of the play is useful. We are confronted in *Edward II* with a drama which, despite its manifest crudities and its obsessive repetitiousness, has an unholy fascination. I have tried to show that the fascination, whatever else it may be, is not the fascination of maturity and genius, and I am accordingly bound to offer some explanation of opinions like Hazlitt's that the final scenes are 'not surpassed by any writer whatever'.[27] Such views have gained wide currency. Now we are familiar enough with the fascination exercised by a psychological aberration which is also intelligent and articulate—the reputation of the later Tennessee Williams (to name only one case) is almost entirely founded on this fascination with disease. When we succumb to the fascination, we confuse the deep satisfactions of great imaginative literature with the idle pleasure of indulging our curiosity about the fringes of human sanity. Delirium is, so to speak, mistaken for the authentic poetic 'frenzy', and neurotic intensity is confounded with imaginative power.

This, I submit, is the kind of mistaken response which leads critics to place a high *literary* value on the last two acts (particularly) of *Edward II*. They have been led by the fascination of the neurotically intense to ignore the extent to which it is dependent on imaginative malfunction —on a neurotic over-insistence on a half-truth about the human condition. It is the function of criticism, however, to stand for health in the broadest sense of that term: and I wonder, as I read those critics who give way to the fascination of *Edward II*, whether they have not abandoned this function and constituted themselves apologists for the neurotic elements that, in an imperfect world, are to be found in the best of us.

Be that as it may—and I do not claim to have demonstrated anything —*Edward II* fails to address itself to much that is human in us; it uses a shrunken language to tell a tale of men who are less than men. Which makes me the more surprised to find the editors of this play, Charlton and Waller, who have hitherto sturdily resisted the blandishments of the critical establishment, agreeing at the end of their (otherwise) excellent Introduction that *Edward II* is superior to *Richard II*—though, to their credit, they do so grudgingly:

It is no doubt futile to make too close a comparison between Shakespeare's loosely-built drama with its wealth of discursive poetry and Marlowe's grimly realistic tragedy. No doubt the latter is the better play and leaves the sharper impression on the mind; it has less grace, less poetry, less humanity, but more power and a better form...[28]

This is astounding. These editors have shown themselves alive to the 'formalist fallacy' which has led to so exaggerated an estimate of *Edward II*; they have conceded that the playhas 'no moral pattern', that it operates by means of a 'complete detachment from ordinary human sympathies', and that it displays 'the inhumanity of *Tamburlaine* or *The Jew*, without the *élan*, the poetry, the *amour de l'impossible* which makes us forget temporarily their extreme exaggeration'.[29] And then we are exhorted to prefer it to *Richard II*! What can 'power' mean, if it is independent of 'grace', 'poetry', and 'humanity'? It would seem that it is as I have argued: the 'grim realism' is a function of inhumanity.

But this is a degradation of the term 'realism' as much as it is of the term 'humanity'. Marlowe's is no more than the reporter's realism, the kind which finally shirks a whole dimension of the real—the moral. The equable tone in which Marlowe enunciates his horrors, the strange bareness of diction, is not the result of a classical restraint, or of some new discipline of art: it is a kind of indifference both to humanity and to art. The play is amoral, not by intention, but by default.

One cannot finally avoid making moral discriminations: one can only be betrayed into superficial and inconsistent ones, by pretending not to be making them. One cannot dispense with the concept of purpose in human affairs: one can only become an unwitting apostle of meaninglessness by affecting to ignore it. Marlowe's attempt to do without the conceptions of moral order of his own day deprived him of dramatic, as well as moral, logic. It left his play a prey to all the disordered forces of personality which lie in wait for the man who loses sight of the elusive and fine-drawn filament of purposiveness, without which life is a mere labyrinth, and consciousness a Minotaur.

SHAKESPEARIAN HISTORY:
CRITIQUE OF 'ELIZABETHAN POLICY'

If there were no other connexion between Marlowe's *Edward II* and Shakespeare's *Richard II* it could be fairly conclusively demonstrated that the reigns of these two kings were linked in Elizabethan historical imagination as *loci classici* of deposition, and consequently they were constantly being called in evidence in disputes about the subject's right to rebel or the king's duty to govern. The advocates both of royal absolutism and of the right to resistance agree to regard them as test cases for their theories.[1] Yet Marlowe, as we have seen, is largely indifferent to this kind of interpretation. The nearest approach to political preoccupation in his play is Mortimer's tautological

> For howsoever we have borne it out,
> 'Tis treason to be up against the king;   I. iv. 280

which precedes a plan for evading popular condemnation on this score, while still rebelling. Rebellion for Marlowe is a necessary pre-requisite for the kind of overreacher he makes out of Mortimer, but the rebellion is conceived as a kind of personal and moral insurrection against the human condition which, because it has no imaginatively cogent social context, is almost totally devoid of political content.

Shakespeare's *Richard II*, on the other hand, appears at times to be remembered only for its political statements—whether Gaunt's patriotism or Richard's version of the Divine Right of Kings—so that it has become important to be clear what we mean when we talk of *Richard II* as a 'political' play. In an obvious sense the designation has some point: the play's most memorable scene is a ceremony of deposition taking place in Parliament; the morality of resistance is a crucial issue for nearly every character in the play—from York to Bolingbroke; even Richard's personal disaster is continually presented as 'kingly woe' and, as was not the case with *Edward II*, we are made to feel that the kingly component in his grief is both central and real:

> Oh that I were as great
> As is my grief, or lesser than my name!

Or that I could forget what I have been!
Or not remember what I must be now!　　　III. iii. 136

Yet there's such a thing as having too much of a half-truth—or so I find myself reflecting as one scholar informs us that Shakespeare 'uses Richard II as the accepted pattern of a deposed king...to set forth the political ethics of the Tudors in regard to the rights and duties of a king', or that Gaunt's scene with the Duchess of Gloucester (I. ii), since it 'does not further the action', 'can have been introduced only to restate the Tudor theory of kingship'. It may be, as Professor Campbell alleges, that *Richard II* is 'a play dealing with the problem of the deposition of a king'; but as one follows her bleakly from one Shakespearian political 'formulation' to the next (with passing regrets for the finer passages represented here only by a vestigial trail of dots) and sees each sentiment neatly labelled and disposed—'accepted Tudor philosophy', 'a proper scene to introduce a play of kingship', 'the orthodox Tudor position', 'York replies with sound doctrine', 'the most important pronouncement of the divine right of kingship'—one has sneaking regrets for the play which had once been a source of pleasure. Illicit pleasure, if we are to believe Professor Campbell, who is very stern in the reproof of 'democratic' views of the equality of critics and readers—views which would absolve us of the depressing necessity of submitting to her scholarly expertise.[2] Nor is *Richard II* a special case. In a similar way, it appears, native intelligence unenlightened by scholarship is prone to miss the point of the Henry IV plays, in which

a series of comic interludes interrupts the continuity of the historical pattern... and because these interludes have been built about the character of Falstaff, they have obscured the history play they were meant to adorn...Falstaff is historically an intruder though certainly a 'delectation'.

So sharp is the division between the 'historical' and the 'delectable' that Falstaff is only admitted to Professor Campbell's study under the cautionary sub-heading: 'The Problem of the Soldier'.[3]

I have mentioned this extreme example of the politico-historical interpretation of Shakespeare partly because it is representative of an alarmingly prevalent trend in the work that is being published on the Histories (and so needs refutation), but also because it indicates to what absurd conclusions one may be led if one neglects to check the formulated 'doctrine' of a play qualitatively against a sense of its imaginative totality. This is, of course, the subjectivity Professor Campbell deplores, but it can hardly lead us further astray than her historicist assumptions have led her; and it may on the other hand preserve for us the *Richard II* which is a source of insight and pleasure.

But before attempting to define this imaginative totality, there is more to be said about the political orthodoxy which is, in Professor Campbell's disquisition, a mere fixed point of reference. It is not merely that she has assumed an extremely simple and direct relationship between Elizabethan political speculation and Shakespeare's historical *oeuvre*—even to the extent of deducing his purposes in writing the plays from current views on the political uses of history[4] (she entitles her book *Shakespeare's 'Histories' : Mirrors of Elizabethan Policy*); like Tillyard and Ribner she has also fastened, in her exposition of 'the Tudor theory of kingship', on a single aspect of sixteenth-century political theory—what might be called the Administration's ego-image—and labelled it 'orthodoxy'. If this designation is correct, either the Tudor propaganda machine was one of unparallelled efficiency, or else the Elizabethans were sadly deficient in independence of mind and critical awareness—neither of which was the case.

There is plenty of evidence that Elizabeth's subjects were uneasy about the tendency of monarchic power to subordinate all traditional restraints to 'The Will of the Prince'. In an interesting didactic piece, dating probably from the last years of Elizabeth's reign, Fulke Greville, Lord Brooke, discriminates sharply between the 'Youth' of a state, when kings 'striue to improue...fraile humanity', and its dotage, when 'though Kings, *Player*-like, act Glorious part, / Yet all within them is but Feare and Art'. Power, in the latter kind of state, is a mere husk from which the kernel of mutuality has been removed. And in another poem, Greville gives a precise account of the process by which power is emptied of all real content:

> Our modern Tyrants, by more grosse ascent,
> Although they found distinction in the State
> Of Church, Law, Custome, Peoples gouernment,
> *Mediums* (at least) to giue excesse a rate
>   Yet fatally haue tri'd to change this frame,
>   And, *make Will law, Mans wholesome lawes but name.*[5]

Clearly, then, Professor Campbell's conception of 'orthodoxy' neglects an important distinction between the spirit of the Tudor version of divinely-sanctioned kingship, and the medieval view upon which it was, to some extent, parasitic. John Danby puts it well: in both, he suggests, absolute obedience was enjoined on the individual to both his temporal and his spiritual overlord. This obedience was urged in the name of an ideal order, compact of Reason and Nature. The Middle Ages supplied feasible grounds for such an obedience. The absolute principle was in fact vested in institutions. Society by intention aimed at equity and the realisation of the absolute shape. Heresy consisted in denying the Spirit rather than the letter of the law. Ideally, the social configurations were not themselves absolute... Under the conditions of Tudor Despotism the medieval world-view became, however, less credible. Heresy now consists in challenging the letter of the social order in the name of any spirit whatsoever. Authority is vested in a person. Elizabeth is absolute in the realms of both Pope and Emperor. She claims, in addition, to be the Virgin Queen. According to her Homilies rebellion is always and absolutely wrong... By the sixteenth century the argument for unconditional obedience becomes more and more an ideology and less and less a way for the spirit. It is political propaganda in moralistic disguise. The duties imposed are the will of the Prince not the will of God. Under the Tudors the discrepancy between the ideal programme and the actual performance—apparent even to the Friars in the Middle Ages—is more obvious than ever... Society was supposed to be an ideal order—Troilus' Cressida. The same system in actuality could behave like Diomed's bitch.[6]

One may object that the change is not in the 'actuality' but in men's ability and willingness to recognise it; but the two changes are connected, and their effect is cumulative: a new cynicism in political behaviour produces a new hard-headedness in political observation. But the existence of this hypercritical cloud of witnesses in turn drives the administration into increasingly naked appeals to 'the will of the prince', giving rise eventually to hysterical propaganda of the kind represented by the 'Homily against Rebellion'—the harried tone of which gives clear indication of the growing influence of the forces it opposes.[7] What these forces were I cannot go into here. What they drew upon, however, is very much to the point.

Although it less and less answered to the realities of political existence, the medieval ideal continued to be invoked with varying degrees of disingenuousness, and thus it was able to remain 'in suspension', as it were, in that extraordinary fluid compound we call Elizabethan culture. As a body of political commonplace it was available for transformation by the individual into more than a polemic platitude—into a coherent and creative vision of man in society. Throughout the sixteenth century there were men who held the old ideal with a humane breadth of vision which liberated them to contemplate the shortcomings of their own particular politic order.

So much that is valuable has been written on the subject that one can afford to be sketchy, suggesting the flavour of the medieval view as it survived in Shakespeare's England, rather than attempting to chart its total configurations. The origins of society, for this view, are not to be traced to expediency,[8] to the subordination of brutish man to an order which, though aimed at his benefit, is not rooted in his nature (though Hooker, interestingly, adopts the Hobbesian position that positive human law must presuppose the will of man to be 'obstinate, rebellious, and averse from all obedience unto the sacred laws of his nature; in a word,...presuming man to be in regard of his depraved mind little better than a wild beast';[9] and in this he points forward rather than backwards); but rather society originates in a natural desire for communion, for the 'good of mutual participation' which Hooker mentions elsewhere,[10] and the political order is subordinate to that fullness of personal life which it is intended to serve:

For hither tendeth all prudence and policy: to bring the whole country to quietness and civility, that every man, and so the whole, may at last attain to such perfection as by nature is to the dignity of man due...[11]

These words, given to Thomas Lupset in Starkey's dialogue of the 1530s, show how naturally the medieval emphasis on the personal ('every man, and so the whole') could be wedded to Renaissance conceptions of 'the dignity of man'. It is continuity of a fruitful and significant kind.

As long as the political order subserves a rich individual human life within that order, the stress in doctrines of rule must fall on responsibility rather than prerogative. 'Power and reygne is, to haue many, whom thou mayste succour and ayde in ryght and honestie', said Vives.[12] The familiar metaphors of rule—the prince as father of the commonweal, as its physician, as the life-giving sun—all emphasise his responsibility rather than his right. The magistrates, for Calvin, had been 'appointed protectors by God's ordinance' of the 'freedom of the people'—a conception which (to anticipate a little) led him to a qualified defence of the magistrate's right to resist the prince.[13]

The rights of the prince, then, are something given him so he may exercise his paternal function the better. But they are given him by the people, in whom the ultimate sanctions of sovereignty reside. Hooker, in a section aimed at demonstrating the king's lawful supremacy in ecclesiastical matters, nevertheless gives full weight to the contractual conception:

Unto me it seemeth almost out of doubt and controversy, that every independent multitude, before any certain form of regiment established, hath, under God's supreme authority, full dominion over itself...God creating mankind did endue it naturally with full power to guide it self, in what kind of societies soever it should choose to live...and that power which naturally whole societies have, may be derived into many, few, or one, under whom the rest shall then live in subjection.

And elsewhere,

By the natural law...the lawful power of making laws to command whole politic societies of men belongeth so properly unto the same entire societies, that for any prince or potentate of what kind soever upon earth to exercise the same for himself, and not either by express commission immediately and personally received from God, or else by authority derived at the first from their consent upon whose persons they impose laws, it is no better than mere tyranny.

Laws they are not therefore which public approbation hath not made so...[14]

There were ways around this stout contractualism which the apologists of absolutism were quick to sniff out; but they were all obliged to pay it lip-service, so deeply grounded was it in the national consciousness.

The fundamental reality, then, was the human mutuality and sociable accord in which man fulfilled his potentialities, and the king was important only in so far as he symbolised the total aspirations of the whole.[15] The sun was accorded the highest place in the heavens because it shone, because it fructified, because it gave light and heat to the whole world, and that exalted position simply enabled it to perform this function the better.

The sacredness of the king was not an arbitrary dogma: it expressed, in the way that came most naturally to a culture dominated by theological modes of thought, the sacredness of that mutuality of which he was both protector and symbol. It was not in his 'body natural' that he was divine, but in his 'body politic'; and the body politic was a mystical unity in which every member of the commonwealth was incorporated. The death of one subject was the loss by the king of 'one of his mystic Members'. The rights of the subject form an indivisible organic unity with the rights of the king: for Shakespeare's King Richard to 'take Herford's rights away' is for him to destroy the foundations of his own power, not simply in terms of the possible consequences, but because he has violated the natural law which binds human society into one irreducible whole—it is tantamount to not being himself (II. i. 195–9). The attribution of quasi-divine status to the king was thus not so much the deification of mere flesh and blood (as Richard would have it) as an insistence on the permanence and transcendent value of the *corpus mysticum* (or, in modern terms, the social organism, the solidarity of mankind) the significance of which was somehow gathered up into, and incarnated in, the king's body politic.[16]

Tudor absolutism, in its extreme and defensive manifestations, was a sadly gelded version of this mutuality, in which right had been divorced from responsibility, the contract cancelled, and in which duty devolved exclusively upon the subject. Like Shakespeare's Richard II, the Tudors tried to retain the sacredness of status without fully accepting the sacred function. They rejected, above all, the notion that failure to be fathers and physicians to the commonweal jeopardised their claim to absolute obedience. It is not surprising, in view of this, that the portrait of an unjust king insisting noisily on the sanctity of his kingship caused alarm amongst Elizabeth's senior counsellors—it was a little too close to the bone, even without the suspicious connexion with Essex. The fascinating fact, however, is that Shakespeare, by placing the advocacy of the old divine kingship in the hands of an unstable Richard and the older generation of statesmen, reveals his awareness that it can no longer stand unqualified. I shall be returning to the matter of divine right in the more particular context the play provides, but we may note here that Shakespeare's endorsement of the *ideal* is complemented by an acute awareness of its uneasy relationship to hard political facts.

The rarefied atmosphere of medieval political theology is, however, only a part of the political air that Shakespeare breathed; for he wrote the history plays towards the end of a century of bitter and acrimonious debate. And when we descend from the Hookers to the prolific tribe of clerical propagandists, a radical disparity of temper is immediately manifest. Conceptions which, in the genuine thinkers, had been a real attempt to crystallise the nature and significance of human society, become on this level mere tools of polemic. But it is not simply that most sixteenth-century political writing is crudely propagandist and as such can throw little light on the things for which we value the Histories; there is something more important here. It is that the didactic aims and the barrenly polemic tone of these tractates result in the evasion of the very issues which make the bone-structure of Shakespeare's 'political thought'. The plays provide evidence that Shakespeare has pondered the unproductive violence of political controversy in his age and has seen through it to the deeper issues it evades. But we will appreciate his intelligence better by pausing for a moment over these minor figures.

The first thing that strikes one on turning to the writers who figure in a study like Christopher Morris's *Political Thought in England: Tyndale to Hooker* (London, 1953) is (with few exceptions) the extreme thinness of the material. Political *rationalisation* there is a-plenty, but of political thought precious little. In fact it would be more helpful than misleading to describe the bulk of the pronouncements about the subject's right to resist a tyrant—to take a key issue—as the resultant of the writer's personal religious commitment and the faith of the reigning monarch. One has only to consider how the protestant insistence, under Henry, on the duty of *submission* 'for conscience' sake', becomes, under Mary, the duty of *resistance* 'for conscience' sake', to realise how extensively the theory is moulded by the personal dilemma of the theorist. And with the second reversal which brought Elizabeth to the throne, the rationale of resistance passes bodily from the protestant Ponet (say) to the Jesuit Parsons, with scarcely a jot of modification.[17]

Post-Reformation political theory is founded on an inherent contradiction. The extirpation of popery was achieved partly by appealing to private conscience as final arbiter in matters of religion; but, the Reformation once accomplished, conscience must necessarily be commanded to discontinue its revolutionary activity. The trouble was that conscience the dog, once roused, would not to kennel, and it remained to plague its masters with its unpredictable vagaries throughout the next two centuries.

Henry and his advisers, in fact, impaled themselves on the horns of a very old dilemma: every soul must be obedient to the powers that be (so St Paul urged—Romans xii. 1); yet equally clearly Christians, like the Apostles, must obey God rather than men (Acts v. 29). It was obviously true that men must render unto Caesar the things that were Caesar's, and to God the things that were God's, but how were men to know which was which? It is characteristic of sixteenth-century political theorising not only that this question is never satisfactorily answered (perhaps it never could be), but that the problem is scarcely acknowledged to exist, each writer simply regarding as irresistible the higher duties which his own conscience commended to him. But it is equally characteristic of Shakespeare to be continuously preoccupied with the rival claims of private conscience and public weal (see, for example, *Richard II*, ii. iii. 139 f.). He could never have been guilty of the evasive naïvety of the French authors of the *Vindiciae Contra Tyrannos* (1579), for instance, who claim to

> obey *Caesar* while he commands in the quality of *Caesar*: but when *Caesar* passeth his bounds when he usurps that Dominion which is none of his own,... they then esteem it reasonable not to obey *Caesar*...[18]

The frequency with which Caesar's 'bounds' are invoked in this way is only equalled by the stubbornness with which the invokers refuse to define them. Shakespeare, by contrast, is continually placing us in situations where, through a Gaunt, a York or a Bolingbroke, we are forced to decide whether Richard is commanding 'in the quality of Caesar', or whether he 'usurps that Dominion'. The answers, understandably, are not immediately extractable, but their obscurity is due rather to the innate complexity of the problems than to any real evasion of the issues.

Shakespeare, indeed, voices the dialogue of sixteenth-century political controversy much more clearly than he adjudicates between the two sides. Take Gaunt's colloquy with the Duchess of the murdered Gloucester in Act I, Scene ii, where the official doctrine of submission— 'Put we our quarrel to the will of heaven...'—is confronted by the Duchess's urgent demand for action. It has been customary to assume that Gaunt here speaks for the author and for the play as a whole, as if this were the only line that the playwright could take. But for every Bilson who threatens subjects with 'damnation by Gods own mouth if they resist', every Carpenter who exhorts us when oppressed to 'arme our selues with patience' and to 'pray to God for redresse', there is a Parsons to remind us that 'God wil not alwayes bynde himselfe to woorke miracles, or to vse extraordinary meanes in bringing those things to passe, which he hath left in the hands of men, & of common wealthes to effectuat, by ordinary way of wisdome and iustice', or a Goodman to urge the people to take the judicial sword in their own hands when the magistrates 'cease to do their duetie', in the confidence that 'God...him self is become immediatly their head (Yf they will seeke the accomplishment of his Lawes) and hath promised to defende them and blesse them'.[19] And not only is Gaunt's doctrine simply one of several alternatives available to Shakespeare, it is opposed in this scene by a conception of family solidarity which has just as deep roots in Elizabethan thought, and which is given equally potent poetic expression. We can only regard his prohibition of rebellious activity as finally binding if we are deaf to the plangent power of the Duchess's 'Desolate, desolate, will I hence and die'.

The absolute opposition of conservative and radical opinion on this matter of resistance to the ruler is due to the evasion of a consideration which was well put by George Buchanan in 1579. It may be true, he argues,

that God, angered at the people, sends tyrants...who punish those who deserve to be punished...but it is equally true that God has called poor and almost unknown men from the ranks of the common people to execute vengeance on an arrogant and worthless tyrant.[20]

The issue really is not whether the prince may be opposed—comes a change of government and, handy-dandy, which is the true-man? which is the rebel?—but what conditions constitute sufficient provocation for opposition. What conditions transform the malignant rebel into a divine minister, the patiently borne 'scourge of God' into an intolerable instrument of Satan? From Gaunt, through York, to Bolingbroke, Shakespeare gives us the whole range of possible answers to this question, and frees them furthermore from their dangerous bondage to abstraction by presenting them to the imagination embodied in a personal moral dilemma. There is a concreteness about his dramatic gift which prevents him making the pedant's mistake of regarding a political theory as more important than, or even separable from, the man that holds it: the focus is on political man, not political theory. But the indirect result of this concentration is a particularity and an awareness of complexity which constitutes the most important kind of 'political thought'. It is a reminder that, though summary and doctrinaire solutions may avail in books, they will not avail in life.

It is hard to conceive of a greater contrast than that between the clear-cut prescriptive utterance of the theorists, and the rhythmically-evoked uncertainties of York:

> If I know how or which way to order these affairs,
> Thus thrust disorderly into my hands,
> Never believe me. Both are my kinsmen:
> Th'one is my sovereign, whom both my oath
> And duty bids defend; th'other again
> Is my kinsman, whom the king hath wrong'd,
> Whom conscience and my kindred bids to right.
> Well, somewhat we must do.   II. ii. 109

York inherits the insoluble problems bequeathed by a century of theory which had concerned itself exclusively with general questions of abstract right, and he expiates in mental anguish the intellectual pusillanimity of the theorists.

It would be possible to show at length how all the key questions posed by the deposition of Richard are given contradictory answers in the political writings of the sixteenth century—how monarchy is, for the conservative thinkers, divinely ordained, a result of a direct delegation of power from God, to whom alone the king, who is the Lord's anointed, is accountable;[21] while for the writers who (for one reason or another) find themselves in opposition, monarchy is a mere matter of expediency in a particular society,[22] a result of the people's delegation of power by means of a contract which binds the king as much as it binds the people;[23] how the divine right of the king is opposed by a conception of the king under the law;[24] how the king's right to the property of his subjects is affirmed by some,[25] denied by others;[26] how some feel that royal status is only justified if it reflects personal worth,[27] while for others the king's personal attributes are irrelevant:

> Though kinges forget to gouerne as they ought,
> Yet subiectes must obey as they are bound;[28]

how royal absolutism is for some a blasphemy,[29] for others a glorious and beneficent institution;[30] how for some the king who must be obeyed is the legally succeeding heir, all other claimants being usurpers, while others see the duty of Christian submission as equally binding in the case of a *de facto* king like Bolingbroke;[31] how the very deposition of Richard is given a series of different interpretations, ranging from the view that it is a primal sin which brought civil war to English Eden, to the view that the accession of Henry IV was God-ordained;[32] how there are even a few discordant voices to remind us that the legality of the Tudor monarchs themselves is dependent on the legality of the deposition of that 'lawful king' Richard III.[33] But these barren controversies—barren because neither party takes cognizance of the views of the other, except as a position to be rebutted—are so remote from the ambiguous, morally puzzling world of *Richard II* that it seems pardonable to pass over them in order to focus attention on the real questions which are obscured by the hot clouds of polemic.

When, for instance, John Carpenter distinguishes evil laws that 'are to be yeelded vnto for conscience sake' from 'diuellish, vngodly and superstitious lawes and decrees' which 'nature, reason and autenticall examples...teach men that they obserue not',[34] we know well enough what he means —a crude distinction between civil legislation and popish tyranny. But how is the man of good-will to decide when the tyrannous shades off into the blasphemous, especially when so many discordant voices offer to instruct him? Can we estimate the justice of the cause, by studying the motives of the partakers? For instance, if we grant, with Parsons, that 'wicked mē...troblesome...for their owne interests and appetits' should not gain the ear of a good subject, but only those who rebel 'vppon iust and vrgent causes',[35] how does one tell them apart, since the wicked and troublesome men invariably claim just and urgent causes? So at least York is forced to ponder when he meets his nephew at Berkeley (II. iii); and the discrimination is not made any easier for him by the presence of that arch-opportunist Northumberland in Bolingbroke's entourage. Bolingbroke's causes may be just and urgent, but is not Northumberland troublesome for his own interest and appetite? The inextricable mingling of just grievance with illicit ambition in the rebelling party is one of Shakespeare's personal contributions to an understanding of the real nature of sedition.

Again, it may be, as the authors of the *Vindiciae* claim, that 'that must euer be accounted just, which is intended only for the publique benefit, and that unjust, which aimes chiefly at private commodity', but rebels are not in the habit of declaring the 'private commodity' at which they indubitably aim; and I have yet to discover the rebellion which was not abundantly equipped with arguments from 'the publique benefit'. Neither is it particularly helpful in so complex a business of sifting motives to be informed that the unjust party is to be detected by the fact that they 'breake the Lawes, and protect those that violate justice, and oppresse the Commonwealth'.[36] In a period of political crisis these are the very questions which are unanswerable: What are the laws? Where is justice? Justice to whom, anyway? In the world of *Richard II* king and rebels alike have broken the laws and violated justice; indeed it is precisely in such soil, where injustice has run riot, that sedition takes root. The trouble with a dictum like Goodman's, that only 'just' power is God-ordained,[37] is that it excludes everyone from grace, since justice to the many will always entail injustice to a few. How does one do in a world riven with faction, where kings are men, and rule over men who are, as Richard complains, at times little better than beasts? Everyone would agree with Ponet that 'the princes watche' *ought* to

defende the poore mannes house, his labour the subiectes ease, his diligēce the subiectes pleasure, his trouble the subiectes quietnesse. And as the sunne neuer standeth still but continually goeth about the worlde, doing his office...so ought a good prince to be continually occupied in his ministerie not seking his owne profit, but the wealthe of those that be committed to his charge;[38]

but do we depose him when he fails to discharge this god-like function? If not, it is necessary for the Bolingbrokes of this world to explain when, and why, the mere human fallibility of a prince becomes culpable and deposable folly, since, as Thomas Bilson observes, God requires 'many things in a prince, the breach of which is not deposition'.[39]

And if we admit the possibility of rebellion upon just causes, we must be prepared to define the authority upon which the rebel proceeds; else the simplicities of sworn allegiance hold the only key to the situation:

> My Lord of Herford here, whom you call king,
> Is a foul traitor to proud Herford's king...
>
> And you that do abet him in this kind
> Cherish rebellion, and are rebels all.
>
> *Richard II*, IV. i. 134 and II. iii. 145

This task of re-defining the sanctions of monarchy Bolingbroke conspicuously fails to undertake, and the result is a profound uncertainty about the legitimacy of the rebel's cause.

And if, following Bishop Ponet's plenary absolution, a private man 'commaūded or permitted by common autoritie vpon iuste occasion and common necessitie' kills the tyrant, does the ethical problem end there?[40] Exton thought not, with his 'would the deed were good!'. Indeed, as Ponet himself observed, albeit in a different connexion,

it is not the mannes waraunt that can discharge the, but *it is the thing it selfe that must iustifie thee*. It is the mater that will accuse thee, and defende thee: acquyte thee and condemne thee: when thou shalt come before the throne of the highest and euerlasting power, wher no temporal power will appeare for thee, to make answer or to defende thee: but thou thy self must answer for thy self, and for what so euer thou hast done. And therfore christen men ought well to considre, and weighe mannes commaundementes, before they be hastie to doo them...[41]

'The thing it selfe' is indeed the core of Exton's (and Bolingbroke's) self-accusation.

Nor is any but the most rigid doctrine of legitimacy a solution to these problems; for, as that wise man Sir Thomas Smith points out, there are princes that are tyrants by entry but kings by administration (Henry IV perhaps?); others succeed lawfully but are tyrants nevertheless (Richard III?); and some 'both in the comming to their Empire, and in the butte which they shoot at, be kings, but the maner of their ruling is tyrannical' (Richard II?).[42] It is in such a fog-bound world, from which all the traditional landmarks have been removed, that York gropes for integrity and fails to find it. Nor can we blame him. There is an extraordinary and appropriate tenderness about Richard's gesture of understanding:

> Uncle, give me your hands; nay, dry your eyes—
> Tears show their love, but want their remedies;   III. iii. 202

for Richard himself is lost in the same half-lit territory of moral confusion.

If then we are to talk of Shakespeare's Histories as reflecting 'Elizabethan policy', it is not the resonant platitudes of the 'Homily against Rebellion' or the propagandists we have been considering that can be adduced with any show of relevance. All these writers have, in one way or another, come to grief in 'the narrow Channel' Edmund Bolton mentions,

which now and then shifting it self, as the Sands about remove, doth notwithstanding evermore lye between that *Scylla* of the Peoples Liberty and the *Charibdis* of Royal Prerogative; which, being in some parts thereof invisible, and in others illimitable, brings present Destruction...[43]

They have been betrayed by their own simplifications. It is rather to the wary ambiguities of a Thomas Smith—significantly, a professional diplomat, not, like most of our other authors, a clerical propagandist —that we must turn to find a historical temper comparable to Shakespeare's.[44]

The basic political reality, for Smith, is a state of flux:

For the nature of man is neuer to stand still in one maner of estate, but to grow from the lesse to the more, and decay from the more againe to the lesse, till it come to the fatall end and destruction, with many turnes and turmoyles of sicknesse and recouering, seldome standing in perfect health, neither of a mans bodie it selfe, nor of the politique bodie which is compact of the same.

'With many turnes and turmoyles of sicknesse and recouering, seldome standing in perfect health'—it might be the epigraph at the head of Shakespeare's Histories; just as another of Smith's *dicta*, as he discusses whether a corrupt state should be overthrown, might provide an epilogue:

The iudgement of the common people is according to the euent and successe: of them which be learned, according to the purpose of the doers, and the estate of the time then present. Certaine it is that it is alwayes a doubtfull and hasardous matter to meddle with the chaunging of lawes and gouernement...[45]

The amalgam of empirical openness with a kind of agnostic caution is characteristic of the best political thinkers of the period ('to bear a tolerable sore is better than to venture on a dangerous remedy' is the quintessence of Hooker's conservatism).[46] And we are here very close to the political climate of *Richard II* which, though it is a play that *exploits* the clear-cut principles of the sixteenth-century propagandists, is subtly and pervasively sceptical about those absolute rights and wrongs so readily bandied about in a century of fierce political debate. What Shakespeare perhaps adds to the amalgam is an awareness, incipiently tragic, of a kind of historical necessity against which even the best type of conservatism is ultimately powerless—the necessity is called Bolingbroke.

9

SHAKESPEARE'S POLITICAL
AGNOSTICISM: 'RICHARD II'

I

One of the things that remains with me most strongly after a performance or a reading of *Richard II* is a sense of the riddling complexity,
almost the inextricability, of justice in the world Shakespeare has
presented. The trouble begins in the first scene. Richard wants to be
certain that in Bolingbroke's quarrel with Mowbray he is dealing with
'some known ground of treachery' and not with 'ancient malice'. But
not surprisingly, in view of the paradox inherent in the concept of
'*known* treachery', Gaunt can only offer an approximate sifting of his
son's motives, and it is Richard who gives us the certainties of the
encounter:

> High-stomach'd are they both and full of ire,
> In rage, deaf as the sea, hasty as fire.   I. i. 18

And if there is a slight air of amused condescension about this characterisation, it is nevertheless not much help in clarifying the issues.

This, however, is no more than a prelude to the introduction of an
offstage character whose disturbing presence in a way broods over the
entire action—the dead Duke of Gloucester.[1] Bolingbroke makes the
matter appear relatively plain: Mowbray, he alleges, plotted Gloucester's
death,

> And consequently, like a traitor coward,
> Sluic'd out his innocent soul through streams of blood.

     I. i. 102

But the context is highly suspicious. The charge follows a piece of
blustering rhodomontade where extreme conventionality and the sense
of a prepared speech ('First—heaven be the record to my speech...
Now Thomas Mowbray do I turn to thee...') is matched by an
extraordinary silence about the crimes that have provoked this storm
of abuse. There follow fifty-odd lines of mutual recrimination before
Richard finally manages to bring Bolingbroke to the point: 'What
doth our cousin lay to Mowbray's charge?' And then the king sows
new doubts by adding, in a style as high-flown as Bolingbroke's,

> It must be great that can inherit us
> So much as of a thought of ill in him.   I. i. 85

Furthermore, Bolingbroke's accusation is followed by lines revealing both an incipient arrogance which regards the castigation of vice as a personal prerogative, and an inflated, over-dramatic sense of personal righteousness:

> Which blood, like sacrificing Abel's, cries
> Even from the tongueless caverns of the earth
> To me for justice and rough chastisement;
> And, by the glorious worth of my descent,
> This arm shall do it, or this life be spent.   I. i. 104

(In scripture it was to Jehovah that Abel's blood cried from the ground—Genesis iv. 10.) This may be the tone demanded by convention in these circumstances, but it is none the less disturbing.

Clarification, however, appears to be imminent, for Mowbray, having answered with circumstantial precision the first charge of misappropriating state funds, turns to the second matter. But instead of clarification we get—

> For Gloucester's death,
> I slew him not, but to my own disgrace
> Neglected my sworn duty in that case.   I. i. 132

What sort of an exculpation is this? Was his 'duty' to prevent the murder? Or to perform it? To whom was it 'sworn'? And why did he 'neglect' it? Perhaps he did not slay the unlucky duke, but the duke was slain. One's instinctive impulse is to scan the faces of the assembled company, each of whom, since he is content to let this pathetically inadequate 'explanation' pass without comment, is suspect of knowing more of the matter than he cares to say. But, as if by tacit agreement, Mowbray is not pressed to expand his cryptic statement, and very shortly we are to see Richard attempting with an uneasy flippancy to cover the sore with a plaster—

> Forget, forgive, conclude and be agreed:
> Our doctors say this is no month to bleed.   I. i. 156

—and Gaunt abetting him in what is patently a muffling-up of abuses.

Now it is commonly assumed either that Shakespeare, careless in his exposition, has forgotten to give us the facts of the case, or that he assumes in his audience a knowledge of history which will clear up the whole mystery. The first hypothesis I neglect, as it seems positively the last resort of criticism; but the second is so often propounded that it needs an answer. It should be remembered, then, that Holinshed is a very bulky book, the reign of Richard alone occupying a hundred-odd folio pages of double-column text; that there are in its pages many dukes of Gloucester, and even professional students of the work suffer from some initial confusion about their identities; that this particular Duke of Gloucester does not get very extensive treatment, and what treatment he does get suggests that he was one of those 'too fast growing sprays' that might reasonably have been trimmed by the royal shears;[2] and that very few playgoers prepare for their afternoon's entertainment by reading the play, let alone its verbose and tedious source. It is worth noting, too, that—as is not the case with certain teasing questions in the other Histories—we cannot refer back to Shakespeare's own dramatisation of the events for an 'authorised version'. I assume, therefore, that most of Shakespeare's audience was dependent on the playwright for all but the broad outlines of the plot, that Shakespeare knew this, and that he deliberately put this scene of obfuscation and mystification *before* Act I, Scene ii (which shows some signs of dispelling the mystery), because he wanted to establish, right from the start, the moral impenetrability of the political order. He was in fact cultivating that special alertness in an audience, which springs from the necessity to take bearings in territory which is not only new and strange, but explicitly treacherous. Listened to in this spirit, the first scene leaves us with a bewildering assortment of contradictory impressions, not only about the Gloucester affair, but also about such matters as Richard's ability personally to fill out the dignity of his office, the extent to which Mowbray's honour is a rhetorical affectation, or the significance of Bolingbroke's appeals to his 'descent'.

The trial by combat, however, with its public procedure, established ritual, and martial sublimation of private rancours, promises, if not a final clarification of these confused matters, at least their decent interment. There is a clean impersonality about the conduct of affairs, the offer of a fresh start: after the turbid confusions of the first scene, the ceremonial anonymity of the combatants is refreshing. Mutual recrimination gives way to formula, hysterical defiance to the incantations of the two Heralds; the event is framed by protocol and punctuated with fanfares. The combatants respond to this new atmosphere with positive gaiety.[3] Mowbray, 'sprightfully and bold, / Stays but the summons...' (I. iii. 3–4); Bolingbroke, 'lusty, young, and cheerly drawing breath', couches his farewell to his father in a banquet metaphor. Gaunt responds with an exuberant paternal benediction. But it is

Mowbray who catches most precisely the sense of liberation from a
crushing, stifling subjugation to indirection and subterfuge:

> Never did captive with a freer heart
> Cast off his chains of bondage, and embrace
> His golden uncontroll'd enfranchisement,
> More than my dancing soul doth celebrate
> This feast of battle with mine adversary.   I. iii. 88

It is all very infectious stuff, so that when the king throws his warder
down it is not just Bolingbroke and Mowbray who are bitterly
disappointed: we too feel ourselves being dragged back into the morass
of concealed motive and 'misbegotten hate'. The formality appropriate
to the execution of justice has transmuted itself into the suspect
formality of the staged act of state—for there is something inescapably
histrionic about Richard's exquisite timing of this *coup*. Policy has
supervened upon the 'feast of battle'.

The king's explanation of this startling decision is even more unsatisfactory (I. iii. 125–44):[4] for though he appeals against the horrors
of 'civil wounds plough'd up with neighbours' sword' to an ideal of
peace, peace is conceived here as a sweet sleeping infant who must not
be waked—thus confirming our suspicions that order is preserved in
Richard's England only by dint of political sedation—and war is
presented less in terms of destruction and bloodshed, than as an
aesthetically displeasing cacophony of 'boist'rous untun'd drums',
'harsh-resounding trumpets' dreadful bray' and 'grating shock of
wrathful iron arms'. The fastidious grace of figure hints at an inappropriate detachment in the speaker. And although 'eagle-winged
pride', 'sky-aspiring and ambitious thoughts' and 'rival-hating envy'
may answer to much we have been noting in Bolingbroke and Mowbray, a justicer more confident in his justice could have dispensed with
a few of those compound epithets. The sense that rhetorical resplendence
masks an obscure malady is frequent in this play—whether we are
hearing Northumberland's sugared phrases in praise of Bolingbroke
(II. ii. 6–18), or Bolingbroke's elaborate declaration of submission to
Richard (III. iii. 32–61).[5]

Into such a prepared atmosphere Mowbray's heart-felt plaint, with
its hints of a submerged continent of past association, if not complicity,
falls with double force:

> A heavy sentence, my most sovereign liege,
> And all unlook'd for from your Highness' mouth;

> A dearer merit, not so deep a maim
> As to be cast forth in the common air,
> Have I deserved at your Highness's hands.   I. iii. 154

It takes a very determined regophile to avoid feeling that Mowbray's punishment—so feelingly evoked as an alienation from all that dimension of human intercourse which relies on the friendly arts of language —is too cavalierly imposed, a misgiving which is strengthened when Richard, on a whim, makes the disproportion between the two sentences even more glaring. The sense that there is something radically amiss just below the surface becomes acute when the king extracts what is, in effect, an oath of perpetual enmity from the two rivals:

> You never shall, so help you truth and God,
> Embrace each other's love in banishment,...
> Nor never write, regreet, nor reconcile
> This louring tempest of your home-bred hate...   I. iii. 183

If this is what peace sounds like as it 'draws the sweet infant breath of gentle sleep', there is something to be said for terminating its slumbers.

The first three scenes thus establish a moral climate—indirection, obscurity of motive, the promise of clarification which is, in the event, withheld, and a profoundly uneasy sense that no one really holds the reins of justice. I would like to mention one other instance in the play where Shakespeare returns to this theme, particularly because it is frequently dismissed as an irrelevance: I mean the quarrel-scene which opens Act IV. That this is a thematic development is made plain by its obvious parallel with the first scene—the tabling of accusations, the wordy warfare of challenge, and the visual parallelism provided by the down-flung gages, besides of course the royal (or quasi-royal) arbiter who provides so instructive a contrast with the Richard of the first scene. But there is more to the parallel than an edifying comparison of administrative acumen with bungling amateurism. Consider precisely what happens when Surrey steps briefly centre-stage and shouts,

> As false, by heaven, as heaven itself is true.   IV. i. 64

The scene has opened with the disconcerting spectacle of Bagot (last seen flying to join the king in Ireland) now in Bolingbroke's Parliament, apparently protected, accusing another of Richard's friends of— amongst other things—disaffection to Bolingbroke! This new political line-up cannot fail to produce some initial disorientation in an audience's mind. The agenda states that the deliberations are about Gloucester's death; for despite all the confident assertions on the part of Gaunt and York, the jaws of justice are still chewing on this indigestible morsel. Richard's attempt to close the matter had simply banned discussion by the same token as it had banished those who had broached it. Now apparently Bolingbroke is determined to drag the matter to the light and finally lay the aggrieved ghost of his murdered uncle. But Bagot's 'evidence' is a ramshackle affidavit: apart from the personal rancour which smoulders visibly below the surface ('My Lord Aumerle, I know your daring tongue / Scorns to unsay what once it hath delivered'), Aumerle is quoted as having entertained disparaging thoughts about the banished Bolingbroke, at 'that very time' that Bolingbroke was not banished, nor likely to be.

Nevertheless, a certain elucidation seems to be at hand as one noble after another comes forward to confirm the main outline of the charge. At this point, Surrey, simply an anonymous 'Another Lord' to us in the audience, joins the baying pack, has his credentials approved —''Tis very true; you were in presence then, / And you can witness with me this is true.' The delirious accelerando is at its peak. And then Surrey drops his bombshell. It is a superb *coup de théâtre*, and one calculated to remain in the minds of an audience much more firmly than its overt importance would suggest. As Shakespeare gives us it, there is not much doubt of Surrey's bona fides: he emerges as the champion of unpalatable truth prepared to face the joint fury of the liars, while Fitzwater, who has headed the pack, falls into incoherent mouthings—'he lies, / And lies, and lies'—before giving way to the ultimate feebleness—'Besides, I heard the banished Norfolk say...' (There was another boy too, but he ran away!) What then does this powerful theatrical climax say? To me it says, as plainly as may be, 'Don't look for full explanations, clear conceptions of right and wrong, or even for justice in this environment. They are not to be had.' Fitzwater indeed, with a devastatingly unconscious irony, gives us a lucid diagram of the forces at work:

> As I intend to thrive in this new world,
> Aumerle is guilty of my true appeal.   IV. i. 78

In proportion as he intends to thrive, to that precise extent Aumerle becomes guilty. Reputation, honour and integrity are all subject to the mechanics of ambition. Bolingbroke, at whose *fiat nox* the 'new world'

has come into being, knows well enough what all these protestations
are worth:
> Little are we beholding to your love,
> And little look'd for at your helping hands.   IV. i. 160

I would argue, therefore, that there is a moral obscurity about the
play which is more than a result of the complexity of the issues faced
by the characters: it is an opacity in the texture of the drama which has
been deliberately cultivated—most notably in the case of Bolingbroke's
rebellion—a matter to which I now turn. Shakespeare can seldom have
thrown so little light on a key motivation as he does on the process by
which Bolingbroke moves towards his goal (if indeed we can be sure
that the throne of England *is* his goal—so ill-lit is this territory). And
he does this, I suggest, because he is directly concerned with the
almost palpable darkness in which the politic mind shrouds itself.
'Opportunism', as Brents Stirling reminds us in an excellent essay on
Bolingbroke's quest of the crown, 'is essentially a tacit vice', and 'although the opportunist is aware in a sense of the ends to which his
means commit him, he relies upon events, not upon declarations, to
clarify his purposes.'[6] Or, as John Palmer puts it, Bolingbroke 'never
permits himself to have a purpose till it is more than half fulfilled'.[7]

Our uncertainty about his real motives dates from the very first
hint of his return from banishment (II. i. 224 f.). Northumberland, who
has constituted himself head of the reception committee, offers Ross
and Willoughby so many different inducements to go with him 'in
post to Ravenspurgh'—ranging from righteous indignation at Herford's
wrongs, through chagrin at England's declining role in European
affairs, to a very self-regarding fear for their own financial skin—that
we are in no position to know upon which of these grievances the lords
are acting. The ambiguity is most intense in what looks like Northumberland's manifesto of the rebel cause:

> If then we shall shake off our slavish yoke,
> Imp out our drooping country's broken wing,
> Redeem from broking pawn the blemish'd crown,
> Wipe off the dust that hides our sceptre's gilt,
> And make high majesty look like itself,
> Away with me...   II. i. 291

We never discover whether this is an offer to reform Richard, or
whether the king himself is the pawn-broker, the dust on the sceptre
(the possible pun on 'guilt' makes the confusion worse) which is to be

'wiped off'.[8] Is 'high majesty' to be rehabilitated in Richard's person or by finding a new incumbent for the throne? When we add to this, the fact that Bolingbroke is announced to have his invasion force already mustered, in the same scene where Richard proposed the seizure of his lands, we are ready to add a pinch of sceptical salt to Northumberland's protestation in a later scene that 'the noble Duke hath sworn his coming is / But for his own...' (II. iii. 147–8). We have been led to see Bolingbroke's return as the rallying signal for all the elements of discontent in England—whatever *his* ostensible (or real) motives may be—and no number of formal declarations can completely obscure this vision.

Bolingbroke's entire campaign is dotted with *ad hoc* policy statements of this kind, run up hastily for the occasion, designed to answer immediate objections without ever becoming involved in larger moral questions (cf. especially the meeting with York in II. ii). Half the time they come, not from his own mouth, but from those of his supporters, while he stands silently by—Richard's characterisation of the usurper as the 'silent king' crystallises for the audience much that is puzzling about his nature. It is startling but true that, as one critic points out, 'we discover in the end that he has taken Richard's throne without ever directly accusing him of anything'.[9] This is inescapably the same world as that in which Richard is the one person who never, by word or deed, acknowledges that the Duke of Gloucester is dead.

Thus in a play about deposition Shakespeare has (apparently deliberately) withheld from scrutiny one half of the moral equation—the motives of the rebel. It is as if we had here a first sketch, a mere outline, of the somnambulist power-lust of a Macbeth: Bolingbroke too 'moves like a ghost' 'towards his design', and his ominous silence is, as it were, the state of soul which is given voice in Macbeth's speech:

> Let not Light see my black and deepe desires:
> The Eye winke at the Hand; yet let that bee,
> Which the Eye feares, when it is done to see.
>
> *Macbeth*, I. iv. 51

But precisely because the silence is never interpreted within the play —except perhaps in the final speech—the task of balancing Richard's kingly rights against Bolingbroke's neglected duty becomes extremely problematical. One can neither be wholly glad for Bolingbroke's regal qualities, nor entirely condone Richard's unregal ones. One is tempted to fall back on the Gardener's external estimate of the situation as a fairly literal 'balance of power', in which 'their fortunes both are weigh'd' (III. iv. 84–9) or to accept Richard's image of Fortune's buckets:

> Now is this golden crown like a deep well,
> That owes two buckets, filling one another,
> The emptier ever dancing in the air,
> The other down, unseen, and full of water.   IV. i. 184

It is a mean image for a mean process in which one man's 'lightness' is another's 'heaviness', where the 'emptier' man is always in the ascendant, and into which personal worth hardly enters. And although Richard here reverses the Gardener's judgment about whose scale is the heavier, he agrees to regard the operation of political fortune as entirely capricious. This, of course, is not the final word on the subject, but I have chosen to emphasise first the extreme dubiety which surrounds the discussion of legitimacy and justice in *Richard II*, because it strikes me as one of the primary impressions one takes away from the play.

II

But the rights of a king are not just an external political matter, and they can only be regarded thus by dint of a separation of person and office which this play most emphatically does not make. Shakespeare is as much concerned with the quality of the adjustment his political man makes to this world of moral opacity and obscure inequity, as he is with the world itself. And the second salient feature of *Richard II*, as I see it, is the fact that no one in the play seems to have found a way to make his peace with that world: certainly not York, or his even more confused son, Aumerle; not Bolingbroke; Gaunt's solution is only possible because he can presume on 'an ague's privilege'. Not even Richard (*pace* the worshippers of the 'martyr-king' or the 'royal poet') has been able to find a mature, responsible, fully human way of preserving his integrity in face of the threatening realities of political life. Each makes his own characteristic and disastrous capitulation.

To start with Bolingbroke. We have seen that Shakespeare's treatment of the man is largely a series of vast lacunae, so that the understanding of his character is dependent on the tricky business of interpreting his silences. But they are silences of a definite shape and outline and they are filled out by the overt acts of state which separate them, or —sometimes more revealingly—by the garrulity of his comrades-in-arms. In fact there is a good deal on which to build an estimate of the man. His silences are, to put it sharply, the void where moral consciousness should be at work.

Bolingbroke has, broadly, two modes of utterance: the one a rhetorical, somewhat elaborate mode of public justification, courtly compliment or formal sententiousness—

> As I was banish'd, I was banish'd Herford;
> But as I come, I come for Lancaster   II. iii. 112–13

> I count myself in nothing else so happy
> As in a soul rememb'ring my good friends   II. iii. 46–7

> Where'er I wander boast of this I can,
> Though banish'd, yet a true-born Englishman   I. iii. 308–9

—the style which Hotspur is later to characterise as 'a candy deal of courtesy'; the other is a strongly contrasted, terse, clipped utterance, in Rossiter's phrase, 'the voice of the efficient staff officer'[10]—'My Lord Northumberland, see them dispatch'd' (III. i. 35); 'I thought you had been willing to resign...Are you contented to resign the crown?' (IV. i. 190 and 200); or 'But for our trusty brother-in-law and the abbot... / Destruction straight shall dog them at the heels' (V. iii. 135–7). Both styles, be it observed, proceed from the 'official' man and not from the deeper levels of consciousness; and if the voice of command is less offensive than the voice of courtesy they are both, nevertheless, the products of calculation—the smiling or frowning transposition of the same incurably public tonality. Until the last scene of the play Shakespeare gives us little hint that there is a man behind the official mask: he is simply one of those 'who moving others, are themselves as stone', 'the Lords and owners of their faces'.

Nevertheless, a close scrutiny of Bolingbroke the courtier can tell us a good deal. We discover, for instance, that his submissiveness is a scrupulously modulated effect which he will not expend unnecessarily on (say) a Berkeley:

> My lord, my answer is—to Lancaster,
> And I am come to seek that name in England,
> And I must find that title in your tongue,
> Before I make reply to aught you say.   II. iii. 70

This is plainly the arrogant reality that York detects, a few lines later, in the kneeling figure of his nephew:

> Show me thy humble heart, and not thy knee,
> Whose duty is deceivable and false.

BOLINGBROKE. My gracious uncle—
YORK. Tut, tut! grace me no grace, nor uncle me no uncle,
    I am no traitor's uncle.   II. iii. 83

But even without York to prompt us with his shrewdness, the uneasy
liaison of formal obeisance with the pride of 'braving arms' is plain
enough, especially in Bolingbroke's instructions to Northumberland in
Act III, Scene iii:

> Noble lord,
> Go to the rude ribs of that ancient castle,
> Through brazen trumpet send the breath of parle
> Into his ruin'd ears, and thus deliver:
> Henry Bolingbroke
> On both his knees doth kiss King Richard's hand...
>
>   III. iii. 31

The insolent blast of the 'brazen trumpet', with the correlated contempt
for the 'ancient castle' of royalty, has a swaggering lilt about it as it
sounds in Richard's ruined ears (Coleridge was certainly correct to
regard the ambiguity of the possessive adjective as purposeful) and
delivers its full-line fanfaronade of self-estimation: 'Henry Bolingbroke!'[11] This martial flourish forms a sinister commentary on the
large gesture of submission (why 'on *both* his knees'?), which is
further amplified when Northumberland, the bearer of the message,
significantly fails to kneel to Richard at all.

These two contradictory strains persist throughout the speech:

> If not, I'll use the advantage of my power
> And lay the summer's dust with showers of blood
> Rain'd from the wounds of slaughter'd Englishmen—
> The which, how far off from the mind of Bolingbroke
> It is such crimson tempest should bedrench
> The fresh green lap of fair King Richard's land,
> My stooping duty tenderly shall show.   III. iii. 42

The insulting march of triumphant force, scarcely masked by the
enamelled artificiality of 'crimson tempests', 'fresh green laps' or
'grassy carpets', is held in check by a thin syntactical thread—'The
which...'. And the contradiction gradually becomes cynically overt, as
Bolingbroke proposes to 'march without the noise of threat'ning
drum', a parody of peace,

> That from this castle's tottered battlements
> Our fair appointments may be *well perus'd*.   III. iii. 52

All this is caught up in the thunder image (ll. 54–60) where the domination-theme, with its emphasis on 'terror' and 'thund'ring shock', has completely swamped the sham submissiveness. Boling-broke's description of himself as 'yielding water' is patently at odds with the thought which has provoked the image, and he has great difficulty in extracting himself from the rebellious implications of his utterance. (If the Quarto spelling 'raigne' in line 59 is correct, he does not extract himself at all.) [12]

Such lapses in his public *persona* are rare, but they do help to reinforce Richard's damaging portrait of the vote-catching politician in Act I, Scene iv, 'Wooing poor craftsmen with the craft of smiles', as a necessary tactic in a campaign aimed at egocentric aggrandisement on a really vast scale:

> Off goes his bonnet to an oyster-wench;
> A brace of draymen bid God speed him well,
> And had the tribute of his supple knee,
> With 'Thanks, my countrymen, my loving friends'—
> As were our England in reversion his,
> And he our subjects' next degree in hope.   I. iv. 31

Formulations like *the craft of smiles*, *his supple knee*, help to crystallise our sense of this man who is all outside, as does York's reprise of this tune in the last act—when there is no longer any suspicion of distorting malice in the speaker: 'whilst he, from one side to the other turning' (note the sharply observed gesture of the great man being consciously gracious),

> Bare-headed, lower than his proud steed's neck,
> Bespake them thus, 'I thank you, countrymen'.   v. ii. 19

There are frequent occasions in the play when we are made aware like this of a Bolingbroke who tends lovingly his public image; a Bolingbroke who, for instance, at the moment of arrogating to himself the kingly prerogative of weeding the garden of the state, is at great pains to clear himself 'here in the view of men' (III. i. 6). The justifica-tion he offers for his execution of Bushy and Green is full of carefully calculated effects: first, he parades a chivalrous magnanimity towards Richard—

> a prince, a royal king,
> A happy gentleman in blood, and lineaments,
> By you unhappied...   III. i. 8–10

—which he has never displayed in his real relations with the king; he al-ludes darkly to unspecified misconduct which has 'Broke the possession

of a royal bed, / And stain'd the beauty of a fair queen's cheeks'—
thus casting himself in the role of Protector of Wronged Womanhood,
and Stern Castigator of Moral Degeneracy, without being obliged to
relate this lurid picture to the apparently harmonious relationship that
subsists between Richard and his queen.[13] It is in this situation, significantly, that Bolingbroke adumbrates the Pilate image which dogs him
to the end of the play (cf. v. vi. 50): his aim in this public display of
righteousness is, he tells the condemned men, 'to wash your blood /
From off my hands' (III. i. 5–6). But guilt cannot be dealt with exclusively on the public level, and Richard with immense force is later to
turn Bolingbroke's image against him:

> Though some of you, with Pilate, wash your hands,
> Showing an outward pity—yet you Pilates
> Have here deliver'd me to my sour cross,
> And water cannot wash away your sin.   IV. i. 239

And, we might add, no more can 'a voyage to the Holy Land' wash
the blood from a hand that is really 'guilty' (v. vi. 49–50), for this is
still expiation on the public level.

Richard's symbolic revenge upon his rival is to make him enact in
public the deed which he has all but obscured from 'the view of men'
by his careful attention to the euphemistic forms of political existence—
he makes him 'seize the crown'. Bolingbroke, understandably, is
abashed at so naked a declaration of illicit purpose, and has to be jogged
into action: Here, cousin, seize the crown.
> Here, cousin...   IV. i. 181

The tableau Richard proposes ('on this side my hand, and on that side
thine') exposes Bolingbroke's discreet campaign as one man's brazen
attempt to wrest a golden bauble from the grasp of another. His
hesitation is the hesitation of a man who knows that this is one deed he
cannot simply 'bid his will avouch'. It is the hesitation of guilt.[14]

But apart from the inner emptiness which Bolingbroke's window-
dressing leads us to suspect, that skilfully cultivated image is considerably
tarnished by the methods he is obliged to use and the company he
keeps. One thinks especially of Northumberland in this connexion—
the 'fiend' whose brutal tormenting of Richard in the Parliament scene
causes even Bolingbroke to whistle him off (IV. i. 271). It is Northumberland who unfurls that all-too-familiar document of the police-
state—the prepared confession, drawn up to the specifications of the

new regime, not by the accused, but by his accusers, that the souls of
men may *deem* the prisoner worthily condemned, whatever the true
facts of the case may be. It is Northumberland, not Bolingbroke, who
is seen callously enforcing the order for the separation of the queen
from Richard, and rejecting the queen's naïve request for joint banishment with a Machiavellian chuckle over the absurd notion of preferring
'love' to 'policy' (v. i. 84). And it is Northumberland, not Bolingbroke,
who articulates the complete deprivation of moral consciousness which
makes all this possible:

> My guilt be on my head, and there an end.
> Take leave and part, for you must part forthwith.   v. i. 69

No one who believed in the possibility of guilt could take it upon himself so nonchalantly—it is a mere gesture of impatience. Yet Bolingbroke, ultimately, must own Northumberland, for he is an embodiment
of that aspect of Bolingbroke's own will to power which he has not the
courage to act out in his own person, a revelation of that side of his
nature which can only work by delegation. And he must also own
Exton, that new and appalling parasitic growth in the garden of the
state, that Bolingbroke's 'broad-spreading leaves' have sheltered and
brought to maturity.

Exton's mentality is that of the new boy in the gang, anxious to
prove his mettle by alacrity in carrying out orders or, better, by
anticipating them, a thriver in the 'new world' whose every faculty is
fixed upon the face of the fortune-maker, noting each change of mood,
each flicker of emotion. He will become 'the king's friend'. Yet for all
his appalling guilty-innocence he is such a child-like son of ambition—
so anxious to have his wobbly divinations confirmed, even by a
servant ('Was it not so?...did he not?')—that we are left less preoccupied by *his* guilt, than by the silent king who finally gives utterance
to what is in him—'Have I no friend will rid me of this living fear?'
and looks 'wishtly' at Exton. That look, marking his explicit willingness to exploit the crude ambitions of a small man on the make,
establishes a bond with Richard's murderer which no amount of
hysterical denunciation can nullify. Bolingbroke's sentence on Exton is
no more than an articulation of his own inner state —'The guilt of
conscience take thou for thy labour... / With Cain go wander through
shades of night...' (v. vi. 41–3).

In this last scene, Shakespeare lets us see briefly the moral chaos that
lies behind Bolingbroke's somnambulistic pursuit of power: what he

most desires he knows, when he has it, for poison. Richard's corpse, the last of the rebels to grace his triumphant suppression of sedition, is in truth his 'buried fear'—not a 'living fear' now finally laid to rest, but a fear deeply hidden which now rises to consciousness and actuality to torment him. He may, as he says, 'love him murthered', but that does not mitigate the fact that it is only 'murthered' that he loves him, and (by a secondary ambiguity) it is the fact that he is 'murthered' that he loves. It is ironic that a course of action which he had initiated as the avenger of Abel (I. i. 104) finds him at its conclusion the patron of Cain. It is only now that the lightly-invoked 'crimson tempest', Bolingbroke's courtly blood-rain metaphor (III. iii. 42 f.), yields up its disquieting meaning:

> Lords, I protest my soul is full of woe
> That blood should sprinkle me to make me grow.   v. vi. 45

For blood *must* sprinkle him to make him grow: his fertility, his flourishing state, would be impossible had not the king's blood stained the king's own land, just as his continuing 'growth' is only possible because, in Carlisle's words, 'The blood of English shall manure the ground' (IV. i. 137). Yet grown he has, and it is as impossible for him to relinquish the fruits of blood, as it was inevitable that he should shed it. Blood and growth in Bolingbroke's world are inseparably intertwined—this is Shakespeare's paradoxical precipitation of a simultaneous sense of inevitability and of moral misdirection which has hung about the figure of the successful rebel.

The inevitability is important; for when we have noted the dangerous emptiness of Bolingbroke the public man, his commitment to indirection and violence and his ineradicable blood-guilt, we have not said the last word. His political virtues make his success irresistible. He is, for instance, a determined realist, knowing well enough that one cannot hold a fire in one's hand 'By thinking on the frosty Caucasus' (I. iii. 294–5), and this quality, the lack of which leads Richard to so many phantasmic solutions to his problems, enables him to expose the element of histrionic fraud in Richard's grief—'The *shadow* of your sorrow hath destroy'd / The shadow of your face.' He is, besides, as so many commentators have noted, a capable administrator in precisely the situations where Richard has failed—in the handling of faction in his own court, for example, or in the pardoning of a Carlisle who has played Gaunt to his Richard. But the inevitability (and so perhaps the excusability) of his rise depends finally, not, I think, upon his personal weight, though this is considerable and of the right political kind, but upon Richard's emptiness—to reverse the metaphor of the buckets. As Harold Goddard remarks, Richard is a vacuum into which Bolingbroke the whirlwind rushes.[15] The kind of responsibility that this kind of weakness must bear for the excesses of strength is suggested by Lawrence's emphatic overstatement of an essential truth:

No man...cuts another man's throat unless he wants to cut it, and unless the other man wants it cutting. This is a complete truth. It takes two people to make a murder: a murderer and a murderee. And a murderee is a man who is murderable. And a man who is murderable is *a man who in a profound if hidden lust desires to be murdered.*[16]

Richard, as I see him, is just such a murderee.

III

Shakespeare's King Richard has evoked some of the most contradictory critical responses in the whole range of Shakespearian studies. To some he is the epitome of political ineptitude, a pitifully effeminate, ineffectual man, and these critics scold and browbeat their way through his long self-revelations in an ecstasy of castigation. To others he is the poet-king, the Christ-like martyr to bestial ambition, the 'fair rose' withering on the tree of the State, who achieves in the end a lyric poet's victory over a hostile environment. Each of these views seems to me to entail some subjugation of what one *does* feel about Richard, to what (on political or aesthetic grounds) one feels one *ought* to feel. Furthermore the separating off of the two views of Richard—as political being and as private man—is based, as Michael Quinn points out, upon 'a modern separation of politics and ethics which would have been largely incomprehensible to an Elizabethan and particularly unreal in a discussion of kingship'.[17] The separation, one might add, is also unacceptable to anyone who has grasped the distinctively human and dramatic nature of Shakespeare's approach to the political order. Quinn goes on to argue that the characters in *Richard II*

are required to appear on more than one battlefield simultaneously, and that the audience is required to assess them according to several different standards, and that the consequent judgments do not entirely agree; the final verdict must be ambiguous...

But since the ambiguity of the reaction to Richard which Shakespeare evokes in us does not issue in confusion (as it does with Marlowe's

Edward, or his Jew of Malta) it becomes important to define that reaction as precisely as possible.

The most obvious starting point, perhaps, is the political ineptitude which is so clearly mapped out by Gaunt in Act II, Scene i. Here is a king whose decisions are all short-term, who meets a financial crisis with the seizure of the nearest source of negotiable capital (Gaunt's estate); who takes no account of estranged nobles or angry commons as long as his royal magnificence meets no serious check; for whom the territorial acquisitions of the past are no more than invested securities which can be turned into capital when the need arises; for whom the anguished protests of friends goaded into reluctant opposition are only the 'frozen admonitions' of 'lunatic lean-witted fools'; a king who feels himself so far above the law as to be able to violate with impunity the very laws of succession that brought him to the throne; a king so politically unsophisticated that he can hear the uneasy mutterings of rebellion—'those thoughts / Which honour and allegiance cannot think'—and invest the possessor of those thoughts with full viceregal powers, 'For he is just, and always loved us well'. And Shakespeare makes us see that this is more than the folly of a political innocent—for Richard is intelligent enough when he chooses—'We thank you both, yet one but flatters us...' (I. i. 25); or 'Well you deserve. They well deserve to have / That know the strong'st and surest way to get' (III. iii. 200–1)—it is an irresponsibility which has more than a tincture of pure malice in it. Richard is no mere 'young hot colt' as York hopefully opines (II. i. 69), the unfortunate victim of an impulsive nature; for 'will doth mutiny *with wit's regard*' (II. i. 28), as becomes plain when we consider the exquisitely modulated brutality of his attitude to the dying Gaunt:

> Now put it, God, in the physician's mind
> To help him to his grave immediately!
> The lining of his coffers shall make coats
> To deck our soldiers for these Irish wars.
> Come, gentlemen, let's all go visit him,
> Pray God we may make haste and come too late!   I. iv. 59

'Amen' comes the prompt response of the malicious coterie to whom grief at parting, draymen, governmental extortion and death are all alike raw material for the parade of cynical wit. And Richard, in this scene, is more teacher than pupil. Those last two lines might understandably be taken for the utterance of Richard of Gloucester, so close are they to the sardonic-brutal tone of joyous viciousness. So might the veiled threat against Bolingbroke which mingles deadly malice with a kind of schoolboy levity:

> He is our cousin, cousin, but 'tis doubt,
> When time shall call him home from banishment, ·
> Whether our kinsman come to see his friends.   I. iv. 20

I think it is considerations of this kind that have led some critics to write off Richard as 'so vile a sample of royalty' that not even his later developments can redeem him.[18]

But even if we confine ourselves to the first two acts (before Shake-speare's exploration of Richard in depth is properly under way) there is more to him than this. The frivolity, here maliciously sinister in timbre, is elsewhere patently defensive. It is the verbal playfulness of a mind unsure of its own best insights:

> Wrath-kindled gentlemen, be rul'd by me,
> Let's purge this choler without letting blood—
> This we prescribe, though no physician;
> Deep malice makes too deep incision.
> Forget, forgive, conclude and be agreed:
> Our doctors say this is no month to bleed.   I. i. 152

The metaphor is continually wavering between being turned to entirely purposeful account—'Deep malice makes too deep incision'—and a kind of self-depreciating frivolity which will make retreat easy should the parties prove intractable—'though no physician', 'Our doctors say...'. It is the hesitant reticence of a man ill at ease when demanding that others 'be rul'd' by him, happier to 'prescribe, though no physician'. It is the same quality of self-doubt which makes it possible for Mowbray and Bolingbroke to defy him later in the scene, and which makes him, in turn, swallow the bitter draught with affected lightness:

> We were not born to sue, but to command;
> Which since we cannot do to make you friends...   I. i. 196

This is a weakness in a king, sure enough; but after the roar and swagger of Bolingbroke's self-confidence, which it follows—'O God defend my soul from such deep sin! / Shall I seem crest-fallen in my father's sight...', etc.—there is a certain redeeming awareness of limitations which suggests it might be a human strength. Indeed the Richard we see in Act I, Scenes i and iii, though he is shown to be ominously unable to enforce his will, is not lacking in dignity: Shakespeare establishes this first, before letting us see the other facets of his character. True, by the end of Act II, sympathy has swung away from the king, but this is only in preparation for the new Richard of Act III, Scene ii, whose 'ability to express feeling', as Traversi points out, is attractive after the 'practical coldness' of Bolingbroke.[19]

Strikingly it is when Richard is already ceasing to *be* king, that he presents to the world for the first time a fully-formed royalty of demeanour and utterance:

> We are amaz'd, and thus long have we stood
> To watch the fearful bending of thy knee,
> Because we thought ourself thy lawful king;
> And if we be, how dare thy joints forget
> To pay their awful duty to our presence?   III. iii. 72

The measured, regal tread of these lines (and those that follow), their formal equilibrium yet sharp cutting-edge, is the best argument for Richard's cause that is offered anywhere in the play. Yet this same man, later in the scene, is seen lost in the extravagance of indulged grief to the utter subversion of his royalty. Throughout the play our feelings about Richard fluctuate in this way, each new development reminding us that there is more in any man than may be cramped into a proposition of moral approbation or disapprobation.

Yet not quite 'in this way'; because, from the time of Richard's landing in Wales (III. ii), there is a steady tendency for the weighing of pros and cons to coalesce in a single act of imaginative apprehension, an understanding of Richard's inner state which is itself an act of judgment. And as the focus becomes deeper, thus rendering superfluous both approval and hostility, one begins to sense a deficiency, an emptiness at the heart of Richard's address to the world which denies him (and with him the play) either the triumph of tragic stature or its profundity.

There are many ways of defining this deficiency, and I would prefer not to be committed to any one way of seeing it, since each critical methodology does some kind of over-conceptual violence to the wholeness of the dramatic reality. So I shall try to approach the matter from several different angles. On one level the failure is related to a narcissistic-exhibitionist streak in Richard's character[20] which leads him continually to attempt to focus all attention on himself—as (perhaps) in the interruption of the trial by combat at Coventry, and certainly in the Deposition scene ('Now, mark me how I will undo myself') which reaches its climax when Richard calls for a mirror, the very symbol of his self-regarding malady (though it is much else as well). We are frequently made aware that he has his eyes upon his audience, carefully gauging their reactions, sensitive especially to contempt or hostility— 'Mock not my senseless conjuration, lords' (III. ii. 23); 'We do debase ourselves, cousin, do we not?' (III. iii. 127); 'Well, well, I see / I talk but idly, and you laugh at me' (III. iii. 170–1); or that moving moment when a grateful recognition of human warmth and sympathy is mingled with the Narcissus-actor's moment of triumph—'Aumerle, thou weep'st (my tender-hearted cousin!)' (III. iii. 160). Significantly, . this last sentiment is prelude to an extravagant indulgence of grief which deviates, as Johnson complained, 'from the pathetic to the ridiculous'.[21]

Nor is this simply a matter of psychopathy, for the suspicion that Richard is acting his emotion very often subverts the seriousness of his utterance. The tableau element in the spectacle of the returning king fondling 'his earth' is sufficiently self-conscious to alert us to other elements of self-dramatisation in his speech (III. ii).[22] It is the same with the Richard of the Deposition scene, a man who is 'pathetic and yet too self-conscious to be entirely tragic, sincere yet engaged in acting his own sincerity, possessed of true feeling and elaborately artificial in expressing it'.[23] In so far as Richard shares this propensity for self-dramatisation with Bolingbroke, the mode is part of a larger treatment of 'the theatricalism of politics'; but whereas the staging of scenes is for Bolingbroke a mere political device, it is for Richard a deeply personal necessity.[24]

For Richard's instinct to stage-manage his appearances is an attempt to establish control over a reality which he does not wish to understand. By wilfully projecting a chosen ego-image upon reality, he can avoid knowing the extent to which he must bear responsibility for his own catastrophe: thus, by crowning himself a 'king of grief' he is spared the necessity of enquiring into the causes of that grief. There is something both pathetic and evasive about the way Richard clings to this image of himself:

> You may my glories and my state depose,
> But not my griefs; still am I king of those.   IV. i. 192

But we may wonder to what extent he is their 'king'. He was much nearer the truth, one feels, when he cried,

> A king, woe's *slave*, shall kingly woe obey.   III. ii. 210

Yet even here there is equivocation: if a slave to woe, then no king; yet because the woe is his, it is 'kingly' and he justified in 'obeying' it. It is all part of his purposeful apotheosis of *grief considered apart from its cause* as an absolute, and so unquestionable, state of being. The truth is that the grief has grown, by indulgence, disproportionate to any conceivable cause, has indeed begun to engulf Richard himself, so that he cries out in anguish, 'O that I were as great / As is my grief' (III. iii. 136–7). Each time he gives way to this huge inexplicable woe, his estrangement from reality and his need for grief increases.[25] In an image of cloying excess, he renders his enslavement to this voluptuous mode of relief:

> That bucket down and full of tears am I,
> *Drinking* my griefs...   IV. i. 188

When Northumberland presents him with the record of his 'crimes', it is the tears filling his eyes that prevent his reading, though the same tears cannot blind him to the sins of others (IV. i. 244 f.). And one does not have to be insensitive to the real pain in Richard's voice, to catch also the muted terror of a man who is being violently wrenched out of a fantasy-world where he is spared the agonies of self-knowledge:

> Must I do so? and must I ravel out
> My weav'd-up follies?   IV. i. 228

The weaving image catches very precisely Richard's sense that it is wantonly destructive to undo a work of neurotic concealment which has been years a-making.

But the agonies of self-knowledge pursue him: for it is not the face 'like the sun', the idealised portrait of the *roi soleil*, that confronts him in the mirror he has called for, but a face that has simply trimmed and countenanced folly, now to be finally out-matched by a superior face-maker (IV. i. 281–8). This face Richard cannot contemplate and he smashes it in a frenzied gesture which is both a renunciation of self-knowledge and an expression of self-loathing. And even that gesture is inescapably histrionic.

A secondary line of defence against hard truths is built around a kind of generalised and self-regarding pathos. Sometimes it is the elegiac note of *de casibus* tragedy that signals the retreat—

> For God's sake let us sit upon the ground,
> And tell sad stories of the death of kings   III. ii. 155–6

—where an almost hysterical urgency ('For God's sake') contrasts strangely with the child's fable-making he proposes ('sad stories'). There is about this strain a hectic exaggeration ('*All* murthered'), and a neurotic demand upon the world that it shall share his grief—the aim is to 'send the hearers weeping to their beds' (v. i. 45). It is Richard himself who provides the critique of such a retreat from responsible engagement with the world: it is refuging one's shame, bearing one's misfortunes 'on the back / Of such as have before indur'd the like' (v. v. 26–30).

Sometimes again, the retreat is made in terms of a slack stoicism:

> Mine ear is open and my heart prepar'd.
> The worst is worldly loss thou canst unfold.
> Say, is my kingdom lost? why, 'twas my care,
> And what loss is it to be rid of care?   III. ii. 93

The sententiousness and the facile catechetical technique reveal this as factitious, possibly consciously so; and the reality behind the triteness is a vision of universal chaos which, as Traversi notes, 'is itself a hysterical evasion of the truth'.[26]

> Cry woe, destruction, ruin, and decay—
> The worst is death, and death will have his day.   III. ii. 102

But this speech, and Richard's whole stance in this scene, represent a more subtle kind of evasion: it is an attempt to anticipate calamity, even to initiate it, so as to avoid submitting to the tutorship of circumstance. Richard will draw the sting of every ill chance, bring it under his governance, by a willed pessimism. Bushy and Bagot *have* made their peace with Bolingbroke; he will have it so. He is now in 'that sweet way to despair' and

> By heaven, I'll hate him everlastingly
> That bids me be of comfort any more.   III. ii. 207

Johnson is right to note the effort of mastery in these lines: 'nothing is more offensive to a mind convinced that its distress is without a remedy, and preparing to submit quietly to irresistible calamity, than those petty and conjectured comforts which unskilfull officiousness thinks it virtue to administer.'[27] But there is here, as well, a leaping over all obstacles to despair, a panting eagerness to touch the bottom of his griefs so that he may rest in them.

It is this mental characteristic which makes possible the alarmingly rapid capitulation to Bolingbroke. For Richard puts the words of usurpation in Bolingbroke's mouth for him. It is he who first mentions deposition:

> What must the king do now? Must he submit?
> The king shall do it. Must he be depos'd?
> The king shall be contented. Must he lose
> The name of king? a God's name, let it go.   III. iii. 143

The sense of psychic disintegration, a complete 'letting go' ('Now, mark me how I will *undo* myself'), is linked here with a feeling of overwhelming relief as the burden of responsibility is relinquished. Again the regressive strain is apparent. By the end of the scene Richard, like a distraught child, no longer knows whether he is coerced or willing; he only knows he wants it all over:

> What you will have, I'll give, and willing too,
> For do we must what force will have us do.
> Set on towards London, cousin, is it so?   III. iii. 206

It is the same impatient longing for the rest of annihilation, the fretful cry of a man prolonged too long in pain, that rings across Westminster Hall:

> Whither you will, so I were from your sights.   IV. i. 315

These two cries prompt in Bolingbroke two decisive actions—the journey to London (meaning deposition) and the committal to the Tower (meaning murder).[28] This is what I meant by saying that, 'in a profound if hidden lust', Richard is a 'murderee'.

There is thus nothing inherently surprising about finding Richard espousing a kind of nihilistic fatalism. He tells the queen,

> I am sworn brother, sweet,
> To grim Necessity, and he and I
> Will keep a league till death.   V. i. 20

There is a tension here between the voluntary oaths of the *fratres jurati*, to which Richard refers, and the concept of 'Necessity'; for Necessity neither requires nor invites cooperation. One feels that it is the necessity of his death which is the real subject of Richard's pact: it is a kind of self-destructive *entente cordiale*, 'for I must nothing be' (IV. i. 201). The sense of nothingness springs partly from his inability to envisage any mode of existence for himself once he has ceased to be king. So completely has he translated his sense of himself into the 'name' of the king, that the usurpation of the name by another leaves him a mere shell—'Nothing can we call our own but death' (III. ii. 152). The last stages in this process of disintegration are reached in Act V, Scene v, in the endless meaningless activity of the imprisoned mind (again presented in a theatrical metaphor—'Thus play I in one person many people'). It is a breeding act which is ultimately and endlessly sterile, because self-confined—'A generation of still-breeding thoughts' (and I am sure there is some play here on the 'still-born' 'still-breeding' parallel). This movement of thought culminates in

> But whate'er I be,
> Nor I, nor any man that but man is,
> With nothing shall be pleas'd, till he be eas'd
> With being nothing.   v. v. 38

It is fatally confusing to try, as Wilson Knight does, to relate this position to 'the faith of high tragedy', or to see it, with R. M. Frye, as a 'Christian analysis of contentment'.[29] Certainly there is something tough-minded here which commands respect in a way Richard does not elsewhere. But in a very literal sense, it is nihilism—not the emptying of the soul in preparation for faith, nor a glad acceptance of release from temporal bondage—but a desire for the obliteration of consciousness, for the 'ease' of death, for 'nothing'. It may be something bleaker than the voluptuous death-worship of Romanticism, but close attention to the despairing cadences makes nonsense of any attempt to see Richard as the triumphant martyr that his comparisons of himself with Christ might suggest him to be. He is desolation itself. And the death-in-battle that finally consummates his long courtship of sorrow and annihilation is not so much a 'last redeeming act of will', as a reflex of desperation ('Patience is stale, and I am weary of it'—v. v. 103): it is 'proud and ignorant and hopeless'.[30]

When I suggest that this, at rock-bottom, is Richard, I do not mean to apply any moralistic blanket-judgment, nor to indulge in that coarse bullying of 'fine temperament' which Yeats diagnosed at the root of much adverse comment on Shakespeare's king.[31] Indeed the full recognition of Richard's 'emptiness' is only open to those who have seen how close he comes to being 'full'. For, at times, he is capable of seeing himself with great clarity—

> Nay, if I turn mine eyes upon myself,
> I find myself a traitor with the rest   iv. i. 247

—or the bitter perception of an ironic fitness in his own fall—

> I wasted time, and now doth time waste me,   v. v. 49

where the vision of a temporal order laid waste by his very prodigality with time is firmly linked to an awareness of his own spent and shrunken ('wasted') stature. But he retreats from such searing insights, and the position into which he retreats may be broadly described as 'nihilism'.

So when, in the finest speech in the play, he does achieve a poised objectivity which crystallises much of our sense of the world in which he acts, it is important to be clear what it is that is being offered us.

> For within the hollow crown
> That rounds the mortal temples of a king
> Keeps Death his court, and there the antic sits,
> Scoffing his state and grinning at his pomp,
> Allowing him a breath, a little scene,
> To monarchize, be fear'd, and kill with looks;
> Infusing him with self and vain conceit,
> As if this flesh which walls about our life
> Were brass impregnable; and, humour'd thus,
> Comes at the last, and with a little pin
> Bores through his castle wall, and farewell king!
> Cover your heads, and mock not flesh and blood
> With solemn reverence; throw away respect,
> Tradition, form, and ceremonious duty;
> For you have but mistook me all this while.
> I live with bread like you, feel want,
> Taste grief, need friends—subjected thus,
> How can you say to me, I am a king?   III. ii. 160

The crown is hollow partly because there is no man to fill it, Richard having attenuated his manhood into the symbolic regalia of royalty which thereby becomes hollow. But 'crown' is also the physical head of the king, the hollow skull which is the reality beneath the skin, just as death's court is the reality at the centre of the king's court. Thus the shadow of worldly power is only one manifestation of that vast shadow world which is physical existence, and in both cases the reality behind the shadow is Death—skull, death's-head, buffoon. The hollow-ness is an insubstantiality at the heart of appearance, whether it is the hollowness of the skull, the hollowness of the grave-mound (identified with savage bathos as a ghastly kind of pie filled with bones—'that small model of the barren earth / Which serves as paste and cover to our bones' (III. ii. 153-4)) or the hollow resonant space in the courtyard of a castle, enclosed by those pompous walls of flesh against which Death conducts his mock-siege. But the other function of the images of hollowness is to present a vulnerability so piteous as to fall victim to a little pin—a pathetic and childish inadequacy appropriate to children's games or a puppet show—Bye, bye, Punch! Farewell King!

There are thus two complementary movements in the speech: one penetrating vertically the surface of 'tradition, form, and ceremonious duty' to reveal a personal emptiness and a sinister manipulator behind the scenes; the other a horizontal, temporal process leading, by way of a bitter anticlimax, to the same revelation. For Death's 'little pin' is, quite precisely, an instrument of deflation, a trivial, absurd and horrible exposure of 'self and vain conceit'. Both movements combine to degrade humanity to such a level that 'respect', even self-respect, must be thrown away. Unlike Lear's, Richard's discovery that royalty is not agueproof, though moving in proportion as it is desperately needed, does not lead to the release of a 'royalty of nature' which is common to all men. Rather it induces in Richard a sense that he is 'subjected'. To the end he is unable to enter into any kind of constructive or co-operative relationship with the forces of life and death; he can only accept this 'subjection' with bitter irony, and become sworn brother to grim Necessity, an accomplice in his own murder.

Richard, like Bolingbroke, though in a completely different manner, has failed to make anything creative of the political chaos into which he was born.

IV

What then must we say of the York who follows the moderate's *via media* between these two extremes?

Shakespeare is exceedingly gentle with the old man, allows no one to mock him, permits him to grasp pretty clearly the military and political realities of strife-torn England, and depicts him as genuinely concerned to discover a course of action compatible with integrity and rectitude. He gives full weight to the mitigating circumstances of his age, and to the impossible false situation into which Richard's insensitivity and lack of prevision have thrown him. He lets him berate both Bolingbroke and Richard with a directness and forcefulness which shows him to possess a developed moral intelligence that puts them to shame. In the early stages of the play he displays that tenderness of conscience towards other human beings for lack of which both Bolingbroke and Richard stand convicted. And he has an engaging kind of proud humility which is not afraid to expose its uncertainties to the gaze of others.

Yet, for all the sympathetic understanding he commands, York seems also to have failed the test imposed by this time of trouble.

> Well, well, I see the issue of these arms.
> I cannot mend it, I must needs confess,
> Because my power is weak and all ill left.
> But if I could, by Him that gave me life,
> I would attach you all, and make you stoop
> Unto the sovereign mercy of the king;
> But since I cannot, be it known unto you,
> I do remain as neuter.   II. iii. 151

There have been stern moralists, or strategists, prepared to reprimand York for not bluffing the situation out, for lacking that rigid adherence to the forms of government which would have led him to adopt a posture of righteous punitive wrath which he could not, in fact, have made good. But it is hard to *feel* anything wrong with this ingenuous and endearing honesty. The trouble begins with that word 'neuter'. It might appear to be no more than a formal articulation of the attitude of neutrality he has adopted throughout the scene. Yet it is a new departure. And it is a piece of self-deception. The two grammatical senses of the word subvert York's conscious meaning—the 'neuter' verb, which is an intransitive verb (in the terminology of Shakespeare's time, 'neither active nor passive'); and the 'neuter' gender. The second undertone is the most damaging, for it is a man who speaks, claiming a kind of 'neutrality' which is proper only to inanimate nature, impossible to man—just as impossible as to be neither active nor passive. York's self-delusion lies in his wishful espousal of a neutrality which is not in nature, and in the next lines we see what that neutrality (friends with both and foes with neither) means in practice:

> So, fare you well,
> Unless you please to enter in the castle,
> And there repose you for this night.   II. iii. 158

It means making a crucial decision blindfold, and pretending that there has been no decision. For York to entertain the rebel leaders in a castle he claims to hold for the king is, within his own terms of reference, treason. It is a dim realisation that the time for consideration has somehow passed him by in the night, like a station where he intended to alight, and that he is now committed beyond recall to a cause he never consciously chose, that stops his speech and sets the tears flowing when he next meets Richard (III. iii). He has tried to find out right with wrong—which may not be.

(The later developments of York's character seem to me to be on a much smaller scale, like an unfinished sketch. One senses an overall intention—perhaps to show how bad conscience sets its teeth and hardens into doctrinaire inflexibility, even to the denial of that very love of kindred which first brought him in behind Bolingbroke—but it is fitfully executed and does not engage our sympathies on the same level as the York of the first three acts.)

I suggest, then, that in Bolingbroke, Richard and York, we are confronted with three attempts to solve the problem of responsible, morally sensitive behaviour in a world torn by political strife. And each attempt Shakespeare leads us to see as seriously defective in some direction.

Is this then merely a play of tragic cynicism about the possibility of integrity in the political sphere?

v

'Cynicism' is probably too strong and too shallow a word for the prevailing climate of the play, but its agnosticism, to my mind, is very deeply rooted. When we consider the order-vision (largely theological in orientation) which has an indisputable place in *Richard II*, it is surprising to discover how little it shifts the balance of judgment in a less pessimistic direction: the real power of the play is deployed elsewhere.

There is, however, one scene which is frequently urged as a notable exception to such generalisations—the Garden scene (III. iv). Here, for once, the complexities of the action seem to be unravelled and laid out for our inspection. Here there is a hint of some comprehensive harmony. Critics have been quick to pounce on the Gardener's pronouncements as a key to the puzzle: 'the gardener', we are told, 'gives both the pattern and the moral of the play'.[32] But I find it hard to see in what sense the commonplaces in which he deals really mesh with the world presented elsewhere in the play. It is not a fecund blossoming Nature that is invoked as the political archetype, but a pruned and trimmed formal garden with its 'knots' and props, a place where even Spring must be regarded as 'disorder'd'. The whole emblematic scheme implies, not a Nature with which man may enter into fruitful partnership, but a Nature which may be wilfully and deliberately cut down to size (for 'All must be even in our government'), disciplined into productivity. If we are to take the Gardener's aphorisms as the good advice that Richard most needs, they seem oddly unhelpful. Has he not cut off the head of that 'too fast growing spray', Gloucester, and had nothing but trouble for his pains? Has he not wounded the bark of those 'over-proud in sap and blood' to prevent them confounding themselves 'with too much riches', only to have them rise in rebellion against his 'burthenous taxation'? The metaphor is fundamentally misleading in that it makes of a complex two-way process—the government of rational independent beings—a simple instrumental act —lopping away 'superfluous branches'. Richard's problem is that his subjects are not such complaisant stocks as the Gardeners have to rule over. They answer back, they demand justice, they hit out at their would-be pruner. The Gardener would have us believe that it is lack of diligence, the 'waste of idle hours', that has 'thrown down' Richard's crown. But his real problem was to know what to be diligent about, there being no convenient gardening manuals to make all plain to him. There is throughout the Gardener's pronouncements a sententious crudity and a lack of particularity which simply does not answer to the realities of Richard's predicament.

It would be pleasant to suppose that Shakespeare was here taking a very hoary political allegory and showing up its deficiencies by applying it to a knotty case. But he provides no ironic context (unless we count the queen's wry comment, 'My wretchedness unto a row of pins, / They'll talk of state...'). And since Shakespeare (unusually) permits these rustics to speak in fairly dignified blank verse, I am inclined to suppose the discrepancy to have escaped his notice. As at the end of *Richard III*, the pressure of imagination has fallen off, and Shakespeare here propounds traditional remedies which are too feeble for the seriousness of the disease.

Two moments in the scene convict the rest of shallowness: one occurs when the emblematic mode (in which State equals Garden, but the term Garden is not permitted to do more than embellish the conception of the State) gives way to metaphoric exploration and fusion:

> He that hath suffered this disordered spring
> Hath now himself met with the fall of leaf.   III. iv. 48

Here Richard's degradation submits him to the seasonal revenge of outraged Nature; it is not so much the unfortunate result of a failure of foresight, as an involuntary participation in the inscrutable cycle of natural existence. He has 'suffered' spring, painfully and passively—for how could he have done otherwise? But he has also actively 'suffered' spring to be, and to be what it is—'disordered'. He is both victim and architect of his own miseries. Such an ambivalent rendering does some justice to the Richard we have seen acting and suffering in the rest of the play—a man at times strangely passive yet determined to impose his will on those around him. But it recognises that prudential 'trimming' and 'dressing' is subject to larger and less controllable necessities.

The second moment occurs when the Gardener is lured out of his realm of moralistic abstraction into the particularities of the king's situation. With the introduction of those letters that 'came last night', the metaphor changes abruptly:

> King Richard he is in the mighty hold
> Of Bolingbroke. Their fortunes both are weigh'd;
> In your lord's scale is nothing but himself,
> And some few vanities that make him light.
> But in the balance of great Bolingbroke,
> Besides himself, are all the English peers,
> And with that odds he weighs King Richard down.
>
> III. iv. 83

Gone is the pretence that one can, by wise husbandry, circumvent the operation of mere opportunism. Fortunes are weighed, and it is numbers that count. There may well be some correlation between the 'balance-of-power' and the 'garden-of-the-state' views, but, as they are presented here, one is the moralistic platitude, the other the stern, if regrettable, reality. The bulk of the Garden scene, then, I see as a surrender to the kind of over-simplification that Shakespeare eschews elsewhere in *Richard II*. The other manifestations of his concern with order are much more pertinent and integral.

The Divine Right of kings, of which Richard is so persistent an exponent, is such a manifestation, but it would be a mistake to imagine that it is urged simply as a key to understanding, or as a panacea for the ills of the play-world. When Shakespeare puts the advocacy of this doctrine primarily in the mouth of the kind of king we have seen Richard to be, he is subjecting it to a severe, if implicit, critique. For from one point of view, the king's view of his status as quasi-divine, and his faith in the efficacy of his 'Name', are simply further examples of his tendency to regressive thinking, leading here to a childish belief in a kind of magical nominalism. If we are hesitant to apply such categories to a sixteenth-century play, Shakespeare gives us a broad enough hint of psychological malfunction when he places the key enunciations of Divine Right in a scene where Richard is see-sawing violently between blind despair and a wildly precarious elation and over-confidence (III. ii). There is more than a suspicion that in this doctrine we have a theological fantasy of omnipotence, not completely under conscious control, which is proclaimed to allay Richard's anxious doubts about his personal adequacy to a threatening political situation. It is surely a strange doctrine that makes it possible for man 'that but man is' to patronise the very earth, doing it 'favours' with his 'royal hands' (III. ii. 11). Certainly Richard's convictions are badly out of touch with the *political* realities, to go no further:

> For every man that Bolingbroke hath *press'd*
> To lift shrewd steel against our golden crown,
> God for his Richard hath in heavenly pay
> A glorious angel: then, if angels fight,
> Weak men must fall, for heaven still guards the right.
>
> III. ii. 58

This is not the authorially-endorsed omnipotence of a Tamburlaine—

> Draw forth thy sword, thou mighty man at arms,
> Intending but to raze my charmed skin,
> And Jove himself will stretch his hand from heaven
> To ward the blow...   *I Tamburlaine*, I. ii. 177

—but self-delusion, declared to be such by the recollection that even the Son of God (cf. the presumptuous implication of filial status in 'his Richard') did not use his legions of angels, but preferred to die rather than violate the natural process of cause and effect. There is, besides, a cynical substratum of meaning suggested by the concealed play on 'press'd'—'golden crown'—'pay'—'angel'—as if Richard somewhere inside himself regarded the whole confrontation as a merely mercenary matter where '*angels* fight'. Carlisle, incidentally, has already rejected this notion of a divine providence divorced from human foresight and prudence, pointing out that heaven yields 'means' which 'must be imbrac'd / And not neglected';

> else, heaven would,
> And we will not; heavens offer, we refuse
> The proferred means of succour and redress.   III. ii. 29

In any case the seriousness of the sanctions invoked is 'placed' by Richard himself when, in the next line, Heaven takes him at his word, and deprives him of all but angelic help. He is forced then to confess that his angelic legions are symbolic rather than actual, depend, indeed, upon the actual for their existence:

> AUMERLE. Comfort, my liege, why looks your grace so pale?
> RICHARD. But now the blood of twenty thousand men
> Did triumph in my face, and they are fled;
> And till so much blood thither come again,
> Have I not reason to look pale and dead?   III. ii. 75

To the extent that Richard is aware that his fantasy is fantasy, we are not here dealing with serious psychic disturbance. His response to Aumerle's 'Comfort, my liege, remember who you are', indeed, sounds more like a parody of the kind of 'comfort' such remembrance brings him, than a serious resort to transcendentalist royalism:

> Arm, arm, my name! a puny subject strikes
> At thy great glory.   III. ii. 86

But when Richard himself ceases to believe in the divine sanctions of royalty, their claim to serve a normative function in the play is correspondingly weakened. In fact, one of the clearest things about *Richard II* is the way it tests conceptions of abstract right against a world largely hostile to such conceptions. As one critic puts it,

Shakespeare's contribution as poet...lies chiefly in his evocation of the paradox inherent in the idea of divine right, inheritable, after all, by human blood and placed in the unreliable keeping of human temperament...[33]

Yet Richard's right remains a key question in the play, and it would be foolish to pretend that it is not in a real sense 'the king's blood' that stains 'the king's own land' in the closing scenes. Although the indelibility of the sacramental anointing is called in question by Richard himself, when he claims to wash off with 'tears' the balm which 'Not all the water in the rough rude sea' could remove (IV. i. 207 and III. ii. 54–7), we are still left wondering whether his kingship can be so easily dissolved as he affects to think. And though with his own breath he releases 'all duteous oaths', denies his 'acts, decrees, and statutes', and invokes God to pardon all oaths that are broken to him (IV. i. 210–15), the sick state of Bolingbroke's conscience at the end of the play is clear enough evidence that it is no such simple matter. At all events, one wonders whether the 'sacred state' of a king can simply be 'denied'. Shakespeare seems to be using the *character indelibilis* to hint at possible final sanctions behind the expediency which hedges kingship about, even though those sanctions have no clear practical bearings.

He does not, however, insist on Richard's sacred *rights*, so much as on the *wrong* of Bolingbroke's usurpation. Whatever we may think of the religious bonds of kingship, Bolingbroke's violent dissolution of them stands condemned as something that 'may not be' (II. iii. 144). Though there is much in the action which makes us see his rise to power as 'inevitable', though inexorable catastrophe seems to brood over the king's cause, just as effortless triumph seems to attend Bolingbroke, yet this is the kind of 'inevitability' which cannot abrogate personal responsibility either in Richard or in Bolingbroke. It is an amoral process which only takes on moral meaning in the consciousness of the participants. And this meaning is given a decisive twist against the rebel cause in the picture of inner disarray with which we are presented in the last scene. It is as if Shakespeare says: Right may be problematical, but violent wrong carries its own judgment within itself. We may be uncertain about much else in the political sphere, but the greed of power to be its own 'carver' (II. iii. 143)—the metaphor implies ill-bred and indecent haste to 'feed'—cannot be excused. 'To find out right with wrong—it may not be', even though there is no other clearly discernible way to find it out. This is the Shakespearian 'agnosticism'—not a retreat from moral responsibility, but a refusal to accept moral over-simplifications. Richard's culpability can no more excuse Bolingbroke's aggression than Richard can take refuge against his own sins in over-riding conceptions of his kingly right.

Thus, when York, describing Richard's maltreatment at the hands of the London populace, offers a conspectus of the events of the play, our reaction to the summing up is extremely complex:

> ...had not God for some strong purpose steel'd
> The hearts of men, they must perforce have melted,
> And barbarism itself have pitied him.
> But heaven hath a hand in these events...   v. ii. 34

For we know that York too hath had a hand in these events, and this is half pious rationalisation. Yet the sentiment does answer to the strange inevitability I have mentioned; and York's discreet bewilderment about what that 'strong purpose' might be is ours as well. The Elizabethan theatre-goer who knew his chroniclers might have called to mind the decades of civil butchery over which the 'strong purpose' worked itself out, but if he did he would have been invoking a very different Providence from that comfortable institution which orders all for the best, and that right quickly. Providence, in these terms, becomes a tortuous, blind purging of ancient wrongs 'With many turnes and turmoyles of sicknesse and recouering', a process too vast to be ever fully understood.

But perhaps Shakespeare's most subtle presentation of a pattern in the events he dramatises is his picture of a transitional age in which that tower of conservative strength, John of Gaunt, can be the father of Henry Bolingbroke. For in a very real sense the play is concerned with the clash between traditional statecraft—the garden view of politics, if you like—and that new world of Northumberlands and Fitzwaters whose emblem is the Balance of Power.[34] When one looks closely at the men who give voice to the traditional sanctities of government, and do so with weight and gravity, they turn out to be all old men—Gaunt, York, Carlisle. They are full of recollections of the great age of English power under 'noble Edward' (II. i. 171–83), of 'that young Mars of men', the Black Prince, with whom they shared their 'hot youth' (II. iii. 89–101), of 'that England that was wont to conquer others' (II. i. 65), so bitterly different from the England they now see. Like old men they mutter in corners about new-fangled court fashions, or grumble about the passion for 'lascivious metres' that has accompanied the decline of the martial virtues (II. i. 17–26). Collectively they represent a formidable body of traditional wisdom and expertise, which Richard ignores at his peril. It is as a summation of that wisdom that we need to see Gaunt's great speech of lament over the royal throne of kings (II. i. 31 f.). It is a compelling vision of the past and a passionate denunciation of the present, but it is not a set piece which jumps out of its frame to demand absolute and univocal assent. It is an old man's profession of faith privately confided to another old man. The very rhetorical structure, with its piling up of short appositional phrases, is expressive of the old man 'lacking *breath*' yet 'new *inspir'd*', so that, as Wilson Knight remarks, we feel 'a gathering power...breaking through the impediment of age'.[35] And part of the poignancy of the speech springs from the fact that the order it praises, like Gaunt himself, is dying.

The same sort of thing must be said about Carlisle's spirited defence of Richard in the Parliament scene (IV. i. 114 f.) which, for all its generosity of feeling and passionate sincerity, is in some sad way out of place. Bolingbroke may respect the 'high sparks of honour' he sees in Carlisle, but he cannot really hear what is being said. All Carlisle achieves is to delay the deposition for the space of forty-odd lines, before he is hustled off the stage like the lamentable old anachronism he is.

Which is not to say he does not speak truth. He does. And we in the audience take his point much more clearly than Bolingbroke can, the more so since this is one of the few voices raised in the fourth act which speaks with real humility ('Worst in this royal presence may I speak, / Yet best beseeming me to speak the truth...') and without some damaging ulterior motive. But it is a truth which we perceive to be no longer viable, a truth which fails somehow to engage with the realities of Bolingbroke's new world. In an appalling way Northumberland's cynical comment is the right one:

> Well have you argued, sir, and, for your pains,
> Of capital treason we arrest you here. IV. i. 150

The old world-order which is shown in its death-throes is what Gaunt calls 'Christian service, and true chivalry' (II. i. 54), and it is profoundly involved with the religio-military ideals of the crusades. It thrives on ritual and ceremony, and receives its first serious set-back in the scene where the trial-at-arms is not permitted to take its course: Richard, though involved in its forms, is sufficiently contemptuous of its ideals to substitute those methods of indirection and subterfuge which finally issue in the triumph of Bolingbroke. He has kept its husk in his notions of kingship, but thrown away the kernel of 'Christian service', and his commitment to the manipulative arts makes him fair game for the superior manipulator.

There is a fascinating moment in the fourth act (another of Shakespeare's 'irrelevances') when this vast geological change in cultural ideals comes suddenly into focus, and momentarily we pause, as on the summit of the last and highest ridge to survey the land we are leaving behind. It is when Carlisle (appropriately) speaks the epitaph on another representative of the chivalric ideal—Thomas Mowbray:

> Many a time hath banish'd Norfolk fought
> For Jesu Christ in glorious Christian field,
> Streaming the ensign of the Christian cross
> Against black Pagans, Turks, and Saracens;
> And, toil'd with works of war, retir'd himself
> To Italy; and at Venice gave
> His body to that pleasant country's earth,
> And his pure soul unto his captain Christ,
> Under whose colours he had fought so long. IV. i. 92

We look back across a long dramatic vista to that dancing feast of battle where we last saw Norfolk, hear Bolingbroke's unusually warm response to the memories it evokes ('Sweet peace conduct his sweet soul to the bosom / Of good old Abraham'), and realise that Boling-broke will come vainly to covet such a death, that indeed none of those present will give their bodies to pleasant earth, but to hollow English tombs in ground manured with English blood.

There is about the evoked image of Mowbray something of the poignancy of lost felicity—Adam's last glimpse of the Gates of Eden. And it is in this light that we need to see the ideals of Gaunt or Carlisle. They may be that to which the play aspires, but they are also that away from which, inexorably, the play moves. Our sense of the justness of the Christian-chivalric ideal is coloured by its poignant impossibility. Though Bolingbroke stands condemned by the canons of political equity laid down by his father, he is, for the play, Necessity. Again there is this paradoxical shock and recoil, a breaking down of all simple one-way attitudes, which is of the essence of the play's 'agnosticism'.

When I search for some analogue for what might be called the imaginative 'flame-colour', the characteristic lambency of *Richard II*, I am tempted to invoke the shade of the Preacher:

> What does man gain by all the toil
>   at which he toils under the sun?
> A generation goes, and a generation comes,
>   but the earth remains for ever...
> The wind blows to the south,
>   and goes round to the north;
> round and round goes the wind,
>   and on its circuits the wind returns.
> All streams run to the sea,
>   but the sea is not full;
> to the place where the streams flow,
>   there they flow again.   Ecclesiastes, i. 3–7 (RSV)

But this will not do. Because at the root of this kind of disillusion lies capitulation, and a despair which levels all human endeavour to a desert—'All things are full of weariness; a man cannot utter it'.[36] Shakespeare contemplates the 'Vanity of vanities' as steadily as the Preacher, but his world is not flat and empty, because he sees at the heart of futility those crucial human acts of total discrimination which bring into being both good and evil—acts which we can only call 'moral' if we realise how vastly we are extending the depth and range of that all too familiar word.

10

SUPERNATURE AND DEMONISM IN ELIZABETHAN THOUGHT

The modern reader of *Doctor Faustus* normally experiences a pang of disappointment when he realises that Marlowe is not going to question the phenomenon of witchcraft itself; but he then promptly assures himself that in this matter Marlowe is simply following the universal belief of his own day. When this assumption is made, as it frequently is, a large area of the witchcraft symbol is immediately placed beyond the range of conscious art. But the assumption is quite erroneous. Marlowe's decision to treat demonic and other supernatural phenomena as simple facts of nature was actually a surprising piece of conservatism on the part of a man who, in other fields, seems to have been an intellectual radical.

The first observation one wants to make about sixteenth-century demonology is that there is none—at least no coherent and agreed system under which demonic manifestations could be understood and explained. The whole subject was in the melting pot of vehement argument and revision. Even the appearance of uniformity encouraged on the continent by the ubiquitous glare of inquisitorial fires was superimposed on an older scepticism. Witch persecution was a relatively new thing.[1]

The underlying scepticism became explicit in the sixteenth century when a German doctor, John Wier, published a book offering medical explanations for many allegedly demonic manifestations,[2] thus breaking the demonological monopoly of *Malleus Maleficarum*, a textbook by two inquisitors which had held the field since the late fifteenth century. In fact Wier merely reproduced a number of objections to demonic existence which the inquisitorial authors imagined they had laid to eternal rest in their volume. The *Malleus*, in its 'Objections' sections, provides clear evidence that, even at the height of the witch mania, the old naturalistic questions were being asked and that the witch-mongers felt it necessary to answer them. Wier's limited dissent was taken much further in 1584 by the Englishman Reginald Scot. His conclusions were so sweeping that, had they been widely accepted at the time, there would have been no further history of witchcraft to be written after the sixteenth century. 'There will be found', he says,

among our witches onelie two sorts: the one sort being such by imputation, as so thought of by others (and these are abused not abusors) the other by acceptation, as being willing so to be accompted (and these by meere cousenors).[3]

There is a tendency to regard Scot as a solitary and storm-tossed humanitarian beacon in a sea of raging prejudice, but it is only in the comprehensiveness of his denunciation that he is unique. The book is widely and approvingly cited by authors who are trying to establish similar positions, and the ideas can be parallelled in many less revolutionary manuals.[4] The medical explanation of the incubus delusion or of supposed transformation into bestial shapes,[5] the attribution of demon-possession to a disease of the 'phantasy' or to 'melancholy',[6] the discovery of a connexion between nervous states and demonic apparition,[7] or the application of canons of rational probability and internal consistency to supernatural phenomena,[8] are all so widespread as to be almost commonplace.

James I is probably remembered more widely as the author of *Daemonologie* than as a sceptic in things supernatural. Yet the truth of the matter is that, after the publication of that youthful piece of recondite erudition, he came increasingly to doubt the witchcraft phenomena, and devoted a great deal of time to exposing fraud or delusion in alleged cases of demon possession.[9]

The sceptical rationalism that was abroad is exemplified by Edward Jorden, 'Doctor in Physicke', who published, in 1603, an important book in which 'the Suffocation of the Mother', or what we would now call hysteria, was subjected to detailed scrutiny in order to distinguish it from 'possession', examples of which

being verie rare now adayes, I would in the feare of God aduise men to be very circumspect in pronouncing of a possession: both because the impostures be many, and the effects of naturall diseases be strange to such as haue not looked throughly into them.

Jorden hoped that by his medical expertise 'the vnlearned and rash conceits of diuers, might be...brought to better vnderstanding and moderation; who are apt to make euery thing a supernatural work which they do not vnderstand'. Jorden's emancipation was so complete that he was prepared to humour ignorance to the extent of going through the motions of a mock exorcism when the patient insisted he was 'possessed';

so that if we cannot moderate these perturbations of the minde, by reasons and perswasions...we may politikely confirme them in their fantasies, that wee may the better fasten some cure vpon them...[10]

Against this background it is possible to see how far Marlowe's choice of the *Faustbook* as a source committed him to anachronism and reaction.

It is not just witchcraft, either, that is under assault in Elizabethan England: the whole angelic–demonic world, populated with anthropomorphic beings of assorted shapes and functions, has come into question. The protestant, in reaction against popish legends of saintly miracles, is very insistent on the patristic doctrine that the age of miracles has passed; and this notion has the indirect effect of casting doubt on everything supernatural.[11] Perhaps the insistence is, in fact, a theological retreat before the oncoming wave of scientific rationalism. In any case, the whole supernatural order, the angels and demons with substantial bodies, are beginning, in educated circles, to look a little rusty and archaic, as we may gather from an anecdote in Sir Thomas More's *Apologia pro moria erasmi* (1520):

I met an old man once in a bookshop,...a Doctor of Theology of more than thirty years' standing. When I chanced to remark in his hearing that Saint Augustine held that devils all had substantial bodies, the theologian scowled and tried to browbeat me for advancing so daring a heresy. 'I don't hold the view myself, Father,' I said, 'nor do I blame Augustine for holding it. To err is human. I believe most of what he writes, but I don't believe every word either in his books or in anyone else's.' The man was already in a rage because I had dared to insult one of the Church Fathers.[12]

The progressive weakening of old superstition is often signalled by a new kind of flippancy about the devil. The following passage from Nashe is a good example of emergent scepticism broadening into satire (he is dealing, in an apparently serious context, with the ubiquity of the demonic hordes):

There is not a roome in anie mans house, but is pestred and close packed with a campe royall of diuels...Infinite millions of them wil hang swarming about a worm-eaten nose...Vpon a haire they will sit like a nit, and ouer-dredge a bald pate like a white scurffe...The *Druides* that dwelt in the Ile of *Man*...are reported to haue beene lousie with familiars. Had they but put their finger and their thumbe into their neck, they could haue pluckt out a whole neast of them.

There be them that thinke euerie sparke in a flame is a spirit...which may verie well bee...It is impossible the gunnes should goe off as they doo, if there were not a spirit either in the fier or in the powder...If the bubbels in streames

were wel searcht, I am perswaded they would be found to be little better...
Not so much as Tewkesburie mustard but hath a spirit in it or els it would neuer
bite so.[13]

The light-hearted tone is a symptom of profounder modifications in
the relationship that was conceived to exist between the human and the
supernatural planes. As early as the twelfth century, Abailard had
suggested that, rather than whispering incitements to depravity into the
ear of the tempted man, the devil made use of the 'inherent lure of
things', and proposed some quasi-mechanical chain of causation,
which he explained in terms of occult but natural 'virtues'.[14] By the
mid-sixteenth century it was possible for Louis Lavater to write, in
connexion with 'supernatural' manifestations, 'Many things in very
deed are naturall, althoughe wee can not fynde any naturall reason for
them'.[15] One is continually running across passages where a theory of
supernatural agency is rejected in favour of astrological causation. The
fact that these rationalisations no longer appear very rational should not
blind us to the trend of this thought—a steady subjugation of unexplained phenomena to the only known forms of causation which
would fit the facts.

Lavater takes the increasing reliance upon naturalistic explanations to
be some sort of cultural coming-of-age, a by-product of protestant
enlightenment:

Whereas nowe adayes fewe stand in feare of spirites, many might be easily
found, who would seeke them, feele them, yea and also handle them...A man
may soone persuade a childe that ther is a black man, a tall woman, which wil
put chyldren that crie in their budget &c. but after they are come to maturitie
of yeares, they will no more be feared with visions and such like persuasions...
Even so when we were children in the Scriptures...we might be easily seduced
to beleeue many things: But nowe that we reade them...and do dayly profit
in them, we do not suffer our selues to be so mocked...Things are set vp in the
fields to feare away the birdes, whiche at the last also they perceyue to be but
trifles, and are not dryuen away any longer with suche toyes.[16]

The newly mature now mock the bogeys of their youth. The word
'conjuror' is beginning to acquire its present connotations of chicanery.[17]
It is in this context that Nashe raises his voice in protest against these
'great famous Coniurers and cunning men', who are scarcely a month
in town,

but what with their vaunting and prating, and speaking fustian in steede of
Greeke, all the Shyres round about do ring with their fame: and then they begin

to get them a Library of three or foure old rustie manuscript bookes, which they themselues nor anie els can read; and furnish their shops with a thousand *quid pro quos*, that would choake anie horse; besides some wast trinkets in their chambers hung vp, which maye make the world halfe in iealouzie they can coniure.[18]

We are here, at one leap, carried forward into the world of Jonson's Subtle and Face, with the sun of reason shining down from a clear sky. Or so it would appear. But as we read on in this pamphlet, it becomes plain that Nashe's emancipation is a highly selective, not to say sporadic, affair. His one foot on solid ground is very little use to him as long as his other foot is caught fast in a bog of clinging superstition. In this respect he is probably more truly representative than such a monument of intellectual autonomy as Reginald Scot. He is a man of the Renaissance. He was also a friend of Marlowe's.

For Marlowe's position with regard to the supernatural order has a similar ambiguity. There is, of course, considerably more to it than the crude demonological anthropomorphism of his source-book: there is also in *Doctor Faustus* a metaphorical hell inhabited by elusive demons who appear not simply under mechanical compulsion from the conjuror's incantation, but because of the subtle affinity of evil for evil. And yet the view of magic as a direct and simple means of coercing the devil forms another stratum in the play. The inconsistency—I shall be discussing its dramatic effects in the next chapter—is, in historical terms, a doomed attempt to retain an older mechanistic demonology alongside the newer interpretation of the devil as symbol; and it reflects an important tension in that acutely transitional age.

The conception of hell itself was being assailed by the same sceptical and rationalistic trends, and it is worth glancing at the process, I think, in order to define precisely where Marlowe is to be located in the spectrum of Elizabethan supernaturalism. It is true that, apart from the avowed 'atheists', there are few who deny categorically the physical place called hell, 'Within the bowels of these elements' (v. 120), and many who insist on it with great literalness.[19] Yet there was in Christianity from the start an emphasis on the 'privative punishment' of hell, which was seen as more important than mere physical torment, and in the sixteenth and seventeenth centuries this was increasingly emphasised at the expense of the medieval, localised hell—about which Augustine himself had been dubious.[20] 'It is the constant and concurrent judgement of the ancient Fathers', declares a seventeenth-century preacher, 'that the torments and miseries of many hels, come farre short, are nothing, to the shutting out everlastingly from the kingdome [of] heaven...'[21] 'The cursse of GOD', according to a popular catechism which ran through fifteen editions between 1572 and 1614, 'conteineth al the torments that can bee deuised', and hell-fire is simply a way of expressing that pain.[22] Many theologians held hell to be a torment of the faculties rather than of the body. For others it was simply the indefinite prolongation of temporal states of consciousness which thereby became intolerable. In short, there seems to have been a fairly general consensus of opinion which would have concurred with the preacher who declared, somewhat maliciously: 'hell is *profundum, a depth*. To define the locall place of Hell, it is too deepe for me: I leaue it to deeper iudgements.'[23]

These men don't much mind if hell is taken metaphorically, as long as it is acknowledged to be real:

If it be metaphoricall, as *Austin* seemes some where to intimate, and some moderne Divines are of minde: and as the *gold, pearles* and *precious stones* of the *walls streets and gates* of the heavenly Ierusalem...were metaphoricall; so likewise it should seeme that the fire of hell should also be figurative: And if it be so; it is yet something els, that is much more terrible and intolerable.[24]

The vulgarised physical hell is becoming incommensurate with the known depth and subtlety of evil. But, by the same token, hell as a metaphor has been greatly enriched:

The wicked man cannot want furies, so long as he hath himselfe. Indeede the soule may flye from the body, not sinne from the soule. An impatient *Iudas* may leape out of the priuate hell in himselfe, into the common pit below; as the boyling fishes out of the Cauldron into the flame. But the gaine hath beene, the addition of a new hell without them, not the losse of the old hell within them. The *worme of Conscience* doth not then cease her office of gnawing, when the fiends begin their office of torturing. Both ioyne their forces to make the dissolutely wicked, desolately wretched. If this man be not *in the depth of Hell, deepely miserable, there is none*.[25]

When, in *Doctor Faustus*, the worm of conscience and the tormenting fire *do* 'ioyne their forces' in a single intense metaphor—

> Why, this is hell, nor am I out of it.
> Think'st thou that I, who saw the face of God...
> Am not tormented with ten thousand hells
> In being depriv'd of everlasting bliss?—   iii. 78

Marlowe has the best of both worlds—the medieval, for which damnation has such a sharp physical actuality, and the modern with its insight into the depths of the damned mind. More frequently though, as I shall argue, the two versions of hell militate against each other, providing two rival accounts of the same phenomena, each of which invalidates the other.

It is possible to see now why Marlowe's residual attachment to the old pneumatology might prove an embarrassment: it is the 'advanced' thinkers who are taking seriously the evil symbolised by hell and the demonic order. They have realised that a devil who can be ordered about like an errand boy is a paltry enemy beside the real forces ranged against humanity, just as the playhouse Satan is a vulgarisation of the Prince of the Power of the Air. The devil is not fearsome because of his blazing eyes and cloven hoof, but because he knows the heart of man, with all its potentiality for evil and can, with infinite subtlety, exploit his knowledge. To reinterpret Satan in this way is no more than to give the devil his due, as Scot saw:

for some are so carnallie minded, that a spirit is no sooner spoken of but immediatlie they thinke of a blacke man with cloven feet, a paire of horns, a taile, clawes, and eies as broad as a bason &c. But surelie the diuell were not so wise in his generation, as I take him to be, if he would terrifie men with such uglie shapes, though he could doo it at his pleasure...But in truth we neuer haue so much cause to be afraid of the diuell, as when he flatteringlie insinuateth himselfe into our harts, to satisfie, please, and serve our humours, entising vs to prosecute our owne appetits and pleasures, without anie of these externall terrors.[26]

As Scot saw, to rob Satan of his gimcrack stage appurtenances was simply to take him more seriously, which involves taking the evil he represents more seriously. 'The diuell of late is growen a puritane', Nashe warns us, 'and cannot away with anie ceremonies...Priuate and disguised he passeth too and fro...'[27] This new Satan lives closer to the pulse of man, seated in the blood, not so inescapably 'other' as his older stage counterpart had been, nor so easily recognised. We shall see that the demonic order in *Doctor Faustus* is at times invested with a comparable kind of seriousness about evil; but the inconsistent vulgarised version is strong enough in the play to subvert this vision repeatedly.

And yet there is more in Marlowe's 'medievalism' than mere reaction, more in his vacillation than a simple inconsistency. Like many of his contemporaries, he was not prepared to let modern revaluations of the devil turn him into a purely subjective phenomenon. He wants to retain the vivid reality of the medieval Satan alongside the psychological profundity of the new Satan. He is attempting to stand in the eye of the hurricane of intellectual evolution. Because there are moments in *Faustus* where he achieves just this (I have noted one of them already —'Why, this is hell...'), it is helpful to consider the movement in Elizabethan thought which was attempting a similar kind of reconciliation—not so much to show Marlowe's synthesis anticipated in the demonologists (who are an undistinguished crew and don't get very far with the problem), as to expose the materials out of which he made the synthesis.

The terms of the debate are conveniently laid out in a book occasioned by a disputed case of 'possession'. The possessed man was one William Somers of Nottingham who, after astounding the countryside with his antics, was cured by a minister who had built up a local reputation as an exorciser. The cure and the exorcism were subsequently 'discovered' to have been 'fraudulent', Somers confessed his deception—and was immediately 'repossessed'. Controversy raged. Two serious-minded clergymen in the area, however, retired to their study and produced a set of *Dialogicall Discourses of Spirits and Diuels*, in which some progress was made towards understanding the nature of the problem.[28] Their names were John Deacon and John Walker.

It is clear from the early stages of this book that the real issue is not Somers, nor the phenomenon of possession, but the reality of the spirit world. It is on this position that Pneumatomachus, whose name explains his function, launches his attack:

Sir, I take those your supposed spirits for none other matters at all, but the good or euill *motions* and *affections* arising in men: as also those your imagined *Angels*, I hold them to bee nothing else but the *sensible signes* or *tokens* of Gods vnspeakable *power*.[29]

This is one-half of the equation—the *avant garde* half, one might say— and it is an opinion that filled many writers of the period with misgivings. Nashe had met with it:

Some men there be that, building too much vpon reason, perswade themselues that there are no Diuels at all, but that this word *Daemon* is such another morall of mischiefe, as the Poets Dame Fortune is of mishap: for as vnder the fiction of this blinde Goddesse we ayme at the folly of Princes and great men in disposing of honours, that oftentimes preferre fooles and disgrace wise men...so vnder the person of this olde *Gnathonicall* companion, called the Diuell, we shrowd all subtiltie masking vnder the name of simplicitie, all painted holines deuouring widowes houses, all gray headed Foxes clad in sheepes garments; so that the Diuell (as they make it) is onely a pestilent humour in a man...that violently carries him away to vanitie, villainie, or monstrous hypocrisie.[30]

Nashe himself seems to have no very clear opinions on the subject, but for many such doctrine was dangerous in the extreme: Calvin devotes a section of the *Institutes* to the refutation of 'those men...who babble of devils as nothing else than evil emotions and perturbations which come upon us from our flesh', for he saw, quite properly, that the allegorisation of the spiritual world would end in a denial of its reality.[31]

Deacon and Walker, however, are not content to perpetuate the simple subjective/objective either/or. They have felt the force of Pneumatomachus's position, and as soon as Orthodoxus sets about to refute Pneumatomachus he is involved in allegorical interpretations of scripture which seem almost indistinguishable from Pneumatomachus's original position:

Those scriptures which attribute to...*spirites*, a *corporall forme*...may (at no hand) be expounded literally; but must rather be *metaphorically*, and *spiritually* vnderstood...

The devils have an '*actuall*, or *powerfull possession*' but they do not '*essentially* enter into any mans *minde*'. They are 'essential and spiritual' but not 'corporall'. Even temptation is explained by Physiologus in terms of appeals to the four faculties, and he concludes,

It is verie apparant that, those sundrie *tentations* wherewith *Satan* assaulteth mens *minds*, they do ordinarily arise, first, from *external alurements*, and so proceede... to the *mind* it selfe: and that therefore, we neede not imagine anie such *mental possession* for *Satan*, before he can bring the *bodie* of man to...disordered actions.[32]

One tends to shake one's head and mutter something about scholastic hair-splitting. Why, this is precisely what Pneumatomachus said in the first place! And yet it is not. He had claimed that spirits were '*none other matters at all, but* the good or euill motions and affections arising in men', and it is against this 'nothing but' that Orthodoxus and Physiologus take up arms. They are concerned to vindicate the demonic order as independent of the human mind, while at the same time affirming the intimate connexion between the two. It is like Mephostophilis, for whose apparition Faustus's 'conjuring speeches' are 'the cause', and who yet comes '*per accidens*' (iii. 47–8).

Behind the ponderous machinery of scriptural exegesis, invoking of 'authorities' and logic-chopping into which the book now degenerates, lies the germ of an important synthesis: evil is both subjective and objective. It is something freely embraced, but also something that violates the personality. 'Spirites and diuells', says Orthodoxus, 'are able (like *councellors*) to perswade the *wil* vnto something. [But] they cannot possibly *compel* the *wil*, the same (by nature) reiecting al maner of *compulsion*'; and yet elsewhere he makes the idea of demonic viola-tion, of 'effectual *tormenting* and *tempting*', quite explicit.[33] Daneau appears to be moving toward the same position when he claims that Satan is given coercive power over the wicked which they cannot resist, and yet, 'notwithstanding, there was neuer yet any Sorcerer, but he was lead amisse through his owne fault...'.[34]

The power of the devil is proportional to the receptivity of the tempted man, but it is also disproportionate. Man chooses evil; but there is a more terrible sense in which evil chooses him.

It would be rash to claim that the average Renaissance demonologist saw all the implications of this paradox. For the most part it is no more than an unperceived contradiction in his premisses. But a sensitive mind working within this framework, feeling the validity of the symbolic interpretation of hell and its inhabitants, but aware too of the apparently objective force of evil, could arrive, as we shall see Marlowe sporadically did, at a vision of man as continually threatened by uncontrollable forces which he himself has called into existence, and at a vision of evil both as prior and self-existent, and as the creation of man.

Thus, the creative mind playing over the debated territory in its own culture may not merely assimilate what is offered, but may think through it dramatically, and so transform it into a new kind of truth. For is it not true that we feel evil primarily as the external violation, the distorting and deforming of personality by forces which the personality itself can neither own nor control? And isn't it also true that these external coercive forces are the creation of personality, and that in our more lucid moments we know them for our own offspring? The peculiarly Elizabethan thing about Marlowe's confrontation of the crux is that he is not so sure as we that the objective appearance can be reduced to subjective hallucination. His consciousness is pre-Cartesian, in the sense that it does not accept subjective and objective as mutually exclusive categories.

The Elizabethans, as a recent writer on the subject has suggested,

lacked our conception of the cleavage between the objective and the subjective ...it was not that they were without a theory of mental process, or neglected to distinguish the forms impinged upon the intellect by the outside world from combinations of these forms which the soul itself originated. It was rather that they were not so sure as we of the inviolability of the personality, not sure that alien personalities could not come into the mind in a manner much more immediate than anything our theories of suggestion and hypnotism admit of.[35]

At its best, Marlowe's drama gives us the feel and body of this violation of personality at the very moments when we are most aware that Faustus has, in the fullest sense, damned himself. And Shakespeare draws on the same insight in the dramatisation of his Witches—for the conception of evil in *Macbeth* has a good deal of affinity with the best things in *Faustus*.

But the moment Marlowe slackens the paradoxical tension, his synthesis relapses into the two mutually destructive alternatives—the blazing torture-house and the hell of the mind; the basin-eyed, hoofed-and-horned monster and the subtle exploiter of human weakness; the crudely literal and the powerfully symbolic. *Doctor Faustus*, from this angle, displays a series of partial adjustments to a cultural tension in its age, rising at times—but only at times—to a new and authentic insight.

11

THE NEW WINE
AND THE OLD BOTTLES:
'DOCTOR FAUSTUS'

It must be a fairly common experience to come away from a performance (or a reading) of *Doctor Faustus* with very mixed feelings. It is an
intensely puzzling play. The scenes leading up to Faustus's death are
sufficient to convince us that, in Marlowe, we are dealing with a mind
of some distinction; but like so many of the play's high points, the final
soliloquy is followed by a scene of acute bathos:

> O, help us, heaven! see, here are Faustus' limbs,
> All torn asunder by the hand of death.   xx. 6

The descent from authentic imaginative vision to the silly or the
commonplace can occur within the space of a line. The justly famous
definition of hell ('Hell hath no limits, nor is circumscrib'd / In one
self place...—v. 122) is immediately succeeded by

> And, to be short, when all the world dissolves
> And every creature shall be purify'd,
> All places shall be hell that is not heaven.

Although this expands discursively the vision of a hell co-extensive
with the consciousness of the damned, the poetic flame has died to an
ember—'to be short' is the key to the tone: Marlowe's fitful muse has
deserted him again. The same contradiction between the perceptive
and the perfunctory, the profound and the trivial, runs throughout the
play, the most obvious and frequently deplored sign of it being the
comparative barrenness of the scenes that occupy the central section.

Though it is plainly a very serious play, *Faustus* is bedevilled by a
kind of naïve absurdity. It is chronically over-explicit: obvious ironic
points (as with *The Jew*) get hammered home in asides (MEPHOSTO-
PHILIS. 'What will not I do to obtain his soul!') or in that totally
superfluous extra line which Marlowe cannot resist adding—

> How pliant is this Mephostophilis,
> Full of obedience and humility!
> *Such is the force of magic and my spells.*   iii. 33

Partly, it is primitive dramatic technique, unable to handle transitions adequately—'But, leaving this, let me have a wife...for I am wanton and lascivious and cannot live without a wife' (v. 141)—but it issues too in an inappropriate, skittish irresponsibility in the playwright:

> To him [Beelzebub] I'll build an altar and a church
> And offer lukewarm blood of new-born babes.   v. 13

Or

> at midnight I will send for thee.
> Meanwhile peruse this book and view it throughly,
> And thou shalt turn thyself into what shape thou wilt.
>
>   vi. 174

Even Faustus's power fantasies, which are clearly supposed to be 'placed' by the context, have a dangerously uncontrolled kind of puerility. Marlowe obviously knows they are absurd; but if he knew *how* absurd, could he permit them to enunciate themselves so flatly?

> [I'll] make a bridge thorough the moving air
> To pass the ocean with a band of men.   iii. 107

(Why 'with a band of men', if this is not random amplification of a thought that is cherished at the same time as it is consciously rejected?)[1]

Primitive technique is also evident in the handling of soliloquy, where mental conflict is frequently represented geometrically as a simple pendular oscillation between two largely unrealised extremes—in this case, God, Beelzebub:

> Now go not backward; no, Faustus, be resolute:
> Why waver'st thou? O, something soundeth in mine ears,
> 'Abjure this magic, turn to God again!'
> Ay, and Faustus will turn to God again.
> To God? He loves thee not;
> The god thou serv'st is thine own appetite,
> Wherein is fix'd the love of Beelzebub.   v. 6

Like Richard III's very similar soliloquy on the eve of Bosworth, this is not so much the presentation of inner debate as a preliminary sketch for that presentation; and the somewhat monotonous self-apostrophe is a very crude way of representing a man communing with his own soul. We get the histrionic gestures, the broad outlines, but there is no inner reality.

Then there are those subtle felicities in the play which are no sooner perceived than one starts wondering whether they are not perhaps accidental; there is that curious loose-jointed fragmentariness of Marlowe's writing—a quality consistent with the assumption that the verse was assembled piece by piece from a stock-pile of previously written lines and paragraphs—and this view is lent some plausibility by the number of lines remodelled from other plays;[2] and there are all the minor inconsistencies of a work insufficiently digested, ideas which have not undergone that inner chemistry of creation which could assimilate them to one complex imaginative organism, but which survive on the surface of the work as excrescences belonging rather aggressively to one historical epoch. As I shall try to show, the unity of *Doctor Faustus* is, in many respects, something that we have to create for ourselves, answering questions that were for Marlowe insoluble, pursuing implications further than he was able or prepared to pursue them, making choices between incompatibles that appear side by side in the play as we have it. All of which makes it extremely difficult to find a *point d' appui* from which to tackle the play.

After such a comprehensive vote of no-confidence in an author, it may seem odd to undertake an investigation at all; but what is good in *Faustus* is good in such a uniquely interesting way that none of these obvious deficiencies has been sufficient to keep the play off our stages or our bookshelves. We continue to be fascinated, though we are at the same time dissatisfied.

Part of the fascination, of course, lies in the complete critical discord the play has induced. The commentators and scholars who have written about it find it notable for such a diversity of incompatible qualities that one sometimes wonders if they are talking about the same play. Frequently they are not. Out of the patchwork of reported playhouse text and presumed incomplete author's manuscript corrupted by putative censor and editor, one can make almost anything. And it is all too easy to excuse faults in *Doctor Faustus* by attributing them to the collaborator (s?). The simplest and fairest way out of these perplexities is to treat the text we now have as an undoubted literary fact, and refer to its author, by a convenient ellipsis, as 'Marlowe'. Even the poet's most ardent admirers admit he must have at least planned the whole, and most critics would go further. The prose scenes are not unlike the unfunny low comedy of *The Jew*, and there are many of the tell-tale Marlovian verbal tricks in the disputed verse scenes as well. The categorical refusal to admit them as Marlowe's seems to me to be founded on an inflated notion of his poetic infallibility.[3]

As I have suggested, the textual confusion is matched by critical discord. There is, however, agreement on one point: this is not simply a dated didactic essay on the dangers of a forgotten art. It is not a play about black magic. And yet, equally clearly, if the play has any subject at all, it is magic. The dilemma gives rise to two interpretative extremes: the advocates of the first extreme are so anxious to do justice to Marlowe's avowed subject, so conscious of the play's firm roots in sixteenth-century soil, and so suspicious of the analogical habits of modern criticism, that they will not discuss it at all except in terms of Lutheran or Calvinist theology, medieval demonology or Renaissance pedagogy.[4]

Appalled by this spectacle of acute scholarly myopia, the second group of critics flies to the opposite extreme. They give us a Marlowe who is a fully-blown nineteenth-century agnostic, or a Faustus damned in the teeth of justice by a Marlowe who has been cowed by a barbarous theology into committing intellectual 'apostasy'.[5] Or we get Faustus as pre-Marxian man, ignorant of the nature of his problem, but feeling his way towards cultural unification and deeply in need of the 'saving power of social integration'.[6] Interpretations such as these, which laudably attempt to account for the continuing felt relevance of the play, nevertheless imply a Marlowe miraculously emancipated from the vagaries of the historical process and are obliged to fly in the face of the explicit sense of the text.

But both these extremes of interpretative method are founded upon a false dilemma; either (it is assumed) Marlowe is a true child of his time, or he is our contemporary. The truth of the matter is that he was neither. He was the product of his own age in much the same sense that we are of ours. Standing at the centre of a vast network of conflicting ideas, his ears teased with distant sounds of systems falling into ruin and his soles tickled with new growth underfoot, his mind half free, half bound, and a huge assortment of contradictory propositions on every conceivable subject awaiting him in his library, he was a man neither essentially 'medieval' (whatever that means) nor 'modern', but committed in his time to thought, experiment, living, discussion, discovery. This, as I understand it, is what it means to talk of Marlowe (if we must) as a 'man of the Renaissance'. But in virtue of his humanity and his art, and because history is not a series of compartments but a continuum, he is also our contemporary. The problem is not in which of these two ways we are to regard him, but how we are to relate them in a single critical vision of the play. *Doctor Faustus* may reflect a particular cultural crisis in the age of the Renaissance; but that crisis is an important part of the past which has made our present what it is; so that when we confront the play, we are also confronting ourselves.

I

One of the cultural conflicts in which Marlowe clearly found himself involved (and yet a conflict which is not merely 'historical') was the clash between certain varieties of optimistic humanism propounded by the apostles of perfectibility, and an older mistrust of human aspirations to the divinity of knowledge. It was a clash between 'vnsatiable speculation' (to adapt a phrase of approbation coined by the English translator of Marlowe's source-book), and the medieval conception of *curiositas* (the same activity viewed from a diametrically opposite viewpoint).

It would be rash to suggest, of a play which is 'about' so many things, that this is its real subject—for *Faustus* is almost the spiritual auto-biography of an age. But Marlowe lets us be in no doubt that this is *one* of the things it is about: Faustus's 'friendful fortune', he tells us in the Epilogue,

> may exhort the wise
> Only to wonder at unlawful things,
> Whose deepness doth entice such forward wits
> To practise more than heavenly power permits.
>
> Epilogue, 5

The play is, on one level at least, a critique of the philosophy which permitted Pico della Mirandola, in an account of the Creation, to put the following words in the mouth of God:

Neither a fixed abode nor a form that is thine alone nor any function peculiar to thyself have we given thee, Adam, to the end that according to thy longing and according to thy judgement thou mayest have and possess what abode, what form, and what functions thou thyself shalt desire. The nature of all other beings is limited and constrained within the bounds of laws prescribed by Us. Thou, constrained by no limits in accordance with thine own free will, in whose hand We have placed thee, shalt ordain for thyself the limits of thy nature...[7]

For Pico, the road from the doctrine of 'unlimited man' led direct to Cabbalism and magic.[8]

By casting his fable in the most traditional of Christian dramatic forms—the *psychomachia*, the battle for a soul—and by the explicit moralisation of the Prologue and the Epilogue, Marlowe reveals his conviction that traditional wisdom still has something to say to Pico and the humanists. His problem was to discover what this something was.

In the Epilogue (quoted above) he appears to regard the humanist aspiration fairly simply as a doomed attempt to transcend the inherent limits of the human condition. As such it is primal sin, and it aligns the aspirer inevitably with Lucifer. The diagnosis was a commonplace of Christian thought in the Renaissance. Here is a German variation on the theme:

Adam would know, and therefore labours for much knowledge and so *eats of the Forbidden Fruit*, that he may live and become a great one, *even God*; and for this only end the whole world now-a-days applies itself to all studies; because it desires not to die in obscurity and oblivion, but to live and flourish, not in the lower degrees of estimation, but in the chiefest seat of reputation and honour, and withal to know all things that it possibly can... wherefore every day he works more and more...that if it were possible to know more than God, that with *Lucifer* he might be equal with him.[9]

'We have in these our miserable dayes,' complains an English writer, 'as curious a generation as ever was clasped vnder the cope of Heaven.'[10] 'These times are sicke,' cries another, 'of *Adams* disease, that had rather eate of the *tree of knowledge*, then the *tree of life*.'[11]

At its crudest this complaint is no more than the instinctive recoil of dogged ignorance from the labour of knowledge; but in some writers, and the German humanist Sebastian Franck (quoted above) is one of them, it becomes a perceptive analysis of the tendency of knowledge to become a kind of metaphysical property-owning—that mere accumulation of information for purposes of personal aggrandisement which is the occupational disease of the scholar and the academic. Anyone who has browsed amongst the writings of the lesser fry of humanism will know how well the cap fits many of Marlowe's contemporaries.[12]

But it is not an infection peculiar to the Renaissance—and this is one reason why the play still *feels* relevant: it is a perennial disease of the personality, a retreat from the self-knowledge that should be the end and the beginning of all other knowledge, into a spurious kind of erudition. The living word is ousted by the dead letter. Kierkegaard called it 'knowledge become fantastic':

The law for the development of the self with respect to knowledge, in so far as it is true that the self becomes itself, is this, that the increasing degree of knowledge corresponds with the degree of self-knowledge, that the more the self knows, the more it knows itself. If this does not occur, then the more knowledge increases, the more it becomes a kind of inhuman knowing for the production of which man's self is squandered, pretty much as men were squandered for the building of the Pyramids...When the will becomes fantastic, the self likewise is volatilised more and more.[13]

No play which offers an account of so perennial a human problem is likely to become dated; and Marlowe's decision to tackle it is the more interesting for the fact that he has also apparently grasped the possible validity of the soaring humanist aspiration:

> Learned Faustus...
> Did mount him up to scale Olympus' top,
> Where, sitting in a chariot burning bright
> Drawn by the strength of yoked dragons' necks,
> He views the clouds, the planets, and the stars,
> The tropics, zones, and quarters of the sky,
> From the bright circle of the horned moon
> Even to the height of *primum mobile*;
> And, whirling round with this circumference
> Within the concave compass of the pole,
> From east to west his dragons swiftly glide
> And in eight days did bring him home again.   Chorus, 1

In this fine enactment of the sweeping exhilaration of flight—the objective correlative of the Faustian aspiration—we get something very different from the guilt-laden quest of self-gratification (mere *curiositas*, knowledge become fantastic) that the Prologue had envisaged:

> And glutted now with learning's golden gifts,
> He surfeits upon cursed necromancy.   Prologue, 24

This Faustus is more at home in the limitless possibilities of Pico's world. He travels and observes with the sharp disinterested passion of the scientific pilgrim.

Now Marlowe's problem was to harmonise these two visions of the world, not by annihilating one in the interests of the other—that had been done only too often already—but by penetrating the layers of polemic vapourings which obscured the subject, to uncover that deeper level where they were, if not reconciled, at least held in paradoxical synthesis: 'The price of knowledge is damnation: and it is worth the price', perhaps.[14] But the minute one states the paradox like this, it is plain that it won't do. First, because, as I shall argue, Faustus's quest is only incidentally for knowledge; its primary objective is reputation and power. Secondly, because his path to it is manifestly damnable and Marlowe is at some pains to keep it that way. And finally, because the play has a pervasive tone of homiletic demonstration which will not openly admit that the humanist term in the paradox has any validity at all: Faustus's knowledge is *not* worth the price, and the overt intention of the drama is to make this abundantly evident. The play opens and closes with explicit condemnation of his 'devilish exercise'. Thus the kind of positive vitality which magic acquires at times is something the play is trying (and, as I shall argue, failing) to contain. There is not paradoxical harmony, but a tension and over-strain which Marlowe is not able to encompass within a single dramatic vision. His emancipated 'modern' self is at war with his Christianity, and he is not sufficiently far above (or perhaps—it is the same thing—not sufficiently *inside*) the conflict to be able to establish a truce.

I have put the case in this explicitly biographical way, because it seems clear that there are links between the play's divided energies and the career of a theological student turned 'free-thinker'—however imperfectly he may have effected the conversion. Indeed one suspects that it was the very partiality of his change of heart that made it impossible for him to make his peace. The revolt, in *Doctor Faustus*, against traditional evaluations of the human situation, manifests simultaneously a disinterested concern with human emancipation and an acute personal bondage to those evaluations which can only be broken (and that only temporarily) by a shallow and childish aggressiveness. Hence the vein of undirected frivolity which I have noted in the play: it is the aimlessness that results when an intellectual revolt is mobilised against the only ground of evaluation that the rebel knows. The revolt against traditional wisdom is necessarily self-defeating as long as it is conducted on traditional grounds. This is the Marlowe, at all events, who emerges from the Baines Note and Kyd's deposition.[15]

But there is, if I am not mistaken, a slip of the pen in the text of *Faustus* which confirms the biographical inference that Marlowe was trying, at a deep level, to work out his own salvation by means of the play:

> Cut is the branch that might have grown full straight,
> And burned is Apollo's laurel bough
> That sometime grew within this learned man.   Epilogue, 1

As far as I can discover, Apollo's laurel was not awarded to doctors of divinity, but to musicians, artists and poets. Having in a mood of desperate self-rejection consigned himself and his opinions to the depths of hell, may it not be that Marlowe is now writing his own epitaph, the epitaph of a gifted man gone irreparably astray? Certainly there is much in the play to suggest an involvement too deeply personal to be mastered imaginatively.

If this hypothesis is granted, it is easier to understand the near-delirium into which Marlowe's mind is plunged when he comes to write Faustus's death-scene; easier to understand the impression the play gives of falling over itself in breathless haste to arrive at this hideous consummation, beside which everything else seems trivial and nuga-tory. But it also enables us to explain the strange way in which Mar-lowe's choric moralisations of the action fail to mesh with the dramatic actuality: for the attempt to impose a formal moral is the rearguard action of a guilty conscience against a personality still in a state of desperate insurrection; and a self which can consign itself to eternal perdition is not a self which can mediate between the warring factions of personality, nor transubstantiate the battle into art.

II

Marlowe, then, is torn between traditional Christian and Renaissance humanist evaluations of the aspiration to knowledge. But he can have been only dimly aware of the conflict; for when he undertook to dramatise the *English Faustbook*, he accepted a plot which was essentially committed to the traditional view. It appears to have been what he consciously wanted: the basic fact around which the play is organised is that Faustus is damned. There is no sign that he intended to mitigate this, and many signs that he wanted it to be patently clear.

He could for instance have reprieved Faustus and reinterpreted the fable, by appealing to the generally accepted notion of an innocent 'white magic'. All he had to do was to show Faustus enforcing the service of hell by the good offices (previously obtained) of a heavenly spirit ('Theurgy'), or binding the spirits of evil by a reverent use of the divine name, or employing the occult virtues of stones, herbs, numbers, symbols, names, to reduce the demons to awed submission—all of these techniques to be preceded by elaborate purification rituals, lengthy prayers and periods of abstinence—and his soul would have been in no danger.[16] Instead we have a Faustus fresh from his cups (ii. 24), already in a state of spiritual rebellion ('Divinity is... / Unpleasant, harsh, contemptible, and vile'—i. 107), calling up a spirit which is clearly out of his control ('I am a servant of great Lucifer / And may not follow thee without his leave'—iii. 42), by means of a deliberate blasphemy against the Trinity ('*Valeat numen triplex Iehovae!*'—iii. 16) and proceeding to the pact which clearly labels him no magician but a witch.

Marlowe's refusal to extenuate is too comprehensive not to be deliberate. We are to be in no doubt that Faustus is committing a guilty act; and it is in order to preserve this pivotal fact immune from the assaults of scepticism that Marlowe, in the play, takes cognizance neither of the rationalism which doubts the phenomenon of witchcraft itself, nor of the rationalisation which regards it as harmless.

But though the fable fitted Marlowe's conscious aims well enough, it brought troubles with it, in the shape of that anachronistic rout of stage devils and the old cloven-hoofed Satan. They may have been native to the *Faustbook*'s conception, but they were at odds with many of the best things in Marlowe's. The tendency of the older diabolism to stress the objectivity of the demonic world, and to take a fairly literal view of the methods by which a man became entangled with it, was countermined by Marlowe's instinctive exploitation of hell as symbol. Faustus's incantation, Mephostophilis concedes, may have been the cause of his appearance, yet only *per accidens*:

> For when we hear one rack the name of God,
> Abjure the scriptures and his saviour Christ,
> We fly, in hope to get his glorious soul;
> Nor will we come unless he use such means
> Whereby he is in danger to be damn'd.   iii. 49

In place of Faustus's philosophy of manipulation ('Did not my conjuring speeches raise thee? Speak'), rises the vision of a separate and autonomous order of spiritual forces which respond to human action according to laws of their own nature, and with which Faustus has unwittingly become embroiled.[17] This more complex relationship between tempter and tempted opens ironic vistas which lie beyond the compass of a mechanical view of the incantation as effective cause. By hinting that Mephostophilis is a metaphysical resultant of events in Faustus's consciousness, the sense of evil that the fiend represents is given increased depth and power.

Yet the disturbing thing is that these lines are spoken by an actor who, only a few minutes before, has appeared in all the trappings of the old ranter who used so amiably to distribute fireworks, advice and cracked pates among his auditors in the old days. Furthermore, he is attended by a troop of slapstick clowns of the same kidney and is provided not only with the traditional hell-mouth, but with a specially constructed dragon as well (iii. 21).[18] The pantomime devils who 'give crowns and rich apparel...dance and then depart' (v. 82—when

Faustus enquires, 'What means this show?' Mephostophilis replies, with strict veracity, 'Nothing, Faustus'), or the infernal sewers who cross the stage with covered dishes, marshalled by chief waiter Mephostophilis (Scene xviii), undermine the real impressiveness of the denizens of hell elsewhere—as for instance at that superb *coup de théâtre* in Scene vi:

> FAUSTUS. O Christ, my saviour, my saviour,
> Help to save distressed Faustus' soul.
> *Enter* LUCIFER, BEELZEBUB, and MEPHOSTOPHILIS.
> LUCIFER. Christ cannot save thy soul, for he is just;
> There's none but I have interest in the same.   vi. 85

Marlowe appears to be uncertain how seriously he is taking the evil represented by the demonic order. Nor is it particularly helpful to appeal to the earlier morality drama from which these scenes of diabolic clowning clearly derive, since the question of seriousness is even more acute there than it is in *Faustus*. To wed the absurdity of evil to the power of evil is a problem Shakespeare solved magnificently in the *Macbeth* witches; but Marlowe cannot be said to have got very far with it.

The contradiction is woven into the entire dramatic fabric. We have seen the sense in which Marlowe may be said to be making a heroic attempt to wed the imaginative efficacy of the old to the psychological profundity of the new; but in the case of the demons, we usually get no more than an oscillation, or two alternative accounts of the one event. Thus, a man's perilous capacity to be his own tempter, so clearly enacted in the first scene (Faustus's rejection of learning), is reduced near the end of the play to a simple matter of demonic violation:

> 'Twas I that, when thou were i' the way to heaven,
> Damm'd up thy passage; when thou took'st the book
> To view the scriptures, then I turn'd the leaves
> And led thine eye.   xix. 93

Or Mephostophilis, requested to describe hell, gives first of all the traditional, localised underworld—

> Within the bowels of these elements,
> Where we are tortur'd and remain for ever—   v. 120

but then replaces it with the uncircumscribed state of mental torment to which I have already referred (ll. 122–7). The juxtaposition may perhaps be made workable by treating Mephostophilis's first answer as an attempt to fob Faustus off with the 'scholarism' he already knows. But the 'vast perpetual torture-house' image persists throughout the play, and is physically 'discovered' in the penultimate scene:

> There are the furies, tossing damned souls
> On burning forks; their bodies boil in lead:
> There are live quarters broiling on the coals,
> That ne'er can die: this ever-burning chair
> Is for o'er-tortur'd souls to rest them in:
> These that are fed with sops of flaming fire
> Were gluttons and lov'd only delicates
> And laugh'd to see the poor starve at their gates.
> But yet all these are nothing; thou shalt see
> Ten thousand tortures that more horrid be.　　xix. 118

I suppose there is a sense in which these lines reflect Faustus's bondage to the medieval horrors of his own consciousness. But the bondage is also Marlowe's, as is the hint of schoolboy sadism in the facilities of the rhythm. There is an obsessive preoccupation with 'furies' and infernal torments which can be traced from *Tamburlaine* right through Marlowe's dramatic career.[19] It is one of those matters on which his imagination appears to have dwelt with unwholesome insistence, with hideous fascination that is always trying to shake off its horror by parody and overstatement. I cannot believe that the man who wrote these lines was wholly in control of the impulses that express themselves in the verse. As Benvolio remarks of the Faustian rhetoric, 'Blood! he speaks terribly. But, for all that, I do not greatly believe him.' In any case, this gross physical hell combines with the 'Shagge-hayr'd Deuills'[20] and the dismembered corpse of the last scene to superimpose a relatively superficial image of hell upon a dramatic metaphor of great force and range. Hell can never be an anachronism as long as it is used to give shape to the forces which are felt to be ultimately destructive of human significance; but a hell which destroys a man by tearing him limb from limb is an anachronism in the world of serious evil which the best parts of *Faustus* offer to the imagination. Its relative superficiality is reflected in the verse which presents it, relying as it does so heavily on the external and the sensational.

III

But at times the vacillation between subjective and objective accounts of the demonic order gives way to a new synthetic insight in which the objective force of evil is retained at the same time as Marlowe recognises its psychological roots. His success in dramatising Faustus's crises of conscience by the device of the two angels breaks down the subjective/ objective either/or and triumphantly has it both ways.

These figures, who had been literal entities in the old *psychomachia*, become in *Faustus* something much more elusive. It is true that they are abstractions, belonging to no specific time and place, speaking an unmoved, formalised verse from some point clearly outside the area where the play's decisions are taken. Yet the very abstraction keeps them sufficiently unindividualised to be functions of Faustus's conscience, and sufficiently removed from the sphere of dramatic action to symbolise an order outside it.

> BAD ANGEL. Go forward, Faustus, in that famous art.
> GOOD ANGEL. Sweet Faustus, leave that execrable art.
> FAUSTUS. Contrition, prayer, repentance, what of these?
> GOOD ANGEL. O, they are means to bring thee unto heaven.
> BAD ANGEL. Rather illusions, fruits of lunacy,
> That make men foolish that do use them most.
> GOOD ANGEL. Sweet Faustus, think of heaven and heavenly things.
> BAD ANGEL. No, Faustus, think of honour and of wealth.
> FAUSTUS. Wealth!   v. 15

Far from being clumsily primitive, this is an immensely dramatic procedure. The first effect of the interruption is to arrest all action on the stage, and to focus attention on the protagonist, suspended in the act of choice. Not until he speaks do we know to which voice he has been attending. It is the act of choice in slow motion, a dramatisation of his strained attention to the faint voices of unconscious judgment. At the same time, his unawareness of the Angels' presence has the effect of revealing his blindness to the real issues at stake—what he takes to be a decision between contrition and wealth, the forms in which the Angels' exhortations have crystallised in his mind, is a primal decision between good and evil. And his unconscious echoing of their words is a parable of his inability to evade moral categories. The course of self-gratification on which he is embarked is no more his own than are the Angels; yet it is, by the same token, as *much* his own as they are. He is an involuntary participant in the moral order, yet he shapes the moral order by his action.[21]

Marlowe's dramatic point is not that evil is only the basin-eyed monster of legend and good the angelic visitant—i.e. merely objective; nor that they are only manifestations of states of consciousness—i.e. merely subjective; but rather that they have the kind of reality which is appropriately represented by an actor in a play. They are real enough to have voices of their own. It is as if the play moved on a plane at right-angles to the one whose axes are 'subjective' and 'objective'; its co-ordinates are heaven and hell considered as primal symbols, and ranging in their suggested provenance from the purely subjective hallucination to the stonily objective fact.

The paradox of man's submission to the values which he helps to create, his unfree freedom, is not, like some of the paradoxes in the play, a symptom merely of tension between the old and the new. It is a central synthesis and a real insight. At times the same interpretation extends to the other supra-human entities. The Lucifer, for instance, who appears at the opening of Scene iii may be taken as an extension of Faustus's own consciousness, provided we do not take the further, illegitimate step of making him *nothing but* an extension. The stage direction reads, '*Thunder. Enter* LUCIFER *and four* Devils [*above*]: FAUSTUS *to them.*' Faustus is here to conjure the devil; but before he has called, hell has answered. The devil, obeying laws of his own nature, is already present, thus rendering the whole ritual grotesquely superflu-ous. Lucifer's presence is another embodiment of the radical moral polarisation implicit in all human activity. Hell exists independently of Faustus's need of it. Yet, his incantations do have a specific result, for Mephostophilis finally appears before him, less 'pliant' than Faustus imagines, but nevertheless a palpable change in the moral landscape which must, in some measure, be attributed to Faustus's activity—in a sense he *has* brought Mephostophilis from hell. He is also, significantly, responsible for the fact that the 'too ugly' face of hell is given a 'holy shape' which conceals its true nature from his eyes (iii. 25-35). The evil Faustus invokes is both his own and not his own.

At moments like this, the sense of the transcendence of evil, which is such a stumbling-block to the modern reader of *Doctor Faustus*, is given a dramatic validity which is not dependent on the metaphysics of the audience. Our own puny individual evil, we recognise, is watched over by vaster forces that can make of it something so diabolical that we no longer know it as our own. By the evil act we give hostages to powers we may not be able to control. Though not corporeal, not even perhaps an entity at all, the demonic is real. Diabolism of this kind springs from a determination to take man's individual and collective powers with the utmost seriousness. It is a vision of humanity continually threatened by obscure forces of anihilation which are both internal and external—a humanity, in short, capable of tragic stature.

But the hard fact of the case is that this is an insight gained and lost again a dozen times in the course of the play, and it is never held with that firmness and assurance which could make it a master-conception. Rather it is Marlowe's fleeting perception of a dramatic felicity which he knows neither how to control nor how to build into the structure of the drama.

IV

Just as, in the treatment of the supernatural order, Marlowe seems to waver between a rather leaden-footed literalism and real imaginative insight, so in the characterisation of the sin for which Faustus is ultimately damned, he seems uncertain of his ground. At times it is seen homiletically as mere presumptuous pride, 'a devilish exercise'. At times (as it acquires a real dramatic weight and body) it is seen, less simply, as a legitimate aspiration somehow tainted at its source. And at times it is simply endorsed with a kind of naïve enthusiasm which is very like the wide-eyed wonderment of the *Faustbook*.

It is this uncertainty, I think, that has encouraged critics like Professor Ellis-Fermor to see Faustus's sin as a harmless variety of humanist aspiration (for her, Marlowe the humanist is obliged to damn his hero only because he has been guilty of intellectual apostasy in the face of a menacing orthodoxy).[22] This is to respond to something which is certainly present in the play; but it is something of which the play is not, so to speak, aware.

We have seen already how Faustus's exploratory urges could be taken to symbolise the intellectual expansionism of the Renaissance; and it is true that many even of his power fantasies are connected with the widening geographical and mental horizons of that period: true for instance that he proposes to 'search all corners of the new-found world'. But for what? 'For pleasant fruits and princely delicates' (i. 83). Helen may be the paradigm of classical beauty, the resuscitated body of antique learning, but she is raised in order to become Faustus's paramour, and to 'extinguish clear / Those thoughts that do dissuade me from my vow' (xviii. 94). Indeed, most of Faustus's 'humanist' impulses, closely scrutinised, resolve themselves into a familiar and explicit form of hedonism and epicurean self-indulgence. There is no doubt that Marlowe sets out to place very firmly the damnable nature of Faustus's ambition; and if we are to allow any force at all to Ellis-

Fermor's mitigating contentions, we must do so by positing a Marlowe divided against himself, here as elsewhere. In fact, I believe, he was. But it is necessary, first of all, to see how hard he worked to show us the dangers of the Faustian path.

When one considers Faustus's motives for taking up the magical arts, it becomes clear that Marlowe wants us to detect a serious moral weakness at the root of the decision. There is, for instance, his contempt for the laborious particularity of the academic disciplines—'too servile and illiberal for *me*': the revealing stress on the personal pronoun ('Thou art too ugly to attend on *me*') is the dramatic embodiment of the psychological state which Marlowe sees to be attendant on such an intellectual attitude. Faustus prefers the grandiose cult of universals: he will 'level at the end of every art'. But there must be no hard work: the drudgery is to be deputed to his 'servile spirits' (i. 96). The irksome burden of unanswered questions can be shrugged off, for the spirits will 'resolve me of all ambiguities' (i. 79); and it's a desire for the fruits of knowledge without its pains which makes him long to 'see hell and return again safe' (vi. 172). He shares that perennial human conviction that there's a short cut of knowledge, some formula that makes it unnecessary to go about and about the hill of truth—a conviction that is aptly symbolised in the delusions of magic. The art into which the two infamous magicians initiate him is one of those reassuring skills which demand exactly the knowledge one possesses— astrology, tongues, mineralogy (i. 137)—yet promise immediate and infallible results. Cornelius and Valdes are the direct ancestors of our Pelmanists and Scientologists, and Faustus has plainly been reading their illustrated brochure when he remarks,

> Their conference will be a greater help to me
> Than all my labours, plod I ne'er so fast.　　　　　i. 67

It is plain, then, in the opening scenes, that Marlowe is giving us a portrait of an egocentric abuse of knowledge; Faustus belongs to that class of scholars who are, in Nashe's words,

ambitious, haughty, and proud, nor do they loue vertue for it selfe any whit, but because they would ouerquell and outstrip others with the vaineglorious ostentation of it. A humour of monarchising and nothing els it is, which makes them affect rare quallified studies.[23]

It is certainly a desire for 'vaineglorious ostentation' which makes Faustus aspire to the status of an Agrippa, 'whose shadows made all Europe honour him' (i. 116). 'Be a physician Faustus,' he advises himself, 'and be eterniz'd for some wondrous cure' (i. 14—the vaguely indefinite 'some' is an index of the extent to which aspiration is divorced from reality, while 'eterniz'd' reminds us how constantly Faustus makes his felicity reside in the mouths of men). For such an academic megalomaniac, the triumphant university disputation is the most delectable of memories:

> I...have with concise syllogisms
> Gravell'd the pastors of the German church,
> And made the flowering pride of Wittenberg
> Swarm to my problems as the infernal spirits
> On sweet Musaeus when he came to hell...   i. 111

It is with such relish that he finds himself able to equate Wittenberg's 'flowering pride' with a swarm of infernal bees! And the relish is there because he has set all his pleasure upon the subjugation of other beings to his personal gratification. But this is an appetite which reasserts itself at the very moment of its satisfaction; for, once subjugated, the divines of Wittenberg can no longer minister to his sense of power, and he must go in search of increasingly larger spheres in which to exercise his passion for domination. Which is the plot of the play.

If there is one key motif in the scenes leading up to the signing of the pact, it is this 'humour of monarchising', an obsessive preoccupation with power: power over the grand forces of nature—winds, storms (i. 57), the Rhine (i. 88), the ocean (iii. 41), the air (iii. 107); power over national and international destinies ('The Emperor shall not live but by my leave, / Nor any potentate of Germany'—iii. 112 and cf. i. 86, 91–5); power over the storehouses of nature ('I'll have them fly to India for gold, / Ransack the ocean for orient pearl'— i. 81 and cf. i. 74, 143–6), over the plate-fleets of Spain (i. 130); even the disposition of the continental land-masses (iii. 109–10) and the movements of the celestial bodies (iii. 40) are to be at his command. Those of his dreams which are not merely anarchistic nihilism—as the ocean overwhelming the world, the moon dropping from her sphere (iii. 40–1) or the petty prosecution of private revenge (iii. 98)—are simply variations on a single theme: 'I'll be great emperor of the world' (iii. 106). His mind, like Epicure Mammon's, thrown into near delirium at the prospect, casts up this strange farrago of preposterous fantasies in the future tense ('I'll...I'll...I'll...'). Like Mammon, too, Faustus earns our contempt by assuming that the beings of superior power with whom he traffics exist merely to gratify his whims.

Such ambitions are not only damnable, they are laughable, and in terms of the chosen peripateia they are clearly to be regarded as arrant folly and presumption. But Marlowe, we recall, is the author of *Tamburlaine* (*Tamburlaine* the indulgence *ad absurdum* of the 'humour of monarchising', not the moral fable critics have made out of it). And the more I look at the verse in which Faustus's grandiose visions are expounded the less certain I am that Marlowe has wholly dissociated himself from his hero—any more than the anonymous author of the *Faustbook* had done. In both the play and its source book, there are long stretches where a naïve wonder at the subtleties of the witch completely submerges the moral condemnation of witchcraft—an ambiguity which results from the shallowness of the initial condemnation. At such points in the play (and I would include nearly all the central section, Scenes viii–xvii, under this heading) the verse is strangely neutral morally—Mammon's foamings at the mouth provide an instructive contrast—has no clearly placed tone, only a shallow fluency and prolixity that suggest it came a trifle too easily to its author. It is neither the clear moral evaluation of a diseased mind, nor the enactment of a kindling imagination, but the indulgence of an abiding mood or mode in Marlowe's rhetorical poetic.

This becomes clear if we consider one passage where we do get a genuine presentation of the quickened pulse and soaring imagination of a man awestruck before a new universe of meaning and potentiality:

> O, what a world of profit and delight
> Of power, of honour, of omnipotence,
> Is promis'd to the studious artisan!
> All things that move between the quiet poles
> Shall be at my command: emperors and kings
> Are but obey'd in their several provinces,
> Nor can they raise the wind or rend the clouds;
> But his dominion that exceeds in this
> Stretcheth as far as doth the mind of man.   i. 52

By charting so subtly the accumulating emotion behind the words, this masterfully articulated crescendo gives to the word 'dominion' a richer and more human meaning than it has elsewhere. 'Power' in these terms is not merely a presumptuous aspiration beyond the human condition, but a very nearly legitimate ambition closely, though ambiguously, related to the passion for mastery that leads to knowledge and 'truth'. If this vein had been more diligently uncovered in the rest of the play, we might have had a tragedy. But even this fine passage is immediately followed by a piece of rant in the Tamburlaine vein, which tips the delicate balance between an imaginative sympathy which is itself a judgment, and a top-heavy moral censure:

> A sound magician is a demi-god;
> Here tire, my brains, to get a deity!

The overstrain in the verse—expressing itself here in a syntactical incoherence—is not, I suggest, a dramatisation of Faustus's mental state.[24] It is too imprecise and too hectic to be that. Rather it is Marlowe forcing an insurrectionary line of thought to discredit itself by over-protestation. Again, awareness of a tormenting ambivalence at the heart of all speculation, unsatiable or otherwise, has given way to flat homiletic demonstration.

The element of demonstration is strong in *Faustus*—most notably in the rejection of learning which opens the action. Faustus here indulges in a conventional, if not an academic, exercise: the 'Dispraise of Learning'. But both his methods and his conclusions are strikingly different from the Christianised pyrrhonism of his models. Faustus does not, in the traditional manner, indicate the shortcomings of human wit by showing how far each science falls short of its own avowed aims, and how far of divine omniscience; nor does he conclude with an exhortation to study only to know oneself and God. Instead he refers all learning to his private satisfaction, and finishes by rejecting 'divinity' along with the rest.

The startlingly egocentric nature of his rejection can be estimated by comparing a contemporary survey of the same area—Cornelius Agrippa's *De Incertitudine et Vanitate Scientarum*. Agrippa, like Faustus, has bidden *on kai me on* farewell; but for what reasons? Because the philosophers 'striue and disagree emong themselues in all things', one sect subverting another; because their reason 'cannot perswade no constant or certaine thinge, but doth alwayes wauer in mutable opinions'; because Logic, the philosopher's tool, is 'nothinge els, but a skilfulnes of contention and darkenesse, by the whiche al other sciences are made more obscure, and harder to learne'; because their conclusions ground themselves upon authority where they should build upon experience.[25] Here is Faustus surveying the same territory:

> Is to dispute well logic's chiefest end?
> Affords this art no greater miracle?
> Then read no more, *thou hast attain'd that end*;

A greater subject fitteth Faustus' wit.
Bid *on kai me on* farewell...   i. 8

The shifty way in which one section of philosophy (Logic) is equated
with all of Aristotle, and then used to discredit philosophy itself, makes
one doubt that there was ever a serious intellectual objection here at all.

Again, Agrippa has no time for Physic, which he finds to be 'a
certaine Arte of manslaughter...aboue the knowledge of the lawe',
because it cannot predict what it claims to control, yet, unperturbed by
this technological breakdown, makes increasingly extravagant claims
for its efficacy.[26] Faustus:

> The end of physic is our body's health.
> Why, Faustus, *hast thou not attain'd that end*?
> Is not thy common talk sound aphorisms?
> Are not thy bills hung up as monuments,
> Whereby whole cities have escap'd the plague
> And thousand desperate maladies been cured?
> Yet art thou still but Faustus, and a man.   i. 17

Of 'the Lawe and Statutes' Agrippa complains that they are merely a
compound of men's uncertain opinions, 'altered at euerye chaunge of
time, of the State, of the Prince', and cannot, consequently, represent
any real principle of justice.[27] For Faustus the disillusionment expounds
itself in words like 'petty' and 'paltry'. The failure of Law to realise
in the temporal sphere the justice that humanity demands of the divine
order is far from his mind:

> This study fits a mercenary drudge
> Who aims at nothing but external trash,
> Too servile and illiberal for me.   i. 34

In each of these cases, the rewards of learning are conceived entirely in
terms of the recognition and acclaim which are accorded to the
practitioner. Where Agrippa refers a science to the principles which it is
supposed to embody, and finds it wanting, Faustus refers the whole
body of human learning to his private satisfaction—'The god thou
serv'st is thine own appetite'—and when he discovers, either that the
offered satisfaction is already available to him, or that it is one he does
not covet, he passes on. Agrippa is by no means a profound thinker:
but beside Faustus's glib superficiality, Agrippa's carefree *a priori*
pyrrhonism seems eminently sane.

Now it may be that we have here Faustus's mental history in a
conventionalised form; but if so, it is the mental history of a shallow

mind—a sophist's mind: and the telescoping of time (if that is what it is) has the dramatic effect of heightening the sense of shallowness. It is important to realise that the investigation is no more than a façade (note the tone of pert self-congratulation and the glib transitions—as if the books were all ready with the markers at the relevant pages), and that the real decision has been taken in the first four lines, where Faustus exhorts himself to 'be a divine in show / Yet level at the end of every art'. Divinity, of course, was the science which claimed to do just this, and Faustus has already made the 'end of every art' antithetical to the study of God.

There is a peremptory haste about the whole sequence, punctuated as it is by the clap of shut books and the breathless snatching of the next ('Galen come... Where is Justinian?...'), and as a result, when the abrupt slackening of pace does come, it is doubly arresting:

> These metaphysics of magicians
> And necromantic books are heavenly;
> Lines, circles, letters, characters:
> Ay, these are those that Faustus most desires.   i. 48—B text

At once the factitious clouds of sophistry disperse, and, gloating over his symbolic hieroglyphs in irrational fascination, Faustus finds his true tone. The seriousness of his commitment to a thorough-going rationalism is indicated here by the interesting, though not surprising, fact that he does not apply the same rational canons to the 'arte magick': it is enough that 'these are those that Faustus most desires'.

Faustus's condemnation is thus writ large (too large, as I see it) in the opening scene. In order to regard him as a premature Promethean hero of the Enlightenment, one must either regard all enlightened Prometheans as damnable (this is roughly Miss Mahood's position),[28] or admit that, judged by enlightened criteria, he is a decidely damp squib. In anybody's book the attitudes he adopts are unworthy.

And yet there is here that same absence of moral orientation of the *energies* of the verse, however loudly the attitudes expressed may call out for censure. As with the presentation of Faustus's power fantasies, there is an emotional indirection making it almost impossible to be sure that Marlowe has not gone a-whoring after the strange gods he appears to abominate. To a dangerous degree Faustus *is* Marlowe, and the play is a vehement attempt to impose order on a realm of consciousness which is still in insurrection.

Perhaps this is why Marlowe overdoes the condemnation. This

frivolous academic opportunist, who has clearly learned very little from his encyclopedic education, cannot engage our sympathies very deeply. The narrow moral categories of the Prologue seem entirely adequate to encompass the significance of such a presumptuous fool:

> ...swollen with cunning of a self-conceit,
> His waxen wings did mount above his reach,
> And, melting, heavens conspir'd his overthrow. Prologue, 20

This is the tone and manner of homiletic demonstration, not of tragic paradox, and it is in harmony with the Faustus of the early scenes.[29]

On the one hand, then, we have a conscious and studied rejection of Faustus's position, which phrases itself in explicit moral comment and in an only slightly less explicit ironic exposure of his dubious motivation. On the other hand, there is an unrecognised hankering after the pleasures of magic, which turn, as the play progresses, into something very like the pleasures of the senses—'all voluptuousness'. This split in sensibility, between the conscious design and the subconscious desire, is a familiar strait of the Puritan imagination—which finds its illicit Comuses and Bowers of Bliss too powerfully attractive to be dealt with on any but a moralistic level. Yet the moralisation which promises to free the mind from the tyranny of the sensory, this theoretical world-negation, simply hides the secret appetites from sight, and sharpens them as it prohibits their gratification. Thus it gives rise simultaneously to moralistic excess, and to a hectic and unwholesome obsession with the lost joys of mere sensuality. As we shall see, it is a peculiarly protestant dilemma in more ways than one.

v

If there were no more than this in *Doctor Faustus*, it would not exercise the kind of fascination it does. But there is also a desperate fatalism about Marlowe's vision, a sense that all the most desirable and ravishing things, man's fulfilment itself, are subject to a cosmic veto. A tragic rift yawns between the things man desires as man, and the things he must be content with, as sinner. And it is partly against this dark fatality that Faustus mobilises his doomed revolt.

I have described the rejection of learning as peremptory and wilful. But there is one significant moment where Faustus is brought up short for a moment, darkly brooding over one of his texts; and because the subject of his contemplation introduces one of the most impressive movements in the play, it is worth examining the passage carefully.

Stipendium peccati, mors est: ha, *stipendium*, etc.
The reward of sin is death? that's hard:
Si pecasse negamus, fallimur, & nulla est in nobis veritas:
If we say that we have no sin
We deceive ourselves, and there is no truth in us.
Why then belike we must sin,
And so consequently die,
Ay, we must die, an everlasting death.
What doctrine call you this? *Che sarà, sarà*:
What will be, shall be; Divinity adieu.

i. 39—B text punctuation and lineation

Scholars have provided the biblically unlearned with the second
halves of Faustus's texts—'but the gift of God is eternal life', and 'if we
confess our sins, he is faithful and just to forgive us our sins...'—and
we have been made aware that Faustus's argument only holds good in
the absence of Grace.[30] Paul Kocher has even unearthed an example of
this precise syllogism, duly refuted by a theologian.[31] Any member of
Marlowe's audience, we gather, could have given this crude sophistry
its logical quietus. And so he might; but whether he would thereby
have been rid of the problem is another question.

For as the sixteenth century became the seventeenth, and as a distorted
Calvinist theology grew increasingly vocal in English pulpits, the
possibility of reprobation without appeal became one of the most
earnestly discussed topics of English theology. In the year Marlowe
took his B.A., the debate flared up as a Cambridge graduate and future
archbishop, Samuel Harsnett, denounced the preachers of a reprobation
which had, he claimed, 'grown high and monstrous, and like a Goliath,
and men do shake and tremble at it'.[32] Series of manuals offering to
satisfy the reader about his election or otherwise were printed and reprinted. Cases of conscience like the famous one of Francis Spira,
which may have influenced *Faustus*, encouraged unholy and obsessive
speculation about one's eternal destiny.[33] There was a distinct feeling in
the air that, though damnation was a certainty unless steps were taken
to avert it, salvation was a problematical and tricky business. And there
is plenty of evidence to suggest that Marlowe at Cambridge was
thoroughly exposed to this opinion and the debates it provoked.

It doesn't require much imagination to see how this kind of thinking,
robed with all the grandeur of theological authority, might prey upon
a mind already open to suggestions of guilt and worthlessness. Those
who thought it necessary to preach against the doctrine were certainly

aware of the savage self-contempt which it reinforced in unstable personalities.

But Faustus's syllogism is not simply a theological curiosity, nor is it a position to be rebutted and then forgotten. It has an alarming kind of internal and experiential logic which survives refutation. The predestinarian crux is the basilisk eye of Christianity. It proposes the desperate and totally destructive possibility, to which, in his blacker moments, man is prone to yield. Faustus is a little chirpy about it at first—'Why then belike we must sin, and so consequently die...'—but he immediately feels the dark compulsion of the idea: 'Ay, we must die, an everlasting death.' It is the siren song of annihilation, inviting the guilt which is an inescapable component of personality to rise and engulf the whole being. Faustus reacts vigorously and, as I have said, peremptorily: 'What doctrine call you this?...Divinity adieu.' But in that brief brooding pause we have seen his rebellion from an angle which reveals it as, in some sense, a revolt *for life*, not against life. Magic is at least one way of escaping the gloomy pessimism of this doomed view of human existence. The essential pessimism of *Marlowe*'s vision lies in the fact that magic is also, for the play, delusion.

It is, I suppose, fairly obvious that the deity of *Doctor Faustus* is not the God of Love, the Good Shepherd, but either the avenging Jehovah of the Old Testament, or his Christian offshoot, the Calvinist tyrant of mass reprobation. This God, in less troubled days, had been Tamburlaine's patron and protector:

> There is a God, full of revenging wrath,
> From whom the thunder and the lightning breaks,
> Whose scourge I am, and him will I obey. *II Tam.* v. i. 182

In *Tamburlaine* this deity was transparently a theological 'front' for a bloody-minded aggressiveness in the Scythian general, if not in Marlowe himself. But in the period between *Tamburlaine* and *Faustus*, complacent identification with this appalling God has given way to torment and horror before it. In a very real sense, *Faustus* is an unsuccessful attempt to evade the fatal embrace of this murderous and irresistible deity—Marlowe's attempt as well as Faustus's.

The escape route is remarkably congruent with what we know of Marlowe's own revolt, for Faustus's rebellion takes the shape of a flirtation with a kind of free-thought that was fairly widely disseminated in Renaissance Europe.[34] He questions the immortality of the soul (iii. 64); he asks, and apparently wants to be informed, about the origins of the world (though the form of his question labels him an incurable theist—vi. 69); he wonders whether hell exists, or if it does whether it has anything like the horrors depicted by the theologians (iii. 61–3; v. 116–40), and his scepticism has the characteristic Epicurean tinge that tended, in the sixteenth century, to go with the release of the 'advanced thinker' from the oppression of threatened punishment— he wants to spend his 'four-and-twenty years of liberty' 'in all voluptuousness' (iii. 94 and viii. 61).

But like that of most of the 'atheist' rebels of this period, Faustus's free-thought is far from being untroubled. It is deeply involved with personal pressures, and still joined, by the umbilical cord of a terror-which-is-still-faith, to the theism it purports to reject.

Faustus's learned discussions with Mephostophilis, for instance, have a persistent and revealing tendency to finger the wound in his own consciousness—and this despite the fact that he is, ostensibly, searching for the new and startling truths which his liberation from old dogma should have freed him to contemplate:

> Are all celestial bodies but one globe
> As is the substance of this centric earth? vi. 36

When Mephostophilis proves to be stonily orthodox, he is not content, and raises the problem of the eccentric motion of the planets:

> But have they all
> One motion, both *situ et tempore*?

But again he is disappointed, for Mephostophilis merely falls back upon the hypothesis of the poles of the zodiac. His impatience is clear: 'These slender questions Wagner can decide: / Hath Mephostophilis no greater skill?...These are freshman's suppositions.' And again he circles nearer his objective:

> But, tell me, hath every sphere a dominion or *intelligentia*?

asking in effect, How true is the spiritual order allegedly governing the material universe? Here Mephostophilis is again reactionary, for the intelligences had already been expounded as metaphors for behaviour according to rational laws, yet he asserts their objective existence.[35] (It is one of the play's most telling ironies that the new diabolic knowledge, for which Faustus sells his soul, should prove to be nothing more than the old scholastic cosmos which he has contemptuously rejected in its favour.)

There is a little more elementary astronomical catechising, which

Mephostophilis answers conservatively,[36] whereat Faustus concedes, 'Well, I am answered', in a voice that implies he is not; then, precipitately, he rushes on to his true question:

> Now tell me who made the world.

This is his real point of attack; for it is the divinely created, providentially ordered universe that he is so reluctant to accept. The answer he receives is presented with tremendous dramatic force as an upheaval in hell. Mephostophilis refuses to answer, and his sullen recalcitrance grows into a menacing anger, so menacing that Faustus sees, for the first time since his original encounter with the demonic world, the repellent face of evil:

> Ay, go, accursed spirit, to ugly hell!

The fiend's abrupt departure and his subsequent return with Lucifer and Beelzebub at precisely the moment when Faustus calls upon Christ is, as James Smith points out, an apt representation of the emotional upheaval which the very asking of the question provokes in Faustus's consciousness.[37] For his particular form of scepticism is accompanied by, perhaps derived from, a profound emotional involvement with the ideas he rejects; and if his atheism is superficial, it is superficial because his theism is ineradicable.

The same tension between attraction and repulsion is discernible in the exaggerated gestures with which he dismisses the 'vain trifles of men's souls' (iii. 64), and the 'old wives' tales' of an after-life (v. 136), but especially in the ambiguous attitudes that he adopts towards hell itself. It is interesting to note that on this issue (the existence of hell) he also employs the same wary catechising technique, pouncing on discrepancies, and driving home with the question which he hopes will extort the desired information. When Mephostophilis declares himself to be 'for ever damn'd with Lucifer', Faustus is immediately on the alert:

> Where are you damn'd?
>
> MEPHOSTOPHILIS.   In hell.
>
> FAUSTUS. How comes it then that thou art out of hell?   iii. 76

The fiend's answer has gone down in the annals of theatrical history, but its revelation of a hell that is co-extensive with the existence of mind is precisely the reverse of what Faustus was seeking: it was not hell, but the power of the sound magician, that was to stretch 'as far as doth the mind of man'. Yet Faustus is not answered: his view of hell continues to fluctuate wildly throughout the play.

That hell is 'a fable' (v. 128) is only one of the positions he adopts: if it is 'sleeping, eating, walking and disputing', as Mephostophilis suggests, then he'll 'willingly be damn'd' (v. 139-40). On the one hand, he 'confounds hell in Elysium'—meaning, I take it, that the two are a single state, the classical Hades where his ghost will be 'with the old philosophers' (iii. 62-3); on the other hand, Mephostophilis is exhorted to 'scorn those *joys* thou never shalt possess' (iii. 88) and Faustus acknowledges that he has 'incurr'd *eternal death*' (iii. 90). It is only after he has asked for and received a description of hell from a being to whom he is talking only because he believes him to have come from hell, that Faustus declares hell to be a fable. Yet, a few scenes later, Lucifer's genial assurance that 'in hell is all manner of delight' (vi. 171) sends him grovelling for a sight of the fabulous place.

But there's a deep consistency here. Hell is a fable only as long as it's a place 'where we are tortur'd and remain forever'. If it affords 'all manner of delight', he believes in it. He'll scorn the joys he'll never possess only because he does not believe them to be joys. He'll willingly be damned provided he can have damnation on his own terms— 'sleeping, eating, walking and disputing'. The consistency resides in his determination to submit all moral categories to his personal convenience; and the ultimate failure of such an enterprise is figured in the continual presence of the melancholy fiend who knows better than to attempt it. On Mephostophilis's terms—being in hell and knowing it —one can be damned and preserve one's dignity; on Faustus's—being in hell and pretending it's heaven—one can only prevaricate and rationalise, writhing on the pin which holds one fast to an inexorably moral universe.

Moral systems can only be overthrown on moral grounds. What revolutions in morality humanity has seen, have all been conducted in the interests of some higher principle which has hitherto been over-looked. Faustus's reorganisation of morality can make no such claim; it aims merely at making the universe more convenient to live in—'if I may haue my desire while I liue, I am satisfied, let me shift after death as I may', as Robert Greene put it.[38] It lacks even the Utilitarian grace of considering the convenience of mankind as a whole. It is Faustus's private revolution, the objectives of which would be utterly subverted if all men were to participate in its benefits. Marlowe draws with perception and firmness the disastrous blindness implicit in this epicurean individualism. One sees, in the scenes depicting Faustus's

accommodation to damnation and the creed of hell, the kind of meaning
that could be given to his rejection of the traditional wisdom: it is a
rejection of the 'communal' element in human endeavour; and one
immediate result is a dangerous isolation which Marlowe dramatises
in the long midnight colloquies with the non-human Mephostophilis.

Very often of course it is necessary to cut oneself off from the
assumptions that come most easily; but equally often, the severing of
bonds is succeeded by a servile commitment to the party that promises
emancipation. In Faustus's case the commitment is to the non-human
and for the greater part of the play he is shown trying to be 'a spirit
in form and substance', to the consequent atrophy of his specifically
human potentialities. 'He is not well with being over-solitary.'

This is why his eleventh-hour return to the domestic limitations of the
scholar's life, and his poignant reaching out for human contact, are so
extraordinarily moving—at last his estranged and suppressed humanity
has risen to demand its due. When the First Scholar regrets that Faustus
has given his friends no opportunity to pray for him (xix. 69–70), he
is speaking not only of the loss of divine grace, but also of the communal human support which men can give each other, from which
Faustus, by his 'singularity', has cut himself off.[39]

It is when this doomed attempt at autarchy and self-signification
collides with the demands of a nature still fundamentally religious, that
the play again moves into a region of tragic potential:

> GOOD ANGEL. Faustus, repent; yet God will pity thee.
> BAD ANGEL. Thou art a spirit; God cannot pity thee.
> FAUSTUS. Who buzzeth in mine ears I am a spirit?
>   Be I a devil, yet God may pity me;
>   Yea, God will pity me if I repent.
> BAD ANGEL. Ay, but Faustus never shall repent.   vi. 12

The Angels withdraw, leaving Fauṣtus to the bottomless solitude of
moral responsibility:

> My heart is harden'd, I cannot repent.
> Scarce can I name salvation, faith, or heaven,
> But fearful echoes thunders in mine ears,
> 'Faustus, thou art damn'd!' Then guns and knives,
> Swords, poison, halters, and envenom'd steel
> Are laid before me to dispatch myself;
> And long ere this I should have done the deed
> Had not sweet pleasure conquer'd deep despair.   vi. 18

Beneath the rhetorical symmetries of the Angels' speech lies the tragic paradox of a consciousness ruinously divided against itself—a consciousness powerfully drawn by 'salvation, faith and heaven', yet deafened by the 'fearful echoes' that thunder in his ears when he names them, by those magnified reverberations of his own despairing self-accusation. The sense of imprisonment within the self is so overwhelming that he can only frame it in terms of external coercion—'My heart is harden'd'. To ask whether he is in fact coerced, or whether he only imagines he is, is meaningless. Unless we blind ourselves with a drastically over-simplified view of volition, we must recognise in Faustus's predicament a perennial human impasse.

The situation is given added depth as he goes on to specify the 'sweet pleasure' in a way that transcends mere 'voluptuousness' and becomes a passionate love of beauty:

> Have not I made blind Homer sing to me
> Of Alexander's love and Oenon's death?
> And hath not he, that built the walls of Thebes
> With ravishing sound of his melodious harp,
> Made music with my Mephostophilis?
> Why should I die, then, or basely despair?

Why indeed? The music is so entirely present in the lyric cadence of these lines that it becomes more than an infernal palliative. And the mention of Mephostophilis does not so much ironically discredit the vision, as transform the fiend into a sweet musician in consort with all the singers of antiquity. Faustus's religious consciousness, his desperate self-rejection, and his love of beautiful things, are here locked in internecine conflict, none prevailing yet none yielding. It is one of the finest moments in the play.

If one had to select a single scene as the imaginative heart of the action, I think it would be this one (Scene vi), with its appalling and giddy oscillation between the profundities of despair and the escapist frivolities of the Pageant of the Sins; with its superb dramatisation of Faustus's love–hate relation with God, when he calls on Christ and is confronted by Lucifer. If he is torn more violently than this by his divided nature, he cannot survive.

But increasingly, from this point onwards, the hardness of heart, and the corresponding stiffness of mind, provide him with an assured resting place—'Now Faustus must / Thou needs be damn'd... Despair in God, and trust in Beelzebub' (v. 1–5). He resolves the agonies of choice by falling back on an assumed external fate; and though he wavers and has to exhort himself to 'be resolute', his resolution never takes cognizance of the contrary impulse towards repentance. The two are absolutely dissevered. He seems to prefer damnation; for, as a reprobate, he is in a position to exercise that limited variety of 'manly fortitude' which consists in scorning the joys he never shall possess. His is the kind of mind which prefers consistency to integrity. He is stiff to maintain any purpose. And in that stiffness he goes to hell.

I have called this movement in the play (the movement concerned with Faustus's desperate attempt to defy a reality of his own nature) tragic, because it leads us beyond the homiletic framework of the opening scenes, and asks us to conceive of a conflict between immovable conviction and irresistible doubt on the battleground of the individual consciousness. At such moments, the evaluation of Faustus's moral condition is no longer possible in terms like the Chorus's 'swollen with cunning of a self-conceit'. Marlowe's attempt to impose order on his rebellion moves out of the sphere of moralistic abstraction into a world where the felt reality of the heavenly values constitutes their sole claim to serious attention.

And it is a basic element in Faustus's damnation that salvation and the means to it should never seem more than 'illusions, fruits of lunacy'. Although that salvation is a continual theoretical possibility, there is a blockage in Faustus's consciousness which makes 'contrition, prayer, repentance' appear always to be unreal alternatives. And the blockage is Marlowe's too. Why else can it be that the heavenly can only be represented in the faint efflorescence of the Good Angel's utterances, or in the Old Man's appeal to a 'faith' which claims will triumph over 'vile hell' (xviii. 124), but which is imprisoned within its own theological concepts? There is a crippling generality about the salvation the Old Man offers:

> I see an angel hovers o'er thy head
> And with a vial full of precious *grace*
> Offers to pour the same into the soul:
> Then call for *mercy*, and avoid *despair*.   xviii. 61

As spiritual counsel this is hopelessly inadequate, and the reply Marlowe gives Faustus—'I feel / Thy words to comfort my distressed soul'— seems forced and unconvincing.

The final declaration of Marlowe's failure to give body to the heavenly order is the creaking machinery of the descending 'throne' in Scene xix. The only face of God that we see—and see with frightening immediacy—is one from which Faustus recoils in horror:

> See where God
> Stretcheth out his arms and bends his ireful brows.
> Mountains and hills, come, come, and fall on me,
> And hide me from the heavy wrath of God!
> No, no.   xix. 150

The conception of divine justice which prevails is Lucifer's—'Christ cannot save thy soul, for he is just' (vi. 87). Justice expresses itself in the total rejection and annihilation of 'distressed Faustus'.

Under the species of the nature of God, a man figures to himself the friendliness or hostility of the universe, and the possibilities of his existence within it. Marlowe's view of the matter appears to be black in the extreme. The play is permeated with a strong sense of man's alienation from the order of things, a deeply felt 'sense of sin', which seems to dominate its vision. As J. B. Steane points out, the 'lurking sense of damnation *precedes* the invocation' of hell.[40]

It is in the sense that the world of the play is hostile to the only values that can redeem it that Faustus's damnation may be said to be imposed from above. Yet there is an urgency and a personal heat behind this terrible paradox which, though it defeats the synthesising activity of Marlowe's art, commands attention and, indeed, a regretful respect. Though the play's grasp of reality is sporadic, its reach is tremendous. We are watching a man, I suggest, locked in a death embrace with the agonising God he can neither reject nor love. It is the final consummation of the Puritan imagination.

Yet, though this may be the tragedy of Christopher Marlowe, it is not *The Tragicall History of Doctor Faustus*. The tragic dilemma we sense behind the play is *behind* it. It is not officially recognised as a powerful and autonomous insight of revolutionary import. Instead Marlowe tries to accommodate it, by means of the *psychomachia* form, to the old frontiers and boundaries of moralised experience. And it refuses to submit.

The apotheosis of Helen, for instance, which is supposed to be firmly placed as a narcotic which 'may extinguish clear / Those thoughts that do dissuade' Faustus from his vow, nevertheless overflows the moral banks Marlowe is constructing.

> O, thou art fairer than the evening's air
> Clad in the beauty of a thousand stars,
> Brighter art thou than flaming Jupiter
> When he appear'd to hapless Semele,
> More lovely than the monarch of the sky
> In wanton Arethusa's azur'd arms,
> And none but thou shalt be my paramour.   xviii. 112

Up to this point, the image's sensual potency has been qualified by the destruction with which it is associated—'burnt', 'sack'd', 'combat', 'wound'; but here the flame of passion flares up so fiercely that it transfigures even so moral an epithet as 'wanton'. The conflict is sharp in this scene, for these lines are immediately succeeded by the Old Man's

> Accursed Faustus, miserable man,
> That from thy soul exclud'st the grace of heaven
> And fliest the throne of his tribunal seat!   xviii. 119

It is clear that this comment cannot contain the Helen vision; but equally clear that Marlowe expects it to. The 'humanist' and the moralist in him are again at war.

Thus Marlowe comes within hailing distance of that internalisation of moral sanctions by which drama can *lead* into wisdom instead of *pointing* at it, only to abandon it for easier simplifications:

> Faustus is gone: regard his hellish fall,
> Whose fiendful fortune may exhort the wise...

This, cheek by jowl with Faustus's last moments, is the critical paradox of the play at its most acute. I suppose it might be argued that the Epilogue merely condenses, into conventional and manageable form, a dramatic experience too vast and chaotic to be left unformulated; but I am inclined to think that the effect is simply bathetic.

VI

It remains now to trace the last movement of the drama: the movement which begins, rather startlingly, with a Faustus resolutely confronting his imminent damnation:

> What art thou, Faustus, but a man condemn'd to die?
> Thy fatal time draws to a final end.   xv. 21

Sandwiched between the unfunny farce of the Horse-courser and the crude practical joke of the false leg, this is astonishing. It is the first sign of a sudden seriousness that comes over Marlowe when he faces imaginatively the possibility of final destruction—I say, over Marlowe, not over Faustus, because it simply cannot be rationalised as 'character-development'. It is too sudden, too unmodulated, and goes with a new poetic conviction which has been totally lacking since Faustus boarded his dragon for Rome. After the inept flounderings of the central section, something has again gripped Marlowe's imagination. It is not the possibility of repentance, for the moments where Faustus toys with this idea are the flattest and feeblest in the final section. It is the possibility of irretrievable catastrophe, damnation deserved and beyond appeal. Given this possibility, Faustus can recover his dignity, and Marlowe his seriousness—which happens most impressively in the prose scene with the Scholars.

This is a piece of chamber-music finer, I think, than the symphonic grandeurs of the subsequent soliloquy—finer, because more assured, more poised, and less frenetic. The cheerful, well-meaning super-ficiality of the 'sweet chamber-fellows' ('Tis but a surfeit, sir; fear nothing') is a foil for Faustus's unflinching contemplation of his own state ('A surfeit of deadly sin...'). He is gentle, but inexorable:

> Ay, pray for me, pray for me; and, what noise soever ye hear,
> come not unto me, for nothing can rescue me.   xix. 80

There is human warmth, there is humility and there is a new maturity in this Faustus. He has passed beyond egotism, yet not far beyond, for there is a momentary resurgence of the old braggart self, which has to be soberly checked. Above all, the prose charts meticulously the ebb and flow, the very pulse beat of consciousness as Faustus works his way painfully to the enormously difficult confession—'Ah, gentlemen, I gave them my soul for my cunning'. Note how skilfully the impro-visatory syntax is used to render Faustus's faltering progress:

Ah, gentlemen, hear me with patience, and tremble not at my speeches. Though my heart pants and quivers to remember that I have been a student here these thirty years, O, would I had never seen Wittenberg, never read book! and what wonders I have done all Germany can witness, yea, all the world, for which Faustus hath lost both Germany and the world, yea, heaven itself—heaven, the seat of God, the throne of the blessed, the kingdom of joy—and must remain in hell for ever. Hell, ah, hell for ever! Sweet friends, what shall become of Faustus, being in hell for ever?   xix. 42

There is nothing histrionic about this utterance: it is not 'O, I'll leap up to my God! Who pulls me down?', with its inescapably stagey gestural implications, but

I would lift up my hands, but see, they hold them, they hold them—

xix. 58

something real and immediate and unselfconscious.

The discomfited Scholars depart in awkward haste. Mephostophilis and the Angels make their last appearance, and the total destitution and isolation of the damned soul, towards which the play has been moving, is complete. Faustus faces his destiny. It is clearly the culmination of all that has gone before. In order to deal with it, Marlowe invents—and I think the word is justified—a new kind of blank verse and a mode of utterance which has excited admiration now for four centuries. Viewed from behind, through a vista of Peeles and Prestons, it certainly is a startling achievement; but is it the unqualified artistic success it is often claimed to be? Has Marlowe really solved the problems which dogged his steps in the rest of the play? Fine in places it may be, but as a whole...?

Since I am about to depart radically from received critical opinion, I had best begin by attempting to do it justice. The view of the soliloquy as the ironic keystone of a perfect arch has been put well by Helen Gardner:

The great reversal from the first scene of *Doctor Faustus* to the last can be defined in different ways: from presumption to despair; from doubt of the existence of hell to belief in the reality of nothing else; from a desire to be more than man to the recognition that he has excluded himself from the promise for all mankind in Christ; from haste to sign the bond to desire for delay when the moment comes to honour it; from aspiration to deity and omnipotence to longing for extinction. At the beginning Faustus wished to rise above his humanity; at the close he would sink below it, be transformed into a beast or into 'little water drops'. At the beginning he attempts usurpation upon God; at the close he is an usurper upon the Devil.[41]

What I want to ask, is whether 'the great reversal' is not more present in the critic's prose than in the dramatist's verse. With a crucial structural issue like this one, a dramatist cannot afford to rely on verbal and situational associations that span the whole play, and which have to be consciously *made* by the audience. I very much doubt that this response is of the kind we can make while we are attending to the verse, much less listening to an actor. It is the product of subsequent, very literary reflection. Indeed the speech's huge reputation strikes me as a very literary phenomenon (*vide* all the enthusiasm lavished on the quotation from Ovid, which is at best a distraction, in its self-conscious sophistication, and at worst an obtrusion of a somewhat pedantic Marlowe at a moment when all attention should be focused on Faustus). Almost all the critical accounts of the soliloquy I've read seem to assume that we know it to be so good, that we no longer need to read it; and they are notable for *not* looking closely at the text, which is, I think, flawed by serious poetic defects.

One of these is the damaging sense in which this is 'an actor's vehicle'—which is to say, it looks like fine thumping drama, but once one tries to speak it, it becomes embarrassingly stagey. I have already noted one case of this ('O, I'll leap up to my God! Who pulls me down?'), but there are others:

> Earth gape! O, no, it will not harbour me.

> Yet will I call on him. O, spare me, Lucifer!—
> Where is it now? 'Tis gone: and see...

> No, no.

All these lines have gestural implications which are incipiently comic, and depend for their functioning upon an actor who can emotionally intimidate an audience—as, apparently, Alleyn succeeded in doing. In this histrionic context, can one be entirely happy even about

> See, see where Christ's blood streams in the firmament,

fine though it may be in conception? I think it is a real question.

This implied mode of delivery goes with a very heavy reliance on the vocative case and the imperative mood—something to which English style is never very friendly—on apostrophe and on rhetorical question (in 62 lines Faustus apostrophises twenty times). The result, to my ears, is a rhetorical overloading and hectic tone which does not seem properly under control—an impression which is confirmed by the reliance on that familiar rhetorical afflatus, that impetuous, swelling force of unharnessed energy which is so characteristic of Marlowe:

> You stars that reign'd at my nativity,
> Whose influence hath allotted death and hell,
> Now draw up Faustus like a foggy mist...

The meteorological imagery that follows, though striking, does not seem entirely coherent—hence the numerous attempts at emendation.

The impression of a kind of rhetorical overrun, which carries the verse on when the initial impetus of sense has exhausted itself, is confirmed if one compares parallel passages in Marlowe where the same image-complex rolls out in an oddly automatic way.[42] It may be 'apocalyptic', but one has only to compare Macbeth's vision of judgment (*Macbeth*, I. vii) to be aware of the essentially undirected energies of this verse. It is too close in tone and feeling to the random verbal aggression of *Tamburlaine* to be wholly convincing—at least in so serious a context. And the other notable echo in the speech—the remodelling of *Edward II*, v. i. 64–70, substituting 'That Faustus may repent and save his soul' (a very perfunctory line, surely) for 'that Edward may be still fair England's king'—sets one wondering whether there isn't something 'given' rather than 'won' about the apostrophe of the heavens as well. Although I don't dispute that the lines have a very real effectiveness, they still do not seem entirely real, in the way the prose of the Scholars' scene is real; there is an air of contrivance:

> Fair nature's eye, rise, rise again, and make
> Perpetual day; or let this hour be but
> A year, a month, a week, a natural day...

To put it as sharply as possible: do we *need* the repeated 'rise'? would it matter if the 'month' or the 'week' were omitted?

But the gravamen of my charge is that all these elements of self-consciousness and artificiality prevent the speech really taking us into Faustus's consciousness—and again one may contrast the Scholars' scene. What we get is not the flow, the stream of thought, but a series of rapid oscillations. The speech jumps from one mental position to the next:

> Curs'd be the parents that engender'd me!
> No, Faustus, curse thyself, curse Lucifer.
>
> Let Faustus live in hell a thousand years,
> A hundred thousand, and at last be sav'd.
> O, no end is limited to damn'd souls.

It is possible, I suppose, to regard these unmodulated key-changes as a triumphant presentation of a personality in torment and panic disorder, rebounding from one red-hot surface to the next.[43] I can only say that to me it seems too violent and too hectic to achieve such an aim. The poet seems to be himself in a state of near-delirium.

At the same time, this oscillation between extremes—heaven and hell, God and Lucifer ('Yet will I call on him. O, spare me, Lucifer!')—

is a part of the homiletic over-simplification that dogs the play, sign of a sensibility too geometrical, too prone to simple oppositions, operating at one remove from the complex flux of sensation and thought. That one can have a powerful sense of the absolute opposition of good and evil, without resorting to this drastic polarisation, *Macbeth* demonstrates plainly enough. Marlowe, unlike Shakespeare, is too close to his data, too personally entangled, yet at the same time—and perhaps because of the entanglement —detached in an artificial way.

I have put the strictures strongly because contrary judgments are ' very firmly entrenched and some fairly ruthless dissection is necessary if we are to see that the whole does not operate on the level of the best parts of it. But there *are* exceptions; there are unmistakable signs of that imaginative grip and utter seriousness for which one returns to *Faustus*. One is the vision of the wrathful deity, which I have noted as a seminal conception in the play. The inclusive gesture of the God who 'stretcheth out his arms' might have been the in-gathering love of the Good Shepherd, but Faustus can only interpret it in terms of a monstrous looming tyranny directed against the individual, who stands dwarfed by cosmic malevolence. The vision is direct and potent. And there is Faustus's prayer:

> O God,
> If thou wilt not have mercy on my soul,
> Yet for Christ's sake, whose blood hath ransom'd me,
> Impose some end to my incessant pain;
> Let Faustus live in hell a thousand years,
> A hundred thousand, and at last be sav'd.

This has a comparable conviction. Here the very weakness of Faustus's apprehension of Grace—expressed in the theological commonplace— is used to dramatise his desperate clutching at it. The 'incessant pain' remains the dominant reality, redemption the impossible end-point of eternal torment. Prayer is no longer simply the religious extreme of the pendulum-swing, but a reflex of agony inseparable from that agony. The repentance and the revolt are united in a single movement of intense feeling.

These moments are the more impressive in that they show Marlowe establishing some control over his most appalling fear—the fear of final destitution and rejection, figured in the avenging God. And at the end he rises superbly to the occasion with an electrically vital rendering of the very moment of dissolution:

It strikes, it strikes! Now, body, turn to air,
Or Lucifer will bear thee quick to hell!
O soul, be chang'd into little water drops,
And fall into the ocean, ne'er be found.

Enter Devils.

My God, my God! Look not so fierce on me!
Adders and serpents, let me breathe awhile!
Ugly hell, gape not! Come not, Lucifer;
I'll burn my books!—Ah, Mephostophilis!

Here there is a physical particularity, an astonishing evocation of
sensation (the body turning to air and water, magically weightless and
fluid, yet stung into frenzy by adders and serpents of physical agony
that will not let it breathe), and a strange compound of terror at, and
longing for, extinction. The flat either/or of heaven and hell becomes
a fusion in which 'My God' may be addressed either to the Deity or to
the Devils, or in which, as Empson observes, the unaccented position of
the negatives permits 'gape' and 'come' to operate as equivocal
invitations to the very forces from which Faustus is flying.[44] That
irreducible love–hate that Faustus bears toward both God and Lucifer
becomes that cry of erotic self-surrender *and* horrified revulsion as he
yields to the embrace of his demon lover—'Ah, Mephostophilis!'
Marlowe here masters the central paradox of his theism and makes of it
a unique dramatic reality which is genuinely tragic.

It is only a matter for regret that the same judgment cannot be
extended to *Doctor Faustus* as a whole. But, as we have seen, the territory
is no sooner annexed than it is betrayed by those disordered forces in
Marlowe's own imagination which lead him either into hectic exaggeration or into moralistic excess. As a result, what might have been a
central masterpiece of the Elizabethan age remains a sadly imperfect
monument to a gifted dramatist who never really finished anything.

12

MARLOWE AND THE CALVINIST DOCTRINE OF REPROBATION

I have argued in the last chapter that Marlowe's attempt to symbolise artistically his religious conflicts is subverted by the unresolved nature of those conflicts, and by his deep personal entanglement with Faustus's predicament. The aim of this note is to provide some account of pressures in his environment which might have contributed to the internal dissension. However, it is well to be clear that the biographical thesis is dependent on the critical judgment, and that the historical illustration of the former is no more than illustrative. Someone who remains unconvinced by my critical account of *Doctor Faustus* is unlikely to find anything here to clinch the argument. If, however, the critical judgment seems just, and if the reader goes on to enquire how the self-division came about, a certain amount of light can be shed on the matter by pondering the morbid and powerful fascination that the Calvinist doctrine of Reprobation seems to have had for Elizabethan minds.

The first point to be made, is that a sixteenth-century Englishman could not avoid the subject of predestination simply by rejecting Calvinist theology. We may find it fully formed in Aquinas, complete with the radical division between two discrete classes of human being—the predestinated and the reprobate:

Blindness is a kind of preamble to sin. Now sin has a twofold relation—to one thing, directly, viz. to the sinner's damnation;—to another, by reason of God's mercy or providence, viz. that the sinner may be healed...Therefore blindness, of its very nature, is directed to the damnation of those who are blinded; for which reason it is accounted an effect of reprobation. But, through God's mercy, temporary blindness is inflicted medicinally to the spiritual welfare of those who are blinded. This mercy, however, is not vouchsafed to all those who are blinded, but only to the predestinated, to whom *all things work together unto good* (Rom. viii. 28). Therefore as regards some, blindness is directed to their healing; but as regards others, to their damnation...[1]

When Aquinas wants an authority for this, he turns quite naturally to Augustine, who may be said to have anticipated the Calvinist doctrine of reprobation in all but its virulence.

Augustine, for both Puritan and Anglican, was 'the most iudiciall Diuine of all the auncient Fathers'.[2] It was to Augustine that the English Calvinists turned for authoritative support for their views on predestination:

the decree of God in reiecting some, is vnsearchable: and...it doth not at all depend vpon any foreseene contumacie towards the grace of God...For if it were otherwise, we might easily giue a reason of Gods decree. August. epist. 105 saith verie well. *Who* (saith he) *created the Reprobates, but God? and why, but because it pleased him? but why pleased it him? O man, who art thou that disputest with God?*[3]

The obscurantist invocation of divine inscrutability (by way of Romans xi. 20), in order to apply the guillotine to a dangerous debate, is the characteristic resort of the predestinarian, when the monstrous irrationality of this God becomes an embarrassment.[4]

The writer just quoted, William Perkins, is important for our purposes: he became a fellow of Christ's College, Cambridge, in the year Marlowe took his B.A., and was already an influential figure in University theology by the time Marlowe left in 1587. He is one of the key figures in the prolonged dispute between the Arminian Peter Baro, Lady Margaret's Professor of Divinity, and the Calvinist William Whitaker, Regius Professor of Divinity—a clash over precisely this doctrinal issue which can hardly have escaped the attention of a candidate for holy orders resident in the University.[5]

The point to be noted about the doctrine, and particularly about the Calvinist version of it, is that it makes the eternal destiny of the individual a matter already settled, and brands the reprobate indelibly with the mark of Cain. Nothing he can do will make any difference. It makes no odds that he leads an outwardly good life, for God has 'established by his eternal and unchangeable plan', Calvin declares, those whom he will 'devote to destruction'.

We assert that, with respect to the elect, this plan was founded upon his freely given mercy, without regard to human worth; but by his just and irreprehensible but incomprehensible judgement he has barred the door of life to those whom he has given over to damnation.[6]

As a consequence, all the movements of repentance in the reprobate are, in a sense, illusory: often they are merely the physical ravages of sin, issuing in 'melancholy', which is to be sharply distinguished from genuine penitence. 'It is improper', says Calvin, 'to designate as "conversion" and "prayer" the blind torment that distracts the reprobate

when they see that they must seek God...and yet flee at his approach';
this is simply the 'anxiety by which in extremity impious men are
bound and compelled to have regard for what previously they complacently neglected'.[7] Hooker concurs with this:

Contrition doth not...import those sudden pangs and convulsions of mind
which cause sometimes the most forsaken of God to retract their own doings; it
is no natural passion or anguish, which riseth in us against our wills, but a
deliberate aversion of the will of man from sin.[8]

It is possible to see how this position might be justified as an insistence that penitence should embody a real change of heart and
conduct; but in Calvin's English disciples it was given a ferocious
twist. What is medicine to the elect may be poison to the reprobate:
'Conscience beginneth hell in the harts of the vngodlie, and prepareth
Gods children to seeke heauen by vnfained repentance';[9] the sufferings
of the 'very chosen children of God...in the end redounds to their
eternall joy and saluation: Quhair by the contrair, the troubles of the
wicked, turnis at last to their vtter wrack and confusion';[10] the
commandment to believe in Christ (this is Perkins again)

is giuen to the Elect that by beleeuing they might indeede be saued; God
inabling them to doe that which he commands. To the rest, whome God in
iustice will refuse, the same commandement is giuen not for the same cause, but
to another ende, that they might see how they could not beleeue, and by this
meanes be bereft of all excuse in the day of iudgement.[11]

In this kind of hostile universe, it is plain that Adam sinned, not freely,
but 'because he could not resist the ordinance of his God'.[12] Not even
conscience can be relied on to point the way out of this murderous
predicament; for man's conscience itself is endemically evil: 'evil
conscience', says Perkins,

hath spread it selfe ouer mankind as generally as originall sinne; ...The
property of it is, with all the power it hath, to accuse & condemne; and thereby
to make a man afraid of the presence of God, and to cause him to flie from God
as from an enemie.

There are thus two kinds of conscience: the accusing conscience of the
reprobate and the regenerate conscience which, contrariwise, operates
to give 'testimonie...that we are the children of God predestinate to
life everlasting'. There is no escape from the accusing conscience,
because the eternal decree has frozen it in this single posture—man is
'bound in conscience'.[13]

Nor can condemned humanity appeal to principles of justice. Since every man is a sinner, since all flesh is guilty, 'what wrong is offered vnto him if he be cast into the bottome of hell?'[14] Says Calvin,

Let all the sons of Adam come forward; let them quarrel and argue with their Creator that they were by his eternal providence bound over before their begetting to everlasting calamity. What clamour can they raise against this defence when God, on the contrary, will call them to account before him? If all are drawn from a corrupt mass, no wonder they are subject to condemnation! Let them not accuse God of injustice if they are destined by this eternal judgement to death, to which they feel—whether they will or not—that they are led by their own nature of itself.[15]

To be human is to be damnable.

There is, of course, a place for grace in the Calvinist scheme. It is very like the place it has in the world of *Doctor Faustus*: it is the naturally impossible, well-nigh incredible alternative to utter destruction, which is inscrutably and arbitrarily offered to some and withheld from the rest. It cannot be earned by human action. One either has it, or one has not. The granting or refusal of grace is pre-ordained, ineluctable, and unalterable.

The ascendancy of the Calvinist doctrine in England is apparent in the 'Lambeth Articles' approved by Whitgift in 1595:

2. The moving or efficient cause of predestination to life is not the prevision of faith, or of perseverance, or of good works...but only the will and good pleasure of God.

3. Of the predestinated there is a fore-limited and certain number which can neither be diminished nor increased.

4. They who are not predestinated to salvation will be necessarily condemned on account of their sins...

7. Saving grace is not given, is not communicated, is not granted to all men, by which they might be saved if they would...

9. It is not placed in the will or power of every man to be saved.[16]

And if any further evidence is required that the Calvinists commanded a wide audience, one need only consider the astonishingly popular and numerous manuals which, having rubbed salt into the 'wounded conscience', then offered to satisfy the sufferer of his election or reprobation. The titles are probably sufficient indication of the contents:

Robert Linaker, *A Comfortable Treatise, for the reliefe of such as are afflicted in Conscience* [London, 1590]—By 1638 this had run through six editions.

Richard Greenham, *Propositions...specially concerning the Conscience oppressed with the griefe of sinne. With an epistle against hardnes of heart* (Edinburgh, 1597).

——, *Paramuthion, two treatises of the comforting of an afflicted conscience* (London, 1598).

——, *A most Sweete and assured Comfort for all those that are afflicted in Conscience, or troubled in minde* (London, 1595)—Greenham's *Works* ran through seven editions between 1599 and 1611. He left Cambridge ten years before Marlowe's arrival but frequently preached at St Mary's thereafter—see *DNB*.

Richard Kilby, *The burthen of a loaden Conscience* (Cambridge, 1608)—Ten editions by 1630. I can discover nothing about Kilby, but the Cambridge imprint probably indicates that his cure was in that area.

Thomas Wilcox, *Large Letters, three in number, for the Instruction and Comfort of such as are distressed in Conscience by feeling of Sinne and Feare of Gods Wrath* (London, 1589).

William Perkins, *A Case of Conscience...How a man may know whether he be a child of God, or no* (London, 1592)—Twelve editions by 1636, apart from its appearance in the ten editions of the *Works*, 1603–35. Many other of Perkins's tractates come under the same general heading. As I have noted, he was a leading light in Marlowe's Cambridge.

Robert Bolton, *Instructions for Right Comforting Afflicted Consciences* (London, 1630)—Three editions in eight years.

Perhaps the most resounding success of them all was Arthur Dent, whose *Sermon of Repentaunce* (London, 1583)—a piece dwelling alarmingly on the possibility of the reprobate's fruitless repentance—ran through twenty-one editions before 1640, and whose *Plaine mans pathway to Heauen* (London, 1601) achieved twenty-four editions in the same period. The sub-title goes a long way towards explaining this staggering figure:

> *Wherein euery man may clearly see, whether he shall be saued or damned. Set forth dialogue wise for the better vnderstanding of the simple.*

Dent left Cambridge to take up the ministry a year before Marlowe's arrival. The significance of the Cambridge training of many of these writers is not entirely unequivocal, but I mention if for what it is worth.

To such signs of enormous popular interest in the question, one may add the attention devoted to the biographical 'cases of conscience' like Francis Spira's—the protestant backslider who died convinced of his own damnation.[17]

Considerations like these may not perhaps prove the existence of a national obsession at this period; but they do give some indication of the strong pressure the individual was under to suspect that, though honest, well-intentioned, moderately pious, believing himself a believer, he might yet be damned—not merely damned at last, but damned 'before [his] begetting'. Incipient guilt-feelings can seldom have been offered a stronger inducement to take root and flourish.

There was, of course, reaction on the part of the moderate Anglicans. Harsnett's protest in 1584 has already been noted, as has Peter Baro's controversy with the Calvinists, which culminated, in 1595, in his denunciation of the Lambeth Articles quoted above. But Harsnett was hauled over the coals by Whitgift, and Baro was finally obliged to resign his chair at Cambridge.[18] Hooker, in the mid-1580s, preached 'A learned and comfortable Sermon of the certainty and perpetuity of faith in the elect', which was basically an attempt to put a stone between the eyes of the Goliath of reprobation.[19] It was this sermon which sparked off the long contention with the Puritan Travers.

The debate was still raging in the mid-1620s when Donne preached an important sermon against reprobation ('God antidates no malediction; nay not till there be an *inveterate* sinner; *A sinner of a hundred yeares*, at least, such a sinner, as would be so, if God would spare him a hundred yeares here'). The justification Donne offers for this contention is extremely revealing, and reflects light back thirty years onto the tormented Marlowe–Faustus:

Never propose to thy self such a God, as thou wert not bound to imitate: Thou mistakest God, if thou make him to be any such thing, or makest him to do any such thing, as thou in thy proportion shouldst not be, or shouldst not do. And shouldst thou curse any man that had never offended, never transgrest, never trespast thee? Can God have done so?[20]

One of the reasons that Donne, the divine poet, was able to make so much, poetically, of his theism, lies perhaps in the humanity of his conception of God. The Calvinist deity, by contrast, proves intractable to art—and this is true in wider fields than that of literature. Because of its inhumanity it cannot be embodied or given imaginative flesh.

But it would be misleading to regard Donne's statement as totally representative of moderate Anglicanism—or even of Donne's full position. Repentance for the Anglican remained an arduous and difficult art. The doctrine of 'attrition'—a second-class contrition based on fear of punishment, propounded by the Council of Trent—

had been firmly rejected in protestant England.[21] The difficulty of achieving true contrition is frequently enforced by the example of Judas—a line of argument deriving, apparently, from the 'Homily of Repentance' (1562): Judas, we are told,

was so sorrowful and heauy, yea that hee was filled with such anguish and vexation of minde, for that which hee had done, that hee could not abide to liue any longer. Did hee not also afore hee hanged himselfe make an open confession of his fault, when hee sayde, I haue sinned, betraying the innocent blood?...Hee did also make a certaine kinde of satisfaction, when hee did cast their money vnto them againe...It is euident and plaine then, that although wee be neuer so earnestly sorie for our sinnes, acknowledge and confesse them: yet all these things shall bee but means to bring vs to vtter desperation, except we doe stedfastly beleeue, that God...will for his Sonne Jesus Christs sake pardon and forgiue us...[22]

Hooker, too, insists on 'a just sorrow' proportionate to the offence, and 'neither a feigned nor a slight sorrow', and rejects the spurious penitence which does not really hate sin: this is Saul's ineffectual repentance, and is simply not good enough.[23] Penitence, in short, came perilously close to being, like Election, a gift of Grace, thus involving the anxious sinner in a desperate paradox:

> Yet grace, if thou repent, thou canst not lacke;
> But who shall give thee that grace to beginne?[24]

One way out of this murderous antinomy was the epicurean one of laughing it all off, and submerging oneself in a kind of escapist hedonism. This solution (Faustus's in the middle section of the play) was one the theologians were stern to reprehend—though it is possible to see the matter from another angle:

A Cast-away and Alien thus legally terrified, and under wrath for sinne, is never wont to come to this earnestnesse of care, eagernesse of resolution, steadfastnesse of endeavour, willingnesse upon any terms to abandon utterly His old waies, and to embrace new, strict and holy courses. These things appeare unto Him terrible, Puritanicall, and intolerable. He commonly in such cases, hath recourse for ease & remedy to worldly comforts, and the arm of flesh. Hee labours to relieve his heavy heart, by a strong and serious casting his minde, and nestling his conceit upon his riches, gold, greatnesse, great friends, credit amongst Men, & such other transitory delights...[25]

Eliminate the hostile perspective, and you have the Marlowe–Faustus to a tee: living under a precisian theology, yet harbouring strong sensual attachments to this world; presented with a rigid moralistic either/or which was an unreal and shallow dilemma; repelled by the realm of the holy yet unable to shake off the terror of retribution—'*legally* terrified' merely—he can neither go to heaven nor to hell with a good conscience. It is this trapped, claustrophobic situation that imparts a kind of narrowness to the play. And if, like the sudden narrowing of a gorge, this creates a certain turbulent grandeur in the current of the action, the general effect is still one of constriction.

But for the serious-minded the epicurean solution was simply not available. They were trapped under the crushing weight of a cosmic malevolence. On top of the inherent difficulty of true penitence came the suspicion that one was indeed one of those whose penitence is intrinsically and necessarily spurious. A vast fatalistic millstone had been hung about the neck of human endeavour; so

> I do repent, and yet I do despair...
> My heart is harden'd, I cannot repent...
> Damn'd art thou, Faustus, damn'd; despair and die!
> Christ cannot save thy soul, for he is just...
> Thou art damn'd; think thou of hell...

Hooker had tried to break into the vicious cycle of self-accusation in Faustus's kind of mind, and he knew only too well the response such efforts received:

Will you make me think otherwise than I find, than I feel in myself? I have thoroughly considered and exquisitely sifted all the corners of my heart, and I see what there is; never seek to persuade me against my knowledge; 'I do not, I know I do not believe'.[26]

'Damn'd art thou...damn'd!' It is the cry of Francis Spira, dying in 'legal terror':

I am a Reprobate like Cain, or Iudas, who casting away all hope of mercy fell into despaire...having sinned against the holy Ghost, God hath taken away from me all power of repentance...I earnestly desire to pray to God with my heart, yet I cannot; I see my damnation...such are the punishments of the damned, they confesse what I confesse, they repent of their losse of heaven, they envie the Elect, yet their repentance doth them no good...God hath left mee to the power of divels: but such they are, as are not to be found in your Letanie: neither will they be cast out...if I could conceive but the least sparke of hope of a better estate hereafter, I would not refuse to endure the most heavie weight of the wrath of that good God; yea, for twentie thousand yeares, so that I might at length attaine to the end of that misery, which I now know to bee eternall...[27]

The Spira documents are among the most appalling in the history of theological perversion.

Lily Campbell, in an influential study, has argued that we need to receive *Doctor Faustus* as a Calvinist 'case of conscience' if we are to grasp 'the essential dramatic unity of the play'.[28] One may agree. The element of truth in the claim, however, is one which destroys her case for the play's greatness. In order to regard it as possessing an 'essential dramatic unity' at all, one must, by that curious process of mental evacuation which is sometimes mistaken for historical imagination, accept the drastic limitations of a Calvinist cosmos, and refrain from discerning the psychic malfunction upon which it is grounded. One can indeed recreate in this way the kind of topical fascination the play must have exercised in the sixteenth century—if one is prepared to allow guilt to be the fundamental reality of experience. But it is no part of wisdom—and literary criticism is, one hopes, a kind of wisdom —to hand humanity over to impulses which will destroy it; nor is it any part of historical insight to surrender our understanding of the present in order to receive the past. Such historicist self-immolation merely means that there is no self left to discover the meaning the past might have had for it—had it survived. Suspension of disbelief is a very necessary preliminary discipline, but it does not obviate that return upon the self when one enquires what one has received, and evaluates it.

It is a nagging sense that there is some more broadly-based and more humanly intelligible way of looking at the Faustian predicament, a sense that there is a broader wisdom which could include Marlowe's vision within itself, and so *comprehend* it as Marlowe never did, that makes me reluctant to call *Doctor Faustus* a great play. Even if we remain within the field of contemporary theology, one can glimpse a sanity and balance which might have led Marlowe out of his artistic and religious impasse, in Donne's approach to the matter. I do not know whether the echoes (italicised) of Faustus's last soliloquy are conscious in the following passage (though Donne was a great play-goer and Edward Alleyn—the first Faustus—was his son-in-law); but if one takes it as a commentary on Marlowe–Faustus, it is certainly apposite:

Wilt thou...teare open the jawes of Earth, and Hell, and cast thy self actually and really into it, out of a mis-imagination, that God hath cast thee into it before? Wilt thou force God to second thy irreligious melancholy, and to condemne thee at last, because thou hadst precondemned thy selfe, and renounced his mercy? Wilt thou say with Cain, My sinne is greater then can be pardoned? This is *Concisio potestatis*, a cutting off the Power of God...

Truly Origen was more excusable, more pardonable, if he did beleeve, that the Devill might possibly be saved, then that man, that beleeves that himself must necessarily be damned...Beware of such distinctions, and such subdivisions, as may make the way to heaven too narrow for thee, or the gate of heaven too strait for thee. 'Tis true, *one drop of my Saviours bloud would save me*, if I had but that; one teare from my Saviours eye, if I had but that; but he hath none that hath not all; A drop, a teare, would wash away an Adultery, a murder, but lesse then the whole sea of both, will not wash away a wanton looke, an angry word. God would have all, and he gives all to all. And for Gods sake, let God be as good as he will; as mercifull, and as large, as liberall, and as generall as he will... [29]

The diagnosis of an unappeased desire for self-punishment in those who make the way narrower and the gate straiter than it naturally is points the way to that deeper level of self-awareness where the torments of Faustus might at last find their purgation. But Marlowe seems to have been too desperately engaged in his death-struggle with Calvin's God to have time for this kind of self-knowledge.

'AN UNKNOWN FEAR':
'THE TRAGEDIE OF MACBETH'

In approaching a work as manifold and inexhaustible as *Macbeth*, there is considerable danger of losing one's way in the very richness of the play, leaving the reader with a lapful of oddments and annotations, and no coherent image of the whole. It therefore seems worth attempting to state broadly what I see as the *temper* of the play—the spirit in which it appears to have been conceived.

There are some remarks of Nietzsche's, concerned specifically with the temper of Greek tragedy, which are extremely apposite to *Macbeth*. Nietzsche has been enquiring how it came about that a period of prosperity and security gave rise to tragedy which was, in an obvious sense at least, pessimistic; and he goes on,

Is pessimism inevitably a sign of decadence, warp, weakened instincts, as it was once with the ancient Hindus, as it is now with us modern Europeans? Or is there such a thing as a *strong* pessimism? A penchant of mind for what is hard, terrible, evil, dubious in existence, arising from a plethora of health, a plenitude of being? Could it be, perhaps, that the very feeling of superabundance created its own kind of suffering: a temerity of penetration, hankering for the enemy (the worthwhile enemy) so as to prove its strength, to experience at last what it means to fear something?

This 'strong pessimism' and 'temerity of penetration' does not by any means exclude a vision of human potentiality; indeed, as Nietzsche goes on to argue, in a manner it produces that vision:

After an energetic attempt to focus on the sun, we have, by way of remedy almost, dark spots before our eyes when we turn away. Conversely, the luminous images of the Sophoclean heroes...are the necessary productions of a deep look into the horror of nature, luminous spots, as it were, designed to cure an eye hurt by the ghastly night. Only in this way can we form an adequate notion of the seriousness of Greek 'serenity'; whereas we find that serenity generally misinterpreted nowadays as a condition of undisturbed complacence.[1]

Shakespearian tragedy, less than Greek tragedy perhaps, tempts readers to talk of 'serenity'; but the Shakespearian ideals of order and harmony, which are the tautly strung warp of the tragic fabric, easily lose their tension in interpretation and become detached from the frame, and we get readings of *Macbeth* in which evil is somehow *subordinated* to the good and to the natural, and the military victory of Malcolm's forces is seen as the *elimination* of the Macbeth-evil. Against this kind of simplification—one which domesticates the play and draws its teeth— Nietzsche's analogy provides a useful antidote. The good is the after-image of an evil long and steadily contemplated.

There is—to put the matter a little too broadly—a primacy of evil in the world of this play. In a dramatic sense, at least, it is the very virulence of the evil, its positive potency, that gives rise to that organic assertion of health which finally sets bounds to the evil.

So I cannot assent to Roy Walker's account of the play's topography:

Banquo and Macduff, Duncan and Malcolm stand in the sunlight, stand outside the central focus of the tragedy, and thereby intensify it. They are bright figures seen at some distance, moving in a lovely countryside, but seen through the grating of a dark dungeon;[2]

for to some extent (Duncan by his early death becomes the exception) all these 'bright figures' share Macbeth's, and our, incarceration. There is no self-subsistent, chemically 'free' good in the compound: the good is seen either, through Macbeth's, eyes, as that which has been irrevocably lost, or, through the eyes of the Scottish nobles, as that which desperately needs to be recovered. The vision of the natural takes its rise from 'a deep look into the horror of nature': and we must sup full with that horror before we can have any right to the vision. It is not given. Still less is it to be traced to some readily convertible National Fund of Belief—what Professor Elliott is pleased to call Shakespeare's 'Renaissance point of view'[3]—nor, as W. C. Curry would have it, to 'a body of patrimonial doctrines transmitted to the Renaissance from the scholastic philosophers'.[4] Shakespeare's Christianity, though real, is not of this kind.

So when one reads that the essence of Shakespeare's tragic vision is 'the fact that the *infernal* evil working in the heart of man more instantly than his *natural* goodness...can ruin his humanity...unless it is sustained by the *supernal* power of Grace',[5] or that

the kingdom in *Macbeth* shadows forth the kingdom of heaven on earth, obscured for a time by the blanket of the dark but never sundered from heaven. The tragedy is focused on the destruction of awareness of the kingdom of heaven within and the attempt of the human vassals of evil to usurp the divine–temporal kingship,[6] one detects an element in the interpretation which is not to be found in the play, and one could wish for the sensitive critical conscience of a Bradley labouring to exclude those attractive ideas which nevertheless 'fail to correspond with the imaginative effect'.[7] Faced with the equanimity, the easy assurance of the theologising interpreters of this tragedy, one is tempted to bar their advance and challenge them with Baudelaire's question:

> Ange plein de santé, connaissez-vous les Fièvres,
> Qui, le long des grands murs de l'hospice blafard,
> Comme des exilés, s'en vont d'un pied traînard,
> Cherchant le soleil rare et remuant les lèvres?
> Ange plein de santé, connaissez-vous les Fièvres?

('Réversibilité')

I

Nevertheless, it would be over-zealous to deny health, and indeed grace, a part in the dramatic movement. What I am questioning is not their presence but their weight. How much force, for example, is to be allowed to the figure of 'the gracious Duncan'? We might begin by noting that this phrase is Macbeth's anguished outcry *over the dead*, and that Duncan living has a different and lesser function.

In a play where the minor characters tend to be faceless, even nameless, Duncan has his own peculiar style of speech—syntactically involuted, given to elaborate flights of courtesy, just a trifle old-fashioned and quaint:

> ...he can report,
> As seemeth by his plight, of the Revolt
> The newest state.   I. ii. 1

> Is execution done on Cawdor?
> Or not those in Commission yet return'd?   I. iv. 1

> Would thou hadst lesse deserv'd,
> That the proportion both of thanks, and payment,
> Might have beene mine.   I. iv. 18[8]

Or again, isn't there something of the old man's desire to gratify, coupled with an increasing unfamiliarity with the thought-habits of the 'young' in his amusing determination to call Macbeth 'Thane of Cawdor', or in his playful detection of Macbeth's 'great Love' as the hidden spur that brings him home with such speed (I. vi. 23)? (Though this last sentiment may be courteously designed to cover the slight embarrassment when Macbeth himself does not appear to greet the royal guest.)

I mention the individualisation of Duncan first, not because it is the most important thing about him, but because it places certain terminal limits on those other, more important things. Shakespeare gives us no grounds for suspecting that Duncan's virtue exists on a different level of dramatic reality from Macbeth's vice, nor that he is about to take symbolic wing out of the concrete sphere of the action. It is because his virtues are particular and localised, and wedded to a modicum of innocent foibles, that they have the degree of reality that can sustain symbolic extension without becoming attenuated. If Duncan's kingly nature has reverberations beyond the merely personal—and it obviously has—he nevertheless has a solidity and actuality that is the antithesis of arbitrarily imposed symbolic function.

When, as personified royal liberality, he distributes 'signes of Noble-nesse, like Starres' to 'all deservers', the sense of cosmic bounty is qualified by the verse context which suggests the liberality is rooted in very human emotion—'Plenteous Joyes, / Wanton in fulnesse' (I. iv. 33–42): in the same way the diamond presented to his 'most kind Hostesse' is an expression of 'measurelesse content' (II. i. 13 f.). Where the Macbeths see their relation to the king as a 'contention' in showing favours, or a vain attempt to make up an 'Audit' (I. vi. 16 and 27), Duncan expresses his relationship to his subjects in terms of planting and growing, fruition and plenty—images which make god-like liberality a function of nature (I. iv. 28 f.), or in terms of the human mutualities and good fellowship of a 'banquet'.

Nevertheless, the suggestion of his innate generosity is far-reaching and powerful. He is 'fed', not by the strains of homage and adulation, which he accepts completely impersonally, but by the 'commendations' of his friends. He bears his faculties 'meek'. Indeed his courtesy has a continuous tendency to reverse the king–subject relation:

> Where's the Thane of Cawdor?
> We courst him at the heeles, and had a purpose
> To be his Purveyor.   I. vi. 20

He will, that is to say, be servant to King Macbeth, riding ahead to prepare for his coming. The continual insistence on the guest–host relation has the same courteous intention of replacing domination by submission—'Faire and Noble Hostesse / We are your guests to night' are the words of the king who gladly becomes servant and suppliant. 'By your leave Hostesse' is his exit line. This gracious self-effacement is the impressive core of his sometimes florid courtesy. He is a king whom it is no abasement to serve.

Above all, Duncan is trust incarnate; and his trust is neither something arbitrarily 'given', nor an insensitivity to human deviousness, but a necessary expression of royalty. The irony of the following passage has often been noted, but there is more here than a telling entrance for Macbeth:

> There's no Art
> To finde the Mindes construction in the Face:
> He was a Gentleman, on whom I built
> An absolute Trust...
> ...O worthyest Cousin...   I. iv. II

Unless we are to take it as an example of culpable political gullibility (and the tone of saddened realism makes that impossible), this must be seen as a necessary and open-eyed commitment to 'Trust'. There *is* no such art, and Duncan knows it. It simply is insolubly difficult to find a human foundation for 'an absolute Trust'. But Duncan's 'royalty of nature'—to re-apply a phrase of Macbeth's—consists precisely in this: that, knowing the fallibility of human judgment, he nevertheless proceeds to build a new trust as absolute, on the ruins of the old. There is no hint that this trustfulness is reprehensible: rather the reverse. But neither is there any suggestion that it is a manifestation of 'the supernal power of Grace'—not yet. Duncan is an old man and a good king, 'cleere in his great Office'—no more.

But Duncan dead is a new phenomenon: he becomes 'the Lords anoynted Temple', not only, like every Christian, 'the temple of the Living God', but inheritor of the Davidic royalty conferred by the prophet of Jehovah. We might not perhaps pay much attention to Macduff's hysterical mixed metaphor: but it is reinforced by the murderer himself:

> Renowne and Grace is dead,
> The Wine of Life is drawne, and the meere Lees
> Is left this Vault, to brag of.   II. iii. 94

Coming from the lips of Macbeth, these lines have a complex function, and one strand of meaning is surely that he has conferred upon Duncan *in perpetuum* the sanctity his act aimed at challenging. But by making Macbeth spokesman for this insight, Shakespeare imparts a peculiar twist to the sense—Renown and Grace *is dead*. Though it is Macbeth's

self-accusation that speaks, recognising how he has uncreated something which it is not within his powers to recall to life either in Duncan
or in himself, nevertheless he has performed the murder of Renown
and Grace for his world, as well as for himself. For the world of the
play, too, these things are dead. And it is the finality of that act which
gives such poignancy to the image of Duncan that haunts the re-
mainder of the action. Through the perspective glass of Macbeth's
unavailing anguish he becomes 'the gracious Duncan', the sweet
sleeper in an untroubled grave. There is no need for a putative super-
nature infusing Duncan's human nature ('Heavenly peace lives and
moves in him—in, through, and above the admirable traits clearly
recognised by Macbeth . . .'9) to account for the haunting compulsion
of the image: it is haunting because it is lost.

And the loss is total. Though we may not, as spectators, formulate it
to ourselves, it is surely an important element in the dramatic movement that it is not Duncan who is reinstated at the end of the play, but
a young prince who is so far from 'an absolute Trust' as to spend half
of a long scene cautiously withholding his trust from someone who, as
we know, richly deserves it. This replacement of Duncan in the
political order by a man of much smaller stature contributes to an
overall sensation of shrinkage and diminution which hangs over the
concluding movement of the action. But for the Scotland of Acts IV
and V, Duncan is the lost possibility, Malcolm the diminished necessity.
Royalty of nature once slain, only the meaner virtues of circumspection
and prudence can survive.

Consequently, it is a serious distortion of the shape of the play to
attempt to convert Malcolm into the restorer of Duncan's royalty.
Yet there are plenty of critics to claim that he 'reincarnates the humble
benevolence and justness of Duncan', that he is 'the most nearly perfect
picture in Shakespeare of the ideal king', or that 'his unregenerate
manhood is transfigured by grace into divine royalty'.10 Such judgments, apart from exemplifying a strain of pious sentimentality which is
disastrous to this toughminded drama (Banquo has suffered the same
pseudo-canonisation), plainly neglect what Shakespeare has given us in
the few scenes where Malcolm appears.

In the confusion that follows the murder of his father, the first
clearly defined instinct the young prince displays is one of anxious self-
protection, followed by a suspicious and defensive contempt, not just
for the Macbeths—whom he has no special reason to suspect—but for all
the nobles:

> Let's not consort with them:
> To shew an unfelt Sorrow, is an Office
> Which the false man do's easie.
> Ile to England.   II. iii. 135

There is, of course, nothing improbable or improper about this panic, and the suspicion is certainly not misplaced. But the tone is oddly callow; the self-righteousness of the accented 'them' and 'false man', the implied sneer in 'consort', and the syntactical ambiguity (at the colon), which makes Malcolm's sorrow 'unfelt' as much as the false man's, must all be parts of a deliberately calculated effect on Shakespeare's part, unless the sequence was written in a fit of absent-mindedness. The most favourable construction we can put upon the princes' behaviour is that they are too young to feel much more than shock, and too frightened to conceal adolescent callousness and self-concern in the face of disaster. The effect is fleeting but it is hardly the exordium one would choose for the theme of 'the ideal king'.

Malcolm now remains for several acts either 'the son of Duncan' simply, or the subject of Macbeth's calumnies, until he appears in Act IV, Scene iii, talking with Macduff. Professor Knights has warned us that we will be badly misled if we mistake the *dramatis personae* for 'real persons' in this scene, and has insisted on the element of 'choric commentary'.[11] Certainly there is not much enlightenment to be gained by asking what Malcolm 'really is', thus removing him from his dramatic context and forgetting that his reality is a reality only within a complex dramatic movement. But there are frequent occasions in this scene when the energies of the verse direct our attention, not to the choric mouthpiece, but to the character, Malcolm—that is to say, the pressure of individualisation varies from line to line, and with it, the kind of attention the audience gives to the speaker. Malcolm's second speech, for instance, gives us a quite definite state of mind and a correspondingly definite speaker:

> What I beleeve, Ile waile;
> What know, beleeve; and what I can redresse,
> As I shall finde the time to friend: I wil.
> What you have spoke, it may be so perchance.
> This Tyrant, whose sole name blisters our tongues,
> Was once thought honest: you have lov'd him well,
> He hath not touch'd you yet. I am yong, but something
> You may deserve of him through me, and wisedome
> To offer up a weake, poore innocent Lambe

T'appease an angry God.
MACDUFF.   I am not treacherous.
MALCOLM. But Macbeth is.   IV. iii. 8

It is a progressive excursion into distrust: 'What I believe (as I do not believe all I hear)...What know (and that is precious little)...It may be so perchance (there is just a possibility you are speaking the truth) ...'—a distrust which Shakespeare renders by an almost complete absence of explanatory connectives: Malcolm is not willing to offer even his suspicion in an undisguised form. In view of the doubtful impression left by Malcolm's last appearance—and now perhaps it becomes clearer what Shakespeare was doing in that scene—there is no conception of the prince to which we can appeal, as a corrective to this narrowly suspicious exterior. We feel, with Macduff, dismay and a sinking heart. (And it should be borne in mind that we come to this scene directly from the ghastly slaughter of Macduff's family.) And then the speech takes a nastier turn still: again without any connective to cover the modulation, Malcolm mentions Macbeth and Macduff's former love for him. One scents the innuendo, then realises with dismay that Macbeth's lost 'honesty' is being used as a reason for distrusting everyone, and that Macduff's love—a capacity for an absolute trust—is itself being proposed as grounds for suspicion (doubly unjust since Macduff has indeed been 'touch'd'). Once again it is the king faced with the bitter disillusion of Cawdor's treachery—but it is a very different king. Macduff's full-throated indignation as he grasps the drift of the argument is passionately right; and, though Malcolm's neatly balanced antithetical retort is correct too, it has the thinness of mean-mindedness and lacks emotive weight. Something niggling, petty and narrowly suspicious has poisoned the meeting that Lennox envisaged with so much hope in Act III. Malcolm's leaden, despairing cadence—'But Macbeth is'—followed by a half-line pause, hangs clogs on all hope.

It is in this atmosphere that the interview proceeds, and however much Malcolm may unveil the reasonable grounds of his suspicion, and beg

Let not my Jealousies, be your Dishonors,
But mine owne Safeties,   IV. iii. 29

they *are* Macduff's dishonours, and there is something narrow-gutted about these 'Safeties'. Something right-spirited too about Macduff's contemptuous pun—'The Title is affear'd'—a manly indignation beside which Malcolm's utterance sounds querulous. Shakespeare, of course, has the reassuring explanation up his sleeve; but he does not produce it until we have savoured to the full the bitter taste of the new political realities—the post-Duncan *raison d'état*, as it were.

In this situation Malcolm indicates, in passing, where hope lies:

> Angels are bright still, though the brightest fell.
> Though all things foule would wear the brows of grace,
> Yet Grace must still look so.   IV. iii. 22

The good remains unchanged, true to its nature and still potent, however much beset by counterfeits. There are still unfallen angels. Yet good cannot be more fair than fair—for this is to be suspect of being foul. Against evil's assumption of gracious appearance, goodness is defenceless. Its only recourse against the counterfeit is persistence in its own nature. This is the truth *behind* Malcolm's position, and it is a truth for the play at large, the truth of the 'scorch'd snake' and the 'naked babe', the weak things that are, in the end, most strong. But it is not a truth that Malcolm himself appears to grasp. He does not so much assert the impregnability of the good, as the impossibility of discerning it. It cannot be eroded, but neither can it be known. The more angelic, the more suspect. The fact that 'thoughts cannot transpose' the true nature of men and events is not, as with Duncan, the premiss for a magnanimous and courageous trustfulness, but for increased caution.

So it is from the edge of despair (Macduff's despair—for it is largely he who mediates the situation to us), and with a kind of dull incredulity, that we contemplate Malcolm's self-indictment. The timbre of his utterance changes now, and he speaks out of a kind of formal trance; the sense of personality recedes and attention is directed to larger and more general truths about the State and kingship. But we do not remain solely in the realm of the impersonal, for Macduff is a real, physical presence, an impetuous current bearing down the line-end barriers in its course:

> Not in the Legions
> Of horrid Hell, can come a Divell more damn'd
> In evils, to top Macbeth.   IV. iii. 55

And we are directed back to personality again as Macduff's passion for Scotland begins to overbear his moral scruple, producing a sudden coarsening of tone:

> You may
> Convey your pleasures in a spacious plenty,
> And yet seeme cold. The time you may so hoodwinke:
> We have willing Dames enough: there cannot be

> That Vulture in you, to devoure so many
> As will to Greatnesse dedicate themselves,
> Finding it so inclinde.   IV. iii. 70

Apart from the damaging cynicism about Scottish 'Dames' (presumably the same race as the 'widdowes' he is proposing to relieve), there is an extremely distasteful bucks'-party vulgarity about words like 'willing' 'dedicate' (an ugly religious euphemism for 'prostitute') or the punning 'convey'. It is sexuality at its most crude—the gorging excess of a vulture —that Macduff is here condoning. Our alarm cuts right across the 'choric commentary' (if that is what it is) to register a new and menacing development in the situation. Just how many of the values that make peace meaningful are going to be sacrificed in the process of attaining it?

The sense of relief is powerful when Macduff finally repudiates Malcolm. The wave which has been gathering head throughout the scene finally crashes on the shore in a passionate outcry, intensely personal, against the intolerable anguish of Scotland:

> Fit to govern?
> No not to live. O Nation miserable...   IV. iii. 102

It is a kind of vicarious purgation of the outrage which life under Macbeth has become, the bitter comfort of crying out against the universe when there is no more to hope for. Macduff and, I suggest, the audience too, hears Malcolm's sequent recantation from the further side of this corrosive yet soothing despair:

> Such welcome, and unwelcom things at once
> 'Tis hard to reconcile.   IV. iii. 138

One cannot so easily shake off nightmare. We hear the reassuring words as those barely returned from the edge of the abyss—hear them, but are still gripped by less pleasant recollections.

And Malcolm, finally, cannot 'unspeak his own detraction'. To say that he has none of the 'King-becoming Graces' is *not* the same as to say that he has them. The very act of envisaging the corruption of his own nature has tainted him—the more so, since the audience has been given no guide to the reception of these words. Wilson Knight grasped a real truth about this scene, and about the play, when he wrote,

All the persons seem to share some guilt of the down-pressing enveloping Evil. Even Malcolm is forced to repeat crimes on himself. He catalogues every possible sin, and accuses himself of all. Whatever be his 'reasons', his doing so yet remains part of the integral humanism of this play.[12]

Consequently, while accepting Professor Knights's account of the mode in which Malcolm's self-accusation is cast, and of its tendency to adumbrate the positive values that Macbeth's Scotland denies, I see this choric function as subordinated to a more powerful movement which is threatening to engulf the few islands of truly human consciousness that still survive the flood. There is a purgation, but it is dramatic and personal, rather than choric and impersonal. And it is mediated to us through Macduff.

For Macduff, too, labours under this weight of undischargeable guilt. Whatever his reasons for leaving his family—and it is idle to speculate where Shakespeare has given no guidance—he bears a heavy responsibility for their deaths. He may be 'Noble, Wise, Judicious', as Ross claims, but we never know it, and he himself is unable to claim such immunity when he most needs it, but rather accuses 'Sinful Macduff' of some impalpable but criminal neglect. Here we are all 'Traitors / And do not know ourselves'. It appears that all the surviving good has begun to taint.

It is at this point that Shakespeare introduces the eloquent little vignette of the English court and its saintly king (IV. iii. 140 f.). The function of a king, we learn, is to heal, and in this operation he is co-partner with heaven, standing in a special relation to divine grace, the recipient of heavenly gifts. The images are those of bounty and plenitude again: 'sundry Blessings hang about this Throne' as about a productive fruit-tree, and he is '*full* of Grace'. It is one of the rare moments in the play when we get a clear sense of the life-promoting forces of nature, and a momentary lifting of the blanket of the dark.

Much has been made of the alleged compliment to James—though most of this comment is ignorant that James himself was extremely dubious about the practice of touching for the Evil, so that, if it is directed at him, it is anything but a simple compliment.[13] But this is marginal, and those critics who relate the passage to the images of health and sickness, or to the time-honoured similitude of the prince as physician of the Commonweal, are much nearer the heart of the matter. Shakespeare is reminding us of the continuing existence of Duncan's kind of royalty, of the fructifying, health-giving and over-flowing virtues of true kingship.

Yet not even this stands unqualified. Malcolm and Macduff are in exile, and this is an English king. What they glimpse (and, since this is a Scottish play, we with them) is another man's beatitude. For them,

Scotland remains the dark reality to which they must return: the sequence is sandwiched between that long duel of mutual suspicion, and the shattering impact of a deed of unexampled brutality. And a final factor which limits the potency of this beatific vision is the very loose links the passage has with the surrounding material. I know no way of determining whether it is a late addition or not, though Dover Wilson's point that it may be very tidily excised carries some weight.[14] Be that as it may, the transition into and out of the passage is clumsy and the joinery very visible. Macduff's leading question, 'what's the Disease he meanes?', is a primitive device of exposition, which suggests a slackness of imagining, the loss of that purposeful and, at times, frenetic forward drive for which the play is so remarkable. The lapse is not crucial, since, once Shakespeare has made his modulation, he achieves something serene and melodious which we would not be without. But the absence of that structural integrity which puts out root-filaments into the surrounding action means that the connexions between the saintly Edward and the hell that Scotland has become are all of the long-range, image-association kind, which, because they depend heavily on the reader's synthesising activity, are not open to the powerful channelling and focusing effects that occur within a single dramatic sequence. The muted tones are sweet, but they do not carry very far into the circumambient murk.

I would argue, then, that what Professor Knights has called 'the holy supernatural', though a presence in the play, is not a powerful presence.[15] There are certainly 'images of grace', but it is grace invoked in extremity:

> Some holy Angell
> Flye to the Court of England, and unfold
> His Message ere he come, that a swift blessing
> May soone returne to this our suffering Country,
> Under a hand accurs'd.   III. vi. 45

The 'swift blessing' is hypothetical beside the actuality of the 'hand accurs'd'. It is also worth noting that this scene, where many of the images of grace are concentrated, opens with a brilliant piece of equivocating doubletalk, as Lennox skilfully feels out the political alignments of his interlocutor: everyone is committed, like Macbeth, to 'hoodwinking the time' (the phrase comes from Macduff's advice to Malcolm—IV. iii. 72).

Roy Walker tasks the modern reader with a wrong-headed determination not to have the play 'made too Christian'.[16] I suggest, however, that it is not so much a twentieth-century reluctance to enter imaginatively into the religious assumptions of the Elizabethans that creates this resistance, as a sense, emerging from responsive attention to the play, that the Christianity is not so central as one might expect. Or perhaps it would be more accurate to say, the Christianity is less *theological* than the Christian interpreters would have us believe. For if the 'holy supernatural' is less important than critics have argued, the 'holy natural' is central.

II

For there is a grace (as opposed to Grace) which carries considerable weight in the play. It is the dominant characteristic of Duncan, and it is profoundly involved with nature, human and non-human. It is not Grace *above* nature, a quality ultimately superhuman in origin and not answerable to the phenomenal world, but a grace-*in*-nature, an immanent principle of health which, if it suggests the more-than-natural, does so by being transparently grounded in the true nature of things. It makes no direct appeal to the supra-natural.[17]

It is in this working axiom that Shakespeare displays his superiority as a religious thinker over his predominantly theological contemporaries—one of whom was Christopher Marlowe. He does not need the supernatural machinery of angels and demons in order to deal with the perennial human phenomenon of damnation—a state of preter-natural fixity and creative paralysis from which there seems no escape; nor does he require the overtly theological symbolism of Christ's blood streaming in the firmament in order to contemplate that miraculous act of restoration that we call forgiveness—Cordelia is more than sufficient. He knows that values are embodied values or they rapidly convert themselves into 'the dismal shade of Mystery'—that tyrannical and poisonous domination of Person by Concept. Like Blake, he knows that

> ...Mercy has a human heart,
> Pity a human face,
> And Love, the human form divine,
> And Peace, the human dress.

In an age for which the vertical dependence of Nature upon Grace was almost axiomatic, Shakespeare was able to distil, even from the Calvinism that was so influential in England, a vision of nature-as-redemptive which was not dependent on an inhuman kind of trans-cendentalism. Instead of the tyrannous super-deity of some parts of

Faustus, the Jehovah of Marlowe's bad conscience, we have a complete interdependence, perhaps identity, of grace and nature.

> For Mercy, Pity, Peace, and Love
> Is God, our father dear,
> And Mercy, Pity, Peace, and Love
> Is Man, his child and care.

The miraculous thing is that this serene master-conception is at work in a play in which nature-run-wild is contemplated with fierce single-mindedness. (Perhaps the chief interpretative problem with *Macbeth* is to make sense of the interrelations of these two 'natures'; and the chief danger, in interpretation, is to give to one or the other an artificial dominance which the play will not support.)

The portents of the second act, for all their apparent supernaturalism, are examples of this grace-in-nature. The assumption behind the notion of the Heavens 'troubled with mans Act' is one of a fairly intimate and morally stabilised interconnexion between man and the rest of nature. Our problem now is that what was for Shakespeare a metaphor not yet divorced from simple fact has become for us pure metaphor, and fanciful metaphor at that. The most we can generate is an archaic sympathetic shudder—which is precisely not what Shakespeare wanted. Rather we were to see a perfect fitness in these events. They are not somewhat hectically conceived objective correlatives for an emotional state, but the normal outcome of unnatural behaviour. The underlying conception is one of the integrity of all nature, constituted by an innate principle which reacts uniformly to each intrusion of foreign matter—a kind of expulsive reflex directed against evil. Although the instantaneous effect is probably lost to us now, we can still grasp the conception.

Macbeth christens this unity of nature 'the Snake'—

> We have scorch'd the Snake, not kill'd it:
> Shee'le close, and be her selfe, whilest our poore Mallice
> Remaines in danger of her former Tooth.   III. ii. 13

The Snake is not Duncan, for they have killed him. Macbeth is thinking of Duncan's murder as one abortive stage in an attack on a larger, more obscure and (to him) venomous organism, of which Banquo is also a part. He acknowledges that he has declared war on a unity which, when it is 'her selfe', threatens his 'poore Mallice' with a deeper, more enduring malignance than his sporadic violence can muster. It is his sense of the magnitude of the forces with which he is engaged in mortal combat that leads to the violent images of cosmic catastrophe which follow these lines—in order to prevent the snake closing and being herself, 'the frame of things' will have to 'dis-joynt'.

The same awareness of cycles of operation which cannot ultimately be brought to a standstill prompts a musingly enigmatic remark after the Banquet:

It will have blood they say:
Blood will have blood.   III. iv. 121

But 'it' is not merely blood, as Macbeth's explanatory second clause would suggest; 'it' is a dynamic moral order which makes its own exactions from 'the secret'st man of Blood'. Or it is 'that great Bond' (III. ii. 49)—a metaphor which has provoked much ingenious exegesis. The largeness of reference (which is not vagueness) presents Macbeth's profound uncertainty about the nature of this force, which must not only be rendered inoperative (cancelled) but totally obliterated (torn to pieces) if he is to recover his self-possession. He calls it a 'Bond' because it constricts, bounds, binds, pales, closes him in; because he feels it as a legally binding force, drawing its power to oppress him from some eternally established canon; and because, in some obscure way, he feels himself bound by it, as if he had entered into it, were a party to it—as indeed he is; for it is one of those laws which, in Hooker's words, 'do bind men absolutely even as they are men...'.[18] And it is a *great* bond not only because its oppression is monstrous to him, but also because he feels it to have a more than legal validity, to be involved with the great world, the cosmos, the macrocosm. Of the 'great Bond' and 'the Snake', the 'frame of things' which 'will have' what it will, Macbeth appears to be more intensely aware than his enemies.

This unified strength of beneficent 'nature' is presented in many ways. In Duncan, as we have seen, and especially in his relations with his thanes:

DUNCAN.   Let me enfold thee,
And hold thee to my Heart.
BANQUO.   There if I grow,
The Harvest is your owne.   I. iv. 31

The suggestion of a powerfully-knit mutuality, rooted in the natural, is strong here. One senses it too in the compassionate Ross of Act IV, Scene iii, in the brotherly camaraderie of Malcolm's army, or—a metaphorical crystallisation—in the evening evocation of Macbeth's bird-haunted castle, an image, as Professor Knights suggests, of 'life delighting in life'.[19] A similar kind of value is embodied in the 'Babe' imagery which Cleanth Brooks has analysed so persuasively as the tender and vulnerable, yet creative possibility of the future.[20]

But its most startling manifestation occurs when Shakespeare as it were inverts the theme and shows Lady Macbeth converting the incalculable energy of natural affection into the dynamic of murder:

> Come you Spirits,
> That tend on mortall thoughts, unsex me here,
> And fill me from the Crowne to the Toe, top-full
> Of direst Crueltie: make thick my blood,
> Stop up th'accesse, and passage to Remorse,
> That no compunctious visitings of Nature
> Shake my fell purpose, nor keepe peace betweene
> Th'effect, and it. Come to my Womans Breasts,
> And take my Milke for Gall, you murth'ring Ministers,
> Where-ever, in your sightlesse substances,
> You wait on Natures Mischiefe. Come thick Night,
> And pall thee in the dunnest smoake of Hell,
> That my keene Knife see not the Wound it makes,
> Nor Heaven peepe through the Blanket of the darke,
> To cry, hold, hold.   I. v. 40

It need not surprise us that she demands to be *un*sexed in terms that have a ferocious sexual undertone: those reiterated *Comes* are surely a profoundly erotic invitation; she is to be filled 'top-full' by these spirits of sterility; in the passionate thickening of the blood she will achieve remorselessness; her demonic lovers will suckle at her breasts; she will do the deed of darkness, in her sexually inverted state, with her 'keene Knife', under the 'Blanket of the darke'; and there is to be no interfering moralistic heaven to bring about *coitus interruptus*—she will have her fulfilment.

It is the most direct and explicit instance [writes Professor Lawlor] of something that is of the highest importance in the Shakespearian scheme of things. The incalculable force of natural affection is a mighty current. While it runs, however faintly, there is a chance of it leaping unimaginable gaps. Old wrongs righted, the lost found, the dead brought back to life—nothing is impossible while there remain unobstructed the 'compunctious visitings of nature'. To make possible the tragic waste, all occasion of tenderness must be decisively rejected; the current must be finally earthed.[21]

In so far as Lady Macbeth is the real force behind the murder, Shakespeare makes us see the deed as dependent for its energy upon the very nature it violates.

The Snake finally defeats Macbeth's poor malice in the person of Macduff; and the process by which the Thane of Fife is forged into the perfectly adapted instrument of Macbeth's downfall is a beautiful example of the operation of what I called, in connexion with *Richard III*, 'natural', or 'dramatic providence'. This process instinctively phrases itself in terms of season and natural process—

> Macbeth
> Is ripe for shaking...
> The Night is long, that never findes the Day—   IV. iii. 237

and finds its dramatic correlative in that temporal appositeness of plot development, a 'musically' apprehended sense of emotional symmetry and fitness which we noted in the closing stages of *Richard III*. The unfolding of this providence is accompanied by a faint click, as of another piece fitting into place:

> LENNOX. Macduff is fled to England.
> MACBETH.   Fled to England?
> LENNOX. I, my good Lord.
> MACBETH. Time, thou anticipat'st my dread exploits...
>   IV. i. 142

In the long pause that follows Lennox's confirmation, Shakespeare implies an act of ironic recognition, and resignation. We have been here before.

In *Macbeth*, however, the 'providence' is more profoundly related than in *Richard III* to the inner development of the personages in the drama, so that we may almost say that the logic of Macbeth's personal disintegration is the guiding principle of the 'dramatic providence'. The healthful grace-in-nature asserts itself not only through the social organism and in the public realm, but in the self-defeating winding-down of the evil impulse in the individual. Thus the murderous decision that is taken after the Cauldron scene is both a catalyst that is certain to set the social and public reaction going, and a necessary consequence of Macbeth's chosen course.

> Time, thou anticipat'st my dread exploits:
> The flighty purpose never is o're-tooke
> Unlesse the deed go with it. From this moment,
> The very firstlings of my heart shall be
> The firstlings of my hand. And even now
> To Crown my thoughts with Acts: be it thoght & done:
> The Castle of Macduff, I will surprize,

Seize upon Fife; give to th'edge o' th'Sword
His Wife, his Babes, and all unfortunate Soules
That trace him in his Line. IV. i. 144

Considered as a personal action of Macbeth's, this is the necessary consequence of the avid pursuit of the future which makes him continually 'lean away from the Present':[22] Macbeth runs, time runs; and time is continually gaining on him, anticipating him. Ahead of him flies his 'purpose', not possessed in the present, but gradually drawing ahead, passing out of range. Increasingly he is uncertain what his purpose is. He must grapple it to him with a deed, at 'this moment' close the gap between future purpose and present achievement by making them simultaneous—identical twins of acted desire, with no gestation period filled with deliberation and scrupling. And because all his purposes are growing out of date before he can act them, this deed must be the very newest, the 'firstling' of his heart. Having made this decision—not to do anything in particular, but simply *to do*, 'even now', without hesitation, something, anything—it doesn't matter to Macbeth what comes to hand. He stabs the map of his mind with a free-associational pin, and it transfixes the Macduff household at Fife. This is the deed seen through the logic of Macbeth's moral development.

But there are other dimensions. With the random destructiveness of this final decision some invisible but real boundary is crossed. It is not so much the atrocity against women and children (consideration of that is reserved for the next scene) as the fact that the murder is merely instrumental in Macbeth's attempt to prove something to himself. It is not nursed malice (they are 'unfortunate' souls), but murder for thesis, a deed in which all that makes an act recognisably human, whether moral or immoral, has been by-passed. To telescope the interim between the 'first notion' and the 'acting' (in order to obviate the 'phantasma' and the 'hideous dream') is to give to action an automatic, mechanical quality which is truly infernal. And for perhaps the first time in the play, one feels that Macbeth is not beset by that inner compulsion and coercion, the driving fear which has clogged and impeded all his earlier decisions. This, random though it may be, still feels like a real act of volition—the absolutely damnable, freely embraced. Macbeth has crossed a frontier, and, by doing so, has liberated in the audience that impulse which has been mutely calling for his destruction.

Finally, on the more obvious public level, Macbeth here sets a torch to the bonfire that will ultimately consume him. The decision makes the probable enmity of Macduff a certainty, giving Macbeth, on the heels of the prophecy, a very palpable reason why he should 'beware Macduff, beware the Thane of Fife'. Yet there is nothing mysterious or supernatural here. He falls victim to that historical law by which, in Croce's words, 'the man who enslaves another wakes in him awareness of himself and enlivens him to seek for liberty...'.[23] The cosmic necessity of this process is figured in the fulfilled prophecy, just as the principle of degeneration inherent in evil is figured as a kind of dropsy, tending to indefinite distension, which makes the evil-doer increasingly vulnerable, until

> He cannot buckle his distemper'd cause
> Within the belt of Rule.   v. ii. 15

The grace in inanimate nature is in mysterious alliance with the perceptible logic of events, with the disintegration of the personality corrupted by evil—compounding medicines out of the excesses of disease, and with the natural providence in the public sphere, which inscrutably forges instruments of purgation like Macduff.

But Macduff, our special concern at present, is much more than a mute exemplar of the law of retributive reaction. He is a very particular man; and as a man he cannot simply enact 'nature's revenge' without involving himself personally in far-reaching moral problems. For the ethical delicacy of this play, it is not enough that he should proceed directly, in the heat of rage and rancour, to the extermination of the tyrant. He, too, like Macbeth, has a pilgrimage to go, and by studying this journey we can learn much about the kind of goodness Shakespeare is setting against the Macbeth-evil.

The sequence in which Macduff receives the disastrous news from his home is one of the most directly moving things in the play. Emotion elsewhere tends to be either perverted or hopelessly tangled and clotted by self-doubt and suspicion—'O, full of Scorpions is my Minde, deare Wife'. Here it is fine and free-flowing. Before Ross finally delivers his message, he points Macduff the way he must take, in lines that have a magnificent sonority and desolation of movement:

> But I have words
> That would be howl'd out in the desert ayre,
> Where hearing should not latch them.   IV. iii. 193

It is an evocation of that brute pain (the 'Syllable of Dolour' which can only be 'yell'd') that a grief too vast for words gives vent to—the

inarticulate matrix of what is to become, in Macduff, a fine consciousness of 'mission'. The desert is the only place for such grief—private,
limitless, impersonal. And in the succeeding lines Macduff goes into the
inner desert of the mind. Malcolm, pretty disastrously insensitive
throughout this sequence, nevertheless gives us the dark undercurrent
of thought towards destruction which is flowing so swiftly and
treacherously in Macduff's mind:

> the griefe that do's not speake,
> Whispers the o're-fraught heart, and bids it breake.   IV. iii. 209

At the brink where Macduff stands, an infinitesimal joggle, a whisper,
tips over from life into death. There is a child-like frailty of diction in
his distracted questions, as his mind totters on the edge of the unthinkable:

> All my pretty ones?
> Did you say All? O Hell-Kite! All?
> What, All my pretty Chickens, and their Damme
> At one fell swoope?   IV. iii. 216

This is one of the most agonising renderings of the naked voice of
feeling in all Shakespeare, and it focuses attention in a most immediate
way, first on Malcolm's complete misunderstanding of what is happening to Macduff, and second, on a transformation that can properly be
called spiritual that is taking place in Macduff's being. Malcolm wants
Macduff's grief to 'convert to anger', making bereavement immediately
the 'Whetstone' of his sword—a crudity of response which is high-
lighted by the reticent dignity of Ross's demeanour. Malcolm is far too
quick to spot the connexion between Macduff's personal catastrophe
and his own military projects, and so fails to see how much finer a
moral instrument is being forged in Macduff's despair than any facile
revenge-lust could furnish. Ross, by contrast, displays a faith in 'nature'
and a respect for Macduff which lets him bear his own cross, rather than
humiliating him by inept solicitude: he gives him the blunt, brutal
facts—'Savagely slaughter'd'—and then stands down. Malcolm, meanwhile, fusses about with the hearty meddlesomeness of insensitivity—
'What man, ne're pull your hat upon your browes: / Give sorrow
words...', 'Be comforted', and (most revealingly)

> Dispute it like a man.

This is so near to Lady Macbeth's conception of manhood, the mascu-
line ferocity that is really bestiality, that Macduff's quiet vindication of

another kind of manhood carries immense conviction (this is the nature
to whose operation Ross was content to leave him):

> I shall do so:
> But I must also feele it as a man;
> I cannot but remember such things were
> That were most precious to me: Did heaven looke on,
> And would not take their part? Sinfull Macduff,
> They were all strooke for thee: Naught that I am,
> Not for their owne demerits, but for mine
> Fell slaughter on their soules: Heaven rest them now.   IV. iii. 220

Feeling first, action later. Manhood expresses itself in a full and *feeling*
submission to the bitter reality. Only out of this whole-hearted response
to the demands of affection can there come right action. It must not be a
frantic pursuit of forgetfulness and oblivion, but a way to '*remember
such things were / That were most precious*'. And it grows by way of
assuming a burden of guilt. We shall never understand Macduff's self-
accusation here if we interpret act and motive on the level of a shallow
prudential morality—for on that level he is the victim merely of a cruel
miscalculation. But he is here accepting, with an unheroic humility,
his human solidarity with all suffering Scotland, and not only with the
butchered dead—with the Macbeth he has 'lov'd well' too. He takes
on himself a share of the burden of guilt that all men must bear when
the social organism loses its integrity and runs amok among its own
shrines. It is a recognition that heaven does *not* take the part of the
victimised, while man neglects his own implication in the evil of the
oppressor. It is in this sense that 'they were all strooke' for him. They
fell because he did not know that he was 'Sinfull Macduff' and 'Naught',
did not know his own 'demerits', which now press in upon him with
such hopeless insistence.

And yet the knowledge, like all responsible confronting of hard
truth, offers a kind of tough comfort, and is no *cul de sac*: Macduff
now arrives at action—

> O I could play the woman with mine eyes,
> And Braggart with my tongue. But gentle Heavens,
> Cut short all intermission: Front to Front,
> Bring thou this Fiend of Scotland, and my selfe;
> Within my Swords length set him, if he scape
> Heaven forgive him too.   IV. iii. 230

He has been labouring his own salvation at his own pace, and when he
does arrive at the notion of revenge it is neither hysterical (playing the

woman) nor braggart, but appropriately allied with the 'gentle heavens' and a sense that he must be 'forgiven' if he neglects his duty to exterminate Macbeth. That little word 'too' condenses a world of meaning—self-admonition as an antidote to mounting *hybris*; a sense that there is none of us that does not need forgiveness; a capacity for sympathetic self-projection which can spare compassion even for the 'Fiend' himself, feel his plight from the inside; a self-awareness prepared, by the steady contemplation of its own fallibility, to range itself alongside the criminal. The white-hot point of anger is there, too, in 'Fiend of Scotland', but it is held in check by an overriding sense of wise self-doubt. Only on this foundation of acknowledged personal guilt and responsibility can justice justly go into operation. And Macduff, as the one Scot who has fully grasped this truth—Malcolm finds the tune merely 'manly' and is content with an 'enraged' heart —Macduff is the necessary agent of Macbeth's downfall.

So, then, nature is at work in Macbeth to bring him down, in Macduff to create a just avenger. The goodness in Scotland forms an organic unity, and even inanimate nature is convulsed in an effort to shake off the evil. A natural providence inscrutably appears behind the synchronism and unanimity of all these forces, and its eventual success is figured in the progressive fulfilment of the prophecies. What then of the primacy of evil?

One might argue that these forces, though strong, are presented as tender and vulnerable—'a naked New-borne-Babe'. The restorative, regenerating sleep which Macbeth so much desires is also 'the innocent Sleepe' so easily murdered, or 'the Curtain'd sleepe', withheld from the world only by a thin membrane, scarcely withdrawn, easily stirred, and abused by 'wicked Dreames'. Or again, it is noticeable that almost all these manifestations of beneficent nature take the form of a *reaction* provoked by evil: 'In *Macbeth*,' Croce observes, 'the good appears only as the revenge taken by the good, as remorse, punishment...'²⁴ (One could dispute that 'only', but the general point holds good.) But this is no answer, if the reaction is stronger than the evil. How *primacy* of evil? Is it not, rather, doomed?

The answer is, of course, yes. But I am concerned to draw a distinction between the play's *peripateia* and its effect; for I believe that much of its power to grip and, indeed, to terrify, resides in the tension between the qualified optimism of the plot considered as fable, and the 'strong pessimism' of the dramatic actuality. And this tension is only rendered the more intense by being contained within an artistic unity.

III

The primacy of evil in *Macbeth*, that is to say, is not due to its superior force, its inevitable triumph, nor to its being covertly allied to the good in some realm 'beyond good and evil' (though we have seen one sense in which its natural life cycle in the human psyche does tend to complement the healthful operations of 'nature', and there are some grounds for seeing Macbeth's acquiescence in his own destruction as a 'healthy' recognition of his own incurable malady). But evil has the primacy of superior actuality. The feeling is that its capacity for destruction defeats that of goodness for reconstruction. Its assault is not upon the mediocre but upon the best. And its presence in the world of the play is somehow too intense, too real, too pressing to permit us finally to subsume it under goodness, or providence, or nature. As Arthur Sewell points out, all the central images of the play—blood, night, sleep—'evoke in us the very act of annihilating real and solid things, of making blurred the outlines of objects, of mantling the surfaces with darkness'. And none of them is 'regulative; not one steadies us for life in society'; rather they throw us back on the private, the obscure, and the impalpable.[25] In this setting, evil can have a kind of absoluteness.

And if it is objected that this is to make Shakespeare a Manichaean, one may retort that Shakespeare is a Manichaean, and an Augustinian, and a Pelagian—has, in short, some smack of every doctrinal emphasis which represents man's honest attempt to reckon with the problematical in life and morality. There is, besides, a kind of perennial Manichaeism which is only ultimately put aside when men stop taking evil seriously. The truly great writer is both necessarily Manichaean— one thinks of that disturbing masterpiece, Tolstoy's *Kreutzer Sonata*— and necessarily unable to rest in that Manichaeism: he gives us *War and Peace*, or (both stages contained within one vision) *King Lear*. But as the hypersensitive conscience of his age, he cannot avoid feeling the pressure of evil with an alarming absoluteness.

Its *actuality* is one of the notable ways in which Shakespeare's conception of evil transcends the traditional Christian views with which it is sometimes confounded. For scholasticism, evil is nonbeing, and thus unreal, a mere 'privation of what is connatural and due to anyone'.[26]

And while Shakespeare grasps the essential truth in this conception— that to choose evil is to be sucked down into a maelstrom of vacancy and nothingness—he never falls into the slackness and complacence which easily turns evil, for the theologians, into a pseudo-problem. Here is Augustine:

When all good is completely taken away there will remain not even a trace—absolutely nothing. All good is from God; therefore no kind of thing exists which is not from God. Hence that movement of turning away, which we agree to be sin, is a defective movement and a defective movement comes from nothing.[27]

In this passage, and the dozens like it that could be culled from Aquinas and his followers, what might have been a gripping rendering of the truth that evil, for all its force and fury, is an abyss of nothingness, has become a flaccid *dismissal* of evil under the rubric of 'non-being'. Shakespeare grasps both ends of the paradox—the reality and the unreality of evil. And the moments when we are most aware of its reality tend to be also the moments when we sense the central emptiness.

Thus, in place of the reassuring Thomist certainty that 'what is evil simply, is utterly beside the intention in the operations of nature',[28] we get the Shakespearian sense of the interpenetration of the evil in man and external nature:

> Light thickens,
> And the Crow makes Wing to th' Rookie Wood:
> Good things of Day begin to droope, and drowse,
> Whiles Nights black Agents to their Preys doe rowse.
> Thou marvell'st at my words: but hold thee still,
> Things bad begun, make strong themselves by ill.   III. ii. 50

This is what I mean by the actuality of evil. For who will say of this masterly evocation of a particular kind of English nightfall, lines in which there is more essential landscape than most painters achieve in a lifetime, that it is merely pathetic fallacy, Macbeth's projection of his guilty self onto an innocent external world? In a concrete, substantial way the evil is there. Light does not dim, but concentrates, intensifies in small lighted area of sky, with a certain pearling and curdling into a livid glare. The suggestion is one of obstruction and congestion, a defensive consolidation which precedes defeat. And the last black wanderer, in a line that enacts metrically the ungainly flapping flight of the carrion crow, joins the society of evil-doing. The cackling of the 'Rookie Wood', the inherent menace of nightfall, are infallibly translated into a vision of invisible predators consolidating for assault upon all 'Good things of Day'. This is not an imaginative imposition upon external reality, but an eliciting of what was always there—hence the powerful sense of 'scene'. Macbeth's invocation of night is frightening, because the forces he invokes are all too real. It is the consolidating principle of evil in Nature which corresponds to the old Senecan principle of *human* degeneration: *per scelera semper sceleribus tutum est iter*[29]—'Things bad begun, make strong themselves by ill'. The imaginative assent the passage commands makes impossible any simple view of the unreality of evil.

Nor can we dispose of the Witches either, by invoking the scholastic view of evil as illusion. Since order of appearance is an ancient dramatic device for representing other kinds of priority besides the temporal, I take it that the first scene of *Macbeth* is eliminating this interpretation. They are on the scene first—before Macbeth, before we even find out about the battle. We are not shown the real occasion of their meeting, for they issue forth on the point of parting and are gone almost immediately. The image is one of disseminated evil flying forth swiftly over the world, darkening the sky with 'fogge and filthie ayre'. It is as if Shakespeare has foreseen the modern interpretation of the Witches as mere projections of Macbeth's undivulged power-lust, and, with his very first scene, has made it untenable. They are prior.

Yet the power of evil represented by the Witches is ambiguous; for their stage presence combines foreboding with absurdity. Not even the most credulous of groundlings could have missed the element of the grotesque and the ridiculous in this unheralded, abrupt, thirty-second scene of doggerel and melodrama—for even groundlings know when they are at a play. With the Witches, terror is mediated *through* absurdity. The filthy gruel of Act IV, Scene i, for instance, would not have its power to revolt and repel if it were not enunciated in the naïve metric of children's rhyming games—a child-like incantation in which sound precedes sense, yet what sense there is is quintessential malice:

> Double, double, toile and trouble;
> Fire burne, and Cauldron bubble.

The accents of infantile malevolence ('Ile doe, Ile doe, and Ile doe') are alarming because we sense that these figures of childish spite somehow hold the stage, and that the kingdom of the rational and the humane has been given into their power.

The development of the Witch motif is a most complex piece of exposition, but it needs to be grasped if we are to understand the nature of the Macbeth-evil. I shall be ignoring W. C. Curry's gratuitous explanation, influential though it appears to be, that the Witches are evil-spirits disguised as Witches, partly because it is an explanation which is itself in need of explanation—for what *are* evil-spirits?—but more importantly because it is an answer to a pseudo-question which neglects the nature of dramatic illusion. Instead of enquiring how the Witches function within that illusion, Curry asks, 'What are they *really*?' This is simply another version of the biographical fallacy in criticism which insists on knowing what the hero does when alone with his wife, the colour of his hair, and how his father treated him as a child. One might add, too, that even if one admitted the validity of Curry's enquiry, his 'received doctrine of demons' is almost unrecognisably schematised and over-simplified.[30]

If the Witches are not to be taken as relics of an outmoded and largely meaningless cosmology—and I take it they are still effective enough on the stage to discount this way out of the problem—we must try to offer some account of their dramatic efficacy which does not make them dependent on the superstition of the audience. Bradley is helpful here:

The Witches and their prophecies, if they are to be rationalised or taken symbolically, must represent not only the evil slumbering in the hero's soul, but all those obscurer influences of the evil around him in the world which aid his own ambition...Such influences, even if we put aside all belief in evil 'spirits', are as certain, momentous, and terrifying facts as the presence of inchoate evil in the soul itself; and if we exclude all reference to these facts from our idea of the Witches, it will be greatly impoverished...[31]

And Allardyce Nicoll takes us a step further:

We can see in them evil ministers tempting Macbeth to destruction, or we can look on them merely as embodiments of ambitious thoughts which had already moved Macbeth and his wife to murderous imaginings. The peculiar thing to note is that through Shakespeare's subtle and suggestive art *we do not regard these points of view as mutually antagonistic.*[32]

As with the supernatural realm in *Faustus,* a subjective–objective dualism is not very helpful in the understanding of the Witches. They are real and objective enough to have a stage presence, and they are subjective enough to phrase Macbeth's thoughts with an accuracy that sets his heart pounding and his hair on end. It is partly the coincidence, in the Witches, of apparent objectivity with a heart-stopping fidelity to his inmost consciousness that induces in Macbeth the vertiginous sensation that 'Nothing is but what is not'. The dreams of sovereignty which he had supposed to be purely fictitious and internal phenomena now present themselves to him in the guise of achieved fact: 'surmise' appears to have got the better of 'function'. Banquo, who at first found the Witches impossible to classify (see I. iii. 39–47), is not sure, after their disappearance, whether 'such things' were there at all; and his doubt—like Macbeth's anguished question after the 'shew of eight Kings': 'What? is this so?'—phrases something important for the audience; for even if they were 'here', their reality is self-contradictory —'bubbles' of the earth, seeming corporal yet melting into the wind. And the audience, I suggest, is invited to remain, with Banquo, un-committed about the final reality of the Witches, awaiting their validation as the prophecies come to maturity.

Only Macbeth, who is already committed to *creating* a reality for them by action, cuts right through the dubieties that beset us, with a simple indicative equation of prophecy with fact: 'Your Children shall be Kings.' There is more than a suggestion about this third scene that the Witches are parasitic upon reality to the extent that they require a 'host' like Macbeth to confer reality upon them. We only come to 'believe in' the Witches, that is to say, as Macbeth's bloody pilgrimage gets under way and begins to body forth the empty forms projected by the prophecy. And, of course, this is precisely the moment when we also recognise that they are 'really' temptation in its most diabolical form. Essential to the dramatic efficacy of the Witches, then, is the fact that they cannot be classified as either subjective *or* objective; rather the whole movement of the play is a many-sided and progressive revelation of their equivocal relations with reality itself.[33]

Perhaps this is clearest in relation to their prophetic function. In so far as the prophecies are concerned with the future, they represent a retreat from the reality of the present into 'what is not', and the Macbeths' attempt to 'feele now / The future in the instant' is a delusive attempt, under their tutelage, to erect the as yet non-existent into the only reality, and to submit the present to its domination. But in so far as the prophecies progressively translate themselves into fact, one comes to suspect that they may be founded on some superior supra-temporal actuality. The suspicion is strong at the point where Fleance makes his escape by a sheer coincidence which nevertheless has profound ironic fitness. It is as the last 'streakes of Day' fade under 'seeling Night' that the bloody hand secures its invisibility by striking out the last light—the torch that Fleance is carrying. And it is precisely this granting of the Macbeths' reiterated demand for total darkness that ensures the escape of the seed of Banquo who will be 'King hereafter'.[34] The effect is complex and powerful. The sense of that external coercion of accident which goes by the name of Fate is strong enough to set a cold wind blowing out of the wings; and the doubt is only strengthened (as with the later prophecies about Birnam Wood and Macduff's birth) by the knowledge that the explanation is, after all, quite simple and natural.

A similar occurrence in Act v hastens Macbeth's final defeat. He has determined not to go into the field to meet the English force 'beard to beard', confident that his 'Castles strength / Will laugh a Siedge to scorne' (v. v. 1–7). But when the report of the 'moving Grove' reaches him, there is a sudden change of plan:

> Arme, Arme, and out,
> If this which he avouches, do's appeare,
> There is nor flying hence, nor tarrying here.
> I 'ginne to be a-weary of the Sun,
> And wish th' estate o' th' world were now undon.
> Ring the Alarum Bell, blow Winde, come wracke,
> At least wee'l dye with Harnesse on our backe.　　　v. v. 46

The prophecy's fulfilment, which in itself was powerless to overthrow him (there is no indication that his confidence of weathering a siege is misplaced), has produced in Macbeth precisely that state of despairing carelessness and 'valiant fury' without which he would have been invincible. Again the naturalistic, explicable aspect of the supernatural operates transparently, yet only intensifies the supernatural *frisson*: for this concurrence of natural events answers simultaneously precise causation and moral justice. There is a sense in which Macbeth has conferred upon the prophecy all the reality it possesses, and another sense in which he is the slave of the prophecy.

This doubleness, it seems to me, is characteristic of all the predictions and fulfilments in the play—they are both powerless to alter the course of events, and they reflect faithfully the course of events which is unalterable. The very predictions seem to presuppose the effect they will have upon Macbeth—as if a deterministic net had been cast over the whole action. Yet Macbeth proceeds, with every appearance of freedom, to draw the *unnecessary* conclusion from the prophecies: that chance will *not* crown him without his stir. And even that conclusion is presupposed by the prophecy, since a Macbeth who did not stir would have become the vassal of heir-apparent Malcolm, Prince of Cumberland.

It is rather as if Shakespeare were indicating that the germ of all the evil lay in the Witches' intrusion of the timelessly pre-ordained. The Future endowed with a delusive actuality appears as the seed of chaos, 'essentially a disorder-force', as Wilson Knight remarks, 'until it is bodied into the life-forms of the present'.[35] Throughout the play, knowledge of the future makes no difference to that future (it cannot, or it would not then be knowable); it merely encourages the man favoured with prevision to mutilate and misdirect his present in the interests of a future he can neither modify nor avoid. The double nature of the prophecies (as merely descriptive and so powerless to effect what they predict, and yet binding upon Macbeth as a kind of Fate) is reflected in his equivocal attitude to them: in so far as he acts, he takes the future on his shoulders and undertakes to create it, thus becoming the accomplice, or even the master, of his fate; yet he persists in regarding the future as pre-ordained and Fate as his master. The equivocation goes even deeper, for he imagines that the prophetically-revealed, which has become for him a palpable golden crown, can nevertheless be circumvented in the case of Banquo's issue—a contradiction which gives rise to a somewhat puzzling verbal ambiguity:

> Rather then so, come Fate into the Lyst,
> And *champion* me to th'utterance.   III. i. 70

What is Fate doing here? Fighting for, or against him? I think both.[36] Fate is simultaneously Macbeth's pretext for fulfilling the prophecy and the enemy he fights *à l'outrance*. He does not know whose side Fate is on; does not know, to be more precise, that Fate is on nobody's side. He has pawned his freedom to the power which promised him the future, and so he is unable to see himself as wholly free; but to believe that he has been delivered over bound to necessity is intolerable. Yet the accelerating confluence of events and predictions drives him increasingly into fatalistic desperation.

I don't want to make too much of complexities of plot, which tend to operate nearer the surface than other, more important matters; but I believe that, at the successive moments when the prophecies find their simple and all-too-natural fulfilments, the audience experiences a characteristic qualm—a chill of fear at the infinite and patient cunning of things, that diabolical deviousness which is also a kind of justice. To ignore this is to ignore an act of recognition and acquiescence which helps us to orient ourselves within a complex imaginative experience. For with this transitory recognition we admit a suspicion that Macbeth has somehow been, from the very beginning, the plaything of a giant malevolence.

IV

In what sense then is Macbeth free? We have seen how, by his handling of the prophecies, Shakespeare has set us wondering about the very possibility of freedom. He has called into a play a self-doubt which lies in the path of any close scrutiny of one's own 'free' action—the despairing suspicion that it could not have been otherwise, and is therefore meaningless. It is Macbeth's suspicion as he nears the end of his road—either that it could not have been otherwise (that he has been 'paltered with'), or else that the choice offered was only one between equally 'idiot' alternatives, and thus no real choice at all. Yet there is about the famous soliloquy, I think, a very strong sense that it is not a philosophical position so much as an intellectual by-product of behaviour: Macbeth has not thought his way to this position—it has thought him. And we may wonder whether the sensation of fatality is not equally something proceeding indirectly from choice.

It is well to be clear, though, that free-will is not a 'problem' to which Shakespeare is propounding an answer. Rather it is a problematic nexus in human experience to which, as a dramatist, he is naturally drawn. On an obvious level Macbeth is free to refrain from murdering Duncan. On an only slightly less obvious level he was bound to do it. One does not have to opt for one of these versions of the play, for they are both intolerably superficial. What Shakespeare makes us feel, and feel inwardly, is the extremely tenuous division between the 'free' act and the 'determined' one, and the imaginative possibility of a world in which the balance has been imperceptibly tipped towards evil, so that man writhes and sprawls vainly on a greased slope that ends in perdition. The unbalance resides precisely in the problematic nature of the Will.

In every willing there is first of all a multiplicity of feelings: the feeling of a condition to get *away* from, the feeling of a condition to get *to*; then the feeling of this 'away' and 'to'; furthermore, an accompanying muscular feeling which, from a sort of habit, begins a game of its own as soon as we 'will'—even without our moving our 'arms and legs'...Secondly, there is thinking: in every act of the will there is a thought which gives commands—and we must not imagine that we can separate this thought out of 'willing' and still have something like will left! Thirdly, the will is not merely a complex of feeling and thinking but above all it is a passion—the passion of commanding...A man who *wills* is giving a command to something in himself that obeys, or which he believes will obey. But now let us note the oddest thing about the will, this manifold something for which the people have only one word: because we, in a given case, are simultaneously the commanders *and* the obeyers and, as obeyers, know the feelings of forcing, crowding, pressing, resisting, and moving which begin immediately after the act of the will: because, on the other hand, we are in the habit of glossing over this duality with the help of the synthetic concept 'I'—for these reasons a whole chain of erroneous conclusions, and consequently false valuations of the will, has weighted down our notion of willing...[37]

Macbeth, in Act I, knows the 'feelings of forcing, crowding, pressing' that Nietzsche evokes so well here. He is not the commander, but the obeyer, of forces that present themselves as bodily insurrection, anarchy of soul beyond the possibility of conscious control:

> Why doe I yeeld to that suggestion,
> Whose horrid Image doth unfixe my Heire,
> And make my seated Heart knock at my Ribbes,
> Against the use of Nature? Present Feares
> Are lesse then horrible Imaginings:
> My Thought, whose Murther yet is but fantasticall,
> Shakes so my single state of Man,
> That Function is smother'd in surmise,
> And nothing is, but what is not.   I. iii. 136

The 'yeelding' is already fact. The hideous impulsion of the 'horrid Image' overbears all resistance, moral and rational (the thought of murder is the murder *of* Thought), by its own superior actuality. Its hideousness is indeed part of its power, as anyone knows who has stood at the brink of a sheer drop and felt that uncanny and powerful urge to throw himself down. If we attend carefully to Macbeth's voice here, there is a haunting suggestion that the only answer he can give to his 'Why doe I yeeld?' is to evoke for himself the full fascinating horror of the gulf that yawns below him. A few scenes later, he can assign no motive for a deed which becomes increasingly loathsome the nearer he approaches it, except an 'ambition' which, even as he names it, he depicts as an exhibitionist's vanity, futile and self-defeating:

> Vaulting Ambition, which ore-leapes it selfe,
> And falles on th'other.   I. vii. 27

'Then why do I yield?' comes the tormenting and unanswerable question. The 'fine truth of the Macbeth-conception: a deep, poetic, psychology or metaphysic of the birth of Evil' may lie, as Wilson Knight suggests, in the fact that there is no answer to this question.[38]

Of course it is possible to be sunnily rationalistic about this speech: to point out how he is confusing actuality with reality, fact with truth, to deplore his 'muddled conscience', concluding that he is 'a man who fails to think clearly on a moral issue'.[39] And it is undeniable that Macbeth still calls the image of the murder '*My* Thought'—the wedge has not yet been finally driven between the commander and the obeyer in him. But I cannot help feeling that A. P. Rossiter was nearer the heart of the matter when he spoke of 'the upthrust of the essentially guilty undertow of the human mind', something eternally present in consciousness and eternally menacing.[40] Macbeth's 'muddle', in any case, is not so intense as to prevent him seeing precisely what is happening to him—he knows what is and what is not, and knows that they have become inverted. No, there is something much more awesome here than a failure of reason to make necessary discriminations—it is the discovery, too late to prevent it, that one has lost one's footing and that there is nothing now but the long helpless fall into the abyss.

This is not to minimise the truth of Coleridge's contention that Macbeth's is a mind 'rendered *temptable* by previous dalliance of the fancy with ambitious thoughts'.[41] This is plain enough in such things as the self-deluding arithmetic of

> Glamys, and Thane of Cawdor:
> The greatest is behinde   I. iii. 116

(Glamis—one point, Cawdor—one point; Witches—two out of three) when in a very obvious sense the greatest is still *before*. There is a manifest will to self-deception here and elsewhere in the third scene, which prompts Banquo to some fairly pointed observations. But the important point is the impossibility of tracing this guilt to an origin. Macbeth is simply falling in space.

During the descent we have ample time to ponder the nature and the causes of that first false step. All that one feels at this stage is that it has already been taken. And immediately on its heels comes the onset of disintegration. 'Freedom of the will', as Nietzsche observes, 'is the word for that manifold pleasurable condition of the willer who is in command and at the same time considers himself as one with the executor of the command . . .'[42] It is an unimpeded translation of desire into act, unity of being. But with the intrusion of this image which is both horrid *and* desired, the divisive principle is released in Macbeth's nature; his '*single* state', that is, his state of unity, pureness of purpose, harmony of parts ('if the eye is *single*, the whole body is filled with light'), is shaken, and 'Function' must be parted, divided up, one organ functioning in dissociation from another:

> The Eye winke at the Hand; yet let that bee,
> Which the Eye feares, when it is done, to see. 　　I. iv. 52

The kingdom of the body has become a prey to faction and division, and as a direct consequence we cannot talk simply of Macbeth's 'free-will' any more—for he is not one man. For the rest of the play he seeks to find that singleness again, trying to become 'perfect', as he puts it.

Yet there is another sense in which, though not perhaps freely, Macbeth has now willed the evil which seemed to violate him earlier:

> Starres hide your fires,
> Let not Light see my black and deepe desires. 　　I. iv. 50

To know the desires to be 'black and deepe' and still to desire them, to recognise the 'Hand' and then to 'winke', is to implicate oneself in the evil by a willing immersion in the 'horrid Image'.

Bradley showed an awareness of all this baffling doubleness when he saw, as the essential Shakespearian insight in the play, not a lesson in 'the misery of a guilty conscience and the retribution of crime' (or as a nineteenth-century critic primly put it: 'an unparalleled lecture in ethical anatomy'), but a deep feeling for 'the incalculability of evil'—

that in meddling with it human beings do they know not what. The soul, he seems to feel, is a thing of such inconceivable depth, complexity, and delicacy, that when you introduce into it, or suffer to develop in it, any change, and particularly the change called evil, you can form only the vaguest idea of the reaction you will provoke. All you can be sure of is that it will not be what you expected, and that you cannot possibly escape it.[43]

This may seem an oddly agnostic and negative foundation for some-thing I am claiming as a great tragedy, but the interpreters who by-pass the obscure and the incalculable in *Macbeth* in favour of light and clarity always seem to me to offer a shrunken play. Shakespeare had met these well-meaning rationalists in his day:

They say miracles are past; and we have our philosophical persons, to make modern and familiar, things supernatural and causeless. Hence it is that we make trifles of terrors, ensconcing ourselves into seeming knowledge, when we should *submit ourselves to an unknown fear*.[44]

There is a danger of *resolving* things in *Macbeth* which Shakespeare deliberately left unresolved—one of them being the question of Macbeth's freedom. Shakespeare could easily have given us an untroubled, pre-prophecy Macbeth, who possessed, instead of perpetually desiring, 'a clearenesse', who moved by perceptible degrees into the self-divided state of the criminal. But instead, Macbeth walks, on his first entry, right into the arms of the waiting Witches, his whole consciousness before this encounter being narrowed to one prosy remark about the weather, which is itself instinct with the equivocal— 'So foule and faire a day I have not seene'. If Shakespeare had been interested in the crucial act of pure volition which commits a man to annihilation (a pact with Lucifer, for instance), he would have shown it; but that would have initiated a drama in which the moral issues were as perspicuous as they are in *Faustus*. It is a different kind of guilt with which he is concerned—something so obscure in its origins as to appear to have none, a guilt opaque to moral explication.

One senses this opacity in Macbeth's arguments with his wife. Lady Macbeth's skilful manipulation of her husband plays upon his inability to name a time when he was not haunted by the image of the murder. She asks him to accept as his real nature something so close to the truth that it seems pedantic to deny it. She asks him to see himself as the kind of man who murders for ambition, as if the crucial decision were already taken. And it is because Macbeth suspects it *is* already taken, that he has no answer except 'We will speake further' and 'If we should faile?'. When she charges him with 'breaking the enterprise' to her, he is again paralysed by the near-accuracy of her accusation. For he cannot, except on the most literal level, deny that he has broached the matter in that letter to his 'dearest Partner of Greatnesse', when 'nor time, nor place' adhered. Lady Macbeth has merely taken as a proposition what was not yet so fully formed.[45] In Macbeth's guilty silences in these two scenes (I. v and I. vii) we have a powerful presentation of the helplessness of guilt before that which reflects, and thus magnifies, its image. He has silently conceded her claim to know him better than he knows himself. The relationship is summed up, at their first stage meeting, in a few lines of brilliant dialogue:

> MACBETH.   My dearest Love,
> Duncan comes here to Night.
> LADY MACBETH.   And when goes hence?
> MACBETH. To morrow, as he purposes.
> LADY MACBETH.   O never,
> Shall Sunne that Morrow see.
> Your Face, my Thane, is as a Booke, where men
> May reade strange matters...   I. v. 58

Lady Macbeth's Gioconda smile converts the innocent announcement so subtly into guilty innuendo, that Macbeth is no longer certain that it was ever innocent. Immediately he is fumbling. The exchange culminates in that long, pregnant pause (l. 61) during which the black contamination rises to the surface of Macbeth's eyes, and after which his wife can interpret him to himself without fear of contradiction. There is a real sense in which she has here created Macbeth's guilt, and we know that, despite the brilliant and witty insight into her military husband displayed earlier in the scene, she is misreading the 'Booke' here. Yet, as with the crucial issue of the nature of manhood, Macbeth finishes by accepting her view—that to wish is the same as to act, and that he has already determined on the deed.

His capitulation, however, uncovers a central failure in Macbeth's nature—a failure of self-knowledge. His wife's misinterpretation of his genuine scruple as a mere cat's timorousness leaves him powerless because he has no better knowledge of his own real motivation. In a similar way he is paralysed by the shadow of his own potential evil when it rises like a ghost across his path, because he cannot acknowledge it as his own. Its power to tyrannise over his better nature is dependent on his inability to recognise it. If he could say, with Prospero, 'this thing of darkness I / Acknowledge mine', its power to appal and master him would be partially broken. Not being able to say this, yet seeing the evil rising demonstrably from his own 'horrible Imaginings', he is torn asunder, divided against himself, thrown into despair. Because he never acknowledges his potential evil, it perpetually terrifies him in shapes of external coercion.

It is this kind of congenital resistance to the contemplative and the inward which makes almost all his soliloquies involuntary acts of mental laceration rather than purposive reflection. What he wants is medicine—'some sweet Oblivious Antidote' to 'Cleanse the stufft bosome, of that perillous stuffe / Which weighes upon the heart' (and that repeated 'stuffe' indicates how vague is his conception of his own malady). A clean external operation of plucking or razing, a potion, a scientific cure which does not involve himself, but merely operates *upon* the self—this is what he wants. And when the Doctor abandons his mission as scientist and turns theologian ('...the Patient / Must minister to himselfe') Macbeth dismisses the matter with a sourly sardonic laugh:

> Throw Physicke to the Dogs, Ile none of it.   v. iii. 47

The excuse that springs to his lips in Act I, Scene iii, when he has to account for his abstraction—

> My dull Braine was wrought with things forgotten—

embodies a profound unconscious truth: the sea of desires and dreams from which he is now emerging is the neglected underside of his own moral nature—'things forgotten' indeed.

We may go further, and say that the very attempt to transmute himself into King Macbeth is just such a flight from self-knowledge.

When the ambitious man whose watchword was 'Either Caesar or nothing' does not become Caesar, he is in despair thereat. But this signifies something else, namely, that precisely because he did not become Caesar he now cannot endure to be himself. So properly...it is not the fact that he did not become Caesar which is intolerable to him, but the self which did not become Caesar is the thing that is intolerable; or, more correctly, what is intolerable to him is that he cannot get rid of himself. If he had become Caesar he would have been rid of himself in desperation, but now that he did not become Caesar he cannot in desperation get rid of himself. Essentially he is equally in despair in either case, for *he does not possess himself, he is not himself*...

A despairing man wants despairingly to be himself...[Yet] that self which he despairingly wills to be is a self which he is not (for to will to be that self which one truly is, is indeed the opposite of despair); what he really wills is to tear his self away from the Power which constituted it. But notwithstanding all the efforts of despair, that Power is the stronger, and it compels him to be the self he does not will to be...

...to have a self, to be a self, is the greatest concession made to man, but at the same time it is eternity's demand upon him.[46]

At the root of all Macbeth's despairing restlessness, his fruitless search for 'a clearenesse', for 'perfection', lies this failure to *possess himself*, a doomed attempt to tear himself away from his real nature in a 'strange and *self*-abuse'. Yet we should not forget that this breakdown, like the guilty imagining of the murder, is not shown in process of formation, but is one of the pre-existent conditions of the drama; and, as such, it is not insisted upon. The driving energy of the drama lies elsewhere, encouraging us to accept Macbeth's sense of violation and coercion as real. The rational and moral explanation of this sensation, like Duncan's goodness, lies on the fringes of consciousness as something to which we may return later, but not yet.

Meanwhile the initial misdirection brings on a chain of consequences. In the murder sequences, Shakespeare renders the anarchy of Macbeth's

whole nature primarily through its bodily manifestations: the man who
has warped and dislocated nature in order to produce the tension that
will discharge the bolt of murderous desire ('I am settled, and bend up
/ Each corporall Agent to this terrible Feat') is seen blundering round
the stage snatching ridiculously at the phantasmal products of his own
delirium and uttering lines as absurdly melodramatic as they are
grotesque (II. i. 33 f.). Macbeth's spasms of alternate attraction and
terror at the hallucination are so disjointed, syntactically and emotionally, as to suggest incipient insanity. And again 'Function' is self-
divided ('Eyes are made the fooles o' th' other Sences'). The key
changes, but the effect is only intensified as he steadies himself for the
murder:

> Now o're the one halfe World
> Nature seemes dead, and wicked Dreames abuse
> The Curtain'd sleepe: Witchcraft celebrates
> Pale Heccats Offrings: and wither'd Murther,
> Alarum'd by his Centinell, the Wolfe,
> Whose howle's his Watch, thus with his stealthy pace,
> With Tarquins ravishing strides, towards his designe
> Moves like a Ghost. Thou sure and firme-set Earth
> Heare not my steps, which way they walke, for feare
> Thy very stones prate of my where-about...   II. i. 49

Here there is a preternatural sensitivity, especially to sound, an unnatural stillness in which one hears dreams, hears the stealthy pace
which thinks to pass unheard, or hears sounds so distant from habitation
as to be normally inaudible—the witches' sabbath, the wolf—a silence
in which the over-strained hearing would make the very earth cry out.
And combined with this, a suggestion that the senses, the body itself,
has become detached from the observing mind, a strange disembodied
somnambulism in which Macbeth, as in a dream, watches himself
moving 'like a Ghost', beyond possibility of control or recall.

The same 'present horror' persists in the next, connected scene, as
Lady Macbeth registers the night-sounds with a quick panicky intake
of breath—'Hearke'—followed by the long sigh of relief—'Peace'; or
notes the snores of the grooms become suddenly audible as Macbeth
opens the doors. But her self-possession, which goes with an ability to
localise every sound, simply heightens our awareness of the antithetical
condition in Macbeth, who can no longer distinguish inner from outer,
'does not know...what voices are these that groan and cry within and
about him'.[47] The voice that cries modulates without a break into his own
inward crying;[48] the objective event is swallowed in his apprehension

of it—he is not listening *to* the fear of the two awakened sleepers, he is 'listening their fear', hearing it within himself, just as, with the same transitive construction, Lady Macbeth speaks of *thinking* these deeds. The body refuses service—he calls out and does not know it, his tongue rebels and the dry throat will not utter ('Amen / Stuck in my throat').

And then the self-division takes its most terrifying shape:

> What Hands are here? hah: they pluck out mine Eyes.   II. ii. 58

The eye, no longer able to wink at the hand, sees the blood-stained nails descending cruelly to destroy vision itself. The deed, which was his own, has now acquired a life of its own and it threatens the tenderest quick of his being. He does not know whose hands they are: his deed has created a reality of evil outside himself. Yet it is the fact that he also knows them for his own that provokes this frantic desire for blindness, that he may not have to contemplate his deed.

But the self so desperately divided against itself cannot sustain the tension for long, and by the end of the scene Macbeth has moved forward to grasp the only solution that presents itself:

> To know my deed,
> 'Twere best not know my selfe.   II. ii. 72

There is, he sees, no possibility of knowing (grasping the true nature of, and coming to terms with) his deed and also knowing (living amicably with, recognising) himself. It is an absolute antinomy. If he continues to know himself (the self he has been) the deed is incredible and monstrous. If he grasps the reality of the deed he is alienated from himself and can no longer recognise the bloody hand as his own. (It is in the nature of the evil act to drive this wedge between deed and doer, so that acceptance of the deed involves estrangement from the self.) Very well, he will know his deed. He will make his peace with it, build his life around it, accept it as fact. What he will not do is *own* the deed—acknowledge it as the work of the general, Macbeth, loyal vassal of the gracious Duncan. To that self he bids an anguished farewell in these lines, beginning the construction of a new 'self' whose premiss is murder.

v

With this decision, one would expect no more to follow than an extended study in the logic of degeneration, a drawing out of the consequences of total commitment to an act which is irredeemably evil. And this, indeed, is one way (though not the most interesting) of looking at the second half of the play. There is brutalisation, sure enough. The Macbeth who bullies the Murderers in a vain attempt to elicit a hatred for Banquo which will make the murder theirs and not his (III. i); the Macbeth so deeply committed to instrumentalism that men, like dogs, are for him only 'valued' in so far as they will subserve his murderous intent, and who, nevertheless, will 'make love' to the assistance of such 'Mungrels, Spaniels, Curres'; the Macbeth who can answer the Murderer's 'My Lord his throat is cut, that I did for him', with

> Thou art the *best* o' th' Cut-throats,
> Yet hee's *good* that did the like for Fleans:
> If thou did'st it, thou art the *Non-pareill*   III. iv. 16

in a tone naïvely innocent of irony—this Macbeth is a man who is rapidly passing out of the range of any very intense sympathy. The Macbeth of the Banquet scene, too, may be mastering his terrors better than he could before, but he does so on such a shabbily rhetorical level, assisted by the hoary clichés of 'rugged Russian Beare' and 'Hircan Tiger', and the vaunt and swagger of martial defiance, that the claim 'Why so, being gone, / I am a *man* againe' rings very hollow indeed (III. iv. 98–107).

This man, one senses, is in pursuit of total insensibility. Nothing is to make his 'firme Nerves' tremble, or to shake his deep and dreamless sleep.

> Strange things I have in head, that will to hand,
> Which must be acted, ere they may be scand.   III. iv. 138

He has discovered the secret that actions, once performed, will help to deaden and cauterise that inner sensitivity which is his greatest torment. Since the mind, he learns, has a knack of accommodating itself to that to which it has been accessory, he will act first, and thus surgically remove the sensitised zone of self-doubt and self-accusation, which the performed action will burn out in any case. This technique is 'hard use' —the breaking of a young sensitive animal, by systematic and graduated brutality, to force it into 'maturity'; and it ensures 'sleepe':

> Come, wee'l to sleepe: My strange & self-abuse
> Is the initiate feare, that wants hard use:
> We are yet but yong in deed.   III. iv. 141

The prophetic voice that cried to all the house was wrong: Macbeth has found his anodyne.

With the insensibility, perhaps because of it, there goes a willing embracement of evil, known as such:

> I will to morrow
> (And betimes I will) to the weyard Sisters.
> More they shall speake: for now I am bent to know
> By the worst meanes, the worst, for mine owne good,
> All causes shall give way.   III. iv. 131

This is the germ of the proceedings against Macduff's family, which we have noted as a turning-point in Macbeth's relations with himself and with the audience, and the sense of dismal finality is strong in the lines. Macbeth has settled his allegiances in favour of hell.

The chosen evil leads naturally to an imaginatively debauched surrender to the forces of annihilation loose in his own mind. All restraint is to be broken, the winds untied, destruction indulged to the point of utter surfeit. It is the wild dream of a cosmic anarchy where his own internal anarchy will be swallowed up in the roar and shriek of universal disintegration. He projects upon nature his own thirst for the confounding of all distinct sensation and apprehension (which is his torment) in a cataclysm of *general* evil:

> Though the treasure
> Of Natures Germaine, tumble altogether...   IV. i. 58

We cannot grant imaginative patronage, however qualified, to this. The man must be ripped out of the world.

And yet, the sequence in which the evil insensibility is most clearly envisaged and enunciated—Macbeth's late-night colloquy with his wife (III. iv. 121 f.)—is also one of the points in the play where we are most conscious of Macbeth's barbarian energy and courage. 'What a frightful clearness of self-consciousness in this descent to hell,' writes Bradley, 'and yet what a furious force in the instinct of life and self-assertion that drives him on!'[49] Improbable though it may seem, that word *life* is the right word. No interpretation which fails to reckon with the essential ambivalence of our reaction to the 'criminal' Macbeth can hope to do justice to the depth and subtlety of Shakespeare's conception in this play. And those critics who would have us choose between a moral repudiation of the man, and a self-deluding 'justification' of something which is essentially unjustifiable, are simply neglecting the capacity of the mature Shakespeare to encompass extremes of imaginative insight in the one aesthetic experience. The tragic experience transcends both repudiation and justification.

Consider what is happening in the following lines:

> I am in blood
> Stept in so farre, that should I wade no more,
> Returning were as tedious as go ore.   III. iv. 135

It is the point of no return for the man of blood. Macbeth is presented here, paused in mid-stream—note the momentary pondering suspension of the conditional clause which is also a question ('should I wade no more')—knowing he must move soon (since a stream is something one either crosses or does not cross) yet overwhelmingly aware of tedium and of his heavy, impeded movement through the water-blood. It is that imperceptible inter-tidal hiatus when choice presents itself in such a form that there seems no choice—and yet the choice is real and damnable: Macbeth envisages 'returning' and 'going ore' as two equally weighted alternatives, each equally 'tedious', and he does not explicitly opt for either; and yet the decision is there, implied in that indefinable tonal nuance which effectively prefers the tedium of 'going ore' to that of 'returning', and makes its choice within a construction which denies the reality of choice. No simple moralisation will fit the complex reality of this verse, not even the ready-to-hand explanation that Macbeth's freedom has been impaired by his violation of the 'natural law' engraved in his own nature. For while this is a truth the play makes us aware of, it is only one truth. With this passage—and its *modus operandi* is fairly typical of the most gripping things in *Macbeth*—our 'judgment', which might otherwise pronounce univocal sentence on Macbeth, is enclosed within a larger act of imaginative recognition, which says, 'Yes, it is so. That is the way of Mind. This man comes of our stock.' The mystery of will, which is at once *causa sui* and subject to other pressures, presents itself as a problematic nexus at the heart of experience which imagination and intelligence can only bring to this fine focus—never resolve.

It is this capacity of the verse to *imply* judgment without being constricted by it, which makes it possible for Shakespeare to suggest a positive energy of 'life' in the damned Macbeth. For if we look hard at the 'insensibility' that Macbeth pursues, it reveals itself, from another angle, as a quest for 'perfection', a declaration of war on the divisive forces his own act has released. The sense of contraction, constriction, of being 'cabin'd, crib'd, confin'd', is one of the primal modes in which we recognise and define evil, and this restriction of potentiality is instinctively felt as malign; whereas the free play of impulse, talent, imagination—'broad, and generall, as the casing Ayre'—is equally instinctively grasped as a good (III. iv. 20–4). It is delusion to think to achieve it by murder, but we do recognise the essential importance of Macbeth's objectives as he wrestles blindly in his own soul:

> But let the frame of things dis-joynt,
> Both the Worlds suffer,
> Ere we will eate our Meale in feare, and sleepe
> In the affliction of these terrible Dreames,
> That shake us Nightly: Better be with the dead,
> Whom we, to gayne our peace, have sent to peace,
> Then on the torture of the Minde to lye
> In restlesse extasie.   III. ii. 16

At whatever cost he will recover that integrity of impulse and action, that unobstructed discharge of personal energy in which life delights. And something in us responds to these fighting words: for survival, these things must be fought. Macbeth's challenge to Fate, which follows, is in one sense a determination not to succumb to the complete mental collapse that is figured in the dreams, the image of the rack, the 'restlesse *extasie*'. And even the 'firstlings' of action, which are so demonically inhuman, are also felt dimly, and at the same time, as the desperate paroxysms of a nature threatened with a madness of self-alienation. It is true that the campaign proceeds on the assumption that there can be no *returning*, but do we ever really *feel* (as distinct from believing on extraneous grounds) that 'turning back' and 'repentance' (the two senses of the word) are real alternatives for Macbeth? Bradley's enigmatic remark about Lady Macbeth is worth pondering for Macbeth too: 'regarding her from the tragic point of view, we may truly say she was too great to repent'.[50] Doesn't this, however startling it may be theologically, 'correspond to the imaginative effect'?

We might make the same double judgment about the rhetoric by which Macbeth fights off his terrors: it is shallow, yet it embodies a kind of resonant, contemptuous courage:

> Why what care I, if thou canst nod, speake too.
> If Charnell houses, and our Graves must send
> Those that we bury, backe; our Monuments
> Shall be the Mawes of Kytes.   III. iv. 69

And where else can we find such unmanning and appalling terror mastered and focused in intense, fascinated scrutiny, as in the Macbeth of these lines?—

Avant, & quit my sight, let the earth hide thee:
Thy bones are marrowlesse, thy blood is cold:
Thou hast no speculation in those eyes
Which thou dost glare with.   III. iv. 92

Even in its minor manifestations—'The divell damne thee blacke, thou creamfac'd Loone...'—Macbeth's energy of defiance is a force to be reckoned with, something to which we assent at the same time as we recognise its futility. 'It is not merely that he becomes more daring and resolute in action, the more desperate his affairs become', writes Lascelles Abercrombie; '*the whole vitality of the man becomes incandescent.*'[51] It is as if the Shakespeare who knew that the meek must, and do, inherit the earth, also saw from a different point of view (Nietzschean, Lawrencian) what a disaster it would be for the earth if they did, and preserved at the very core of his conception of evil an awareness of dynamism and power: for

> There is a soul of goodness in things evil
> Would men observingly distil it out.   *Henry V*, IV. i. 4

I am insisting on the 'soul of goodness', not merely in the reaction that evil provokes, nor even as generating an additional poignancy and sense of waste—though it does have this effect—but at the heart of evil itself, because there are certain masterly things in the play which cannot be received except on this understanding. Chief among them is Lady Macbeth herself.

It is interesting to reflect on the extent to which this astonishing portrait may have taken its rise from an act of historical imagination. Here is Holinshed on the characteristics of Scottish women:

In those daies also the women...were of no lesse courage than the men; for all stout maidens and wives (if they were not with child) marched as well in the field as did the men, and so soone as the armie did set forward, they slue the first liuing creature that they found, in whose bloud they not onelie bathed their swords, but also tasted therof with their mouthes...When they saw their owne bloud run from them in the fight, they waxed neuer a whit astonished with the matter, but rather doubling their courages, with more eagernesse they assailed their enemies...[52]

Whether he read this passage, or whether, as he might, he deduced Lady Macbeth from the various accounts of bloody viragoes that Holinshed provided, the fact remains that she represents a staggering attempt on Shakespeare's part to feel his way into a kind of womanhood which was barbarian and foreign—an effort of historical projection.

(He did much the same kind of thing when he drew the figure of Coriolanus.) So powerful was this faculty of imaginative projection, however, that it gave to Lady Macbeth a kind of validity and potency, even at those points where she most directly affronts all conventional notions of the feminine or even the human.

It may not be the kind of thing that the super-ego readily approves, but do we not find ourselves, in the theatre, over-awed and startled into a kind of terrified admiration by her unconditional blasphemy against the natural?

> I have given Sucke, and know
> How tender 'tis to love the Babe that milkes me,
> I would, while it was smyling in my Face,
> Have pluckt my Nipple from his Bonelesse Gummes,
> And dasht the Braines out, had I so sworne
> As you have done to this. I. vii. 54

Like the leap from the vertiginous precipice, this violation of the infinitely vulnerable is so exquisitely possible as to transfix the mind that once contemplates it. These are the things one does not dare speak aloud, for fear speech should give them reality. And yet determination in this woman has been fanned to such white heat that she can not only say it, but contemplate the unnameable with an overwhelming actuality. As Coleridge observed, the whole conception derives its alarming power from a knowledge of just 'how tender 'tis to love'.[53] And yet she forces herself to a meticulously precise evocation of the particularities of the deed, right down to the 'Bonelesse Gummes'. The taut intensity of will strained beyond belief is presented in that shocked shuddering pause after 'dásht the Bráines óut...'.

Macbeth is not the only one who is emotionally overborne, and fishes about on the surface of a terrified consciousness for some random reply to words which, it seems, could neither have been spoken nor heard, muttering, 'If we should faile?' Nor is his horrified attraction–repulsion unintelligible when he cries hoarsely,

> Bring forth Men-Children onely:
> For thy undaunted Mettle should compose
> Nothing but Males. I. vii. 73

There is an appalling grandeur in Lady Macbeth's complete subjugation of nature. The sheer resplendence of will has a kind of magnificence which cannot be 'placed' or gainsaid. For the moment the stabbing of an old man in his bed has *become* 'our great quell'.

The same Shakespearian capacity to feel the validity of alien states of mind explains the strange way in which the Macbeths' pagan lightness of conscience—a conscience for which 'things without all remedie / Should be without regard' and 'what's done, *is* done'—comes to seem inevitable. He is creating a barbaric Scottish world in which to unseam a man 'from the Nave to th' Chops' and to 'bathe in reeking Wounds' *is* to be a 'worthy Gentleman' (I. ii. 22 f.). In this world, the grave is peace:

> After Lifes fitfull Fever, he sleepes well,
> Treason has done his worst: nor Steele, nor Poyson,
> Mallice domestique, forraine Levie, nothing
> Can touch him further. III. ii. 23

Macbeth envisages no hell; nor does Shakespeare envisage it for him. It was a singularly inept notion of Garrick's to have the dying Macbeth declaim, like a pasteboard Faustus,

> my soul is clog'd with blood—
> I cannot rise ! I dare not ask for mercy—
> It is too late, hell drags me down; I sink,
> I sink,—my soul is lost for ever !... 54

This is completely foreign to Shakespeare's conception (to say nothing of the execution). Shakespeare's Macbeth lays down the terms of his own damnation—

> Heere,
> But *heere*, upon this Banke and Schoole of time,
> Wee'ld jumpe the life to come. But in these Cases,
> We still have judgement *heere*...— I. vii. 5

and in these terms he receives his 'Justice'—his own 'poyson'd Challice'. Even if the pagan could impose his own pagan naturalism on the universe, as Shakespeare in some measure permits Macbeth to do, he still has 'judgement heere'. Even within this life, the succession of events in sequence, the endless 'consequence' cannot be trammelled up. The ocean laps round the shoal/school of time. One cannot set a terminus to action; it is never 'done'. And Macbeth's willingness to 'jumpe the life to come' cannot free him from the monstrous menace of an infinity and circularity which is as real within time as beyond it. The Justice that works, the Providence in things is a natural one. Shakespeare does not need to demand a Christian repentance of Macbeth; he lets him have damnation on his own terms. The effect is to make it possible for us to grant the pagan frame of reference at the same time as we sense its limitations—as Macbeth himself does when

'Amen' sticks in his throat. There is a breaking down of theoretical and dogmatic barriers as the play enlarges its imaginative frontiers.

Some effect of this kind is necessary, too, to account for the powerful emotional forces released in sequences like the Sleepwalking scene. Pity seems too weak a word for the response this scene evokes. It is something nearer awe. Like the Doctor we 'thinke, but dare not speake', can only murmur 'God, God forgive us all'. The sympathetic movement of feeling fills out our sense that Lady Macbeth has received her profoundly ironic fulfilment, with something less sharply moral. There is a tenderness, a compassion in her, which calls up the equivalent feeling in us:

> Come, come, come, come, give me your hand: What's
> done, cannot be undone. To bed, to bed, to bed. v. i. 63

The tendency of this movement of feeling, as far as one can define something so fragile and elusive, seems to be to free us from the burden of past horror, permitting us to accept this new feminine solicitousness and protective affection as a self-subsistent reality—even though it is woven out of the stuff of past violations of affection. Her sorrow for 'the old man', while also hopeless horror, is, as Mary McCarthy remarks, real 'contrition—sorrowing with. To ask whether, waking, she is "sorry" for what she has done is impertinent. She lives with it and it kills her.'55 The movement of pity and awe in the audience coalesces in an act of imaginative identification which is not extenuation, but simply true judgment.

This is not an isolated moment in the play either. Macbeth's anguished cry, 'O, full of Scorpions is my Minde, deare Wife', with its enactment of the agony, not of a blunt blow producing insensibility, nor a searing wound that may yet heal, but of pain that enters the very marrow of sensation and heightens it, pain moreover shut in upon itself, inescapable and armed with innumerable stings—this cry deepens 'judgment' until it becomes 'recognition'. So does the sequence with which this scene opens, which Granville Barker characterises as 'Lady Macbeth's wan effort to get near enough to the tortured man to comfort him', an attempt in which 'the royal robes, stiff on their bodies—stiff as with caked blood—seem to keep them apart'.56

> How now, my Lord, why doe you keepe alone?
> Of sorryest Fancies your Companions making,
> Using those Thoughts, which should indeed have dy'd
> With them they thinke on... III. ii. 8

As we watch this timorous compassion receive a rebuff—'Be innocent of the knowledge, dearest Chuck...'—and then an embracement which is, in its context, more terrible than rejection—'So prythee go with me'—the moral levee-banks which withhold sympathy are broken and feeling flows freely between stage and audience.

The greatness of *Macbeth* lies in its capacity to encompass so many apparently contradictory ways of feeling about the same phenomena. But such greatness, of course, makes it singularly difficult to say anything clear-cut without resort to paradox: the paradox of an evil which is both primary and unreal; the paradox of a goodness which is supremely real yet does not prevail; the paradox of a Fate which is both prescriptive and binding, *and* powerless to fetter the will; the paradox of a freedom of soul which is both betrayed by its possessor, and subject to external violation; the paradox of an absolving pity which is also a judgment. I know no way of eliminating these paradoxes without minimising Shakespeare's achievement at precisely those points where it is most magnificent, nor without making 'trifles of terrors' and 'ensconcing ourselves into seeming knowledge' when we should be submitting ourselves to the mystery of things. For each paradox represents an approach to central regions of uncertainty and mental anguish in experience, regions where explanation is more likely to be impertinent than illuminating. *Macbeth* is not the play it is because it offers explanations, but because it enables us to contemplate these agonising cruces with steadiness and courage.

All the same, the intrinsic doubleness is perhaps at its most disturbing in the last act. For here Macbeth achieves his 'perfection' and his destruction, the forces of goodness in their moment of triumph seem most empty, and the whole dramatic movement resolves on a single flat note which both concludes, and is desperately inconclusive:

> So thankes to all at once, and to each one,
> Whom we invite, to see us Crown'd at Scone.   v. ix. 40

What is happening in Act v?

VI

Right at the beginning of the act we are given a moralised Macbeth:

> ANGUS.   Now does he feele
> His secret Murthers sticking on his hands...
> ...Now does he feele his Title

> Hang loose about him, like a Giants Robe
> Upon a dwarfish Theefe.
> MENTEITH.   Who then shall blame
> His pester'd Senses to recoyle, and start,
> When all that is within him, does condemne
> It selfe, for being there.   v. ii. 16

Now this, I suggest, is rather what we feel *must* be the case, than what we see on the stage. The Macbeth we see can claim, with some justice, that 'Direnesse...cannot once start me', and Angus's horrifying image of congealed blood, and nightmare paralysis in which the loathed substance will not come free of the hand, is rather a thematic recapitulation, than a preparation for what is to come. We are not to forget the bloody-handed butcher, but neither are we to be limited to this view of Macbeth. For with the arrival of the invading army and the advent of daylight, a load seems to fall from Macbeth's shoulders. Wilson Knight is one of the few critics who has noticed the positive tendency in Macbeth's development now:

He has won through by excessive crime to an harmonious and honest relation with his surroundings. He has successfully symbolised the disorder of his lonely guilt-stricken soul by creating disorder in the world, and thus restores balance and a harmonious contact. The mighty principle of good planted in the nature of things then asserts itself, condemns him openly, brings him peace. Daylight is brought to Macbeth, as to Scotland, by the accusing armies of Malcolm. He now knows himself to be a tyrant confessed, and wins back... integrity of soul.[57]

'Harmonious contact' is putting it strongly, but the point is valid. The invading generals may insist on the relief of the approaching martial resolution—

> The time approaches,
> That will with due decision make us know
> What we shall say we have, and what we owe—   v. iv. 16

but so does Macbeth:

>   this push
> Will cheere me ever, or dis-eate me now.
> I have liv'd long enough: my way of life
> Is falne into the Seare, the yellow Leafe,
> And that which should accompany Old-Age,
> As Honor, Love, Obedience, Troopes of Friends,
> I must not looke to have: but in their steed,

> Curses, not lowd but deepe, Mouth-honor, breath
> Which the poore heart would faine deny, and dare not.
>
> v. iii. 20

This is not despair, nor the self-condemnation of 'pester'd Senses'. It is nearer acceptance—a submission to seasonal mellowing (autumn *not* winter, observe) and a recognition of his fitness for death. It is worth noting that, although the opening lines envisage two possible outcomes of 'this push'—'cheere' *or* 'dis-eate'—the next clause tacitly discounts the first alternative, and prepares for the second—'I have liv'd long enough...' Nor is it a lament for lost felicity: there is something tougher, less self-indulgent, further from contrition about it than that. Logically, at least, the forfeited joys of 'Old-Age' are only invoked to fortify his acquiescence in being 'disseated'. He no longer hungers for these things; they are simply what he 'must not looke to have' (note the prosaic cadence). The pathos of loss is what *we* bring to the speech. Macbeth himself is simply reckoning courageously with a shrunken reality, and recording with scrupulous fidelity—the curses are 'not lowd' it is true, 'but deepe' nevertheless—the realities of his situation. And he is sufficiently accommodated to its ironies to be able to spare a wry pity for the unwilling servant who dares not speak his 'poore heart'. Macbeth, 'sick at heart' though he is, has achieved an honesty as criminal that he never had as a man of honour.

There is the same detached self-observation when, surprised by a breath of supernatural fear at the 'cry of Women', he reflects on the rarity now of such feeling—'I have almost forgot the taste of Feares...' (v. v. 9 f.). He compares the flat deprivation of feeling which is real crime with the stirring, horrific crime of anticipation, like a patient intrigued by his own symptoms, even relishing them a little. There is a faint flicker of the old terror as he recalls his hideous, dinner-table familiarity with evil—'I have supt full with horrors'—but the main effort is to hold his own state steadily before him—to know his deed, and to know what it has done to him.

It is on this basis of known and faced reality that he can achieve the bantering humour of his interview with the Doctor, as he gently ribs the man with the inadequacy of his mystery to 'scowre these English hence', or, in a moment of despairing candour, confesses his grotesque plight—'Doctor, the Thanes flye from me'. The exuberant and exasperated wit of his assault on the Servant in this scene (v. iii) or the grotesquely comic business with the armour combine to give a near jocularity to Macbeth's address to the world. It is the levity of real courage faced with irredeemable catastrophe—sober, yet very much alive. The Doctor responds to the lightened atmosphere with a piece of very ordinary, day-to-day humour:

> Were I from Dunsinane away, and cleere,
> Profit againe should hardly draw me heere.　　　v. iii. 6

But the ordinariness is the point. The portentous world of blood, night and crime has resumed its daylight proportions.

Yet, like all the achieved things in this play, Macbeth's self-possession is under assault. The stasis is temporary. And with the news of Lady Macbeth's death his acceptance gives way to a new tone:

> To morrow, and to morrow, and to morrow,
> Creepes in this petty pace from day to day,
> To the last Syllable of Recorded time:
> And all our yesterdayes, have lighted Fooles
> The way to dusty death. Out, out, breefe Candle,
> Life's but a walking Shadow, a poore Player,
> That struts and frets his houre upon the Stage,
> And then is heard no more. It is a Tale
> Told by an Ideot, full of sound and fury
> Signifying nothing.　　　v. v. 19

This speech presents special difficulties to interpretation. Its direct and powerful effectiveness is manifest, but the range of embodied emotion, and the variety of responses evoked within this brief space, makes critical formulation a very precarious business—hence the flat disagreements: is there 'a touch of tragic grandeur' about this Macbeth, as Bradley suggests?[58] or is it simply 'an abject collapse, where the would-be dominator of the world can see that world only as a procession of fools by candle-light...'?[59] Or is there a triumph of knowledge in the very defeat, as Abercrombie argues?

He has staked everything and lost; he has damned himself for nothing; his world suddenly turns into a blank of imbecile futility. And he seizes on the appalling moment and masters even this: he masters it by *knowing* it absolutely and completely, and by forcing even this quintessence of all possible evil to live before him...Tragedy can lay hold of no evil worse than the conviction that life is an affair of absolute inconsequence. There is no meaning anywhere: that is the final disaster; death is nothing after that. And precisely by laying hold of this and relishing its fearfulness to the utmost, Macbeth's personality towers to its loftiest grandeur...For we see not only what he feels, but the personality that feels it; and in the very act of proclaiming that life is 'a tale told by an idiot, *signifying nothing*', personal life announces its virtue, and superbly *signifies itself.*[60]

This is to record only a tiny sample of the divergent readings one is offered.

We might begin by noting the prevailing tone of the speech—the impotent irritation, almost pique, of 'Creepes' and 'petty pace', the slightly over-emphatic generality of 'Fooles', modulating to a bitter acquiescence with 'Out, out, breefe Candle' followed by *faux conforts* of negation. But the most powerful effect is reserved for the last gesture of renunciation—and this can only be described as savage, a kind of ferocious ennui. The shrillness of tone directs our attention to a constriction of Macbeth's vision, and, as I suggested earlier, to the truth that he is now reaping what he has sown, and cannot, finally, make his peace with its utter negativity. And yet the tone is not merely shrill: it is also, at moments, passionate.

So I don't think it is just the persuasiveness of Abercrombie's prose that makes me feel that he has grasped something important. If we compare Macbeth's fierce brand of nihilism with Richard II's, a difference of temper becomes apparent. There is nothing tearful or self-indulgent about this. It is sternly dry-eyed and rigorous. One does not feel that the negation is an escapist's passivity: rather that it is the only vision left to Macbeth—and he will not blink it. More than this. That it has the sort of validity that derives from strenuousness and rigorousness of imagination—and this is particularly true of the image of the strolling player, 'the walking Shadow', transient apparition upon makeshift stages, himself a mere projection of flickering candle-flame. Here the opening pettishness has gone, and the savagery has not yet supervened, and we contemplate something that looks very much like an imaginative truth to nature. In any case, the movement of feeling in the rest of the speech towards, and away from, this apprehension is so much a flux, a continuum, that gestures of dismissal, like Rossiter's 'abject collapse', simply won't do.

I want, in short, to avoid separating the act of judgment which *sees through* Macbeth, from the act of imagination which sees the world *with* him; and to exclude at the same time the guillotine criterion of philosophic respectability, which would make Macbeth's sentiments appear self-condemned in the very utterance. 'Something might be true,' wrote Nietzsche, 'even though it is harmful and dangerous in the greatest degree; it might in fact belong to the basic make-up of things that one should perish from its recognition.'⁶¹ This kind of truth fixes Macbeth with its basilisk eye, and he stares back unflinchingly. It is another of the moments in the play when we contemplate the actuality of evil, without being overpowered by it.

All the same, 'nothing' is Macbeth's last word, and as he plunges into the violence of battle, the nothingness seems to gain on him. Death, for Duncan, was a thing of ghastly beauty, a ceremonious rite—'Silver skinne, lac'd with...Golden Blood'. Thereafter, once 'Renowne and Grace is dead', it becomes a thing of insane brutality. Banquo dies in an abrupt and overwhelmingly violent crescendo, beginning with the whispered consternation of the Murderers—'A Light, a Light'— rising to Banquo's conversationally-pitched commonplace, and then suddenly blaring forth in 'Let it come down'. A few seconds later all is silent but for the panting of the assassins. But that interval has been filled with the frenzy of 'twenty trenched gashes'—a spectacle of sudden, demonic, ugly brutality—essentially meaningless. Banquo's last healthful words are the most banal in the play, suggesting a pitiful, helpless inconsequentiality about the whole affair (III. iii).

Young Macduff's death (IV. ii) is in the same vein. The word 'traitor', which has hung over the whole scene as something huge, menacing and vague, and which Lady Macduff uses as a vent for her private sense of betrayal, is a mystery to the child. Yet the boy who does not know what a traitor is dies, absurdly, for denying his father to be one. The very ordinary prosiness of the domestic conversation, in the rich poetic fabric of this play, combines with the violent rapidity of a catastrophe ungarnished with words, to produce an effect almost unbearably flat and stark.

Macbeth's death, too, has this blunt-ugly meaninglessness. In the closing scenes of battle, his rhetoric of defiance is increasingly hollow, and Shakespeare permits it to phrase itself in doggerel and jingle:

> But Swords I smile at, Weapons laugh to scorne,
> Brandish'd by man that's of a Woman borne.   v. vii. 12

(This after the slaying of a beardless and untried youth.) Or

> Before my body,
> I throw my warlike Shield: Lay on Macduffe,
> And damn'd be him, that first cries hold, enough.   v. viii. 32

This is not clumsy writing, 'silly and resourceless', as Shaw once claimed,⁶² but a portrait of sham courage—the rant of the rattled gambler playing his last card, or, in Macbeth's metaphor, the grotesque rage of the baited bear. The man is an empty man.

The attempt to make these final moments wholly satisfying to admirers of Macbeth's heroic stature are wilful. With the appearance of Macduff, something snaps in him. He alternates between a black fatalistic remorse, which has a component of shrinking fear—

> Of all men else I have avoyded thee:
> But get thee backe, my soule is too much charg'd
> With blood of thine already— v. viii. 4

and a puerile vaunting which has an edge of hysterical exaltation—

> As easie may'st thou the intrenchant Ayre
> With thy keene Sword impresse, as make me bleed:
> Let fall thy blade on vulnerable Crests... v. viii. 9

(This is the hysterical Richard II of the 'God for his Richard hath in heavenly pay / A glorious angel' phase.) And when Macduff reveals his birth, Macbeth is reduced to a 'cow'd' and muttering renegade who refuses to fight. It is only the threat of extreme degradation—exhibition in a mountebank's booth—that finally induces him to take up his sword and 'try the last'. There is a kind of courage here, but it is animal rather than human. Plainly, for Shakespeare, Macbeth is finished before this moment.

Yet the effect is to make the final settlement somehow empty. With Macbeth's fallen and diminished stature since he took the field, the play-world too seems to shrink. We do not completely lose sight of Macduff's role as the impersonal executor of a justice larger than revenge—

> If thou beest slaine, and with no stroake of mine,
> My Wife and Childrens Ghosts will haunt me still:
> I cannot strike at wretched Kernes, whose armes
> Are hyr'd to beare their Staves... v. vii. 15

—but we do see the inherent brute meanness and meaninglessness of the act of retribution itself. Viewed from a certain angle, the victory of Malcolm and Macduff is a triumph, and a necessary one. But at close range, the killing has the disturbing ambivalence of all acts of violence. This is death in battle rigorously contemplated. It is grotesque and sickening.

It would take more than the conventionalities of Malcolm's final speech to remove this taste from our mouths—even if there were not the mention of 'this dead Butcher, and his Fiend-like Queene' to ensure that we retain it to the end. Malcolm is, of course, right. But the dramatic focus is wide enough to include his kind of rightness within a much larger truth. For Malcolm's callous remark shocks us into a recognition of Macbeth's potential greatness—a greatness that can endure solitude:

Very few people are capable of being independent; it is a privilege of the strong. And whoever tries it, however justified, without *having* to, proves that he is probably not only strong but bold to the point of complete recklessness. For he walks into a labyrinth; he increases a thousandfold the dangers which are inherent in life anyway. And not the smallest of his dangers is that no one can witness how and where he loses his way, falls into solitude, or is torn to pieces by some troglodytic minotaur of conscience. When such a man perishes, it happens so far from human understanding that other men have no feeling for it, no fellow feeling. But there is no return for him—not even a return to human compassion![63]

This is one half of the truth about the final moments of *Macbeth*.

The other half concerns the muted counterpoint which talks of 'planting newly', of 'loves', 'kinsmen', 'Friends' and 'the Grace of Grace'. It is, however, very definitely muted. The mature Shakespeare would not, for instance, have undercut an invocation of 'Grace' with a slightly frivolous word-play of this kind, unless he were deliberately holding something in check. He did not write the triumphant paean of restored humanity that he could have written: first, because this is Malcolm, not Duncan, and destruction has had very much its own way; and second, because the shadow of a vast evil that the play casts still broods over the consciousness. A burst of facile optimism in the Richmond vein would be drastically out of place. Instead Shakespeare permits the mind to play wonderingly over the events of the drama, questioning and probing, toying with words like 'Grace' or 'measure, time, and place', trying to find a meaningful order in it all:

It is not only the pious believer who bends to the will of God, and to Providence which has so disposed when he sees the triumphant and unrestrainable outbreak of vitality, but every serious mind aware of the laws of reality disdains useless regrets and abstains from undue judgments, because no one can say that things would have turned out better if such an event, painful and destructive as it was, had not happened. We ourselves, who suffer from it, would not be what we are without it, and we would not necessarily be better, purer, more intelligent... Then, when the cycle has been completed, and the sky is more serene, the mind tries to find out whether, in all these raptures, follies...and mania of

destruction, if there is no human and moral reasonableness, yet there may be...
a concealed intention on the part of nature...[64]

We are left with an awed sense of the overwhelming potency and
vitality of evil, and with a subdued question about this concealed
intention of nature. It is not a resolution, but a tremulous equilibrium
between affirmation and despair, in which we submit ourselves to an
unknown fear.

'MACBETH' AND THE THEOLOGY
OF EVIL

I have already noted W. C. Curry's claims for the relevance of that 'body of patrimonial doctrines transmitted to the Renaissance from the scholastic philosophers', which he regards as the 'integrating principle' of *Macbeth*. One is tempted to keep the peace by conceding the point: for we may grasp the integrating principle of the play without necessarily being aware of its origins. But his claims go further: Macbeth, he intimates, is a 'Renaissance' figure who 'can be understood and ultimately criticised only by reference to defined standards of moral philosophy', and these standards, we are left in no doubt, are Thomist.[1] A similar claim, though more cautiously phrased, is made by Virgil Whitaker when he says,

Macbeth seems to me Shakespeare's greatest monument to the ethical system that his age inherited from Western Christianity and the classical world, and to which it gave a new and vital expression. For that tradition *Macbeth* is what *Oedipus Rex* was for the Greek—an almost perfect dramatic embodiment.

Whitaker's candidate for the honour of theological godfather is Hooker, whom he regards as 'to a considerable extent responsible not only for the thought but also for the very structure of some of Shakespeare's greatest plays'.[2] These two contentions—and they may serve to represent many more —can be conveniently treated together, since the relevant sections in *The Laws of Ecclesiastical Polity* draw very heavily, and at times explicitly, on Aquinas.

I am not concerned here to press these critics to explain what they mean by an 'integrating principle', or how a theologian can be 'responsible...for the structure' of a work of art—though one scents some misleading double meanings in statements of this kind. Nor is it very much to the point to indicate that Aquinas's works were not in print in England during Shakespeare's lifetime, or to record the opinion of a careful student of both Hooker and Shakespeare that the evidence of the plays demonstrates no more than 'the coincident use of popular ideas and common phrases';[3] for, though Curry and Whitaker slip at times into talking as if it were a question of direct influence, the core of their argument concerns a cultural 'inheritance' or a 'patrimony' which was not dependent on reading this or that book.

Now, the abiding influence of scholastic thought, even on authors who have probably never heard of Aquinas, let alone read him, is patent from the most cursory reading of Elizabethan theologians and preachers. But while it can be readily granted that Shakespeare was exposed to this brand of Christian thought, the real question is what he had made of it by the time he came to write *Macbeth*. Curry and Whitaker clearly regard its effect on the play as crucial and formative. I will try to define in the concluding chapter what I regard as the kernel of truth in this contention; my purpose here is to indicate a number of important elements in the Christian theology of Renaissance England— several of them permanent elements in Christian theology *per se*— which simply do not answer to the realities of *Macbeth*. My objection, broadly, is that the theology is simply not good enough to throw much light on a play of this stature; and I think the point is worth making as long as critics keep on telling us that we cannot understand the play without first understanding the theology.

The doctrine of evil, which one finds in Augustine, Aquinas, Hooker and fairly widely dispersed in sixteenth-century English theological tractates, is built on Aristotelian foundations: it depends on notions of 'form' and final cause, in terms of which every agent acts purposively, and upon a radical distinction between man (a voluntary agent endowed with reason) and the rest of nature (natural agents moved by appetite or superior causes).[4] The implied psychology of evil-doing expounds itself in terms of faculties:

The first active principle in moral actions is the thing apprehended; the second is the apprehensive power; the third is the will; and the fourth is the motive force, which carries out the command of reason.[5]

The personality is a hierarchy in which reason is king, the will chief executive officer, and the physical 'motive force' the subordinated and obedient populace. The first stage in any action (and the stages are schematically separated) is reason's act of apprehension and its ensuing edict.

The good which either is gotten by doing, or which consisteth in the very doing itself, causeth not action, unless apprehending it as good we so like and desire it...Goodness is seen with the eye of the understanding. And the light of that eye, is reason.[6]

For this crucial task, reason is seen as perfectly adequate: for, says Hooker, 'There is not that good which concerneth us, but it hath evidence enough for itself, if Reason were diligent to search it out'.[7] This is part of the consistent apotheosis of reason which made it, in Aquinas, the mediator of the very joys of heaven: '...ultimate happiness is to be sought nowhere else but in an operation of the intellect: since no desire leads us so high as the desire of knowing the truth', and that desire 'rests not until it has reached God'. 'To act virtuously', thus, is to act 'in accord with reason'.[8] It hardly needs pointing out that there is implicit here a fairly optimistic view of human nature and of the powers of reason, to which the passions, though powerful, are regarded as subject in some actual, not merely ideal, way. Without this faith, indeed, Aquinas's whole system would be untenable, and perhaps Hooker's too. But in order to see the world in these sanguine terms, we who live after Freud and Hitler must, I suggest, perform some pretty comprehensive acts of mental suppression. We do not, I think, find this kind of intellectual jettison-operation to be necessary when we approach *Macbeth*.

Since every agent moves to its own 'proper perfection' (and this is assumed, on Aristotelian authority, to be self-evident)[9] every agent must act for a good, since

that to which an agent tends definitely must needs be befitting to that agent: since the latter would not tend to it save on account of some fittingness thereto. But that which is befitting to a thing is good for it. Therefore every agent acts for a good.[10]

(Here the ready optimism manifests itself in the form of tautology offered as proof.) Thus to choose evil, knowing it as such, is impossible. As Hooker puts it,

evil as evil cannot be desired: if that be desired which is evil, the cause is the goodness which is or seemeth to be joined with it. Goodness doth not move by being, but by being apparent; and therefore many things are neglected which are most precious, only because the value of them lieth hid.[11]

So 'evil does not oppose good, except by virtue of a good: and in itself it is powerless and weak, as not being a principle of action'.[12] Evil is 'unintentional in things'.[13] It proceeds from a mistaken choice of 'the lesser good'. 'There was never sin committed', says Hooker, 'wherein a less good was not preferred before a greater, and that wilfully...' And he is here pure Thomist, though the notion is also a commonplace of Christian thought.[14]

Perhaps we can pause here and think back to the Macbeth of Act I, Scene vii. Does a formulation like 'evil as evil cannot be desired' do justice to Shakespeare's conception? Is it even true? Isn't it rather Macbeth's torment that he knows the depths of the evil, the 'deepe damnation' of the deed, and desires it nonetheless?

And in what sense is he shown to be adhering to the 'lesser good' of the crown, when all his talk is of the horrid nature of the deed? After the first euphoria about the 'swelling Act / Of the Imperiall Theame', we hear no more about the sweet fruition of being a king, but watch a man undertaking, in Bradley's phrase, 'an appalling duty'.[15] That Macbeth gets no joy of his kingship once he has it is a commonplace of criticism; but it is equally true that he seems to envisage none *before* he has it. Not only is the crown not 'a lesser good': it is not a good at all, and he knows it.

Or what have the preliminary deliberations of reason, which then issues a directive to will, to do with the 'horrid Image' which assails Macbeth in Act I, Scene iii? That speech strikes me as one very good reason why we should not accept the schematic Thomist account of action; for here reason, will and the 'motive force' are compounded into one chaotic act of imagination, which is no act—merely a 'horrible Imagining'—yet in which the will is so deeply implicated that action seems to follow inexorably from it. This kind of psychological truth is beyond the compass of a faculty psychology.

Or, again, what real truth is asserted if we say that the 'evil' of Macbeth's slaughter of the Macduff household was 'unintentional'? It seems rather to be a retreat from the truth. Answers there are, no doubt, and we shall be considering some of them; but I cannot help feeling that the climate of *Macbeth* is so different, so much more laden with the dark pressure of real evil, that it is a kind of impertinence to explain it in terms of these sunny dialectics.

The theologians, of course, were aware of the problems. They not only knew, they insisted, that reason had been corrupted by original sin, and could be corrupted further by actual sin.[16] We are reminded continually of the way passion can impair reason, and of the way in which the inclination to virtue can be 'diminished indefinitely'.[17] They even saw will itself as subject to the same degeneration: Augustine, for example, was prepared to admit a condition in which 'a man wills to act rightly and cannot' and yet is justly 'judged wrong'; this he saw as 'a just punishment resulting from man's condemnation'.[18] Aquinas, with a quick eye for logical consequences, warned that this doctrine imperilled the whole structure;[19] but the notion of original sin tends always to indefinite extension, and it was to be expected that will, like everything else, would come to be suspected of degeneration.

In at least one Renaissance writer, will itself is conflated with the passions (as the erotic sense of the English word invited one to do) and we get a bipartite division of the soul into 'Mynde, the superiour parte, by whiche alone we are knowen to be menne' and

Wyll...voyde of reason, brute, fiers, cruell, more lyker a beaste, than a man, wherein dwelleth these motions whiche be named either affections or perturbations...[20]

This is Thomism pushed over the brink into the Manichaean doctrine of the two souls of man; but it is done in response to an increasing awareness of the potency both of evil and of the passions. Western civilisation is discovering the limits of rationality.[21]

However, such attempts to reckon seriously with the reality of evil, and to accommodate it to the theological schematum, do not so much solve the problem as create new ones; and it would be possible to quote many passages where this laudable psychological realism necessitated complicated and unsatisfactory logical manoeuvres in order to retain the view of evil as the free choice of the lesser good. Perhaps the most convincing is Hooker's distinction between 'ableness' and 'aptness'—*ableness* to perform the good, an ability which has atrophied in natural man and thus requires the assistance of grace, and *aptness*, the ability of the will 'freely to take or refuse things set before it'.[22] But even this extrication leaves the freedom of the will a sadly shrunken thing, a freedom to choose what one cannot perform. As one seventeenth-century preacher puts it, 'Mens free-will, is only free vnto euill.'[23] In this predicament a minor Jacobean writer exclaims,

One huge rocke I finde in this vast Ocean of our boundlesse Will, common to all men, (and wherevnto all others may be reduced)...I meane an exceeding difficultie to do well: our vnderstandings (I confesse) must labor to find out the truth, but no labour to be compared with the labor to do good...[24]

The emphasis became even stronger in the Calvinist preachers of the period who discerned no finer way of demonstrating the power of God than to denigrate the capacities of man: 'Now therefore to give free-will his packing penny, we may boldly say, that if free-will be, Gods providence is not...'[25]

But the really triumphant solution to the problem of reconciling human freedom with original sin, the supremacy of reason with the corruption of reason, the unintentional nature of sin with man's deliberate choice of it, is Aquinas's. And he achieves this triumph by preventing the two terms of the paradox from ever coming into contact with each other. Each is surgically isolated in its own Article, the opposition reduced to submission by the kind of syllogistic tautology that we have seen, and the conclusion graven in the catalogue of proven propositions, to be invoked whenever the antithetical term of the paradox grows unruly. As a result, all the crucial argument in the Thomist *Summae*, one might say, takes place in the cross-references—'as we proved in Q. LXXI Art. 2', 'see Q. XXIII Art. 1'. When we turn to Q. LXXI Art. 2, we discover that the proof is there, sure enough—all the objections lined up and summarily dispatched; and if we are prone to clutch at offered consolations when faced by irreconcilables and perplexities, there the matter rests. But somewhere between those two passages, as we turned the pages to find the propositional salve, the problem was real, bitter, and insoluble. I must confess to finding Hooker's attempts at synthesis in this area, though less flagrantly sophistical than Aquinas's, a *reduction* of the problem rather than a solution.[26]

Our age has been perhaps less successful than Hooker's in finding the reconciling synthesis within which the contradictions of experience can be resolved. But then it has been obliged to reckon more directly with the outburst of massive and irrational evil. That there have been losses, no one will dispute: but there have also been gains. It has been one of the positive contributions of modern theology to teach men to live with the irreducible paradoxes of human experience (the despair paradox of Kierkegaard, for instance), instead of regarding them as grist to the dialectic mill. When we are invited to become neo-Thomists, we are being asked to surrender all this newly reclaimed territory, and I cannot believe that such a surrender, apart from the intellectual sacrifices involved, is going to help us to understand a dramatist who was so intensely aware of the problematical and the paradoxical as Shakespeare shows himself to be in *Macbeth*.

My second charge against the theology the Elizabethans inherited is that evil tended to be, for it, a pseudo-problem. One would think that Augustine would be the last man on whom one could pin such a charge, but isn't there a blameworthy complacence, to say nothing of logical circularity, about arguments of this kind?—

If you know or believe God is good—and it would be wrong to think otherwise
—He does not do evil. Again, if we admit God is just—and it would be wicked
also to deny this—He both rewards the good and punishes the bad...Con-
sequently, if no one is punished unjustly—as we must necessarily believe, since
we believe everything is ruled by God's providence—God is certainly not the
cause...of evil.[27]

Now this is not the mature Augustinian conception of evil; but it does
represent a perennial tendency in Christian thought to skate over real
problems by dint of a very superficial and unthinking faith. More
blatant examples can be found in Aquinas:

There are in the world many good things which would have no place unless
there were evils: thus there would be no patience of the righteous, if there were
no ill-will of the persecutors; nor would there be any place for vindictive
[*sc.* vindicative] justice, were there no crimes; even in the physical order there
would be no generation of one thing, unless there were corruption of another.
Consequently if evil were entirely excluded from the universe by divine
providence, it would be necessary to lessen the great number of good things.[28]

Blake exploded this line of argument with his exquisite parody:

> Pity would be no more
> If we did not make somebody Poor;
> And Mercy no more could be
> If all were as happy as we.   'The Human Abstract'

But it hardly needed Blake's offices. One immediately wants to ask
Aquinas in what sense good, built on these foundations, remains good,
and whether it is worth the price. But the argument finally lands him in
total paradox:

if evil were taken away from certain parts of the universe, the perfection of the
universe would be much diminished...[29]

There we have it. It is an ancient, and highly respectable opinion; but
its force depends entirely upon the way in which it is held. Aquinas's
way, I think, may be fairly characterised as complacent.

The Calvinist wing of English theology used this doctrine of the
divine sanction of evil to an even more disreputable end: here it
became a kind of divine vindictiveness:

For thogh he wils not sin properly, because he hates it: yet doth he wil the
being of it in the world. For in respect of the counsell of god, it is good that
euil should be. And god wils the being of sin, not because it is his wil to effect,
produce, or giue a being to it, but because his will is to forsake his creature, &
not to hinder the being of euil whẽ he may...[30]

It is the same doctrine—that God wills evil—but the paradoxical tension has been slackened on the other side: whereas it expressed for Aquinas a certain ready optimism about the universe, it expresses for this Calvinist a bitter, misanthropic pessimism.

In a similar way the doctrine of the unreality of evil is a kind of truth; but, in the wrong hands, it becomes mere intellectual pusillanimity, a way of shrugging off a radical problem. It hardly needs urging that, if *Macbeth* presupposes the unreality of evil, it does not presuppose it in this way.

I am not arguing that Shakespeare set about to rebut the theologians' doctrine of evil, as he manifestly did not. His superiority as thinker is very largely a result of his instinctive dramatic concentration on the particular, just as the weakness of Aquinas as thinker lies in his almost complete estrangement from the particular. By going direct to the evil *man*, Shakespeare by-passes many of the dangers inherent in any theoretical discussion of evil. It is not so much that he disagreed with the theologians, as that he had no need of them in this area where his own perception was so much finer and more concrete. By the time he came to write *Macbeth* there was nothing they could teach him, and much he could have taught them. And if his perception was built upon the foundation of a long-established layman's familiarity with theology —which seems more than likely—he had by now so far outstripped his preceptors as to make any interpretation of *Macbeth* in terms of Thomist or Anglican thought more misleading than helpful. Ethical discrimination, and a fineness of moral temper in Shakespeare, may indeed have been strengthened by his cultural involvement with Christianity. But his debt to systematic theology is neither obvious nor demonstrable.

There was, however, one Anglican in Jacobean England who had the imaginative power and depth of insight to encompass the paradox of evil within a Christian frame. A preacher of the 1620s cannot lay any claim to being an influence on Shakespeare; I quote Donne only as an example of the kind of theologian who might be regarded as relevant to the plays of Shakespeare.

Donne's attack on the problem of evil is too complex to be presented here, but we may perhaps get the flavour of it. In a sermon preached in 1624/5, he attempts to reconcile his text, 'There is none good but one; that is, God', with the evident evil in the world. He divides the text, characteristically, into 'two Hemispheares':

The Western Hemispheare, the land of Gold, and Treasure, and the Eastern Hemispheare, the land of Spices and Perfumes; for this puts us upon both these considerations, first, that nothing is Essentially good, but God, (and there is the land of Gold, centricall Gold, viscerall Gold, gremiall Gold, Gold in the Matrice and womb of Gold, that is, Essential goodnesse in God himself) and then upon this consideration too, That this Essential goodnesse of God is so diffusive, so spreading, as that there is nothing in the world, that doth not participate of that goodnesse; and there is the land of Spices and Perfumes, the dilatation of Gods goodnesse. So that now *both these propositions are true. First, That there is nothing in this world good, and then this also, That there is nothing ill.* As amongst the Fathers, it is in a good sense, as truly said...God is no Essence, God is no substance...as it is said by others of the Fathers, that there is no other Essence, no other Substance but God.[31]

Later in the same sermon, Donne reviews the scholastic arguments that evil is 'non-being', and continues,

But if I cannot find a foundation for my comfort, in this subtilty of the Schoole, That sin is nothing...yet I can raise a second step for my consolation in this, that be sin what it will in the nature thereof, yet my sin shall conduce and cooperate to my good.[32]

Evil at the heart of things, yet good also at the heart; a Nature in which nothing is wholly good, yet which is informed and pervaded by essential goodness in such a way as to 'make good of bad, and Friends of Foes'; a world in which evil is too real to be disposed of by a 'subtilty of the Schoole'—this is a style of theology that might have interested the mature Shakespeare, especially as he embarked on an investigation of the proliferating cancer of Macbeth's evil, and searched for the 'concealed intention on the part of nature' in it all.

But when we say this, are we saying anything more than that Shakespeare would have found much in Donne to respond to warmly? that they would have found in each other that sympathetic confirmation and accord that passes between two great minds? The apparent congruence of their thought is only seen in its full significance, when we realise that, in its awareness of complexity and its acceptance of paradox, it is totally *un*representative of contemporary Christian thought.

15

ARTIST AND ETHOS

I

Writing a concluding chapter for a study like this one is rather like climbing a ridge in no-man's land: it is a necessary undertaking if one seriously intends to conquer new territory, but the position is alarmingly exposed. So I shall begin in the region where I feel most confident of saying something moderately conclusive—the proper uses of historical material in the study of literature.

The conception of an 'influence' on a writer is a profoundly ambiguous and dangerous one. It may mean no more than that he has read such-and-such, and retained sufficient memory of it to echo its words or its phrasing. This is best treated as what it is, viz. *allusion*, without any of the preconceptions that enter when one calls it an *influence*. Shakespeare, we know, read the Bible and repeatedly echoed its phrases. But Richmond Noble's careful study of these allusions leaves me, at least, with a clear conviction that in every case the allusion was subordinated to the particular character in whose mouth it was placed, to the specific dramatic situation, or to the larger dramatic movement.[1] R. M. Frye's parallel study of theological allusion in Shakespeare comes out even more strongly against any theory of simple theological influence on his thought, demonstrating time and time again the assimilation of allusion to context.[2] When allusion can be established (and it is harder to do this than the copious annotations in modern editions of Shakespeare might suggest), its implications are generally localised and manageable. We clarify the meaning of a particular passage, but we are not thereby committed to generalisations about the total meaning of the play.

But the term 'influence' can also be used to suggest a larger indebtedness—the kind of central relevance to *Macbeth*, for instance—that we have seen Whitaker claiming for Hooker, and Curry for Aquinas. What should be noted about attempts to establish influence of this kind, however, is that, since they cannot prove *allusion*, their focus is necessarily on the period of gestation *prior* to the play, and such intrinsically nebulous suggestions are as hard to prove as they are to disprove. Which is not to say they are not worth making; what one can say, though, is that the connexion between the work and the alleged influence, the *relevance* of the influence, that is to say, is something which is established critically or not at all. All theories of influence rely upon a prior critical estimation (implicit or explicit) of what the play is about: without this act of definition one cannot even begin to look for an influence. True, once the connexion has been established, what we know of the influence may modify the way we read the work. But at all stages, the relevance of the influence remains in question, and the onus is on the critic who adduces it, to show that it corresponds to something real in the work. One of my chief complaints against the historicist interpreters of Elizabethan drama is that they are so intent on obtaining converts to their 'influence' that they obscure, or even elide, the critical judgment without which their preoccupation is meaningless.

In any case, we need to enquire for what purpose this extra-literary material is being brought into the discussion. Not, I take it, to finish the work of definition the playwright has left incomplete—at least, if this is the purpose, it should be made explicit. It seems rather to be a work of literary supererogation, aimed at plotting the position of the work in the region of discursive thought, or in relation to the history of ideas; perhaps also aimed obliquely at vindicating the claim of imaginative literature to be a kind of knowledge. All this seems perfectly legitimate, and if it is not a strictly literary activity, so much the better; it nevertheless laudably attempts to break down the hermetic isolation in which academic disciplines seem to subsist today, even within the humanities. Its value, of course, will be dependent on the accuracy with which the influence is used to crystallise the true spirit of the work—the accuracy, that is to say, of the original critical judgment.

But if it can be agreed that the act of critical definition is primary, a rather interesting consequence follows: material drawn from the dramatist's own culture has no more intrinsic claim to be regarded as relevant than material from our own, or some earlier culture. Hooker has no more authority than Jean-Paul Sartre in the interpretation of Shakespeare, because what has to be established in each case is a mutually illuminating congruence of thought. We may have discovered from experience that Hooker is more likely to offer this illumination; but mere contemporaneity provides not the slightest guarantee of relevance and may very well prove misleading. To focus attention exclusively on the material contemporary with the writer is to stress the historical *process* which makes one age different from another, at the expense of the historical *continuity* which makes them the same; and the student of literature, least of all people, can afford to neglect the continuity without which he would not be studying literature at all. This is especially true when he is dealing with a major artist, one of whose characteristics, surely, is to get beyond the historically conditioned in his age and to grasp things that only find general acceptance much later in history, if ever—how else can we account for a Bach, a Blake?

Contemporaneity is a misleading criterion of relevance, again, because it fails to consider the *quality* of the thought involved. It is not enough to show that Shakespeare in *Richard II* is confronting the same issues as the political propagandists of the sixteenth century: it must also be shown that he is confronting them on the same level—and this, as we have seen, is very far from the truth. It may be entirely appropriate to explain *The Massacre at Paris* in terms of feeble-minded political polemic (though this is an explanation of something all too explicable), but the obvious relevance of this material to Marlowe's piece of theatrical journalism is founded on a value judgment (equally obvious) about the worth of the play—if it were not so bad, we would not dare to suggest a connexion. This value judgment emphatically cannot be extended to *Richard II*, so we must look elsewhere for parallels, finding, perhaps, Hooker or Sir Thomas Smith—minds, anyway, not utterly incommensurate with Shakespeare's inflexibility and penetration. In a similar way the exaggeration and vulgarisation implicit in the myth of the Machiavel may throw some light on *The Jew of Malta*, but it does not get us very far with *Richard III*, which is confronting the Machiavellian dilemma with a seriousness totally foreign to this kind of popular stereotype thinking. Not even the writings of Machiavelli himself can be profitably compared with Shakespeare's play, until we have seen how Shakespeare presses nearer to the heart of the problem than Machiavelli ever did. Or again, the Calvinist providentialism, though it may help marginally with the interpretation of *Richard III*, is no help at all in explaining the kind of 'providence' at work in *Macbeth*. It operates on a different, and much lower, level. We need someone with Hooker's awareness of complexity if we are to make a comparison at all.

You will notice that in each of these cases the historical material was not introduced under the panoply of 'influence', but as an aid to a more precise definition of the insights the playwright is actually offering. That it was contemporaneous was convenient: people like Smith and Hooker spared me the lengthy necessity of convincing those unable to see that Shakespeare *did* see through, that he *might* have seen through the platitudes of his age. But these men would be no less illuminating if they had written two centuries later or earlier than they did. And even so, they are useful, not primarily because they lead us to the inner core of the plays, but because they are aids to translation—translation of embodied dramatic meaning into discursive meaning: they assist that free transposition of imaginative vision into philosophic or ethical position which, though dangerous and necessarily inaccurate, is still important if the reading of literature is to be part of an integrated wholeness about the business of living.

But the production of discursive parallels is no more than a means to this end. And when we approach a masterpiece like *Macbeth* the problem is to find anything, either in other writers (past or present), or in ourselves for that matter, which really corresponds to this vastness. Like must be compared with like; and what is there which is really like *Macbeth*? The work of art, as it approaches the condition of greatness, becomes progressively incommensurate with any parallels that can be produced. One of the things we mean when we call something a masterwork is that it is unique.

'Tell me, what do you think about greatness?', asks the hero of Mann's *Doctor Faustus*. 'I find there is something uncomfortable about facing it eye to eye, it is a test of courage—can one really look it in the eye?' The temptation, when one is faced by a play like *Macbeth*, is to grow shifty-eyed, shuffle one's feet, and try surreptitiously to trim it down to size—to collate the great with the petty under cover of a sham historicism, and so reduce it to manageable proportions. No doubt there are many thinkers who can throw light on this or that aspect of the play—I have tried to use Nietzsche and Kierkegaard in this marginal way; but I think we are deluding ourselves if we imagine any system, Anglican, Thomist or Existentialist, is going to contain the energies of a work of this stature. Historical criticism, if it is to be useful, needs to know the difference between the greatness which is unique, and the competence for which one can find adequate parallels elsewhere. Shakespeare's contemporaries can indeed show us the fallacies he might have fallen into had he not been great; but criticism, very rightly, is not much concerned with 'what might have been'. The only proper response to *Macbeth* is to meet it eye to eye, and, with what steadiness we can muster, speak the truth about what we see.

The scholarly whittling-down of a work, then, proceeds from an initial critical underestimation of its stature; and the faulty definition of its nature sends the scholar hunting for critical illumination where he can only find specious reasons for his original misjudgment. The only way of avoiding this systematic degradation of literature—and that way is fallible enough—is to be rigorous and scrupulous in deciding what is there in the play, confronting its 'pastness' along with all the other features that present a challenge to assimilation. There will still be plenty of mistakes; but they will not be the huge ones that essentially misrepresent the stature of a work (Curry's tamed *Macbeth*, Tillyard's orthodox Elizabethan history plays, or Lily Campbell's *Henry IV* without Falstaff)—mistakes which appeal, moreover, to the unadventurous, comfort-loving, pusillanimous side of our natures. They will simply locate wrongly the centre of gravity of a play, raising issues that are less than central. But these misplaced emphases can always be absorbed and then corrected by a better critic or a more intelligent reader. They will not make the historicist's unwarrantable claim to superior 'objectivity', and being less heavily armour-plated with erudition, they can be more easily ignored. All of which— absorption, correction, and ignoring—are parts of the thoroughly healthy process of perpetual revision which indicates that work is still very much alive.

There is another side-effect of the scholar's attempt to confine the writer within the pale of the age's commonplace (and this will be the end of my carping): it means that when he turns to a major thinker he does so as to quintessential commonplace, and so misses the real importance of a figure like Hooker. Hooker may distil much that is central to Elizabethan culture, but he does so because what is, for the small minds of the period, a certainty, a fixity, is for him a problem calling for the mobilisation of his entire intellectual resources. The Hooker of the scholarly footnotes, the vade-mecum of stock attitudes, has as little relation to the real Hooker as the Elizabethanism he is used to buttress has to the realities of Elizabethan culture. For this culture is alive, diverse and growing, containing cranks and great minds, entangled with the past and reaching out to the future. The scholarship which has converted this tumultuous age into an era of platitude and conformism has produced a remoteness and separation from twentieth-century concerns which is entirely artificial. It has created the very difficulties of interpretation which it offers, with its scholarly apparatus, to remove. There are foreign things in Elizabethan culture, some negligible because incurably superficial and (mercifully) outgrown, others still disturbing because we suspect an abiding relevance concealed by accidents of historical evolution—of these I shall be speaking soon. But the gulf is not nearly so deep, nor our estrangement so complete, as to necessitate that act of intellectual abdication which the scholars miscall 'historical imagination'.

I have used the case of *Macbeth* to suggest that there are occasions where historical illustration is in danger of becoming impertinent. But *Macbeth* is, of course, exceptional. Where a dramatist is not so magnificently successful in gathering up the cultural *données* into a new artistic unity, the uses of historical knowledge may be wider. In the case of *Doctor Faustus*, it is helpful, I find, to be able to fill out historically the clash between 'vnsatiable speculation' and *curiositas* which is part of Marlowe's subject. But why is it helpful? Isn't it because Marlowe's intentions in this area are largely unrealised ones, and because one wants some explanation of his failure? We only become interested in a poet's intentions when his achievement indicates that he has fallen short of them: intention, that is to say, is a concept necessitated by the existence of unsuccessful art. And the filling out of the intellectual background to *Doctor Faustus*, whether it is by way of contemporary pneumatology or theological notions of the limits of knowledge, is a way of giving shape to elements in the play which, if they had been thoroughly embodied and realised, would have required no such explication. This is a dangerous doctrine, I know, for it is easily perverted into the view that any line or passage which requires annotation to be fully grasped is thereby convicted of being unsuccessful—and this is clearly absurd. But what we are obliged to undertake with *Faustus* is not the annotation of a line or a speech, or even a single scene, but of the whole play. The unresolved tensions at the dramatic level, which prevent an audience from achieving that harmonious and grateful response to something felt as a whole, proceed from a very deep-level failure of conception; and it is the dissatisfaction this produces that sends us out searching for the cultural or social tensions which might correspond to those in the play. Yet even when we locate these pressures, the result is not a substantial change in our estimate of the play: it is just that Marlowe's problems become more intelligible, and his failure perhaps more forgivable. It is the legitimate exercise of historical curiosity in an attempt to understand the checks and blockages to which the creative process is subject; but it does not—unless we are too careless to bother distinguishing our own reconstructive activity from Marlowe's initial dramatic construction—it does not give us a successful and achieved *Doctor Faustus*.

The writer who, in one way or another, is defeated, can often be illuminated in this way. I find it much easier, for instance, to understand the puzzlingly mechanical Providence of *Richard III*, for having looked at the providential theorisers of Shakespeare's age; easier to understand the crudity of parts of *The Jew* in the light of the Machiavel–Jew complex of popular bogeys; easier to understand the clash of metaphorical and grossly literal hells in *Faustus* in the light of the painful evolution of English religious thought away from a primitive anthropomorphism. To understand *how it came about*, but not to excuse. These pieces of background information do not illuminate the artistic fact, so much as the process that produced it: one sees that behind the weakness of artistic embodiment lies a weakness of thought, a willingness to accept from contemporary culture conceptions and attitudes which were intellectually disreputable or personally unsatisfactory. One notes again the extraordinary property of the act of literary expression for showing up the evasions, the blind-spots and the over-simplifications of which the writer himself was possibly not even aware. The dramatic inadequacy results from a failure of penetration; the writer has rested too easily on the conceptions and attitudes of his age, and so has failed to transform and transcend them.

This can be true even when, as with the Marlowe of *The Jew of Malta*, he is in partial revolt against the conceptions and attitudes: Marlowe's assault on the complacent anti-semitism of his contemporaries remains somewhat constricted and unresonant because he has been unable to break out of the narrow categories against which he is revolting. He simply takes the Christian cannon and points it the other way—at the Christians. But by so doing he has assumed an eternal state of war. One see the same thing happening in our own age to a playwright like John Osborne, who is so dominated by the thought-categories of the people he abominates that he can only consume himself away vicariously in the seething bosoms of angry young, or angry middle-aged, men. Either in acquiescence or in revolt, a playwright can be betrayed by the lower levels of thought in his own culture. Without a steady labour of selection and rejection, without a scrupulous evaluation of the quality of contemporary living and a complementary capacity to locate, however intuitively, the real springs of creative life in his society, a writer may find himself committed to the second-rate and the super-ficial. He may fail to be a good dramatist because he has been an insufficiently rigorous analyst of his own culture.

What this line of argument takes for granted, of course, is that literature represents, in D. G. James's phrase, 'a great labour of knowing', and that critical judgment is, in an important sense, a judgment on the *veracity* of the picture of human life that is offered in a work.[3] It is a large claim, but a necessary one. And if it is granted, we can see why there should often be a correlation between the judgment that an element in Elizabethan culture is fallacious, superficial or misleading, and the judgment that a work reflecting it is an artistic failure; why, too, we have to go to the great truth-tellers of Shakespeare's age before we find any parallels to the conspicuous veracity of his plays. And though the correlation between philosophic truth and literary achievement is notoriously treacherous to define, there are good grounds for believing it to exist. In any case, the possibility of its existence alone justifies our keeping open the lines of communication between literary studies and all the other disciplines concerned with distinguishing true from false.

II

I think it is worth trying now to make a few suggestions about the ways in which a writer can enter into creative collaboration with his culture. Obviously a study of seven plays from one period will not support a *quod erat demonstrandum* about so large a matter as the creative process. All I can offer are a few generalisations prompted by my explorations in this field, which do not seem, in the light of general reading and reflection, to be relevant only to the Elizabethan age. The reader is invited to test them against his own impressions, drawn possibly from other periods or other fields of interest.

One requirement for this collaboration, it seems, is that there should be a full exposure to the culture; not only to its formulated orthodoxies, but also to the stresses and strains to which the formulations are subject. The artist must stand at the heart of change. It is not enough, for instance, for him to feel the force of the traditional political wisdom— for this may produce nothing more impressive than the *True Tragedy of Richard III*; nor is it enough for him to be aware exclusively of the political realism which threatens the traditional view—we may simply get the iconoclastic excesses of *The Jew*. It may be true, as Nietzsche claims, that

all those extraordinary furtherers of mankind...have hitherto found their task ...in being the bad conscience of their time. By putting the vivisectionist's knife to the *virtues of their time*, they revealed their own secret: they knew a *new* magnitude of man, a new un-worn path to his magnification. At all times they showed how much hypocrisy, indolence, letting oneself go and letting oneself fall, how many lies, were hidden under the most respected type of their current morality, how much virtue was outlived.[4]

But this is only half of their function, and if they merely aim to short-circuit the current of history in a series of flash revolutions, they will probably be self-defeating. The furtherer of mankind is more than the surgeon of culture, cutting away the dead and diseased tissue, its out-lived virtue. He is also the man who cherishes the living body of contemporary culture, knows the hidden springs of its vitality, the man who can give expression to—and, by the expression, liberate—the virtue that is not yet outlived. He is that unicorn of thought, the conservative-radical. This is perhaps one reason why Shakespeare's politics (particularly) are so puzzling to readers and critics who are addicted to political simplification. They cannot admit that the beast exists at all. How *can* the man, who sees through the sham of royal absolutism so sharply, retain a feeling for the divinity that hedges kingship? Obviously he must be muddled, inconsistent, a radical bogged down in the slough of Tudor propaganda. But it is his critics who are muddled. The great artist, like the goat, has a stomach for all foods, a miraculous organ which can draw nutriment from the most unpromising stuff. In the case of the dramatist, the assimilative faculty seems to operate by penetrating the idea to uncover the man who holds, and so modifies, the idea. Thus Shakespeare gets behind the (to us, repellent) doctrine of passive obedience to the prince, to the John of Gaunt who holds it—a man of some stature, survivor of an older age whose values are now under siege, a passionate patriot and a plain-dealer who earns our respect. He penetrates the public façade of a Bolingbroke to reveal the inner vacillations and the moral chaos that the unbridled pursuit of power necessarily entails. Or, in the opposite direction, he sees through the merely vicious and inhuman in the Compleat Machiavel, to the huge gusto and *élan* which makes a Richard of Gloucester such an irresistible force: the concrete and the dramatic is used as a lever to dislodge the anciently entrenched moral simplifications. Or again, the theological explanations of the nature of evil are tested against the sharper realities of that underworld of half-realised desire which is evil's, and Macbeth's natural element.

The dramatist who is to make anything of the material his culture offers him must be able to think *through* ideas in this way, must be able to use them and not be used *by* them. Unless he can do this he is simply going to reproduce, in the microcosm of the play, the tensions and strains of his own age—and this, I take it, is what *Doctor Faustus* supremely illustrates. There is no Elizabethan play which makes us so acutely aware of the transitional nature of the age. But its capacity to reflect the age is bought at the price of an incapacity to contain what it reflects. Marlowe's undoubted sensitivity to the manifold and chaotic life around him breaks his drama. This is not creative assimilation. It is being at the mercy of a whole flood of impressions and pressures which quickly reduce the creative faculty to impotence. Exposure to the cultural flux is not enough: there must also be a capacity for gestation, an inner chemistry of creation which issues finally in a new and distinctive life—child, perhaps, of parents we know, recognisably related to a particular age and culture, yet containing within itself its own principle of unfolding life.

Neither should we confuse *exposure* to contemporary culture with *topicality*—that chirpy quality of up-to-the-minute minds which has no necessary connexion with an understanding of the present. The great mind can use the topical material—as Shakespeare used the equivocation issue in *Macbeth*: with a lordly assurance so startling that the scholars are still scurrying about trying to find the key to the play in the writings of Father Garnett; but its tendency is always to suspect the merely topical (Shakespeare's only play about Elizabethan England is *The Merry Wives of Windsor*), and, since direct social comment tends also to be superficial social comment, it tries to penetrate the surface of contemporary life to something more durable and stable. *Macbeth* does not so much have 'sources' in Elizabethan thought, as put down roots into its very depths. It may actualise an essential and important aspect of that age, but it also transforms that age, and no Elizabethan who received the full impact of *Macbeth* could have been the same kind of Elizabethan thereafter. We can talk of the Shakespeare who produced the history plays as a man very much alive to the currents of his age; but, although the author of *Macbeth* is no less sensitive to these things, we are much more conscious of the movement inwards, the penetration to the lower levels of the self, for which social, religious and political life provides only an outward garment. Without this penetrating movement, exposure to contemporary life tends always to gravitate towards mere topicality. *Doctor Faustus* was, as we saw, intensely topical in its day; but it was artistically defeated by Marlowe's failure to understand inwardly his own relation to the topical raw material. When, on the other hand, the inward movement, fully developed, is wedded to a total exposure to the multifarious pressures of historical existence, we move into the region of the great masterworks.

But inwardness assumes a self upon which to retreat, a core of assured humanity—precisely what Marlowe seems to have lacked. Which is why I have been so interested in the disruptive forces that are let loose from time to time in his writings: not in order to be able to crow over human fallibility, but so as to be able to offer some account of the strange lack of coherence and stability in his dramatic vision. Ultimately, I'm sure, it is a personal failure, a disquieting void at the heart of the self, that provokes the outbursts of violence, the oscillation between extremes of assertion and distrust, faith and despair, frivolity and bombast. How else are we to explain that dramatic wilderness, dotted with the parched remains of old passions and echoing with howls of inarticulate rage and violence, which is the bulk of *Edward II*?

Yet it is not of course a *purely* personal matter. The internal dynamics of personality are partly a social product and do not exist on some rarefied plane of unmoved movement. Hence my attempts to account for the breakdown of imaginative coherence in *Faustus* in terms of Marlowe's cultural environment. But we may agree to hold Marlowe finally responsible for the breakdown, and if we do, we must attempt the psychological explanation.

Shakespeare, on the other hand, seems to have possessed supremely this inner stability. He was a classic, as Croce remarks, 'because he possessed the strength that is sure of itself'.[5] It is a measure of the creative spirit's independence of the *Zeitgeist*, that Marlowe and Shakespeare were contemporaries. The rich and fruitful Elizabethan culture could not avail for the talented man who lacked the essential personal qualification of 'the strength that is sure of itself'.

So then (if I may be permitted to translate hypothesis into prescription): the creative collaboration of dramatist with culture requires of the writer that he be fully exposed to the traditional and to the new in his environment; that he shall stand at the heart of historical change and know what is going on about him; it demands a faculty of penetration, an ability to think through ideas to persons, and a reconstructive, gestative activity which saves him from being at the mercy of the merely chaotic in his environment; he must be able to see through the topical to the perennial, through the historical to the human, through the problem to the self which *is* the problem. He must have a capacity for inwardness. Above all he must have a self that is infinitely flexible, able to dart itself forth, but calm and firm at the centre. And we may perhaps add (with *Edward II* in mind), he needs a certain purposiveness, a drive towards meaning which will prevent the imaginative debility of a play like that one, in which the waning, perhaps the unforeseen irrelevance of Marlowe's temperamental obsessions, left him with the mere shell of a drama.

This is what is required of the dramatist. But isn't there something required of the culture as well? Don't we habitually assume that Elizabethan culture gave Shakespeare something without which he would not have been the dramatist he is? I have devoted a good deal of space to setting out the things it didn't give him, and the gifts he politely but firmly returned to the sender. But aren't there deeper, more important levels on which he was really nourished by the intellectual and moral life of his age? I believe there are.

III

I am now on ground where I must tread very delicately. For one thing, the evidence we have considered has been drawn mainly from intellectual history, and in so far as this preoccupation with ideas has led to a neglect of social history, it is necessarily partial and inadequately integrated with the whole of Elizabethan life. Then again, the diagnoses one makes about the genuinely fructifying elements in a culture, though they begin as pragmatic judgments—'This moral norm seems to have had good poetic effects', 'Shakespeare drew strength from that generally accepted belief'—turn imperceptibly into judgments about the validity of the morality and the belief. Perhaps it is right that this should happen, but it will be more consonant with the degree of certainty possible in this region, if I can keep the conclusions in the form of questions.

We have seen that, if Elizabethan culture offered an important kind of incitement and encouragement to the dramatist, it did not offer it indiscriminately. The point is elementary, but it needs to be made, lest we forget that Marlowe was exposed to the same forces as Shakespeare and, lower down the scale, Robert Greene to the same forces as Marlowe. Being an Elizabethan did not turn Greene into a Marlowe, nor Marlowe into a Shakespeare. But having reminded ourselves that the process of creative assimilation involves *two* variables—artist and culture—it is permissible, I think, to focus attention on the culture.

The problem, however, is the multiplicity of cultural factors that might be relevantly adduced. If this study had been more slanted towards social history, this would have been the place to relate the peculiarly Elizabethan fusion of courtly and popular modes of thought and expression to the structure of society at that period (though such an analysis would have to take account of the courtly contempt for popular culture—including the drama). Or one might attempt to explain the peculiar concreteness of Shakespeare's approach to theoretical problems, by reference to the day-to-day actualities of life in a small 'organic community' (though one should not forget the element of historical abstraction which necessitates the inverted commas around that phrase). Or, perhaps more importantly, one could trace the Shakespearian vitality of language, and consequently of thought, to something inherent in Elizabethan spoken English—an earthy common sense and suspicion of cant, deriving from proverbial lore, peasant shrewdness and a literary tradition rooted in Chaucer and Langland—claiming, with Leavis, that Shakespeare 'incarnated the genius of the language'. But even here one would have to give due weight to the folio volumes of cant, particularly theological cant, to which Shakespeare's contemporaries gave vent, and recognise what real independence of spirit was needed to shake off their malign influence; one would need to ponder the fact that, in a collection of proverbs like Tilley's, the Shakespearian crystallisation is almost always more pointed and more earthily wise than the popular sayings which presumably gave rise to it; one would have to enquire what our conception of 'the genius of the language' would look like without Shakespeare and Shakespeare's influence on subsequent writers.[6]

Though these are real questions and need answering, they call for extensive study, and study along different lines from those I have been following. There is, however, one point on which many of my lines of investigation do seem to be converging.

Perhaps the most outstanding feature of Elizabethan culture—at least to modern eyes—is its ingrained and ineradicable Christianity. It is a quality which has turned nearly all the historical investigations in this study into matters of theology—something for which I have not apologised since it is inherent in the subject. But what did Shakespeare make of the pervasive religiosity of his age? The question would seem unanswerable; but we do have, in his biblical allusions, an indication of his familiarity with the Scriptures and, more importantly, presumptive evidence—since he echoes some books more frequently and more precisely than others—of his preferences as a reader.

Job and Ecclesiasticus he seems to have known very well and he draws on them in a much more direct way than is usual with his biblical echoes. The other books that seem to be often in his mind are the Psalms, Proverbs and the Gospels. The overtly theological books, the New Testament epistles particularly, do not seem to have occupied him with anything like the same seriousness.[7] The preference for Job could be explained as a poet's gravitation toward some of the finest poetry available to him—perhaps the Psalms too. But the familiarity with the wisdom literature does seem to indicate a natural affinity for the solidly secular, moral sanity of these works, which is the obverse of the minimal interest in Pauline theology. Shakespeare, I suggest, would have been happier with Arnold's style of belief, for which conduct is three-fourths of life, than with the more theoretical, systematic preoccupations of the Paulinists Arnold was attacking.[8] His intelligence is moral rather than theological. The preference for the Gospels among the New Testament books indicates a similar orientation.

But it also accounts for a certain delicacy of conscience which is not to be found amongst the Old Testament writers—a delicacy which permits Shakespeare, for instance, to endorse the positions neither of Richard II, Bolingbroke, nor even York. The delicacy is capable of being transmuted into a formidable indictment of hypocrisy, as we saw happening in the portrayal of Edward IV's court, but it presumes at all events an intensely serious view of moral responsibility.

Christ's approach to this matter is founded on a paradox. On the one hand, the man who says *Raca* (thou fool!) to his brother is in danger of hell-fire, and the lustful thought is tantamount to the lustful act; that is to say, the boundaries of moral responsibility are pushed right back into the inner sanctum of desire and motive, and action is made essentially, indeed portentously, moral at all times. On the other hand, we are not to judge at all, lest we be judged and so receive, 'measure for measure', our own arrogant condemnation—a line of thought that has left clear marks on Shakespeare's ethical thought ('Forbear to judge, for we are sinners all').[9] The balance between these two contrary movements in Christian ethics is beautifully dramatised in the *Macbeth* doctor:

> More needs she the divine than the physician.
> God, god forgive us all!

There is simultaneously the judgment, and the withholding of judgment; the recognition of moral responsibility, and the self-doubting recoil under its weight.[10] This kind of moral sensibility (also in Ross, and in Macduff's 'Heaven forgive him *too*!') is crucial, as we have seen, to the establishment of the positive good in *Macbeth*. I suspect there is a related connexion between the pity which is 'like a naked new-born babe' and Christ's 'Except ye become as little children...'—an insistence on that vulnerable, yet eager openness, an abnormally heightened sensitivity to one's own moral life, and that of one's neighbour, which found classic expression in the Sermon on the Mount.

This ethical climate has a good deal to do with important things in Shakespeare's drama. The heightened moral sensitivity stimulates the probing of motive, the unwillingness to accept public accounts of public actions; and the forbearance, the awareness of fallibility, encourages the creating mind to feel its way compassionately and delicately into the mind of the sinner. There is a rigorousness, almost a ruthlessness of judgment, which will not overlook the smallest foible; and yet a balancing reticence and tact which draws back from the brutality of condemnation. The reticence does not imply condonation; but neither does the rigour imply dismissal. The two together in vital equilibrium provide a guarantee of stability, a kind of base camp for that extraordinary Shakespearian capacity to feel alien states of being from the inside, withholding the pat judgment and yet, by that very reticence, implying a more profound judgment—as in the treatment of Richard II.

On the basis of this Christianly reinforced assurance, Shakespeare could set off so far into the barbaric hinterland of evil that he left his Christian preceptors far behind, producing in *Macbeth* a play which threatens the theoretical structures of Christianity by its supra-theological vitality. Yet it is a play fed at its sources by the ethics of Jesus. For the creating mind that fuses imaginative identification *with* Macbeth, and a moral judgment *on* Macbeth, into a single act of dramatic recognition, is one which has grown accustomed to stretching itself Christianly between trenchant judgment and wise suspension of judgment. Its poise and assurance is supported by the Christianity it has breathed from its earliest years. Which does not necessarily mean that Shakespeare was a 'believer' in the conventional sense—George Eliot in *Middlemarch* seems to have drawn a similar strength from a Christianity she rejected—but that he was supported in a thousand indefinable ways by the Christian climate in which he lived. He could take these things for granted, did not need to be noisily assertive about them, could rest in them.

Related to this ethical sensitivity is a faith in humanity, reinforced by the Christian conception of man as bearing the image of God, which also seems central to the Shakespearian stability. We have seen how Edward IV, desperately groping for the ideal of brotherhood which his whole reign has violated, turns naturally to this conception:

> But when your carters or your waiting-vassals
> Have done a drunken slaughter and defac'd
> The precious image of our dear Redeemer,
> You straight are on your knees for pardon, pardon...
>
> *Richard III*, II. i. 122

And there is more here than a chance allusion. In Shakespeare's imagination the ideal social order, the mutuality of fulfilled human society, is inseparably bound up with the sacredness of the individual. To deface the image, as Edward and Clarence's murderer and Exton know to their cost, is an act of the deepest sacrilege. It may even amount, for Macbeth, to the murder of all 'Renown and Grace'. The morality of existence in society is founded on a religious reverence for life. 'I am a human being', wrote Luther; 'this is certainly a higher title than being a prince, for God did not make a prince; men made him. But that I am a human being is the work of God alone.'[11] The point again is not that this is an exclusively Christian conception, but that it had, in Shakespeare's age, the whole weight of Christian consciousness behind it. In this, too, he could rest with assurance.

The sacredness of the individual, so fundamental to Shakespeare's dramatic vision, was of course more than a matter of individuals: it implied a faith in human society. We have noted Hooker's endorsement of 'the good of mutual participation', and the centrality of this value to the Elizabethan political ideal. With it went an equally important faith—perhaps more classical than Christian in origin—in 'the *common* sense'. 'The most certain token of evident goodness is, if the general persuasion of all men do so account it', as Hooker puts it. And again,

The general and perpetual voice of men is as the sentence of God himself. For that which all men have at all times learned, Nature herself must needs have taught; and God being the author of Nature, her voice is but his instrument.[12]

Civil society, in the Elizabethan vision, was always aspiring—and not aspiring vainly—to the state where it could embody the mutuality which did complete justice to universal humanity. It is a faith that we may regard with the more interest for the fact that it is almost completely lost. The intellectual sector of twentieth-century society is highly suspicious, and not without reason, of 'the common sense' and of the democratic principle on which it is founded. And yet we must recognise that the suspicion is damaging, undermining as it does the genuinely social dimension of the life of the mind, making it defensive where it should be expansive. There is no doubt that much of the assurance of Shakespeare's art proceeds from a faith in human society which is of this order. Can we then regard it as irrelevant to our concerns, something we have outgrown? Can we dismiss the Christian ethics that underpinned the structure, as no longer tenable? Do we wholly understand ourselves, when we are resolutely secularist, or regretfully anti-Christian? (These are not rhetorical questions—unless we are confident enough to imagine we hold the answers.)

Can we, for instance, exclude from our conception of the human, the impulses that Hooker sees as man's natural desire after spiritual things, and still lay claim to a real inclusiveness:

For man doth not seem to rest satisfied, either with fruition of that wherewith his life is preserved, or with performance of such actions as advance him most deservedly in estimation; but doth further covet, yea oftentimes manifestly pursue with great sedulity and earnestness, that which cannot stand him in any stead for vital use; that which exceedeth the reach of sense; yea somewhat above the capacity of reason, somewhat divine and heavenly, which with hidden exultation it rather surmiseth than conceiveth; somewhat it seeketh, and what that is directly it knoweth not, yet very intentive desire thereof doth so incite it, that all other known delights and pleasures are laid aside, they give place to the search of this but only suspected desire...For although the beauties, riches, honours, sciences, virtues, and perfections of all men living, were in the present possession of one; yet somewhat beyond and above all this there would still be sought and earnestly thirsted for.[13]

The trouble, of course, is that Hooker is offering this very real insight into the nature of human aspiration, as an argument for the necessary existence of a *supernatural* way of salvation. And one of the great obstacles to assimilating the strongly religious vision of the Elizabethans is that it is plainly buttressed by a transcendentalism which is almost totally foreign to the modern mind. It is a crucial question whether we can receive their humane wisdom without their belief in absolutes. We might begin by enquiring what function this transcendentalism serves in Shakespearian drama, bearing in mind that its practical usefulness does not necessarily entail its truth.

It seems to me that an unwillingness to rest in a good which is not *the* good is a quality that distinguishes Shakespearian drama very sharply from its modern counterpart. Hooker again provides a context for discussion:

Another kind [of good] there is, which although we desire it for itself, as health, and virtue, and knowledge, nevertheless they are not the last mark whereat we aim, but have their further end whereunto they are referred, so as in them we are not satisfied as having attained the utmost we may, but our desires do still proceed. These things are linked and as it were chained one to another; we labour to eat, and we eat to live, and we live to do good, and the good which we do is as seed sown with reference to a future harvest. But we must come at length to some pause. For, if everything were to be desired for some other without any stint, there could be no certain end proposed unto our actions, we should go on we know not whither...something there must be desired for itself simply and for no other.[14]

Hooker here recognises the two poles of intellectual and moral activity—'our desires do still proceed'; and 'we must come at length to some pause'—and the function of his absolute, the something that is 'desired for itself simply', is to account both for the 'proceeding' and for the 'pause'. The insatiable desire and the right fulfilment of that desire are contained within the same frame of vision. Now a mind which lives naturally and without constriction within this frame has certain safeguards against the debilities and diseases which have followed the shattering of the frame. It does not 'go on it knows not whither' in an endless quest for meaning which, in proportion as one recognises its endlessness, becomes increasingly meaningless. It is not tempted to turn the quest itself into the only true meaning, thus depriving itself of any possible reason for continuing the quest. Somewhere at the depths of its consciousness it whispers, 'It is an axiom of nature that natural desire cannot utterly be frustrate.'[15] It is not trapped in the anguished desperation of one waiting eternally for Godot, and believing at the same time that the activity is meaningless. It is not subject to the necessary and irreversible rout of all its aspirations.

On the other hand, because there is an absolute in which the mind *can* rest, it does not stop off at the half-way-houses of '*a* positive meaning' (Ibsen's social emancipation or Brecht's economic gospel) but enquires its way to *the* meaning, and will not be deflected. Its 'desires do still proceed', and its exploration is continually gaining in depth. The transition from the history plays to the tragedies by way of *Henry IV* is a very good example of this forward and inward movement; and it is hard to imagine a development so rapid and so purposeful without a firm conviction at a fairly deep level that there was a truth to be discovered. The moments when this conviction appears to falter, though they may produce (in *Troilus and Cressida*) a powerful drama of disillusion which is very 'modern' in its courageous confrontation of corruption and meaninglessness, display neither the steadiness nor the inevitability of the Shakespeare we agree to call a classic. There is something both rash and tentative about them, a strange air of disorientation.

Now I am not suggesting that Shakespeare would not have achieved his tragic vision if he had been an atheist. He may very well *not* have 'believed in God' in the conventional sense. What I am suggesting is that the deepening of his personal vision was reinforced, given a certain purposiveness and seriousness in relation to his whole cultural environment, by its congruence with Christian thinking about the absolute good, and the absolute truth. And that the loss of that absolute has made the creative exploration of human life harder to justify, prone to fall into purposelessness, liable to stop short at the moment when it should be pressing on. This disabling condition would not be sufficient to defeat genius, but lesser mortals may very well be inhibited by it.

In another respect the absolute appears to be relevant to the Shakespearian achievement; its irrefragable existence provides a sheet-anchor for a mind deeply committed to realism about human nature. The realist's road is a dangerous one to travel. It can very easily end in fierce disillusion, bitter vituperation or the languors of total despair. Telling the hard truth about the way we live is something that only the strongest man can endure, and even he may go mad, as Nietzsche did, when he is deprived of human support. The indigenous Elizabethan transcendentalism was able to give Shakespeare the kind of support that prevented his realism toppling over into brutality, sentimentality or despair. The brute facts of human existence (the Machiavellian facts, for instance) did not erode the ideal but merely developed the tension between ideal and actual (neither of which could be relinquished) to the point of tragic intensity. His realism was saved from corruption by the salt of an inalienable ideal. It was not, to repeat, the fact that Shakespeare believed in God that gave him a sureness deeper than theological commitment. But the kind of mind which had his deep faith in time-as-redeemable could find in Elizabethan Christianity the support of common preoccupations and a common sureness.

To regard time as redeemable is to have faith in humanity, despite

335

the charges that realism can bring against it—for all these threads are part of the one web of meaning. But it is also to believe that the universe is not ultimately hostile to human fulfilment. It involves a belief in providence. What Shakespeare distils from the muddles and misconceptions of Elizabethan providential theorising is a faith in a universal moral order which cannot finally be defeated, and we have seen reason to enquire whether this is not a necessary faith for the dramatist—as necessary as the realism which continually threatens it. It is a factor at least which connects Greek tragedy with Shakespearian tragedy.[16] Fortified by this conviction a poet is not tempted to make the shrug his final attitude to the endemic injustice of human life—a sham solution that the theatre of the absurd is perpetually in danger of embracing. The shrug is, in any case, incompatible with the extremely serious view of moral responsibility which is characteristic of Shakespeare; and perhaps that view of moral responsibility is incompatible with a morally fortuitous universe? What Shakespeare has done, in a sense, is to take the step of faith necessary to the survival of moral sensibility, and projected his personal sense of meaningfulness onto the world at large, positing an activity of choice and discrimination which is not finally at odds with 'nature'. The absence of this conviction in Marlowe issues alternately in a hard-bitten, defensive cynicism (the *Jew of Malta* phase), or, reinforced by the external pressure of Calvinist notions of reprobation, gives rise to a gnawing fear that all may be irrational, that a monstrous cosmic injustice may have the last say (the *Faustus* swing of the same unquiet pendulum). The effect, in dramatic terms, is disabling and disruptive. It may be true—it is what I have argued—that Shakespeare confronts this fear; but he is not, like Marlowe, intimidated by it.

But the important thing about Shakespeare's 'providence' is that, increasingly as he moves towards the tragedies, it is a natural providence —and here perhaps there is some hope of effecting a *rapprochement* with the Elizabethans. For there is an abiding tendency in Elizabethan thought to translate the absolute in terms of 'nature'—and this is true even of the theologian Hooker, who resists strongly the puritan attempt to cut across the operation of natural causes with theories of divine intervention: 'Nature hath need of grace, whereunto I hope we are not opposite, by holding that grace hath use of nature.'[17] Shakespeare's mind, as a dramatist's must be, is even more deeply committed to the natural. But his view of nature is informed and transfused with the kind of faith Hooker reserves for the absolute. The principle of health—

grace—is not in heaven, but in nature, and especially in human nature, and it cannot finally be rooted out. It is faith in this principle—not necessarily as redeeming the world nor even prevailing, but as inalienably present—which, in *Macbeth*, makes possible the stability, the solid ground of assurance from which Shakespeare can explore and submit himself to the unreal-reality of evil, without fear of losing his bearings.

Finally, his exploration of evil involved calling in question the beneficence of nature itself—as *Lear* shows even more clearly than *Macbeth*; and there is nothing factitious about this questioning. But at the deepest level it is true, I think, that one only questions one's basic convictions in this frightening and ruthless way, when one is sure at the bottom of one's soul that they can stand the fierce heat in the crucible of doubt. And, partly, this sureness is a sureness in society, something for which one feels invisible human support on all sides from the best minds and the most sensitive consciences of one's age.

Although Shakespeare's Christianity (if we can use the ellipsis) is not a transcendental solution to the enigmas of life, it does draw its strength from a belief in the absolute; though it implies no denial of evil and chaos, it does have its eyes fixed on the shining forth of the good. It has somehow converted the hope we must all entertain (however desperately) when we reflect on the future of the human race, into something more durable than hope. It lives, in the broadest sense of the term, in a state of faith. But the faith is not the *subject* of the plays, which are thoroughly secular and thoroughly empirical in tone. Although the vision of evil in *Macbeth* has been stabilised by it, the play is not a statement of faith, but an exploration of the totally destructive possibility which threatens it. The permeating faith in man, in society, in nature, which lies always at the back of Shakespeare's agnosticism, his despair, the vision of destruction, the vision of predation, the vision of evil, is a salt which never loses its savour. But it does not, either, become the predominant flavour.

It may strike the reader as odd that, having objected so noisily to Christian interpretations of Shakespeare, which (after all) claimed no more than a certain doctrinal parallelism, I should now produce a Shakespeare more pervasively Christian than that of the Christianisers. But this is precisely my point: if Shakespeare is Christian at all, he is Christian at a much deeper level than that of theological conformity. If he has the abnormally developed assimilative faculty of the great artist, this only means that he will draw the more deeply and extensively on the Christianity of Elizabethan culture. Indeed if he was to stand at the centre of his age and feel its heart-beat on his own pulse, he *had* to be Christian in some sense. To have been anything else in that age would have involved preferring a shallow emancipation to the ground of all that was best in Elizabethan culture. But because the assimilation was a creative assimilation, because it went with a capacity to penetrate the surface manifestations of culture, Shakespeare releases for us, more vividly than any theologian could have done, the perennial relevance of Elizabethan Christianity. What this relevance might be, I have tried to suggest.

To detect lost truths in the past is bound to look like an attempt to set the clock back—an activity which we, still deeply involved with a post-Darwinian evolutionism, are very nervous about; and I would like to disavow here any ambition to revive the historical myth of an ideal Elizabethan society which was somehow superior to our own. I do not know how such a theory could be tested, let alone proven. But when we respond to certain qualities of a culture, feeling their force and their validity to be still real, we are in fact exercising 'historical imagination' in its true sense. We confront the past, conscious simultaneously of its pastness and its presentness. We accept the challenge to self-definition which its dual nature offers, and we tackle the task of 'translation' without which the perception of value degenerates into mere anachronistic nostalgia. This reciprocal illumination of the present by the past, and the past by the present, gives to contemporary consciousness a broader base, and a wider range of possibilities than would otherwise be open to it. What it means today to be human is enriched by a sense of what it has meant in the past, and what it always will mean.

If this enrichment is to go on, the Elizabethan ideals which retain their relevance must be kept alive in whatever forms of survival present themselves: they are already very much alive in the minds of a responsive modern audience at a Shakespeare play, and we have at our disposal means of increasing both the responsiveness and the audience. What is more, this continuing imaginative vitality in the plays provides assurance that, when we criticise our own culture in terms of the Elizabethan vision, we are not merely building sand ramparts against the tide of history, but fostering a life which is altogether present. It is one way, after all, of expressing our concern for the evolution of society —which consists in a perpetual rediscovery, in new contexts, of the truths by which we live, and a steady labour to embody them more fully in the life-forms of the present.

BARABAS AND THE HISTORICAL
JEW OF EUROPE

William Rowley, in a satirical squib of the 1600s, pictures himself and some like-minded friends scouring London for the lost French knight, M. l'Argent—for lack of whose company they were somewhat dumpish and melancholy. Eventually they arrive at the 'kennell of a most dogged usurer', and beat upon his door.

We might now heare the tongueless staires tell us (by force of an oppressive footing), that there was somebodie descending, which was better verified by a rewmatique disposition of the descender, for (with small interims) now and then we might hear on[e] hawking and vomitting the best part of his corruption, that was his fleame; for there was no part of him lesse harming (yet that noisom enough). Anon his gouty footmanship had reacht the dore, where after the quest of, who was there, and our most humble answere, the locks and bolts were set at liberty, and so much of the dore was opened as we see the compasse of a bakers purgatory or pillory, for even so showed his head forth the dores; but as ill a head in forme (and worse in condition) then ever held a spout of lead in his mouth at the corner of a church: an old moth-eaten cap buttoned under his chinne, his visage (or vizard) like the artificiall Jewe of Maltaes nose, the wormes, fearing his bodie would have gone along with his soule, came to take, and indeed had taken possession, where they peept out still at certaine loope holes to see who came neere their habitation; upon which nose, two casements were built, through which his eyes had a little ken of us. The fore part of his doublet was greasie sattin, stil to put him in mind of his patron Satan, the back part eight penny canvas, a thing (worse than comparison) that loves not halfe himselfe...his industrie is to maintaine his scalpe in a warme cap, his stinking feete in socks, his nose in sacke, his guts in capons, and his brains in mischiefe.

To this lumpe of iniquity, this living carrion, this house-kept fox that's only preserved to stinke...wee (to show our humillitie) bent ith' hammes, and gave him worshipful salute.

Having explained their quest and their great anxiety to meet with Monsieur Money, they are alarmed at the sudden change in their informant's countenance:

This was pitch throwne upon burning toe, and oyle upon that to quench it withall: that face that was wilde-fire before, was now hell-fire, raging and boyling as if the poore harmlesse wormes should then have suffered torment: some flew out with feare, others were murthred even in their cabbins, that the blood ranne about his guiltie nose with the very suddaine screwing of his face; yet after coller had procured a foaming vent, he randed out these sentences— Money? vengeance and hell so soone as Money! he will not bide with me...¹

We have here, in a fairly developed form, a stock myth of Elizabethan popular culture: the Usurer with the monstrous fiery nose, racked with avarice, consumed with gout and miscellaneous corruptions, ally of Satan and the object of a ferocious, almost pathological, loathing. Interestingly enough, Rowley acknowledges in passing the stage character who had done much to fix the characteristics of the Usurer-Jew firmly in the popular imagination—Marlowe's Barabas.

It has recently been shown that Barabas, and much else in *The Jew of Malta*, derives from an earlier Jew-play now only extant in a German version which was taken on tour by the *Englische Komoedianten*.² It is possibly the play of the Jew 'showne at the Bull', which Gosson mentioned in 1579,³ and probably the primary source for *The Merchant of Venice*. It is based, somewhat tenuously, on the career of Joseph Nassi, Duke of Naxos and favourite of the Turkish court—a man whose immense wealth and influence bred rumour and fable throughout Europe. Since there is a direct source, there is no longer any necessity to posit Marlowe's personal acquaintance with Nassi's career (though he was interested in Levantine affairs) nor to deduce a Marlovian research project into the vicissitudes of European Jewry. Given the outlines of his source play, he could have filled in the rest with miscellaneous knowledge and a keen nose for human hypocrisy—the latter, I suspect, the most important factor.

What follows is not, therefore, offered as an account of the origins of Marlowe's play, but as an aid to understanding the attitudes in his audience upon which Marlowe drew, and to which at times he capitulated. As with *Faustus*, he is here relying upon some pretty vulgar vulgar-superstition, material which is often intractable to a fully artistic moulding and which invites the stock response rather than the imaginative self-inspection. Marlowe seems to oscillate between satisfying the lower appetites of his audience, and putting a diagnostic finger right on the pressure-points of European anti-semitism. The play is alternately sensationalist in the *Massacre at Paris* mode, and acutely intelligent in a mode all its own. Those who are interested in localising this ambiguous relationship with the audience may find some illumination in the current image of the Jew, which Marlowe exploits so inconsistently.

The first and most striking feature of the Elizabethan Jew-image is the fact that it had persisted almost entirely without first-hand experience. The Jews had been expelled from England in 1290 after a long period of extortion and persecution. The Jews that were known in the country between that date and the resettlement in 1656 amount to only a few hundred, and most of these were either real or pretended converts seeking assimilation (real or apparent) into the English community. The Jews known to have been present in sixteenth- and seventeenth-century London were prosperous merchants, some of them trusted advisors of the government, and in no significant way related to the Shylocks and Barabas's of the stage.[4] The myth was thus largely dependent upon the folk wisdom embodied in proverbs and cant sayings, or upon literary sources, mainly Continental ones. It was, accordingly, free to develop unconstrained by the facts of experience. 'Where there had been physical contact at one time,' writes one historian, 'its effects may live on traditionally after the separation, in a few well-marked but ossified traits, expressions, similes, maxims, all the more tenaciously adhered to because they are looked upon as ancestral wisdom, henceforth incapable of correction.'[5] Thus when Launcelot Gobbo puns on the proverb 'worth a Jew's eye',

> There will come a Christian by,
> Will be worth a Jewess' eye,   *Merchant*, II. v. 41

he brings into play the memory of the time-honoured royal practice of extorting Jewish gold with the threat of mutilation.

A dynamic element in the formation of the myth was, of course, the influence of the Gospels, which neglected the semitic origin of Christ and his disciples and referred to his opponents, somewhat inaccurately, as '*the* Jews'. In Christian Europe the word acquired its primary colouring from this constantly re-iterated usage; and the medieval stage reinforced the lesson of Jewish villainy in contemporary terms, dressing the villains of the passion story in Jewish cloaks and horned hats, often completing the identification with the appendage of the Jew badge—a circle of yellow cloth on the arm, instituted in 1215—and the use of current Jewish names.[6] This, together with the exigencies of dogmatic theology, which made it necessary to label the medieval Jew the enemy of Christendom, resulted in an almost universal opprobrium being attached to the Hebrew race.[7]

Intimately bound up with the theological antagonism are the repeated tales of Host desecration. The stories follow a standard pattern: the

Jew bribes a Christian to secure the consecrated wafer, mutilates it by pricking it or stamping upon it; blood miraculously flows from the wafer or the Christ-child appears in it, whereupon the infidel is paralysed, struck dumb or rendered insensible in some instructive way, and the army of the Church, otherwise the mob, carries the un-hallowed dog off to a well-deserved and generally horrifying death. The last act of the story is sober fact, as many contemporary accounts bear witness; the rest, since there are never any witnesses of the sacrilege, is a matter for speculation.[8]

With the arrival of the angel of death in the form of bubonic plague, the antagonism took a pathological turn. The Spanish Jews, it was alleged, acting under orders from a council of world jewry, had 'dispatched messengers with boxes containing poison and with threats of excommunication, forced them to poison brooks and wells.'[9] Though the reports were violently self-contradictory and though no evidence was ever adduced, there was very little doubt in the public mind that the Jews were responsible for the ravages of the black death; as late as 1580, when an epidemic broke out in Aix, an English doctor was to diagnose its cause as 'poison which the Jews rubbed on the knockers of doors'.[10]

The poison allegation, which recurs monotonously throughout the medieval period and later, had its roots in the large number of Jews who did, in fact, practise medicine. Once Christendom had found some reason, however tenuous, for suspecting the Jews, it was almost inevitable that the deaths of Christian patients should be attributed to their Jewish physicians, and, by the same logic, the cures were attributed to sorcery. By the time Dr Johann Eck wrote his *Ains Judenbüchlin* in 1541 he could claim that

when they come together at their festivals, each boasts of the number of Christians he has killed with his medicine, and the one who has killed the most is honoured.[11]

Queen Elizabeth's Jewish physician, Dr Lopez, was one of the most notorious victims of popular frenzy on this subject.[12] 'Canst thou impoyson?' enquires a character in Marston's *Malcontent*; and Malevole replies, 'Excellently, no Jew, Potecary, or Polititian better'.[13]

The 'Polititian' allusion is a reminder that the Elizabethan Machiavel-monster, and English fantasies about Italy, that 'academie of man-slaughter, the sporting place of murther, the apothecary shop of poyson',[14] are part of the same vicious ethnocentric complex that gave rise to Elizabethan anti-semitic frenzy. The fusion is complete by the time Webster produced his Romelio, who enters 'in the habit of a Jew', and gloats thus:

> Excellently well habited! why, methinks
> That I could play with mine own shadow now,
> And be a rare Italianated Jew;
> To have as many several change of faces,
> As I have seen carved upon one cherry stone,
> To wind about a man like rotten ivy,
> Eat into him like quicksilver, poison a friend
> With pulling but a loose hair from's beard, or give a drench
> He should linger of nine years, and ne'er complain,
> But in the spring and fall, and so the cause
> Imputed to a disease natural; for slight villanies,
> As to coin money, corrupt ladies honours,
> Betray a town to th' Turk, or make a bonfire
> A th' Christian Navy, I could settle to't
> As if I had eat a politician,
> And digested him to nothing but pure blood.[15]

As the dreaded year 1500 approached and the Turkish threat became a matter of grave concern, the figure of Antichrist loomed large on the theological horizon. Prophecies were anxiously scanned and the pronouncements of the Schoolmen were systematised into a quasi-dogmatic eschatology. Antichrist was to be the offspring of a union between the devil and a Jewish harlot, and he was to found his empire upon Jewish support. Immured behind the wall of the Caspian mountains, waiting for the word of command, was a vast horde of 'Red' Jews, who would sweep across Europe, meeting up with their European compatriots and 'seducing many nations'.[16] It was, I suppose, inevitable that in these years of mounting international and psychological tension the burden of guilt should be thrown upon a non-conforming, alien minority such as the Jews. In an age of rabid and mutually suspicious nationalism, any group so conspicuously supra-national as world-Jewry must have seemed profoundly menacing. Since they were awaiting a Messiah, and since the Messiah had already come, it was self-evident that their Messiah must be Antichrist. It had long been known, in any case, that whenever in Jewish ritual they prayed for the destruction of those who worshipped false gods, they were in fact praying for the annihilation of Christendom.[17] The Jew was the inveterate enemy of mankind—'A crucifying Hang-man trayn'd in sinne, / One that would hang his brother for his skinne', as an obligingly frank Jew in a seventeenth-century play describes himself.[18]

Furthermore, the Cabbala and the Talmud were reputed to be the root and source of all magic—were they not written in Hebrew, a language no Christian could understand? Moses, their lawgiver, was a magician of some note, as his Egyptian performances avouched. What more natural than that the enemies of Christendom should achieve their ends by witchcraft? Thus the earliest versions of the Faust legend have the Faust figure introduced to the devil by a Jew. Even the demonic orgies of the witches came to be known as a 'Sabbath' and their meetings as 'synagogues', a sinister overtone that the word still retains.[19] Once the equation between Jew and sorcerer had been made, the last barrier of rational constraint was down; the Jew could, with perfect propriety, be held responsible for the failure of crops, the outbreak of fire, devastation by flood, miscarriage or deformity at childbirth, livestock diseases, epidemics.[20] And each allegation that was thus made was followed by ferocious reprisals upon the Jewish community at large, the scenes of carnage fixing the libels all the more firmly in the race memory.

Nor were matters allowed to rest there. The next step was to conflate the devil with his servant—and so we get in woodcuts of the sixteenth and seventeenth centuries a hook-nosed devil who wears Jewish cloak and badge, and takes part in the services of the synagogue or the business transactions at the money-lenders'. In Crete they went so far as to add a black devil to the yellow Jew badge.[21] 'Certainly', says Launcelot Gobbo, that convenient purveyor of vulgar prejudice, 'the Jew is the very devil incarnation.'[22] No one could be very surprised, therefore, when, in the sixteenth century, the Portuguese marranos turned their talents to the construction of engines of war and became military advisors to the Turks.[23] It was all of a piece with their ferocious misanthropism.

Perhaps the most tenacious of all the anti-semitic libels was that of child-crucifixion. One hundred and fifty cases of this charge are on record, Hugh of Lincoln being the most famous English example. Belief in the medicinal value of blood, particularly young blood, was the source of this strange conviction that Jews were in the habit of stealing Christian children, crucifying them and using the blood in their Passover ritual. Frequently the decoy was the daughter of the Jew, for folk-lore permitted him to have extravagantly beautiful daughters, as long as it was understood that the beauty was the fatal façade for a murderous heart. Abigail plays this role in her father's plots, though she does it unwittingly.²⁴

One variant of the theme explains the practice as an attempt on the part of the Jews to cure secret issues of blood from which they were believed to suffer. It was widely held that not only female, but male, Jews were subject to menstruation and that this was the cause of the Jewish smell, *foetor judaicus*, which good Christians found well-nigh intolerable.²⁵ I have already noted (pp. 41–2) Marlowe's neat parody of this absurd and persistent superstition.

It is possible now to see the roots of the pathological disgust which informs Rowley's portrait of the usurer with which we started. One has only to add to this the universal Jewish addiction to usury and the picture is as complete as space will permit. Although the Jews were originally usurers under Christian compulsion, and though they had many Christian rivals in rapacity, the equivalence of Jewish race and the practice of money-lending was so firmly established that by the early seventeenth century one meaning of the fascinating verb 'to judaise' was, as I have mentioned, 'to lend at interest'.

Most of the features of the Jew-myth which have been discussed so far are Continental in origin and could only have percolated into English consciousness by indirect routes. But usury was an acute social problem, and one over which even a Shakespeare was liable to grow overheated, as *Timon of Athens* indicates. The translator of *A general discourse against the damnable sect of Usurers* admirably gives us the social context of the problem in his 'Epistle Dedicatorie' addressed to Sir Christopher Hatton:

I feare me that many occupiers in the world which can not liue by their lawfull trade and beare a countenance, do maintaine themselues by Vsurie. I feare mee that many officers whose allowance is but verie small, and their liuing nothing at all besides, are iolie fellowes, and that by Vsurie. I feare mee, that many gentlemen, whose reuenues are but simple, can bring mighty things to passe, & that by Vsurie...I would that among occupiers many, whiche hauing good trades whereby they may liue well, yet for greedines of more gaine, did not leaue their lawfull callinges, and liue onely by Vsurie: I woulde that among sutche as are called gentlemen, many whiche haue liuinges, and may keepe good houses, did not either sell all, or forsake their home to come into populous townes and liue by Vsurie: I would that many whom God hath blest with ritches of this worlde, whereby they may procure good and commendable trades to liue by, refused not them to liue by Vsurie.²⁶

The advent of a money economy in the 'populous townes', the decay of the great houses which had been the centres of national life, the ruinous competition involved in maintaining a 'countenance' at a Court shored up by chronic borrowing, the sapping of habits of thrift by the increasing availability of credit—all these social changes produced an insecurity that bordered at times on panic. The money-lender, though merely the economic instrument of new desires, had all the resultant tensions and crises laid at his door; and the money-lender was, by an ineradicable popular association, the Jew.[27]

We have seen (p. 41) how this virulent prejudice had become embodied in the very language Marlowe was using: the pejorative sense of the word 'Jew' summed up the history of Judaeo-Christian relations, even for those who were not consciously aware of it. There is, besides, the implication of treachery and double-dealing, which chained the words 'Judas' and 'Jew' together by a pre-conscious association of sound and idea. Thus the English ambassador at Constantinople complains that, despite his kind treatment of Duke Joseph, he has received only 'a Jeweishe reward', and has been 'iudasly and iewisly' dealt with.[28] Or a Christian merchant in a contemporary play, treacherously overtaken by a ferocious and cannibalistic Jew, anathematises his assailant as an 'Inhuman Dogge...true seed / Of that kisse-killing Judas'.[29] Munday has a collocation which combines the betrayer and the usurer:

the Judas broker, that lives by the Bagge and (except God be more mercifull to him) will follow him that did beare the bagge.[30]

'The hat he wears,' says drunken Ithamore, slandering his erstwhile master, 'Judas left under the elder when he hanged himself' (IV. vi. 67).

Munday's allusion provides a broad hint where one of Barabas's dramatic antecedents is to be found—in the figure of Judas of the medieval mystery cycles. In these plays, following an ancient legendary tradition, the hated figure of the betrayer is made doubly loathsome by the addition of the attributes of the money-lender. Judas, who attends to the finances of Christ and his disciples, has made a practice of deducting ten per cent for his own use. When the Magdalen squanders 300 pence worth of spikenard in an act of senseless devotion, Judas is so enraged that he determines not to be cheated of his commission and promptly sells Christ to the Jews for a precise 30 pence, insisting all the while upon his avaricious motivation:

> Mony I wyl non forsake,
> And thei profyr to my plesyng

For covetyse I wyl hem wake
And onto my maystyr I xal hem bryng...[31]

This parallel is more than a matter of antiquarian interest. There is a continuous stage tradition stretching from Judas with his red wig and carrying the standard property of the usurer's bag, down to Shakespeare's 'red-hair'd Jew'.[32] ('His very hair is of the dissembling colour', complains Rosalind when Orlando fails to arrive at the tryst, and Celia corrects her, 'Something browner than Judas's; marry his kisses are Judas's own children'—*AYL*, III. iv. 7.) Marlowe's Jew with the 'artificiall nose' is of the same kindred. Here again a native English tradition comes in behind the Continental one, and puts Marlowe's audience in contact with the underground energies of a perennial anti-semitism.

The chronicle literature which was a part of English historical consciousness unobtrusively performed the same task. In a popular history like Stow's *Annales* (1580), the ordinary reader could ponder stories of Jew-persecution in the twelfth and thirteenth centuries, before the Expulsion; read how King John, attempting to raise a loan from the Jews, was in trouble with a stubborn Hebrew who refused to pay up until the king 'hadde caused every day one of his great teeth to be pulled out by the space of 7 daies, & then he gaue the king 10,000 marks of siluer...'; or read accounts of the martyrdom of Hugh of Lincoln and William of Norwich.[33] Most important, he could learn the precise note of callous indifference that was to be struck when dealing with recalcitrant Hebrews:

A Jew at Tewkesbury fell into a priuie vpon the Saturdaie, and woulde not for reuerence of his Sabboth bee plucked out, wherefore *Richard* of *Clare* earle of Gloucester, kept him there till Munday, at which time hee was found dead.

Stow adds a sinister postscript: 'The said *Richard Clare*...died, and his brother William, by poyson as was thought.'[34] Those who were not addicted to Chronicles could acquire the same attitudes by reading English translations of Continental tales, or breathe the contagion from Chaucer's Prioress. And if any further evidence—apart from Marlowe's play—is necessary to prove the liveliness of the tradition, the succession of Jewish villains in Elizabethan literature puts the matter beyond all doubt.[35]

This murderous folk-tradition lies behind Barabas's pseudo-autobiographical catalogue of villainy (II. iii. 175 f.); he has poisoned wells, practised as a physician, with invariably fatal results; he has worked as a military engineer betraying both sides, before settling down into his conventional role of usurer. It lies behind Friar Jacamo's conviction that Barabas must have crucified a child (III. vi. 50), and behind the whole anti-Christian ferocity of the Jew's moral attitudes. Most of the things the tradition produces directly in *The Jew* are either downright crude, or equivocally undermined by the exaggeration implicit in this kind of stereotype thinking.

But Marlowe does seem to be aware of something else in his material. His satirist's nose quivers at the scent of hypocrisy and, whether from personal knowledge or from instinct, he reproduces with great accuracy the tortuosities and rationalising involutions of the Christian mind when it is obliged to deal personally and financially with the Jew. It is this aspect of the play which remains comically vital still.

There is a story concerning Henry II of France, which Marlowe probably did not know, but which illustrates the point conveniently. The king owed the influential Duke Joseph Nassi, Barabas's historical prototype, the sum of 150,000 ducats; but, since the Jew was his inveterate diplomatic foe, he refused to repay the loan. The reason he advanced to justify his defaulting is worth some attention. He averred that 'both law and religion forbade [him] to repay the debt to his Jewish creditors, because it was altogether forbidden for the Jews to have any business dealings in France, but all their goods rather to be confiscated'.[36] We are left to conclude that it was the veriest coincidence that the king discovered this scruple *after* he had raised the loan and not before, and that it is only out of his royal clemency that he now refrains from exterminating the pestilential race of money-lenders. The fact that it is Henry who is at the mercy of the money-lenders, and not they at his, does nothing to abate the lofty tone of self-righteousness which the king adopts—a tone which is consistently found in the dealings of the Christians with Jewish usurers. For this kind of preposterous sophistry, offered by the Christians without a tinge of irony, Marlowe provides the ironic context.

The tacit assumption in Henry's threat is also typical: he assumes that the Jewish population of France exists solely as a mine from which he may quarry as much gold as he stands in need of. On the basis of the same principle, Peter the Venerable of Cluny had urged Louis VII, in 1146, to confiscate all Jewish goods in order to finance the Crusades.[37] It is the foundation of the endless succession of forced loans and extortions to which the medieval Jewish community was subject; it justifies the unleashing of the mob (a frequent royal practice when the Jewish cow would not 'give down her milk freely'), for the Hebrews, as an accursed race, are very lucky to be allowed to live, are, in fact, the chattels of the kings who magnanimously spare their lives. We are here very close to the moral climate of Marlowe's Malta. Henry's attitude is shared by Ferneze and, later, by Ithamore when he needs money to appease his whore.

From a financial point of view, even conversion to Christianity was a heads-I-win-tails-you-lose affair. Coryat, visiting Venice in 1608, discovered that regrettably few Jews were being converted because on conversion all their goods fell to the state. The rationalisation of this extraordinary ordinance is again the interesting element:

> whereas many of them do raise their fortunes in vsury, in so much that they doe ...flea many a poore Christians estate by their griping extortion; it is therefore decreed by the Pope...that they shall make a restitution of all their ill-gotten goods, and so *disclogge their sovles and consciences*, when they are admitted ...into the bosome of Christs Church.[38]

Again the highminded concern for Jewish moral well-being and the total innocence of irony. It is substantially the same dilemma that Barabas faces: either pay half, or turn Christian (= pay all?), or pay all (I. ii. 68 f.).

The rationalisation goes further. Since it is unacceptable to harry an opponent who differs from you in all good conscience, the Jew must be a deliberate heretic. And it is the almost universal assumption of medieval and Renaissance Christendom that the Jews do, in fact, recognise the truth of Christianity, but from a wilful and cross-grained stubbornness refuse to admit the fact. They were frequently accused of tampering with the text of the Old Testament in order to obscure its Christological meaning.[39] Coryat's encounter with the Jewish community at Venice ended in exasperation because they were 'such refractary people',[40] and Luther, near the end of his life, gave vent to his rage at the incorrigible obstinacy of the Hebrew, declaring that they were the devil's people and not even baptism could effect any permanent change in their nature.[41] The obstinacy which was really galling the Christians was their holding out against the clammy embrace of universal Christendom, their persisting in being the one exception in the Western European conformity. It was a mob rage-reaction against the sole dissenter. Marlowe sees the absurdity of the Christian monomania which regards all divergence from a not very self-evident truth as wilful error, and he starts from a very different position:

> FERNEZE. Why, Barabas, wilt thou be christened?
> BARABAS. No, governor, I will be no convertite.

The religious persuasions of the two protagonists, in so far as they are not mere 'policy', are data, given. The idea of Barabas changing his religion is as ridiculous to Ferneze as it is to Barabas.[42]

In a similar way, Marlowe sees through the Christian notion of the Jews as an accursed race, to the rapacity for which this is no more than a convenient smokescreen, and he has caught both the self-righteous tone, and the logical perversity on which it is founded: 'If your first curse fall heavy on thy head...'Tis not our fault...' The First Knight's preposterous sophistry mirrors the very general belief that the Christian, in hounding the Jews to death, was simply the unwitting instrument of God's inscrutable justice, and could not be held responsible for his actions. He was, rather, performing a meritorious deed, for 'whoso [does] an injury to a Jew [is] a follower of Christ'.[43]

The matter, indeed, went deeper. Since the Jews were accursed *as a race*, they were collectively responsible for the criminal acts of individual Jews. The doctrine of corporate responsibility, a normal adjunct of ethnocentric thinking of this type, went deep into the consciousness of Christendom. Thus John Stow can write, with the casual enormity of the reporter,

The Jewes *at Northampton* crucified a christian boy vpon Goodfriday, but did not throughly kill him, for the which fact manie Jewes *at London* after Easter were drawne at horse tailes and hanged.[44]

It is, I suppose, some mitigation that they waited until 'after Easter', but then it has always been possible for human beings to be neat precisians on some fine point of morality at the very moment when they are enacting some unthinkable crime. Much of the cutting edge of Marlowe's satire derives from a keen delineation of this sort of moral myopia.

If it could not be maintained that the Jew was a wilful heretic, and if one was unwilling to invoke the blanket clause of total Jewish guilt, there was another way of justifying the predatory behaviour of the Christian mobs. Luther again is the text, though he merely repeats what others had alleged: 'The Talmud and the Rabbis teach that it is no sin to kill the Goyim, that is, heathens and Christians, to break an oath to them, or to rob and plunder them. The one and only aim of the Jews is to weaken the Christian religion.'[45] This psychopathic capacity for attributing to one's victims the aggressive feelings, which are the motivating force of one's own persecution, provides Marlowe with a setting for his study of the Machiavellian art of faith-breaking: 'It's no sin to deceive a Christian...etc.' is, as we have seen, no more than a reapplication of the Christian syllogism.

Against this lurid background it is possible to see something sane and courageous in Marlowe's satirical assault on Christian complacency. When he chooses, he can aim his shafts with deadly accuracy. The only pity is that he was not *sufficiently* independent in mind to shake off the crude influence of that mythical Jew who was the inveterate enemy of mankind.

A NOTE ON THE AUTHORSHIP OF 'FAUSTUS'

Despite a pervasive critical stance of scepticism about the authorship of *Faustus*, the bulk of informed opinion seems ready to allow Marlowe a substantial hand in the planning and execution of the play: Sir Walter Greg, who was prepared to allow only eight hundred-odd lines of the play to be authentic Marlowe, nevertheless saw 'no reason to doubt that it was he who planned the whole' (see 'The Damnation of Faustus', *MLR*, XLI (1946), 99). J. D. Jump concurs, in his edition (London, 1962, p. xlvii). Leo Kirschbaum, in 1946, registered a strong protest against the 'impressionistic criticism' which made sweeping judgments about authorship: 'There has been altogether too much cocksureness in the determination of what is Marlowe's and what is not...I am ...convinced that he could and did write slapstick comic scenes and uninspired serious scenes' (*The Library*, XXVI (1946), 247). Since *The Jew* shows very much the same amalgam of competence and incompetence, the more elegant hypothesis is to attribute the amalgam to the same author in both cases. The question, it seems, is still open.

I have little hope at this late stage of effecting a revolution in judgments about the authorship of the central verse scenes, but I list some considerations which do not seem to have been taken into account:

(1) Some time ago, G. C. Taylor ('Marlowe's "Now"' in *Elizabethan Studies in Honour of G. F. Reynolds*, Boulder, Colorado, 1945, pp. 93–100) provided a useful stylistic test for authentic Marlowe, in the playwright's excessive and idiosyncratic use of 'Now...And now ...But now...Now, Faustus...' constructions to open sentences and begin lines. This mannerism occurs with unusual frequency in the disputed papal scenes. There is a parallel tendency, too, to use 'then' in the same way (see especially in the disputed scene xiii, ll. 16, 22, 35, 36, 100).

(2) We have already seen Marlowe in pope-baiting mood in *The Massacre* and *Edward II*, and the same vein in these *Faustus* scenes goes with a characteristic insistence on the 'triple crown' (viii. 84, 180, 191; ix. 47; xii. 10). In *Massacre* (xvi. 47 and xxi. 62) Marlowe had used this

phrase as a kind of derisive shorthand for the papacy, and, in *II Tamburlaine*, I. vi. 62, he even attributes a 'triple mitre' to John the Great of Abyssinia—presumably because of the anti-religious animus of the context. ('Triple' is a favourite Marlowe word—cf. *I Tam*. III. i. 37; III. ii. 112; IV. iv. 78; IV. ii. 30; *II Tam*. II. iv. 100; IV. iii. 118.) The pride of the pope expressed in treading his enemies underfoot (*Faustus*, viii. 90–8) occurs also in *Massacre*, xiii. 5. Trampling on one's conquered foe is, of course, a frequent motif in *Tamburlaine* (cf. *I Tam*. I. ii. 55–7, 219; IV. iv. 140, and of course the ascent of the throne on the back of Bajazeth, which is possibly the germ of the pope's very similar action in *Faustus*).

(3) The distractingly frequent occurrence of Marlowe's favourite words like 'solemniz'd-solemnity' (Chor. I. 25; viii. 55, 82, 199; ix. 32), 'proud-pride' (viii. 77, 82, 93, 119, 132, 177), or 'haughty' (viii. 135, 143) is not of course conclusive, though I think a reader familiar with Marlowe's style might detect a faint oddity about the usages which can be parallelled in other plays. Lines like 'False prelates, for this *hateful* treachery / Curs'd be your souls to *hellish* misery' are equally hard to pin conclusively on Marlowe, but to my ears they have that excess of vehemence combined with a basic lack of conviction which is very like the Marlowe of *Massacre* and *Edward II*. More convincing is the reference to 'superstitious books' (viii. 115—cf. the 'superstitious bells' in *I Tam*. III. iii. 237 and the 'superstitious taper-lights' in a similar context in *Edward II*, I. iv. 98), or the idiosyncratic 'frolic' (ix. 56; cf. *Edward II*, I. ii. 67; I. iv. 73 and II. ii. 62, and *Jew*, Prologue 4—an unusual word in Elizabethan English), and 'overpeer', meaning 'treat with contempt' (viii. 134; cf. *Edward II*, I. iv. 19). Evidence of this kind is necessarily subjective and cumulative, but it suggests that the case for the hypothetical interpolator who wrote scenes viii, ix, xi–xiii is not as watertight as it might be.

(4) Finally, there is one echo of an image complex which is very common in Marlowe at xii. 20: '...magic charms, that shall pierce through / The ebon gates of ever-burning hell / And hale the stubborn furies from their caves.' Cf. *I Tam*. I. ii. 159—'Or meant to pierce Avernas' darksome vaults / To pull the triple headed dog from hell', and *II Tam*. II. iv. 97—'wound the earth, that it may cleave in twain, / And we descend into th'infernal vaults, / To hale the fatal Sisters by the hair, / And throw them in the triple moat of hell.' Cf. also *II Tam*. I. vi. 16–20 and v. i. 44–6 for the same association of ideas. The verbal association which links 'pierce', 'hale', 'vaults', 'triple' is unlikely

to have been reproduced by a mere imitator: it is altogether too pre-conscious to be imitated.

I have found no evidence of this kind about the prose scenes, which strike me as less clearly Marlovian than the verse ones. But it is an open question: there is so little prose that we are certain is Marlowe's, that it seems a little presumptuous to reject the prose of *Faustus*, on the basis of arbitrary notions about the kind of prose he might have written.

The unacknowledged tenderness for Marlowe's reputation, which lies behind much of the attribution of scenes to this or that hypothetical author, is witnessed by the fact that no one has yet suggested that the fine prose of the Scholars' scene (xix) was written by that meddlesome devil of an interpolator. And yet I know of no bibliographical arguments for believing him to be at work in the 'comic' scenes, which would not apply equally to that scene. The bibliographical arguments, in fact, are all founded on discriminations involving *taste* much more radically than they involve *science*. As I say, the question remains open.

NOTES

CHAPTER I

1 R. G. Collingwood, *The Idea of History* (Oxford, 1946), p. 313.
2 Helen Gardner, *The Business of Criticism* (Oxford, 1959), pp. 134–5.
3 H. A. Mason, *Humanism and Poetry* (London, 1959), p. 32.
4 Matthew Arnold, 'On the Modern Element in Literature', *Complete Prose* (Ann Arbor, 1960), I, 20.
5 J. Huizinga, *Men and Ideas* (London, 1960), p. 58.
6 B. Croce, 'Storia, Cronaca e False Storie' [1937], *Filosofia, Poesia, Storia* (Milan, 1951), p. 443.
7 *History as the Story of Liberty*, tr. S. Sprigge (London, 1941), pp. 19–20.
8 *Filosofia, Poesia, Storia*, p. 444.
9 *The Idea of History*, p. 247.
10 'The Task of Cultural History' [1926], *Men and Ideas* (London, 1960), pp. 51–5.
11 E. H. Carr, *What is History?* (Penguin) (1964), esp. chap. I.
12 *The Idea of History*, part V, sect. 4.
13 The whole Croce–Collingwood position has, however, been assailed, from a philosophical angle, by Gilbert Ryle in his *Concept of Mind* (London, 1949), chap. II, sect. 9. The reader who is satisfied by Professor Ryle's account of mind, therefore, will be obliged either to discount my whole argument, or to question that account in the light of historical (and literary) theory and practice.
14 *The Idea of History*, p. 288.
15 B. Croce, *Il Concetto Moderno della Storia* (Bari, 1947), p. 18.
16 *What is History?*, p. 119.
17 See above, p. 5. This again seems to be widely accepted. See E. H. Carr, *What is History?*, pp. 12–23, and R. G. Collingwood, *The Idea of History*, pp. 243 and 281.
18 *Filosofia, Poesia, Storia*, pp. 445, 449 and 451.
19 *Men and Ideas*, p. 54.
20 Matthew Arnold, *Culture and Anarchy*, ed. J. D. Wilson (Cambridge, 1963), p. 44.
21 'On the Modern Element in Literature', *ed. cit.* I, 21.
22 *What is History?*, pp. 26–7.
23 *Il Concetto Moderno della Storia*, pp. 25–6.
24 *What is History?*, p. 131.
25 *Ibid.* p. 29 and cf. pp. 55 and 68.
26 *Il Concetto Moderno della Storia*, p. 19.
27 See for instance the subtle and interesting ententes with 'evolutionism' that

are established by E. H. Carr (*What is History?*, p. 121) and Croce (*History as the Story of Liberty*, tr. S. Sprigge (London, 1941), pp. 51–4).

28 *Culture and Anarchy*, ed. cit. p. 6.

29 *Judgements of History and Historians* (London, 1959), p. 24.

30 L. Trilling, *The Liberal Imagination* (London, 1951), p. 188.

31 *Ibid.* p. 190.

32 *Ibid.* p. 191.

33 L. C. Knights, 'The University Teaching of English and History: A Plea for Correlation', *Explorations* (London, 1958), p. 193.

CHAPTER 2

1 'The "Massacre at Paris" Leaf', *The Library*, 4th series, XIV (1934), 447–69. F. S. Boas, *Christopher Marlowe* (Oxford, 1940), p. 166.

2 For a classic demonstration of this point, see L. C. Knights, 'Shakespeare and Shakespeareans', *Explorations* (London, 1958), pp. 85–91.

3 *Marlowe's 'Doctor Faustus'* (Oxford, 1950), p. 97.

4 See H. S. Bennett's edition (London, 1931), p. 173. One other piece of evidence is that the 'Lyons', whose governor was to murder Dumaine, appears in the text as 'Orleans' (xviii. 129; xx. 11)—a very possible error if memory or dictation was involved.

5 There are some obvious *non sequiturs*, perhaps due to omissions, in Scene vi, between ll. 49 and 50; x. 9 and 10; xiii. 22 and 23. The strongest evidence, of course, is the Collier Leaf.

6 'François Hotman and "The Massacre at Paris"', *PMLA*, LVI (1941), 349–68; 'Contemporary Pamphlet Backgrounds for Marlowe's "Massacre at Paris"', *MLQ*, VIII (1947), 151–73 and 309–18. My argument in this chapter depends a great deal on Kocher's hard work before me.

7 For accounts of French events and their English repercussions at this time, see J. B. Black, *The Reign of Elizabeth* (2nd edn. Oxford, 1959), pp. 145–88 and 360–4; and J. H. M. Salmon, *The French Religious Wars in English Political Thought* (Oxford, 1959).

8 See Kocher, *MLQ*, VIII (1947), 156.

9 Kocher (*PMLA*, LVI (1941), 358) has shown that Marlowe is here following Hotman (reprinted as book x of Jean de Serres's *The fourth parte of Cōmentaries...of the Ciuill warres of Fraunce*, London, 1576). See sigs. 9^r, 15^v, 19^r, 15^r, 1^v.

10 See Kocher, *MLQ*, VIII (1947), 169–70.

11 Cf. viii. 39–45.

12 Henri Estienne, *A Mervaylous discourse vpon the lyfe...of Katherine de Medicis* (Heydelberge [London?], 1575), p. 134.

13 See Kocher, *PMLA*, LVI (1941), 367.

14 See the Catholic tracts, *La Vie et faits notables de Henry de Valois* (Paris, 1589),

pp. 27, 37 and 53; and *Les Meurs humeurs et comportemens de Henry de Valois* (Paris, 1589), pp. 21 and 89 f.; and cf. *Contre-Guyse* (London, 1589), sig. K4^r, which refers discreetly to the minions as 'certayne gentlemen whom the king hath aduanced'; and *An Advertisement from a French Gentleman* ([London?], 1585), p. 39.

15 See Kocher, *MLQ*, VIII (1947), 172.

16 See, for example, *The Restorer of the French Estate* (London, 1589), p. 167; Michel Hurault, *Antisixtus* (London, 1590), p. 23; and his *A Discourse upon the present estate of France* (London, 1588), p. 32; Pierre de Belloy, *A catholicke Apologie* (London, [1590?]), sig. A3^r; Jean de Serres, *A General Inventorie of the History of France*, tr. Edward Grimestone (London, 1607), p. 704; Jean de Frègeville, *The Reformed Politicke* (London, 1589), p. 47.

17 The inflation of Epernoun's role is discussed by Kocher, *MLQ*, VIII (1947), 172.

18 See for instance *Martine Mar-Sixtus* (London, 1591), sig. F3^v; de Serres, *General Inventorie*, London, 1607, p. 661; or *The discouerer of France to the Parisians*, tr. E.A. (? , 1590), p. 13.

19 See especially Hurault's *An Excellent Discourse of the now present Estate of France* (London, 1592), sigs. 29^v–35^r.

20 See Kocher, *MLQ*, VIII (1947), 316.

21 See *Ibid.* p. 313. Friar Clement, the murderer of Henry III, is alleged to have had a dispensation: see *Martine Mar-Sixtus* (London, 1591), sig. C2^r. *Contre-League*, tr. E.A. (London, 1589), p. 52, accuses the pope of declaring the murder of heretic rulers to be meritorious, but does not assert a general dispensation of the kind Guise envisages here.

22 See for instance *Martine Mar-Sixtus*, esp. sigs. C2^{r-v} and E2^v; G.B.A.F., *A discouery of the great subtiltie...of the Italians* (London, 1591), p. 25; De Frègeville, *The Reformed Politicke*, p. 43; and *A Summe of the Guisian Ambassage to...Rome* (? , 1579), sig. Aii^v.

23 See Colynet, *The True History of the Ciuill Warres of France* (London, 1591), p. 407; *Martine Mar-Sixtus*, sig. F2^r.

24 The two lines common to both speeches may have been, in the *Massacre* text, a reporter's insertion; but the congruence of tone is striking even without the verbatim parallel.

25 See *I Tamburlaine*, I. i. 78–80; III. ii. 1–14; III. iii. 138–9, 149–50, 239–40; v. i. 2; v. ii. 258–67; *II Tamburlaine*, I. i. 31–41; II. iv. 103–6; III. ii. 98–105; III. iv. 58; III. v. 55–7; IV. i. 192–8; v. i. 63–72, 203–6; v. iii. 74.

26 T. S. Eliot, 'Christopher Marlowe', *Selected Essays* (3rd edn. London, 1951), pp. 121–2.

27 de Frègeville, *The Reformed Politicke*, pp. 79–80. *Martine Mar-Sixtus*, sig. F4^r, has a parallel piece of threatening prognostication.

28 For the Guise's Spanish alliances and the hostility they provoked, see *An Advertisement from a French Gentleman*, p. 22; *A Caueat for France*, tr.

E. Aggas (London, 1588), p. 8; Pierre de Belloy, *A Catholicke Apologie*, sig. 95ᵛ; Jean de Frègeville, *The Reformed Politicke*, pp. 36 and 64; the Guises were frequently denigrated as 'strangers', both because they came from Lorraine, and because of their Spanish alliances. See Henri Estienne, *Lyfe...of Katherine de Medicis*, p. 133; *The Protestation of...Frauncis...Duke of Allenson* (? , 1575), p. 5. The very real grounds for alarm at Spanish expansionism are well laid out by Hurault in his *An Excellent Discourse*, sigs. 24ʳ–28ᵛ.

29 Other Spanish allusions occur at xvi. 47–50; xviii. 82–5, 105–6.

30 See J. B. Black, *The Reign of Elizabeth*, p. 407.

31 G. B. Shaw, *Our Theatres in the Nineties* (London, 1932), II, 181–2 and III, 317–18.

CHAPTER 3

1 *Works*, ed. E. V. Lucas (London, 1903), I, 42.

2 T. S. Eliot, 'Christopher Marlowe', *Selected Essays* (London, 1951), p. 123.

3 See W. Rowley, *Search for Money* [1609], quoted on p. 339, for a contemporary reference to this piece of theatrical make-up.

4 See also II. iii. 174; IV. i. 24.

5 See Appendix A for an account of Barabas's origins in European Jewmythology.

6 For example, cf. Prologue, ll. 9–13 with *Respublica* (EETS, 1905), ll. 73–4 where Avarice remarks,

> 'For though to moste men I am found Commodius,
> Yet to those that vse me my namme is Odius.'

See also the close parallel between Udall's Vice addressing his 'bags' (ll. 752 f.) and Marlowe's Jew in Act II, Scene i, with *his* bags. Further evidence for the connexion with the Vice is presented by A. Freeman, 'A Source for the "Jew of Malta"', *N. & Q.*, n.s., IX (1962), 139–41.

7 See also the gulling of Lodowick (II. iii. 32–95) and Abigail's entry into the nunnery (I. ii. 331–65) for similarly crass treatments of duplicity.

8 Cf. Tamburlaine, who proposes to assail Atlas before he dies, 'That, if I perish, heaven and earth may fade' (*II Tamburlaine*, v. iii. 60).

9 See I. ii. 326–9; II. iii. 80–5; III. iii. 33–6; III. vi. 40–1; IV. i. 13–16.

10 So argues B. Spivack, *Shakespeare and the Allegory of Evil* (London, 1958), p. 347.

11 Robert Wilson's *Three Ladies of London*, in Dodsley, ed. Hazlitt (London, 1874), VI, 357.

12 *Coryat's Crudities* [1611] (London, 1776), I, 298; *Merchant of Venice*, II. ii. 107–8.

13 *Merchant of Venice*, I. iii. 174.

14 *Merchant of Venice*, IV. i. 79–80. Cf. *Two Gentlemen*, II. iii. 12—'A Jew would have wept to have seen our parting'.

15 See Joshua Trachtenberg, *The Devil and the Jews* (Yale, 1943), pp. 48–52.

16 The principle can be traced in the precept and practice of the Church from the age of the Crusades, through the thousands of pogroms and purges that disfigure European history. Trachtenberg's horrifying study of anti-semitism (see note 15) is a history of the application of the principle that Christians are absolved of all human obligations when they are dealing with a heretic. See Appendix A.

17 *Richard III*, I. iii. 306–8.

18 See Appendix A.

19 *Greene's Groats Worth of Witte* [1592] (Bodley Head Quartos, VI) (London, 1923), pp. 43–4.

20 *Poetry and Humanism* (London, 1950), p. 77.

21 See chapter 5.

22 See *Discourses*, I, 275 (I. xxvii. 2), where Machiavelli deplores the fact that men do not know 'how to be either magnificently bad or perfectly good'.

23 'Machiavelli's Prince: Background and Formation', *Review of Politics*, XIII (1951), 147.

CHAPTER 4

1 See *The Letter Book of Gabriel Harvey*, ed. E. J. L. Scott (Camden Society) (London, 1884), p. 79. The epigram is given in full by Edward Meyer, *Machiavelli and the Elizabethan Drama* (Weimar, 1897), p. 22.

2 Felix Raab, *The English Face of Machiavelli* (London, 1964), p. 53.

3 *Ibid.* pp. 56–7.

4 The disagreement, for example, between Paul Kocher (*Christopher Marlowe* (Chapel Hill, 1946), pp. 194–202) for whom the Machiavellian influence is 'a mirage', and Roy Battenhouse (*Marlowe's 'Tamburlaine'* (Nashville, Tennessee, 1941), pp. 206–16)—'Marlowe's reliance on *The Prince* was conscious and direct.' The sanest discussion is Irving Ribner's 'Marlowe and Machiavelli', *CL*, IV (1954), 348–56.

5 A. H. Gilbert, *Machiavelli's 'Prince' and its Forerunners* (Durham, North Carolina, 1938).

6 See Mario Praz, 'The Politic Brain: Machiavelli and the Elizabethans', in *The Flaming Heart* (New York, 1958), pp. 90–145 (a revision of the 1928 British Academy Lecture), and Edward Meyer, *Machiavelli and Elizabethan Drama*.

7 H. B. Parkes, 'Nature's Diverse Laws: the Double Vision of the Elizabethans', *SR*, LVIII (1950), 403–4.

8 See chapters I and II of Felix Raab's *The English Face of Machiavelli*, pp. 8–76.

9 It is not only the literary critic with partisan commitments who is to be heard claiming Shakespeare as a major political thinker: see Friedrich Meinecke, *Machiavellism*, tr. D. Scott (London, 1957), pp. 40–1—'The

ability to think in terms of inner conflicts, violations and tragic problems, presupposes a more modern and sophisticated mentality [than Machiavelli's], which perhaps only began with Shakespeare. It was in the spirit of the time to delight in tracing precise and rectilinear paths...'—or Christopher Morris, who refers to Shakespeare as 'an almost unrivalled observer of political behaviour' (*Political Thought in England: Tyndale to Hooker* (London, 1953), p. 103).

10 *The Prince*, tr. Luigi Ricci (London, 1935), p. 68 (chap. xv).
11 Innocent Gentillet, *A Discourse upon the meanes of wel governing [Contre-Machiavel]*, tr. S. Patericke (London, 1602), 'Preface to the Third Part'. Gentillet has been much berated by later students of Machiavelli, but he was not altogether a fool. Meinecke, who is one of the few historians who has done more than abuse Gentillet, offers a sane estimate of his work on pp. 51–6.
12 I am thinking particularly of the case L. A. Burd argues in his Introduction to *Il Principe* (Oxford, 1891), pp. 12–30, see esp. pp. 15–16.
13 E. Cassirer, *The Myth of the State* (Yale, 1961), p. 126.
14 *Discourses*, tr. L. J. Walker, i, 489–90 (iii. vi. 41).
15 *The Prince*, ed. cit., p. 8 (chap. iii).
16 *Christopher Marlowe* (London, 1927), p. 93.
17 F. Chabod, *Machiavelli and the Renaissance* (London, 1958), p. 142.
18 '...nelle azioni di tutti gli uomini, e massime de'principi...si guarda al fine'—*The Prince*, p. 79 (chap. xviii); Ricci translates this somewhat glibly as 'the end justifies the means', but the difference is only in explicitness, for this is certainly what Machiavelli implies.
19 *The Prince*, p. 77 (chap. xviii).
20 *Ibid.* p. 74 (chap. xvii); p. 115 (chap. xxvi); pp. 118–19.
21 F. Meinecke, *Machiavellism*, tr. D. Scott (London, 1957), pp. 39–40. Cf. *The Prince*, p. 108 (chap. xxiii)—'men will always be false to you unless compelled by necessity to be true'.
22 F. Meinecke, *Machiavellism*, pp. 4, 5, 6 and 7. I should in fairness note that Meinecke's brilliant analysis precedes a discussion of Machiavelli in which he appears to claim that Machiavelli was aware of these problems. This I am unable to see. It seems to be a confusion between the genuine intellectual explorer (like Meinecke himself) and the man who raises all the crucial questions by being unaware of them—thus provoking Meinecke into creative thought.
23 Ernst Cassirer, *The Myth of the State*, p. 140.
24 *Advancement* (Everyman) (London, 1915), p. 203.
25 *Eccl. Pol.* ii, 21–3 (v. ii. 3–4).
26 See Felix Raab's discussion of such men as Richard Morrison or William Thomas in *The English Face of Machiavelli*, (London, 1964), chapter ii.
27 H. R. Trevor-Roper, 'Niccolò Machiavelli' in *Historical Essays* (London, 1957), p. 63.

28 B. Spivack, *Shakespeare and the Allegory of Evil* (London, 1958), p. 375.
29 Christopher Lever, *Heauen and Earth, Religion and Policy* (London, 1608), p. 8.
30 *The Prince, ed. cit.* p. 78 (chap. XVIII).

CHAPTER 5

1 Used of an earlier scene, in E. M. W. Tillyard, *Shakespeare's History Plays* (London, 1944), p. 208.
2 J. B. Black, *The Reign of Elizabeth* (Oxford, 1959), p. 407.
3 E. M .W. Tillyard, *Shakespeare's History Plays*, p. 208. I am deliberately singling out Tillyard as a target for criticism, partly because his Christian-providential view of Shakespearian history destroys much that I value in the plays, but also because, whether willingly or not, he has become the patriarch of a tribe, the genealogy of which may be traced in Harold Jenkins's critical bibliography, 'Shakespeare's History Plays: 1900–1951', *ShS*, VI (1953), 1–15. Since then we have had G. I. Duthie, in chapter V of his *Shakespeare* (London, 1951), assuming that Tillyard's conclusions have now passed into that region of immutability where further criticism is impertinent; then Irving Ribner's *English History Play in the Age of Shakespeare* (Princeton, 1957)—a book that claims to refine on Tillyard, but frequently repeats his errors; and, recently, M. M. Reese, a more intelligent follower, who sees that Shakespeare was 'not by habit a man who thought in slogans' (*The Cease of Majesty* (London, 1961), p. 91) but does not push his criticism of Tillyard far enough to liberate himself from the ethical claustrophobia of *Shakespeare's History Plays*. These writers would no doubt refuse to be lumped together in this way; but they are united by a common determination to attribute to Shakespeare a more timid and unoriginal Christianity than I can find in him, and by an agreement to regard the historical temper of Hall, and the polemic temper of the Homilies, as relevant to the interpretation of the plays.
4 E.g. Tillyard, *Shakespeare's History Plays*, p. 203—Shakespeare's references to the marriage 'are in the very spirit of Hall's title, *The union of the two noble and Illustre Families of Lancaster and York* and his statement in his preface of the "godly matrimony" being "the final end of all dissensions titles and debates."' (Ribner, *English History Play* (Princeton, 1957), pp. 101, 118–20, accepts this view and the large assumption that goes with it: that the primary purpose of the play is to 'display the working out of God's plan' for England.) Tillyard's reference to Hall's *title* is interesting: I have found nothing in Hall which is half so eloquent on the subject of the 'Tudor myth' as Tillyard himself. I suspect the myth mattered less to the Elizabethans than we have been led to believe.
5 *Hol.* III, 740/2 f. and 742/1.

361

6 For evidence that Shakespeare knew the play, see G. B. Churchill, 'Richard III up to Shakespeare', *Palaestra* (Berlin, 1900), pp. 396–528, and J. Dover Wilson's 'Introduction' to his *Richard III* (Cambridge, 1954), pp. xxix–xxxi.

7 I follow the First Folio arrangement and punctuation here, taking the full-stop after 'distress' to represent (as it often does in the Folio) an interrupted sentence. The elaborate editorial emendations to which this passage has been subjected offer nothing to compare with the taut interplay given in the Folio.

8 I.e. after the coronation of Richard, *Hol* III, 737/1.

9 *Hol.* III, 732.

10 In A. P. Rossiter's *Angel with Horns* (London, 1961), pp. 7–8; John Palmer (*Political Characters of Shakespeare* (London, 1945), pp. 65–117) sees Richard largely from this angle as a 'typical and recurrent example of the political leader' (p. 65). See especially p. 101.

11 For other examples, see I. i. 119–20; I. i. 146; I. ii. 104–8; I. iv. 247–8; II. ii. 46, and Rossiter's perceptive comments on the 'dark monarchy' theme in the imagery of the play (*Angel with Horns*, pp. 10–12).

12 A letter to Forbes-Robertson quoted by J. Palmer, *Political Characters of Shakespeare* (London, 1945), pp. 115–16.

13 Both Marston and Heywood make references to, and parodies of, the famous line, in a way that implies that everyone is familiar with it. See H. H. Furness (ed.), *Richard III* (New Variorum Shakespeare) (Philadelphia, 1908), pp. 421–2.

14 W. J. Birch, *An Enquiry into the Religion and Philosophy of Shakespeare* (London, 1848), p. 198.

15 R. G. Moulton, *Shakespeare as Dramatic Artist* (Oxford, 1893), chapter v; and cf. Stopford Brooke, *On Ten Plays of Shakespeare* (London, 1905), pp. 100–1, 108; H. C. Goddard, *The Meaning of Shakespeare* (Chicago, 1960), I, 40; M. M. Reese, *The Cease of Majesty* (London, 1961), pp. 208–14; Tillyard, *op. cit.* pp. 199–200; 212–13.

16 *Hol.* III, 761/1.

17 See Michael Quinn's intelligent article, 'Providence in Shakespeare's Yorkist Plays', *ShQ*, x (1959), 45–52. I discuss the matter more fully in chapter 6.

18 *Shakespeare as Dramatic Artist*, p. 120.

19 From 'Emotion of Multitude', *Essays and Introductions* (London, 1961), p. 215

20 *Hol.* III, 721. The phrase is adapted by Shakespeare in II. iii. 43–4.

21 See J. Dover Wilson's interesting and plausible reconstruction of the way in which this scene was composed: 'The Composition of the Clarence Scenes in "Richard III"', *MLR*, LIII (1958), 211–14.

22 See especially the explicit identification at III. i. 82, with which cf. e.g. *Respublica* (EETS, 1905), ll. 501–5, 560–3, 1245–9, where the Vice's trick

of accidental veracity promptly emended is exemplified. Several critics have commented on Richard as Vice, the most detailed account being in Anne Righter's *Shakespeare and the Idea of the Play* (London, 1962), pp. 95–7.

23 Probabilities favour a production of *The Jew of Malta* prior to 1592, which is the earliest date for the writing of *Richard III*. See J. D. Wilson's edition of *Richard III*, 'Introduction', pp. viii–x, and H. S. Bennett's edition of *The Jew*, 'Introduction', pp. 4–5.

24 *Our Theatres in the Nineties*, II, 285.

25 The obvious parallel at *Macbeth*, III. iv. 135 gives added sharpness to the comparison.

26 *Political Characters of Shakespeare*, p. 113.

27 A. H. Thompson in a note to v. iii. 177 in his Arden edition of *Richard III*.

28 *Angel with Horns*, pp. 4–5.

CHAPTER 6

1 *Institutes*, I, 200 (I. xvi. 3); I, 199 (I. xvi. 2); I, 208 (I. xvi. 9) and I, 204 (I. xvi. 5). Cf. Andreas Gerardus, *A Treatise of Gods Prouidence*, tr. John Ludham (London, [1600?]), sig. Niii^r—'Contingence or Haphazard cannot truely be auouched, where the due knowledge of Gods prouidence is extant...'

2 Andreas Gerardus, *A Treatise of God's Prouidence*, sig. B8^r.

3 *Institutes*, I, 60 (I. v. 7). Cf. Arthur Dent, *A Sermon of Gods Prouidence* (London, 1611), sig. C4^r—'*God* with great wisdome, doth send forth of his treasure all sorts of callamities: sometime by them to punish the wicked, some-time to exercise the Godly with them.'

4 Thomas Blundeville, *The True Order and Methode of wryting and reading Hystories* (London, 1574), sigs. Fiii^{r-v}.

5 *Summa Contra Gentiles*, III, lxiv (p. 152) (my italics).

6 *How Superior Powers Oght to be Obeyd* (Geneva, 1558), p. 49.

7 'Sermon III' in *Works*, ed. Keble (Oxford, 1863), III, 624–5.

8 Juan Huarte, *The Examination of Mens Wits*, tr. Richard Carew (London, 1594), p. 13.

9 *Ibid.* pp. 14, 15–16, 216.

10 Act I, Scene i, in *Plays*, ed. H. H. Wood (London, 1938), II, 238.

11 See 'Sermon III' in *Works*, ed. Keble, III, 629–32.

12 *The Tradition of the Goddess Fortuna in Medieval Philosophy and Literature* (Northampton, Mass., 1922), p. 220 f. Cf. chap. xxv of *The Prince*.

13 See D. C. Allen, 'Renaissance Remedies for Fortune: Marlowe and the "Fortunati"', *SP*, XXXVIII (1941), 188–97.

14 *Hypercritica: or a Rule of Judgement, for writing or reading our History's* [1618], in J. E. Spingarn (ed.), *Seventeenth-Century Critical Essays* (Oxford, 1908), I, 84–5.

15 Concio, translated by Thomas Blundeville in *The True Order and Methode of wryting and reading Hystories*, sig. Fiiᵛ. Cf. L. F. Dean, *Tudor Theories of History Writing* (Contributions in Modern Philology, No. 1) (Ann Arbor, 1947), pp. 2–3.

16 Jean Bodin, *Method for the Easy Comprehension of History* [1566], tr. B. Reynolds (New York, 1945), pp. 17 and 29. This emphasis on 'choise and election' is parallelled in Patrizzi, translated in Blunderville, *op. cit.* sigs. Diʳ and Civʳ.

17 See Irving Ribner's discussion of this process in 'The Idea of History in Marlowe's "Tamburlaine"', *ELH*, xx (1953), 251–66.

18 Jean Bodin, *Method for the Easy Comprehension of History*, tr. B. Reynolds, p. 51; see also pp. 44–5, 51 and 54; and cf. Bacon, *Advancement* (Everyman) (London, 1915), p. 79.

19 Edmund Bolton, *Hypercritica*, in J. E. Spingarn (ed.), *Seventeenth-Century Critical Essays* (Oxford, 1908), I, 93.

20 *Eccl. Pol.* I, 210 (I. iii. 4). I should perhaps note that Hooker is talking here of 'things natural which are not in the number of voluntary agents'. I am not certain that he intended the position to be extended to the human sphere. It would, however, be entirely consistent with his approach elsewhere to make the extension.

21 George Hakewill, *An Apologie of the Power and Providence of God* (Oxford, 1627), sig. C2ʳ; and cf. pp. 27–38.

22 'Sermon III' in *Works*, ed. Keble, III, 636.

23 *Ibid.* III, 633–4.

CHAPTER 7

1 I. Ribner, *The English History Play in the Age of Shakespeare* (Princeton, 1957), p. 131.

2 F. S. Boas, *Christopher Marlowe* (Oxford, 1940), pp. 172–91.

3 Jean de Serres, *A general Inventorie of the History of France*, tr. E. Grimestone (London, 1607).

4 P. H. D. T., *Histoire Tragique et memorable, de Pierre de Gauerston Gentil-homme Gascon jadis le mignon d'Edoüard 2...Dediée a Monseigneur le Duc d'Espernon* ([Paris?], 1588).

5 'The Meaning of "Edward II"', *NP*, xxxII (1934), 11–31.

6 For the primacy of Holinshed as Marlowe's source, see *Edward II*, ed. H. B. Charlton and R. D. Waller (London, 1933), pp. 31–52.

7 *Hol.* III, 340/1, 349/1.

8 *Ibid.* III, 341/2.

9 *Edward II*, ed. Charlton and Waller (London, 1933), note to v. v. 30.

10 'The Honour of the Garter' [1593], ll. 222–4. Charlton and Waller (p. 21 note) are dubious whether this passage in fact refers to Marlowe's play. But its complete irrelevance in context—it is suggested by the mention of a

sixteenth-century Mortimer whom Peele is eulogising—is best explained as the irruption of a theatrical memory still fresh and powerful. It is the *cry* he remembers, which would be odd if he had only read about it.

11 Cf. W. Empson, 'Two Proper Crimes', *The Nation*, CLXIII (1946), 444–5.

12 See C. F. Tucker Brooke, *Life of Marlowe* (London, 1930), pp. 99 and 107.

13 'Marlowe's "Edward II": Power and Suffering', *CQ*, I (1959), 195.

14 A Latin version is printed as *Vita et Mors Edwardi Secundi* in W. Stubbs (ed.), *Chronicles of the Reigns of Edward I, and Edward II*, Rolls series, vol. 76, pt ii.

15 As given by Stow, *Annales* (London, 1615), p. 226.

16 C. Leech, 'Marlowe's "Edward II": Power and Suffering', *CQ*, I (1959), 190–1.

17 W. D. Briggs, in his edition (London, 1914) of *Edward II*, was the first to point out the similarity. If Shakespeare was a Pembroke's man and acted in Marlowe's history-play—a fact which would explain the odd and unauthorised appearance of 'Tressel' (Trussel) and 'Berkeley' as attendants on Lady Anne in *Richard III*, when Shakespeare was casting about for a couple of incidental names—there could be more than coincidental resemblance involved.

18 A. P. Rossiter in the 'Introduction' to *Woodstock: a Moral History* (London, 1946), p. 65. (Of Marlowe's characters generally, not of this play specifically.)

19 Rossiter again, *op. cit.* p. 65.

20 Harry Levin counted 110 usages of this kind. See *The Overreacher* (London, 1954), p. 115.

21 *The Golden Labyrinth* (London, 1962), p. 58. The whole section on Marlowe, though brief, is extremely penetrating.

22 Thus Charlton and Waller in the Introduction to their edition, p. 63.

23 *Poetry and Humanism* (London, 1950), p. 86 and preceding pages.

24 'Marlowe's "Edward II": Power and Suffering', *CQ*, I (1959), 195.

25 *The Golden Labyrinth*, p. 58.

26 Quoted (without a reference) by Mario Praz, 'Christopher Marlowe', *Eng. Studs.* XIII (1931), 211.

27 Quoted by Charlton and Waller, *op. cit.* p. 54. Lamb had a similarly high opinion of the play. See his *Complete Works*, ed. E. V. Lucas (London, 1903), I, 42.

28 *Edward II*, ed. Charlton and Waller, p. 64.

29 *Ibid.* pp. 55 and 56.

CHAPTER 8

1 L. B. Campbell, *Shakespeare's 'Histories': Mirrors of Elizabethan Policy* (San Marino, 1947), pp. 170–200.

2 *Ibid.* pp. 3–4, 197, 212.

3 *Ibid.* pp. 213, 245.

4 *Ibid.* chapter XI, especially p. 125. Irving Ribner (*The English History Play*, Princeton, 1957) follows her in this highly dubious procedure.

5 *Caelica*, Sonnets CI and LXXVII in *Certaine Learned and Elegant Workes* (London, 1633), pp. 225 and 247–8.

6 J. F. Danby, *Shakespeare's Doctrine of Nature* (London, 1949), pp. 51–2.

7 Irving Ribner makes this point in an Appendix to a book which has nevertheless (inexplicably) treated Elizabethan political thought as if it were epitomised in the Homily. See his *English History Play* (Princeton, 1957), p. 314.

8 See George Buchanan's attack on this notion in *De Jure Regni apud Scotos* [1579], tr. C. F. Arrowood (Austin, Texas, 1949), pp. 46–7.

9 *Eccl. Pol.* I, 239 (I. x. 1).

10 *Ibid.* I, 250 (I. x. 12).

11 Thomas Starkey, *A Dialogue between Reginald Pole and Thomas Lupset*, ed. K. M. Burton (London, 1948), p. 26.

12 L. J. Vives, *An Introduction to Wysedome*, tr. R. Morrison [London, 1544], sig. A viii^v.

13 *Institutes*, II, 1519 (IV. xx. 31).

14 *Eccl. Pol.* III, 343–4 (VIII. ii. 5), and I, 245–6 (I. x. 8).

15 This ideal of mutuality is treated excellently by L. C. Knights in two important studies, to which my debt will be obvious: 'Shakespeare's Politics: with some Reflections on the Nature of Tradition', and 'Poetry, Politics, and the English Tradition', both reprinted in *Further Explorations* (London, 1965).

16 The theory of the king's two bodies is treated in a masterly book of that name by E. Kantorowicz (*The King's Two Bodies*, Princeton, 1957), upon which I have drawn in this paragraph.

17 Robert Parsons, *A Conference about the Next Succession to the Crowne of England* [Antwerp?], 1594; John Ponet, *A Shorte Treatise of Politike Power* [Strasbourg], 1556.

18 Tr. [W. Walker] (London, 1648), p. 36.

19 Thomas Bilson, *The True Difference between Christian Subiection and Vnchristian Rebellion*... (Oxford, 1585), sig. Av^r; John Carpenter, *A Preparatiue to Contentation* (London, 1597), p. 162 and p. 161 marg.; Robert Parsons, *A Conference about the Next Succession*, pt II, p. 68; and Christopher Goodman, *How Superior Powers Oght to be Obeyd* (Geneva, 1558), p. 185.

20 G. Buchanan, *De Jure Regni*, ed. cit. p. 12.

21 This notion, in its pure form, is surprisingly rare however. Charles Merbury (*A Briefe Discourse of Royall Monarchie* (London, 1581), p. 43) appears to espouse it, but elsewhere (pp. 16–36) he argues only that an hereditary monarchy is the most convenient form of government. John Aylmer, in

An Harborowe for faithfull and trewe subiectes [Strasbourg?], 1559, sig. M2ᵛ, similarly appears to be urging the divine origins of monarchy, but elsewhere he defends the 'mixte' rule as being better than 'mere Monarchie' (sig. H3ʳ).

22 A sixteenth-century commonplace: see George Buchanan, *De Jure Regni*, *ed. cit.* p. 57; Robert Parsons, *A Conference about the Next Succession*, p. 3; John Ponet, *A Shorte Treatise of Politike Power*, sig. Aivᵛ; Thomas Smith, *De Republica Anglorum* (London, 1583), p. 17; Hooker speaks for most when he says that, the kinds of government being many, 'Nature tieth not to any one, but leaveth the choice as a thing arbitrary'—*Eccl. Pol.* I, 243 (I. x. 5).

23 The contractual idea is almost universal, though naturally stressed most by advocates of resistance: see *Vindiciae contra Tyrannos* (London, 1648), pp. 46, 47, 51–61; John Ponet, *A Shorte Treatise of Politike Power*, sigs. Aviiʳ⁻ᵛ, Gvᵛ–viʳ; Robert Parsons, *A Conference about the Next Succession*, pp. 24, 73; George Buchanan, *De Jure Regni*, *ed. cit.* pp. 52, 54, 107, 108; Thomas Bilson significantly puts the doctrine in the mouth of the Jesuit in his dialogue, *The True Difference between Christian Subiection and Vnchristian Rebellion*, p. 341; Hooker—*Eccl. Pol.* III, 349–51 (VIII. ii. 9–11)—manages to accommodate contractualism to non-resistance, by locating the original contract in the mists of antiquity, and constituting Custom as its guardian.

24 This axiom, again, is almost universally admitted. The medieval formula had been *Rex infra et supra legem*, the king as *imago aequitatis* as well as *aequitatis servus*. The historical Richard claimed the *imago* without the *servus*—'*quod leges suae erant in ore suo, et aliquotiens in pectore suo: Et quod ipse solus posset mutare et condere leges regni sui.*' (See E. Kantorowicz, *The King's Two Bodies*, pp. 96, 144, 28 n. and *passim*.) But in the sixteenth century the stress fell on *servus* and *infra*, even among defenders of what we should now call royal absolutism, like Charles Merbury (*A Briefe Discourse of Royall Monarchie*, pp. 44–5). Hooker, as so often, speaks for the bulk of English opinion when he says the king's power 'is termed supremacy, as being the highest, not simply without exception of any thing. For what man is there so brainsick, as not to except in such speeches God himself...? Besides, where the law doth give him dominion, who doubteth but that the king who receiveth it must hold it of and under the law?'—*Eccl. Pol.* III, 342 (VIII. ii. 3).

25 E.g. John Carpenter, *A Preparatiue to Contentation*, p. 156.

26 E.g. *Vindiciae contra Tyrannos*, pp. 80–94; John Ponet, *A Shorte Treatise of Politike Power* [Strasbourg], 1556, sigs. Eviiiʳ f.

27 Thomas Starkey, *A Dialogue between Pole and Lupset*, *ed. cit.* pp. 100 and 151.

28 *Gorboduc*, v. i. 50–1. Such dogmatism is the more interesting for the fact that, one scene later, the play insists on the principle of consent in government (see v. ii. 152–9). The contradiction has been traced to the politics

of the two authors, by Sara R. Watson, '"Gorboduc" and the Theory of Tyrannicide', *MLR*, xxxiv (1939), 355–66.

29 *Vindiciae contra Tyrannos*, p. 5; Robert Parsons, *A Conference about the Succession*, p. 35; John Ponet, *A Shorte Treatise of Politike Power*, sig. Biii^r. As we might expect from men with a more intimate knowledge of political affairs, Thomas Starkey (in *A Dialogue between Pole and Lupset*, ed. cit. p. 99) and Thomas Smith (in *De Republica Anglorum*, pp. 7–8) confine themselves to remarks on the evil effects of absolute power on both governor and governed.

30 E.g. Charles Merbury, *A Briefe Discourse of Royall Monarchie*, pp. 1–2, 41–3.

31 Hooker, within a few pages, adopts *both* positions: 'By which of these means soever [conquest or divine appointment] it happen that kings and governors be advanced to their states, we must acknowledge both their lawful choice to be approved of God, and themselves to be God's lieutenants . . .'—*Eccl. Pol.* III, 344 (VIII. ii. 5); and cf. III, 349 (VIII. ii. 8)—'in case it do happen that without right of blood a man . . . be possessed, all those things [coronation rites, etc.] are utterly void, they make him no indefeasible estate, the inheritor by blood may dispossess him as an usurper'. The clash of these two incompatible principles is, in part, the subject of Shakespeare's whole history cycle.

32 On this issue Holinshed, with characteristic ingenuousness, gets himself into hot water with his providential moralising. Not only is Bolingbroke an impudent rebel, 'for which both he and his lineall race were scourged afterwards', his rise to power also reflects 'the prouidence of God . . . & his secret will' which, Holinshed tells us somewhat gratuitously, is 'to be woondered at' (III, 508/2 and 499/2). The tangle is Holinshed's personal contribution to Hall's version. Parsons, in *A Conference about the Succession*, pp. 60–8, uses Richard's deposition, and its beneficial effects, with considerable perspicacity as an argument for political action against unsatisfactory monarchs.

33 A well-aimed barb from Robert Parsons, *A Conference about the Succession*, p. 62, which must have galled the flank of the administration. Burghley made notes from Parsons's tract—see E. W. Talbert, *The Problem of Order* (Chapel Hill, 1962), pp. 66–7.

34 John Carpenter, *A Preparatiue to Contentation*, pp. 156–7.

35 Robert Parsons, *A Conference about the Succession*, pp. 32–3.

36 *Vindiciae contra Tyrannos*, p. 119.

37 Christopher Goodman, *How Superior Powers Oght to be Obeyd* (Geneva, 1558), p. 110.

38 John Ponet, *A Shorte Treatise of Politike Power*, sigs. Fviii^{r–v}.

39 *The True Difference between Christian Subiection and Vnchristian Rebellion*, p. 341 marg.

40 *A Shorte Treatise of Politike Power*, sigs. Gviii^{r–v}.

41 *Ibid.* sig. Diii^r (my italics).

42 *De Republica Anglorum*, p. 6.

43 Edmund Bolton, listing the 'Places of Danger, Syrts, Shallows, and Rocks of most Mischief' that threaten the historian: *Hypercritica* [1618?], in J. E. Spingarn (ed.), *Seventeenth-century Critical Essays* (Oxford, 1908), I, 105.

44 My attention was drawn to Smith by E. W. Talbert's intelligent study of him in *The Problem of Order* (Chapel Hill, 1962). The book provides elaborate documentation of the 'dialogue' element in sixteenth-century political thought, and has made it possible for me to sketch in outlines which would otherwise require extensive argument.

45 *De Republica Anglorum*, pp. 4 and 5.

46 *Eccl. Pol.* I, 482 (IV. xiv. 2).

CHAPTER 9

1 His presence is discernible throughout I. ii, and also at II. i. 105, 124–31, 165, 179, 182; II. ii. 100–2; and he is the subject of acrimonious dispute at the opening of IV. i.

2 See *Hol.* III, 488–90.

3 Cf. M. M. Mahood's excellent exposition of this 'dancing tattoo of language' in her *Shakespeare's Wordplay* (London, 1957), p. 76.

4 Dover Wilson may be correct in regarding this tangle (ll. 131–8) as due to the superimposition of two alternative MS drafts of the same passage. See his *Richard II* (Cambridge, 1939), p. 141. H. C. Goddard, *The Meaning of Shakespeare* (Chicago, 1960), I, 151–2, claims the speech as a Shakespearian exposure of Richard the 'arch-rhetorician' who betrays insincerity by self-contradiction; but the explanation is as complicated as the speech is confusing.

5 D. A. Traversi's chapter on *Richard II* (*Shakespeare from 'Richard II' to 'Henry V'* (London, 1958)) is excellent on the use of rhetoric in the play.

6 'Bolingbroke's "Decision"', *ShQ*, II (1951), 30 (reprinted in abridged form in *Unity in Shakespearean Tragedy* (New York, 1956)).

7 *Political Characters of Shakespeare* (London, 1945), p. 134.

8 See M. M. Mahood's exposition of this speech in *Shakespeare's Wordplay*, p. 82.

9 M. M. Reese, *The Cease of Majesty* (London, 1961), p. 254.

10 A. P. Rossiter, *Angel with Horns* (London, 1961), p. 38.

11 See Coleridge's *Shakespearean Criticism* (Everyman), II, 148–9.

12 E. W. Talbert (*The Problem of Order* (Chapel Hill, 1962), p. 163 and *passim*) has some perceptive comments on this speech and on the scene in general.

13 Dover Wilson, predictably, regards this as 'a loose thread from an old play' (*Richard II* (Cambridge, 1939), p. 181), but the 'Old Play' hypothesis has been well answered by Peter Ure in his Arden edn (London, 1956), pp. xlvi, l–li, and *passim*.

14 Some editors doubt the authenticity of the second 'here Cousin', but the words occur in both Quarto and Folio texts.

15 *The Meaning of Shakespeare* (Chicago, 1960), I, 155.

16 *Women in Love*, chapter II—'Shortlands' (my italics).

17 '"The King is not himself": the Personal Tragedy of Richard II', *SP*, LVI (1959), 169–70.

18 Swinburne's phrase, in perhaps the most preposterous example of this line of argument (*Prose Works*, ed. Gosse and Wise (London, 1926), I, 258).

19 Traversi, *Shakespeare from 'Richard II' to 'Henry V'*, p. 30.

20 This subject is treated (albeit somewhat unsatisfactorily) by J. A. S. McPeek, 'Richard II and his Shadow World', *American Imago*, XV (1958), 195–212.

21 Johnson, however, regards the deviation as Shakespeare's not Richard's. See his note to III. iii. 157.

22 Cf. L. C. Knights, *Shakespeare: the Histories* (London, 1962), p. 35.

23 Traversi, *Shakespeare from 'Richard II' to 'Henry V'*, p. 40.

24 See L. F. Dean, '"Richard II": the State and the Image of the Theatre', *PMLA*, LXVII (1952), 211–18.

25 Richard's paralysis in a posture of grief is duplicated in the diminishing mirror of the queen, the inexplicable, absolute nature of the 'nameless woe' becoming explicit there (see esp. II. ii. 1–40).

26 *Shakespeare from 'Richard II' to 'Henry V'*, p. 31.

27 Note to III. ii. 207–8.

28 This significant pattern was pointed out first, I think, by Brents Stirling, 'Bolingbroke's "Decision"', *ShQ*, II (1951), 33–4.

29 G. W. Knight, *The Imperial Theme* (London, 1931), p. 358, and *passim*; R. M. Frye, *Shakespeare and Christian Doctrine* (Princeton, 1963), pp. 131–2.

30 Michael Quinn, '"The King is not himself": the Personal Tragedy of Richard II', *SP*, LVI (1959), 185; Reese, *The Cease of Majesty*, p. 246.

31 'At Stratford-on-Avon', *Essays and Introductions* (London, 1961), pp. 102–6. Yeats's version of Richard, however, suffers from accepting him too much at his own valuation.

32 E. M. W. Tillyard, *Shakespeare's History Plays* (London, 1944), p. 250.

33 Parker Tyler, 'Phaeton: the Metaphysical tension between Ego and Universe in English Poetry', *Accent,* XVI (1956), 29–30.

34 Tillyard has some intelligent things to say concerning the historical theme in *Richard II* (*Shakespeare's History Plays*, pp. 251–9).

35 G. W. Knight, *The Sovereign Flower* (London, 1958), p. 28.

36 Cf. Yeats's remark on the Shakespeare of the histories: 'He meditated as Solomon, not as Bentham meditated, upon blind ambitions, untoward accidents, and capricious passions, and the world was almost as empty in his eyes as it must be in the eyes of God' (*Essays and Introductions* (London, 1961), pp. 106–7). This is an important, but only a partial, truth. The words describe the author of *Deidre of the Sorrows* better than the author of *Richard II*.

CHAPTER 10

1 See E. T. Withington, 'Dr John Weyer and the Witch Mania', in Charles Singer (ed.), *Studies in the History and Method of Science* (Oxford, 1917), p. 191. The canon *Episcopi*, which was accepted as carrying apostolic authority, had declared the nocturnal flights of witches to be mere delusion and ordered the accused women to be treated accordingly. Sprenger and Institor, in order to justify their own inquisitorial witch-burnings, had to fabricate a wire-drawn reinterpretation of this canon: see *Malleus Maleficarum* [1489], tr. M. Summers (London, 1928), pp. 3–4 (I, Q. 1).

2 *De Praestigiis Daemonum, et incantationibus* (Basel, 1566). The book was well known in England, as constant marginal references show. Dr John Dee was lending it to interested friends in 1597. See his *Private Diary*, ed. J. O. Halliwell (Camden Society) (London, 1842), p. 57. See also Gregory Zilboorg, *The Medical Man and the Witch During the Renaissance* (Baltimore, 1935).

3 *The Discouerie of Witchcraft*, ed. B. Nicholson (London, 1886), 'Epistle to Sir Roger Manwood', p. x.

4 See *Ibid.* Introduction, pp. xliv–xlv. I have found several other approving comments, besides the ones Nicholson gives. But the influence of the book is best measured by the number of refutations it provoked, among them James I's *Daemonologie* (1597), George Gifford's *Discourse of the Subtill Practises of Deuilles* (1587), and Henry Holland's *A Treatise against Witchcraft* (1590).

5 Louis Lavater, *Of Ghostes and Spirites* [1572], ed. J. D. Wilson and M. Yardley (Oxford, 1929), p. 6.

6 *Ibid.* pp. 9–13; John Deacon and John Walker, *Dialogicall Discourses of Spirits and Divels* (London, 1601), Fifth Dialogue.

7 See Thomas Adams, *The Diuells Banket* (London, 1614), p. 172; Thomas Nashe, 'The Terrors of the Night', *Works*, ed. McKerrow (London, 1910), I, 348 and 378; Lavater, *op. cit.* pp. 14–16.

8 Samuel Harsnett's *A Discovery of the fraudulent practises of Iohn Darrel* (London, 1599) is a good example of this rationalistic temper.

9 See G. L. Kittredge, *Witchcraft in Old and New England* (New York, 1956), chap. XVII, and H. N. Paul, *The Royal Play of 'Macbeth'* (New York, 1950), pp. 75–130.

10 *A Briefe Discourse of a disease called the Suffocation of the Mother... Wherein is declared that diuers strange actions and passions of the body of man, which in the common opinion are imputed to the Diuell, haue their true naturall causes...* (London, 1603), sigs. A3ʳ, A2ᵛ–A3ʳ, 24ᵛ.

11 See for example J. Deacon and J. Walker, *Dialogicall Discourses* (London, 1601), p. 326; Scot, *Discouerie, ed. cit.* pp. 125–6 (VIII. i).

12 Quoted and translated by H. A. Mason in his *Humanism and Poetry in the Early Tudor Period* (London, 1959), p. 95.

13 Nashe, *Works*, ed. McKerrow, I, 349–50.

14 *Abailard's Ethics*, tr. J. R. McCallum (Oxford, 1935), p. 7.

15 *Of Ghostes and Spirites*, ed. J. D. Wilson and M. Yardley (Oxford, 1929), p. 52.

16 *Ibid*. p. 185.

17 The commonest accusation levelled against the masters of conjuring is that of 'legerdemain': see Scot, *Discouerie*, p. 237 (XIII. i); Deacon and Walker, *Dialogicall Discourses* (London, 1601), pp. 3, 124 and 326; Samuel Harsnett, *A Discovery of the fraudulent practises of Iohn Darrel* (London, 1599), sigs. A 2ᵛ–A 3ʳ and 16–17. Even those writers committed to a defence of supernatural agency admit that there is much juggling masquerading as occult mastery: see Lambert Daneau, *A Dialogue of Witches* (London, 1575), sig. Biiᵛ; George Gifford, *A Discourse of the Subtill Practises of Deuilles* (London, 1587), sig. A2ʳ; Henry Holland, *A Treatise against Witchcraft* (Cambridge, 1590), sig. E3ᵛ; Nashe, *Works*, ed. McKerrow, I, 378; Lavater, whose main task is to discuss the 'ghostes and spirites' that *do* walk by night, nevertheless spends his first eleven chapters discussing those that don't—the spurious apparitions; see *Of Ghostes and Spirites Walking by Nyght*, ed. cit. pp. 9–53.

18 *Works*, ed. McKerrow, I, 364.

19 See Aquinas, *ST*, III (Supplement), Q. XCVII, art. vii; Adam Hyll, *The Defence of the Article: Christ descended into Hell* (London, 1592), sig. 25ᵛ; 'The Complaint of Dives', in Anthony Munday's *Mirrour of Mutabilitie* (London, 1579), sig. Civʳ; and Robert Horne, *Of the Rich Man and Lazarus* (London, 1619), pp. 76–80.

20 *City of God*, tr. M. Dods (Edinburgh, 1913), II, 377 (XX. xvi); but cf. II, 433 (XXI. ix).

21 Robert Bolton, *Of the Foure Last Things* (London, 1632), pp. 95–6.

22 Edward Dering, *A bryefe and necessary Catechisme* (London, 1577), sig. Biʳ.

23 Thomas Adams, *The Diuells Banket* (London, 1614), p. 186.

24 Robert Bolton, *Of the Foure Last Things* (London, 1632), pp. 101–2.

25 Thomas Adams, *The Diuells Banket* (London, 1614), p. 188.

26 *Discouerie*, ed. cit. p. 426.

27 *Works*, ed. McKerrow, I, 367.

28 The bibliography of this dispute is as follows: in 1598 an account of Somers's exorcising was published anonymously as *A Briefe Narration of the possession, dispossession, and, repossession of William Sommers*. Apparently there was criticism, for, soon afterwards, the exorciser, John Darrell, published *An Apologie, or defence of the possession of William Sommers...Wherein this worke of God is cleared from the evil name of counterfaytinge* (no publication details given). He was then attacked by S. H. (Samuel Harsnett, later Archbishop of York) in *A Discovery of the fraudulent practises of Iohn Darrel* (London, 1599). Darrell countered with [*A Detection of the S*]*innfvl, Shamfvl, Lying, and Ridiculous discours, of Samuel Harshnet* (?, 1600) and published at the same time an account *Of the Strange and Greuous vexation by the devil of 7*.

persons in Lancashire, another of his cures. A fellow minister, George More, now imprisoned with Darrell for his part in the affair, published his own account of the Lancashire possessions in *A True Discourse concerning the certaine possession and dispossession of seven persons... which also may serve as part of an answere to a fayned and false Discoverie* (?, 1600). In 1601, Deacon and Walker published the *Dialogicall Discourses*. Darrell continued to publish recriminatory 'defences' until 1602. H. N. Paul, *The Royal Play of 'Macbeth'* (New York, 1950), pp. 75–130, gives a convenient brief account of the case and of some others of the same kind, in which he connects the attack on the exorcisers with Bishop Bancroft's campaign against the Puritans.

29 *Dialogicall Discourses* (London, 1601), p. 10.

30 *Works*, ed. McKerrow, I, 219–20.

31 *Institutes*, I, 178 (I. xix).

32 *Dialogicall Discourses* (London, 1601), pp. 17, 50 and 45.

33 *Ibid.* pp. 63 and 50.

34 Lambert Daneau, *A Dialogue of Witches* (London, 1575), sig. Ei^r.

35 R. H. West, *The Invisible World* (Athens, Georgia, 1939), p. 165.

CHAPTER II

1 Cf. L. C. Knights's diagnosis of an unresolved conflict in Marlowe between anarchic infantilism and a mature acceptance of the limits of reality: 'The Strange Case of Christopher Marlowe', *Further Explorations* (London, 1965), pp. 75–98.

2 I am assuming the late date for *Faustus* (see J. D. Jump's argument for this in his edition of the play (London, 1962), pp. xxiv–xxvi). The lines re-modelled include vi. 99–101; xviii. 99–100, 101, 106–7; xix. 136–44, 142, 146, 148, 157, 160; the parallels are noted by Jump. In addition cf. xix. 183 with *I Tam.* v. ii. 237, and xix. 156 with *I Tam.* v. ii. 179.

3 See Appendix B: 'A Note on the Authorship of *Faustus*'.

4 I am thinking of critical accounts like those of Clifford Davidson, 'Doctor Faustus of Wittenberg', *SP*, LIX (1962), 514–23; W. W. Greg, 'The Damnation of Faustus', *MLR*, XLI (1946), 105–6; or B. Langston, 'Marlowe's "Faustus" and the "Ars moriendi" Tradition', *G. C. Taylor Studies* (Chapel Hill, 1952), pp. 148–67.

5 The charge is Una Ellis-Fermor's in her *Christopher Marlowe* (London, 1927), pp. 62–3. George Santayana presents this view in its most exaggerated form in his *Three Philosophical Poets* (Cambridge, Mass., 1910), pp. 146–50. J. B. Steane deals well with this perversity in an Appendix headed '"Doctor Faustus": the Diabolonian Interpretation' (*Marlowe: a Critical Study* (Cambridge, 1964), pp. 365–9).

6 Clarence Green, 'Doctor Faustus: Tragedy of Individualism', *Science and Society*, X (1946), 275–83.

7 'An Oration on the Dignity of Man', in E. Cassirer *et al. The Renaissance Philosophy of Man* (Chicago, 1948), pp. 224–5.

8 See F. A. Yates, *Giordano Bruno and the Hermetic Tradition* (London, 1964), chapter v, pp. 84–116.

9 Sebastian Franck, *De Arbore Scientiae boni et mali* [1561], tr. 1640 and reprinted Glasgow, 1888, p. 12.

10 Thomas Wright, *The Passions of the Minde in generall* (London, 1604), p. 315. This is part of a discussion (pp. 312–16) of 'Curiositie in knowing things not necessarie'.

11 Thomas Adams, *The Diuells Banket* (London, 1614), p. 182. Cf. also L. J. Vives, *An Introduction to Wysedome*, tr. R. Morrison [London, 1544], sig. Civ^r, and Phillip Stubbes, *The Anatomy of Abuses* (*The Second Part*), ed. F. J. Furnivall (London, 1877–82), pp. 56–7, for similar sentiments.

12 H. A. Mason (*Humanism and Poetry in the Early Tudor Period* (London, 1959), pp. 27–36) does an effective job of demolition on the pretensions of these self-styled torch-bearers of culture.

13 S. Kierkegaard, *The Sickness unto Death*, tr. W. Lowrie (New York, 1953), p. 164.

14 Lascelles Abercrombie formulates the meaning of the Faust myth thus in *The Idea of Great Poetry* (London, 1925), p. 161.

15 See J. B. Steane's intelligent and balanced analysis of the evidence for Marlowe's intellectual and religious rebellion, in *Marlowe: a Critical Study*, pp. 17–26. P. Kocher is also interesting, though less cautious, on the subject of Marlowe's religious thought: see his *Christopher Marlowe* (Chapel Hill, 1946), pp. 21–172.

16 There is a good summary of the position of natural magic in R. H. West, *The Invisible World* (Athens, Georgia, 1939), pp. 45–7. The methods of 'white' magic are fully described in Agrippa's *Occult Philosophy* (tr. J. F., London, 1651), the last twelve chapters of which are devoted to the rites of purification.

17 The conflict between literal and metaphorical views of the efficacy of the conjuror's incantation has been used by editors to prove dual authorship. See W. W. Greg, *Marlowe's 'Doctor Faustus'* (Oxford, 1950), pp. 102 f. and J. D. Jump (ed.), *Doctor Faustus* (London, 1962), p. xliv. But the contradiction is built into the play. Cf. the literal efficacy implicit in the description of the Magic Books given Faustus by Mephostophilis and Lucifer (v. 160–5 and vi. 175–6)—and this in scenes which are not suspected of being the work of the ubiquitous interpolator. In fact the two accounts of the incantation simply reflect a tension in demonological theory in Marlowe's day.

18 See the reference in Henslowe's property list of 1598 to 'j dragon in fostes' (*Henslowe's Diary*, ed. R. A. Foakes and R. T. Rickert (Cambridge, 1961), p. 321).

19 See, for instance, *I Tam.* II. vi. 5–8; IV. ii. 26–9; IV. iv. 17–22, 38; V. ii.

155–7, 179–84, 193–5; *II Tam.* I. vi. 16–20; II. iii. 18–26; III. ii. 11–13; III. v. 24–9; v. i. 44–6. And cf. *Jew*, III. iv. 96–100; *Massacre*, xix. 10–11 and *Ed. II*, IV. vi. 87–9.

20 From a description of a performance at the Fortune. See J. D. Jump (ed.), *Doctor Faustus*, p. lxi. The tone of the description suggests that this aspect of the play was beginning to appear rather tiresome to the gentlemen-viewers of 1620.

21 Much of this commentary draws on the perceptive essay by James Smith in *Scrutiny*, VIII (1939), 36–55.

22 *Christopher Marlowe* (London, 1927), pp. 62–3.

23 *Works*, ed. McKerrow (London, 1910), I, 351–2.

24 If J. D. Jump is right in glossing 'tire', 'exhaust yourselves' (*Doctor Faustus*, p. 9), this is a very odd usage. But the other explanations ('*attire*' or 'tire' in the sense of tearing flesh from a carcass) are no more satisfactory. Nor is the A-text 'trie'.

25 *Of the Vanitie and Vncertaintie of Artes and Sciences*, tr. J. Sanford (London, 1569), sigs. 64ʳ, 20ᵛ and 21ʳ.

26 *Ibid.* chap. 82.

27 *Ibid.* sig. 160ʳ.

28 *Humanism and Poetry*, pp. 64–74.

29 The same persistent deflation of Faustus's ambitions is carried on in the Clown sequences, whose relation to the main action is well plotted by Robert Ornstein in 'The Comic Synthesis in "Doctor Faustus"', *ELH*, XXII (1955), 165–72. But Ornstein seems prepared to excuse too much, even to the extent of referring the fact that the Clowns are not very funny, to an 'honesty of comic realism'—i.e. real Clowns are not really funny. But the scenes are neither good nor integral enough to qualify for the title of a 'comic synthesis'.

30 See J. T. McCullen, 'Doctor Faustus and Renaissance Learning', *MLR*, LI (1956), 9, for suggestions about the way an Elizabethan might have taken this syllogism. Like most contentions about 'the Elizabethan audience' McCullen's conclusions are to be regarded with caution.

31 'A Dialogue between the Christian Knight and Satan', *The Catechism of Thomas Becon etc.* (Parker Society) (Cambridge, 1844), pp. 626–33.

32 See Lynette and Eveline Feasey, 'Marlowe and the Christian Humanists', *Notes and Queries*, CXCVI (1951), 267.

33 See Lily B. Campbell, '"Doctor Faustus": a Case of Conscience', *PMLA*, LXVII (1952), 219–39. The Spira case was dramatised by Nathaniel Woodes as *The Conflict of Conscience* (1575), and is printed, in its revised form, in Dodsley, vol. VI. I shall be having more to say about Spira in particular, and Calvinist theology in general, in the next chapter.

34 That there was an 'atheistic orthodoxy', certain well-defined channels in which dissent naturally ran, is well argued by George Buckley in his

Atheism in the English Renaissance (Chicago, 1932). The congruence between this kind of free-thought, the opinions attributed to Marlowe by Baines and Kyd, and Faustus's scepticism, is very close indeed.

35 By Pomponazzi, amongst others. See L. Thorndike, *A History of Magic, and Experimental Science* (New York, 1914), v, 104–5.

36 I find myself in disagreement with F. R. Johnson ('Marlowe's Astronomy and Renaissance Scepticism', *ELH*, XIII (1946), 241–54) who is anxious to vindicate Marlowe as an advanced astronomical thinker. But since there were Copernicans in England, a minute divergence from Ptolemy hardly constitutes advanced thought. The speaker, in any case, is Mephostophilis, not Marlowe.

37 *Scrutiny*, VIII (1939), 47.

38 *The Repentance of Robert Greene* [1592] (Bodley Head Quartos, VI) (London, 1923), p. 11.

39 I borrow the term from a sixteenth-century manual of spiritual counsel which deals intelligently with Faustus's kind of malady. Singularity, according to the author, is 'when a parson so restyth to his owne opinion and to his owne reson that he wyll not beleue eny other nor folowe the coũseyl of eny other...' and it proceeds from a *servile* fear of God, where there should be a *filial* fear—William Bonde, *A... Treatyse for them that ben Tymorouse and fearefull in Conscience* [London, 1535], sig. viiiᵛ.

40 *Marlowe: a Critical Study* (Cambridge, 1964), p. 159; the pages that follow this comment bear closely on my argument here.

41 'Milton's "Satan" and the Theme of Damnation in Elizabethan Tragedy', *Essays and Studies*, I (1948), 50–1. See also James Smith's essay in *Scrutiny*, VIII (1939), 36–55, the whole purpose of which is to demonstrate the integrity of the final scene in the play as a whole.

42 E.g. *I Tam.*, I. ii. 50–1; III. ii. 77–81; *II Tam.* II. ii. 13–15.

43 So D.J. Palmer in 'Magic and Poetry in "Doctor Faustus"', *CQ*, VI (1964), 65.

44 *Seven Types of Ambiguity* (London, 1930), pp. 261–2.

CHAPTER 12

1 *Summa Theologica*, II–I, Q. LXXIX, art. 4 (pp. 389–90).

2 William Perkins, *A Discourse of Conscience* [1596], in *Works* (Cambridge, 1603), p. 626.

3 William Perkins, *A Golden Chaine: or, Description of Theologie* [1591], in *Works*, p. 123.

4 Cf. Calvin, *Institutes*, II, 951 (III. xxiii. 4); Luther in *Letters of Spiritual Counsel* (London, 1955), pp. 115–17, 132, and Arthur Dent, *The Opening of Heauen Gates* [1610] (London, 1617), p. 59.

5 See *D.N.B.*, under Baro, Whitaker, Perkins and Harsnett.

6 Calvin, *Institutes*, II, 931 (III. xxi. 7).

7 Calvin, *Institutes*, I, 620 (III. iii. 24). Cf. William Perkins, *A Discourse of Conscience*, p. 643; Alexander Hume, *Ane Treatise of Conscience* (Edinburgh, 1594), chapter V; and cf. Paul Kocher's discussion of the distinction between melancholy and penitence in 'Lady Macbeth and the Doctor', *ShQ*, V (1954), 341–4.

8 *Eccl. Pol.* III, 11 (VI. iii. 5).

9 Richard Greenham, *A...Comfort for all those...afflicted in Conscience* (London, 1595), sig. A3ʳ.

10 Alexander Hume, *Ane Treatise of Conscience*, p. 39.

11 *A Discourse of Conscience*, p. 628.

12 Arthur Dent, *The Opening of Heauen Gates* [1610] (London, 1617), p. 37. Elsewhere (p. 75) Dent refers this notion, correctly, to Calvin.

13 William Perkins, *A Discourse of Conscience*, pp. 621, 658 and 660.

14 Arthur Dent, *The Opening of Heauen Gates* [1610] (London, 1617), p. 60.

15 *Institutes*, II, 950 (III. xxiii. 3). Cf. K. O. Myrick's discussion of this strain in Elizabethan thought in 'The Theme of Damnation in Shakespearean Tragedy', *SP*, XXXVIII (1941), 221–45.

16 As given by E. C. S. Gibson, *The Thirty-Nine Articles of the Church of England* (London, 1902), p. 475.

17 Amply documented by L. B. Campbell, '"Doctor Faustus": a Case of Conscience', *PMLA*, LXVII (1952), 225–32.

18 See *D.N.B.*, under Harsnett, Baro.

19 'Sermon I' in *Works*, ed. Keble (Oxford, 1863), III, 469–81.

20 *Sermons*, ed. E. M. Simpson and G. R. Potter (Berkeley, 1953–62), vol. VII, Serm. 14, pp. 352, 360–1.

21 See J. D. Peterson's discussion in 'John Donne's Holy Sonnets and the Anglican Doctrine of Contrition', *SP*, LVI (1959), 504–18, and cf. with Donne's statements, Robert Bolton's in *Instructions for a Right Comforting Afflicted Consciences* [1630] (London, 1635), pp. 473–8, and Hooker's in *Eccl. Pol.* III, 10 (VI. iii. 4).

22 'The II Part of the Sermon of Repentance', *Certaine Sermons or Homilies* (London, 1623), p. 268.

23 *Eccl. Pol.* III, 10–12 (VI. iii. 4–5).

24 Donne's Holy Sonnet IV—'Oh my blacke Soule!'

25 Robert Bolton, *Instructions for a Right Comforting...*, p. 271.

26 'Sermon I', *Works*, ed. Keble (Oxford, 1863), III, 475.

27 Nathaniel Bacon, *A Relation of the fearefull estate of Francis Spira* (London, 1638), pp. 62, 78, 98, 132, 140. Spira was known in England earlier, from a translation of Matteo Gribaldi's account: *Concerning the terrible iudgementes of God, vpon him that...denieth Christ...* (Worcester, 1550, and London, [1570]).

28 '"Doctor Faustus": a Case of Conscience', *PMLA*, LXVII (1952), 219–39.

29 *Sermons*, ed. E. M. Simpson and G. R. Potter (Berkeley, 1953–62), vol. X,

Serm. 4, pp. 117–18. (Italics mine, Donne's own italics removed, with the exception of the Latin phrase.)

CHAPTER 13

1 F. Nietzsche, *The Birth of Tragedy*, tr. F. Golffing (New York, 1956), pp. 4 and 59–60.

2 Roy Walker, *The Time is Free* (London, 1949), p. 175.

3 G. R. Elliott, *Dramatic Providence in 'Macbeth'* (Princeton, 1958), p. 15.

4 *Shakespeare's Philosophical Patterns* (Baton Rouge, 1937), p. vii.

5 G. R. Elliott, *Dramatic Providence in 'Macbeth'*, p. 11.

6 Roy Walker, *The Time is Free*, p. xv.

7 *Shakespearean Tragedy* (London, 1905), p. 348. This continual return to the initial imaginative response is one reason why Bradley's chapters on *Macbeth* remain the best general account of the play.

8 I have been largely convinced by Richard Flatter's case for the soundness of the Folio text, especially in respect of lineation (*Shakespeare's Producing Hand*, New York, 1948, *passim*); and since no modern editor has taken his arguments to heart, it seemed best to use the Folio text, accepting only the old-established emendations, and assisting the general reader by giving line references to Kenneth Muir's Arden edition of 1951.

9 G. R. Elliott, *Dramatic Providence in 'Macbeth'*, p. 48.

10 *Ibid.* p. 28; H. C. Goddard, *The Meaning of Shakespeare* (Chicago, 1960), II, 132; R. Walker, *The Time is Free*, p. 162.

11 'How Many Children had Lady Macbeth?', *Explorations* (London, 1946), pp. 28–9.

12 G. Wilson Knight, *The Wheel of Fire* (London, 1930), pp. 166–7.

13 See H. N. Paul, *The Royal Play of 'Macbeth'* (New York, 1950), pp. 367–87.

14 *Macbeth* (Cambridge, 1960), p. xxxiii.

15 *Explorations* (London, 1946), p. 30.

16 *The Time is Free*, p. 72.

17 The best exposition of this principle that I know is to be found in the excellent chapter on *Macbeth* in L. C. Knights's *Some Shakespearean Themes* (London, 1959), an essay which meets most of the objections I have been raising to 'How Many Children had Lady Macbeth?' by its deepening and broadening of the provenance of this term 'nature'.

18 *Eccl. Pol.* I, 239 (I. x. 1).

19 L. C. Knights, *Some Shakespearean Themes* (London, 1959), p. 135.

20 'The Naked Babe and the Cloak of Manliness', in *The Well-Wrought Urn* (London, 1949), pp. 21–46.

21 John Lawlor, *The Tragic Sense in Shakespeare* (London, 1960), p. 117.

22 Francis Berry's phrase, in an excellent grammatical analysis of the time-themes in *Macbeth* (*Poets' Grammar* (London, 1958), p. 49).

23 Benedetto Croce, *History as the Story of Liberty* (London, 1941), p. 60.

24 B. Croce, *Ariosto, Shakespeare, and Corneille*, tr. D. Ainslie (London, 1920), p. 229.

25 *Character and Society in Shakespeare* (Oxford, 1951), pp. 99 and 97.

26 See e.g. Aquinas, *SCG*, III. i–xv. This phrase occurs in chapter vii (p. 15).

27 *De Libero Arbitrio*, tr. Dom Mark Pontifex (London, 1955), p. 137.

28 *SCG*, III. vi (p. 15).

29 *Agamemnon*, l. 115 (cited by Dover Wilson, *Macbeth* (Cambridge, 1960), p. 137).

30 W. C. Curry, *Shakespeare's Philosophical Patterns* (Baton Rouge, 1937), pp. 53 f.

31 *Shakespearean Tragedy* (London, 1905), pp. 347–8.

32 *Studies in Shakespeare* (London, 1927), p. 119 (my italics).

33 The very different temper of the interpolated Witch scenes, especially III. v, which distinguish sharply between real and 'artificiall Sprights', show us their 'Masters' and generally make prosaically explicit all that is obscure and alarming in the Shakespearian Witches, supports this view. These scenes are the tidying-up operations of mediocrity in the face of the Mystery of Iniquity.

34 This point was drawn to my attention by Dr B. Joseph.

35 G. Wilson Knight, *The Imperial Theme* (London, 1951), p. 139.

36 R. Walker (*The Time is Free*, p. 93) points out the significance of the double construction.

37 F. Nietzsche, *Beyond Good and Evil*, tr. M. Cowan (Chicago, 1955), pp. 20–1.

38 See G. Wilson Knight, *The Wheel of Fire*, p. 133.

39 A case argued with some conviction by C. G. Clarke, 'Darkened Reason in "Macbeth"', *Durham University Journal*, XXII (1960), 11–18.

40 *Angel with Horns* (London, 1961), p. 215.

41 *Shakespearean Criticism*, ed. T. M. Raysor (Everyman) (London, 1960), I, 61.

42 *Beyond Good and Evil*, tr. M. Cowan (Chicago, 1955), p. 22.

43 *Shakespearean Tragedy* (London, 1905), p. 386.

44 Lafeu in *All's Well*, II. iii. 1–6 (my italics). Amongst my other debts to Wilson Knight, it was he who first made me ponder the relevance of this passage to *Macbeth*: see *The Wheel of Fire*, p. 173.

45 I am unconvinced by Dover Wilson's theory (*Macbeth* (Cambridge, 1960), pp. xxxiv–xxxviii) about the lost scene where Macbeth 'broke the enterprise' to her; and since a single, puzzling reference to an off-stage conversation is unlike mature Shakespearian workmanship, I conclude that the remark refers to what we do know (the letter, which was a compromising enough document, if he knew his wife's propensities) or to the unspoken understanding that is common between people who know each other well. Bradley (*Shakespearean Tragedy* (London, 1905), pp. 480–4) has a very sensible discussion of the matter.

46 Søren Kierkegaard, *The Sickness unto Death*, tr. W. Lowrie (New York, 1953), pp. 152–4 (my italics).
47 R. Walker, *The Time is Free*, p. 66.
48 Editorial head-scratching about the correct place to close the inverted commas is thus beside the point. For this effect only Elizabethan punctuation (or the lack of it) will serve.
49 *Shakespearean Tragedy* (London, 1905), p. 362.
50 *Ibid.* p. 378.
51 *The Idea of Great Poetry* (London, 1925), p. 176 (my italics).
52 The 'description of Scotland' prefixed to *The Historie of Scotland* (London, 1585), p. 21.
53 *Shakespearean Criticism*, ed. T. M. Raysor (Everyman) (London, 1960), II, 221.
54 Quoted by H. H. Furness, Variorum *Macbeth* (Philadelphia, 1873), p. 295.
55 'General Macbeth', *Harper's Magazine*, CCXXIV (June 1962), pp. 36–7.
56 Quoted by Kenneth Muir in the Arden *Macbeth*, p. 84.
57 *The Wheel of Fire*, pp. 171–2.
58 *Shakespearean Tragedy*, p. 365.
59 A. P. Rossiter, *Angel with Horns* (London, 1961), p. 227.
60 *The Idea of Great Poetry* (London, 1925), pp. 176–8.
61 *Beyond Good and Evil*, tr. M. Cowan (Chicago, 1955), p. 46.
62 G. B. Shaw, *Our Theatres in the Nineties* (London, 1932), III, 3.
63 F. Nietzsche, *Beyond Good and Evil*, tr. M. Cowan, p. 36.
64 Benedetto Croce, *History as the Story of Liberty* (London, 1941), p. 62.

CHAPTER 14

1 *Shakespeare's Philosophical Patterns* (Baton Rouge, 1937), pp. vii and 137.
2 Virgil K. Whitaker, *Shakespeare's Use of Learning* (San Marino, 1953), pp. 206 and 299.
3 R. M. Frye, *Shakespeare and Christian Doctrine* (Princeton, 1963), p. 15 n.
4 See *Summa Contra Gentiles*, III. i–ii (pp. 1–7), with which cf. *Eccl. Pol.* I, 200 (I. ii. 1); and *SCG*, III. ii (p. 5), with which cf. *Eccl. Pol.* I, 220 (I. vii. 2).
5 *SCG*, III. x (p. 23).
6 *Eccl. Pol.* I, 220 (I. vii. 2).
7 *Ibid.* I, 224 (I. vii. 7).
8 *SCG*, III. i (p. 121); and *ST*, II–I, Q. LXXXV, art. 2.
9 *SCG*, III. xvi (p. 33).
10 *Ibid.* III. iii (p. 7).
11 *Eccl. Pol.* I, 223 (I. vii. 6).
12 Aquinas quoting Dionysus, *SCG*, III. xi (p. 20). Cf. also III. x (p. 21) and III. xv (p. 31).

13 *Ibid.* II. iv (p. 9) and III. v and vi (pp. 14–15).

14 *Eccl. Pol.* I, 224 (I. vii. 7). Cf. *ST*, II–I, Q. LXXV, art. 1; Q. LXXXII, art. 3 and Augustine, *De Libero Arbitrio*, tr. Dom Mark Pontifex (London, 1955), p. 134 (II. 52).

15 *Shakespearean Tragedy* (London, 1905), p. 358.

16 See for example *SCG*, III. xi (p. 29), and *Eccl. Pol.* I, 234 (I. vii. 7) or *ST*, II–I, Q. LXXXV, arts. 1 and 3.

17 *ST*, II–I, Q. LXXXV, art. 2.

18 *De Libero Arbitrio*, tr. Pontifex (London, 1955), pp. 192–3 (III. 51).

19 *SCG*, III. x (p. 24).

20 L. J. Vives, *An Introduction to Wysedome*, tr. R. Morrison [London, 1544], sig. Cii^v. A similar view of Will as 'idle and desperate' in itself is to be found in Arthur Dent's *The Opening of Heauen Gates* (London, 1617), p. 63.

21 Cf. Patrick Cruttwell's diagnosis of a new tone of scepticism and a new complexity of sensibility in the literature of the 1590s, which he characterises as 'the collapse of reason's authority' (*The Shakespearean Moment* (London, 1954), pp. 23 f.).

22 *Works*, ed. Keble (Oxford, 1863), II, 537–8.

23 Arthur Dent, *The Opening of Heauen Gates*, p. 34 marg.

24 Thomas Wright, *The Passions of the Minde* (London, 1604), p. 319.

25 Arthur Dent, *The Opening of Heauen Gates*, p. 47.

26 See especially the fragment Keble prints as 'Appendix I' to book v of *Eccl. Pol.* (II, 537 f.).

27 *De Libero Arbitrio*, tr. Pontifex (London, 1955), p. 35 (I. i).

28 *SCG*, III. lxxi (pp. 176–7). The reader who is tempted to regard this as a momentary and unrepresentative aberration on Aquinas's part can find precisely the same argument employed by Augustine in *De Libero Arbitrio*, *ed. cit.* p. 76 (II. iii), and by Arthur Dent in his *Opening of Heauen Gates*, p. 68. It is, in fact, a commonplace of Christian apologetics.

29 *SCG*, III. lxxi (p. 177).

30 William Perkins, *A Treatise of Gods Free Grace and Mans Free Will*, in *Works* (Cambridge, 1603), p. 874.

31 *Sermons*, ed. E. M. Simpson and G. R. Potter (Berkeley, 1953–62), vol. VI, Sermon 11, p. 231 (my italics).

32 *Ibid.* VI, 238–9.

CHAPTER 15

1 See *Shakespeare's Biblical Knowledge* (London, 1935), esp. pp. 22–3.

2 *Shakespeare and Christian Doctrine* (Princeton, 1963), esp. pp. 9, 12–13 and 57.

3 D. G. James, *Dream of Learning* (Oxford, 1951), p. 78.

4 *Beyond Good and Evil*, tr. M. Cowan (Chicago, 1955), p. 136 (sect. 212).

5 *Ariosto, Shakespeare, and Corneille*, tr. D. Ainslie (London, 1920), p. 291.

6 I am thinking in this paragraph of studies like Patrick Cruttwell's *The Shakespearean Moment* (London, 1954), L. C. Knights's various essays in this area—'Shakespeare's Politics', 'Poetry, Politics and the English Tradition' and 'The Social Background of Metaphysical Poetry', all reprinted in *Further Explorations* (London, 1965), and F. R. Leavis's influential remarks *en passant* in an essay on Joyce (*For Continuity* (Cambridge, 1933), pp. 215–16).

7 This interpretation is based on the evidence amassed by Richmond Noble in *Shakespeare's Biblical Knowledge*, see esp. pp. 36–8, and the 'Index of Biblical Books', pp. 281–300.

8 See *Literature and Dogma*, chapter 1.

9 *II Henry VI*, iii. iii. 31.

10 See R. M. Frye's comments on this passage in *Shakespeare and Christian Doctrine*, pp. 244–6.

11 *Ibid.* p. 199.

12 *Eccl. Pol.* i, 226–7 (i. viii. 3).

13 *Ibid.* i, 257–8 (i. xi. 4).

14 *Ibid.* i, 254 (i. xi. 1).

15 *Ibid.* i, 257 (i. xi. 4).

16 See in this connexion H. D. F. Kitto's interesting essay, 'A Classical Scholar looks at Shakespeare', in *More Talking about Shakespeare* (London, 1959).

17 *Eccl. Pol.* i, 367 (iii. viii. 6).

APPENDIX A

1 William Rowley, *A Search for Money* [1609] (Percy Society Reprint) (London, 1840), ii, 19–21. The portrait may derive from Nashe's usurer with the 'huge woorme-eaten nose, like a cluster of grapes hanging downe-wardes' (*Works*, ed. McKerrow (London, 1910), i, 162); but it may have been so much of a popular tradition as to require no authorisation. Cf. Mammon the Usurer in Marston's *Jack Drum's Entertainment* (*Works*, ed. H. H. Wood (London, 1939), vol. iii), who is described as the owner of a 'firie' nose (p. 187), is humorously allied with the devil (p. 196), and goes about armed with his 'bagges' (p. 197), and suffering from the gout (p. 196). The stage-Jew of the period (Shylock this time) is described by an actor of the 1630s:

> 'His beard was red; his face was made
> Not much unlike a witches.
> His habit was a Jewish gown
> That would defend all weather;
> His chin turn'd up, his nose hung down,
> And both ends met together.'

(Thomas Jordan, cited by H. H. Furness in the Variorum *Merchant of Venice*, Philadelphia, 1888, pp. 461–2.)

2 See Herman Sinsheimer, *Shylock: the History of a Character* (New York, 1964), pp. 58–61. Sinsheimer's discovery, which was first published in 1947, has rendered most of the earlier source theories obsolete. But the book seems to have escaped attention, and the conjectural sources are still being accumulated in the learned journals.

3 Stephen Gosson, *The Schoole of Abuse* (Arber's Reprints) (London, 1906), p. 40.

4 For the historical material available on the question of Jewish communities in Elizabethan London, see Lucien Wolf, 'Jews in Tudor England' in Cecil Roth (ed.), *Essays in Jewish History* (London, 1934), pp. 73–90; Lucien Wolf, 'Jews in Elizabethan England', *Transactions of the Jewish Historical Society of England* [*JHSE*], XI (1924/7), 1–91; 'The Case of Thomas Fernandes before the Lisbon Inquisition', ed. Cecil Roth from the papers of Lucien Wolf, *JHSE Miscellanies*, part II (1935); C. J. Sisson, 'A Colony of Jews in Shakespeare's London', *Essays and Studies*, XXIII (1937), 38–51; A. M. Hyamson, *The Sephardim in England* (London, 1951), chapter 1; E. R. Samuel, 'Portuguese Jews in Jacobean London', *Transactions of the JHSE*, XVIII (1958), 171–230; Cecil Roth, *A History of the Jews in England* (Oxford, 1949), chapter VI; and John Gwyer, 'The Case of Dr Lopez', *Transactions of the JHSE*, XVI (1952), 163–84. J. L. Cardozo (*The Contemporary Jew in Elizabethan Drama*, Amsterdam, 1925) founds some of his argument on material which has since been superseded, but is nevertheless utterly convincing in his defence of the 'mythical' nature of the stage Jew.

5 J. L. Cardozo, *The Contemporary Jew in Elizabethan Drama*, p. 52.

6 See Leon Fisch, *The Dual Image: a Study of the Figure of the Jew in English Literature* (London, 1959), pp. 13–18.

7 See Joshua Trachtenberg, *The Devil and the Jews* (Yale, 1943), pp. 159–63.

8 J. Trachtenberg, *The Devil and the Jews*, pp. 109–23, has a detailed account of the history of this superstition. It is dramatised in *The Conversion of Ser Jonathas the Jewe by Myracle of the Blyssed Sacrament* (*ca.* 1460, reprinted in J. Q. Adams (ed.), *Chief Pre-Shakespearean Dramas*, Cambridge, Mass., 1924), but with a merciful conclusion, which may reflect a difference between the Continental and English climates of Jew-baiting.

9 H. Graetz, *History of the Jews*, tr. B. Löwy (London, 1892), IV, 109. Stow (*Annales* (London, 1615), pp. 219–20) reports that in 1319 'aboue 12000 Jewes' died in Germany alone for 'consenting' to the poisoning of the water-supply by 'Lepars' and 'Sarazens'.

10 Trachtenberg, *The Devil and the Jews*, p. 107.

11 *Ibid.* p. 93.

12 The tangled threads of expediency and crowd-pleasing that led to this execution are admirably extricated by John Gwyer, 'The Case of Dr Lopez', *Transactions of the JHSE*, XVI (1952), 163–84.

13 *Plays*, ed. H. H. Wood (London, 1934), I, 207 (v. iii).

14 Nashe, *Works*, ed. McKerrow (London, 1910), I, 186.

15 *The Devil's Law-Case*, III. ii, in *Dramatic Works*, ed. W. Hazlitt (London, 1857), III, 53–4.

16 See J. L. Cardozo, *The Contemporary Jew in Elizabethan Drama*, pp. 210 f. and Trachtenberg, *The Devil and the Jews*, pp. 33–41.

17 Trachtenberg, *op. cit.* p. 43.

18 Zariph, in Day, Rowley & Wilkins, *The Travailes of Three English Brothers* [1607], quoted by Cardozo, *op. cit.* p. 149.

19 Trachtenberg, *The Devil and the Jews*, pp. 23, 58–64, 58 f. and 210.

20 See Graetz, *History of the Jews*, IV, 518 and Trachtenberg, *The Devil and the Jews*, pp. 90 and 184.

21 Trachtenberg, *op. cit.* pp. 26 and 30.

22 *Merchant of Venice*, II. ii. 28.

23 Cardozo, *The Contemporary Jew*, p. 97.

24 See Trachtenberg, *The Devil and the Jews*, pp. 124–39. Percy (*Reliques of Ancient English Poetry* (2nd edn. London, 1767), I, 35–6) prints a Scottish ballad on the Hugh of Lincoln legend which exemplifies the pattern.

25 Trachtenberg, *The Devil and the Jews*, pp. 48–52.

26 Philippus Caesar, *A general discourse against... Usurers*, tr. Thomas Rogers (London, 1578), sig.* iv^r.

27 The identification of Jews and Usury is so complete in Rogers's mind that he refers to the expulsion of the Jews in the reign of Edward I, as the banishment of the *Usurers* (*Ibid.* sig. **ii^r). Cf. *The Death of Usury* (Cambridge, 1594), pp. 10, 41–2.

28 Lucien Wolf, 'Jews in Elizabethan England', *Transactions of the JHSE*, XI (1924/7), 69.

29 Sir Anthony Sherley in Day, Rowley & Wilkins, *The Travailes of Three English Brothers* [1607], quoted by Cardozo, *op. cit.* p. 153.

30 Additions to Stow, *Survey of London*, 1618, p. 233. H. Sinsheimer, *Shylock* (New York, 1964), pp. 114–16, gives a brief history of this association of ideas.

31 *Ludus Coventriae*, ed. J. O. Halliwell (Shakespeare Society) (London, 1841), p. 268. There are parallel treatments in the Towneley, Chester and York cycles.

32 See Furness (ed.), *Merchant of Venice* (New Variorum Shakespeare) (Philadelphia, 1888), p. 461.

33 (1615 edn.), see pp. 159, 168, 183 and 190.

34 *Ibid.* p. 191.

35 M. J. Landa, *The Jew in Drama* (London, 1926), pp. 47–85, has an exhaustive list of references to Jews, some of which are disputed by J. L. Cardozo, *The Contemporary Jew in Elizabethan Drama*, chapter IV.

36 Graetz, *History of the Jews*, IV, 634.

37 See A. L. Williams, *Adversus Judaeos: A Bird's-eye View of Christian 'Apologiae' until the Renaissance* (Cambridge, 1935), pp. 393–4.

38 *Coryat's Crudities* [1611] (London, 1776), I, 301.

39 Trachtenberg, *The Devil and the Jews*, p. 15.

40 *Crudities* (London, 1776), I, 303.

41 Trachtenberg, *The Devil and the Jews*, p. 218.

42 Ferneze's sarcastic intent is plain from the context (I. ii. 79 f.). Barabas's term 'convertite' is probably a scornful allusion to the *domus conversorum* where converted Jews were lodged in London for re-indoctrination. See I. Singer (ed.), *Jewish Encyclopedia* (New York, 1903), IV, 636–8.

43 So at least Joseph Pfefferkorn, a 'converted' sixteenth-century German Jew, maintained. See Graetz, *History of the Jews*, IV, 455.

44 *Annales* (London, 1615), p. 200 (my italics). There is a similar case, when 700 Jews perished for an extortionate compatriot who demanded 10 per cent per week on a loan, reported on p. 192.

45 Quoted by Graetz, *History of the Jews*, IV, 585.

INDEX

Authors quoted but not named in the text are listed under the page where the quotation occurs, followed by the number of the note—e.g. 199 n. 23.

INDEX

Authors quoted but not named in the text are listed under the page where the quotation occurs, followed by the number of the note—e.g. 199 n. 23.

INDEX

DATE DUE